Giving Wings to the Gospel

GIVING WINGS TO THE GOSPEL

The Remarkable Story of Mission Aviation Fellowship

Dietrich G. Buss
Arthur F. Glasser

Foreword by Max Meyers

Baker Books

A Division of Baker Book House Co
Grand Rapids, Michigan 49516

© 1995 by Dietrich G. Buss

Published by Baker Books
a division of Baker Book House Company
P.O. Box 6287, Grand Rapids, MI 49516-6287

Printed in the United States of America

Library of Congress Cataloging-in-Publication Data

Buss, Dietrich, G.
    Giving wings to the gospel : the remarkable story of Mission Aviation Fellowship / Dietrich G. Buss and Arthur F. Glasser ; foreword by Max Meyers.
        p.   cm.
    Includes bibliographical references (p.).
    ISBN 0-8010-5230-0 (pbk.)
    1. Mission Aviation Fellowship. 2. Aeronautics in missionary work.
I. Glasser, Arthur F. II. Title
BV2082.A9B87 1995
266'.006'01—dc20   95-14097

To the sons and daughters
of MAF families

Contents

Acronyms

ABWE	American Baptists for World Evangelization
ACROSS	American Committee for the Rehabilitation of Southern Sudan
ADS	Alas de Socorro
AIM	African Inland Mission
AMAF	Australia Missionary Aviation Fellowship
BIOLA	Bible Institute of Los Angeles (now Biola University)
CAMF	Christian Airmen's Missionary Fellowship
C&MA	Christian and Missionary Alliance
CAR	Central African Republic
CBFMS	Conservative Baptist Foreign Mission Society (now CB International)
EAL	Ethiopia Air Lines
EFMA	Evangelical Foreign Missions Association
FAA	Federal Aviation Administration
GMU	Gospel Missionary Union
HCJB	Call letters of short wave Christian radio station "Voice of the Andes" Quito, Ecuador
JAARS	Jungle Aviation and Radio Service
MAF-UK	Mission Aviation Fellowship, United Kingdom
MAF-US	Mission Aviation Fellowship, United States
MAP	Medical Assistance Program
MBI	Melbourne Bible Institute
ME	Missionary Electronics
MWE	Movement for World Evangelization
NTM	New Tribes Mission
OMF	Overseas Missionary Fellowship
ORM	Orinoco River Mission
RAAF	Royal Australian Air Force
RAF	Royal Air Force
RBMU	Regions Beyond Missionary Union
SAIM	South American Indian Mission
SA-MAF	South Africa Mission Aviation Fellowship
SIL	Summer Institute of Linguistics
SIM	Sudan Interior Mission
SSEM	South Sea Evangelical Mission
STOL	Short-takeoff-and-landing
TEAM	The Evangelical Alliance Mission
UFM	Unevangelized Fields Mission
WASP	Womens Airforce Service Pilots
WBT	Wycliffe Bible Translators
WIM	West Indies Mission
WMAC	World Mission Aviation Council
YMCA	Young Men's Christian Association
ZLV	*Zendings Luchtvaart Vereniging*

8

Acknowledgments

In the course of researching and writing this history of Mission Aviation Fellowship, I have received assistance from a host of wonderful people to whom I am deeply indebted. Back in 1983, Herb Morgan, then serving as chairman of the MAF-US historical documentation committee, asked me to undertake an oral history project spanning the early years of MAF. Donna Burns, manager of communication ministries, moved the project forward. As this compelling story started to come into focus, the decision was made to write this history.

President Max Meyers supplied the inspiration to expand the story into a full-fledged history embracing MAF organizations in the United States, United Kingdom, Australia, New Zealand, and South Africa. In 1992, Ghislaine Benney, the newly appointed communications manager at MAF, immediately moved to link the history project to the fiftieth anniversary celebration of MAF.

Working with Ghislaine has been a singular delight. Her contagious enthusiasm made it easy to cross each hurdle. Her sharp eye for detail has strengthened this work in many respects, and her decision to visually enrich the narrative with choice photos and specially designed maps anchors this story in time and place. Ghislaine wrote chapter 22, "MAF-US in Recent Years."

Extended interviews with the founders and other MAF members brought this story to life. I am indebted to Jim Truxton, Betty Greene, Grady Parrott, Claire Mellis, Hobey Lowrance, Darlene Lomheim, Bob Hutchins, Don Berry, Roy and Katie Parsons, Chuck Bennett, Norm Olson, John Fairweather, and Denny Hoekstra. It was a pleasure to meet and interview Stuart King of MAF

United Kingdom while he and Phyllis were visiting California. Others who shared how MAF served them in overseas locations were Dr. Everett Fuller, Bob Hawkins, Mary Hawkins, Ben Elson, Ed Gustafson, Dr. William Rule, Harold Catto, and Leonard Tuggy. My thanks to each of them for their valuable contributions.

Writing about people and events that in many cases took place half a world away is a hazardous task. The possibility of errors of fact and interpretation is endless. To present the story as accurately as possible, senior members of the MAF organizations reviewed the manuscript. Their corrections and comments have been most helpful in revising the text. I want to give thanks to Ian Stacy and Vic Ambrose of Australia, Stuart King of the United Kingdom, and Gordon Marshall of South Africa. For MAF-US, my thanks go to Betty Greene, Grady Parrott, Hobey Lowrance, Don Berry, and Bob Gordon. Grady gave countless hours critiquing drafts and supplying background information and details to round out the story. My special thanks to Grady and Maurine for their warm hospitality during my many extended visits at their home in Placentia. I also want to thank my brother, Dr. Reinhard Buss, and my mother, Martie Johnson Buss, for their close reading of early drafts.

Dr. Arthur Glasser, Dean Emeritus, School of World Mission, Fuller Theological Seminary, who has served on the boards of MAF and Air Serv International, collaborated with me in revising the manuscript. I greatly appreciate his wisdom, insight, and good humor. The Epilogue is directly from his pen.

This history could not have been written without the support of Biola University. A series of release-time grants plus a semester sabbatical gave me time for research and writing. Paul Ericksen, archivist at the Billy Graham Center, supplied copies of MAF personnel correspondence that ran into thousands of pages.

I want to thank the Baker Book House editorial team, Dan Van't Kerkhoff, Mary Suggs, and the production staff for turning a manuscript into this attractive book.

Finally, without the encouragement and support of Dr. Edward H. Norman, this manuscript would not have seen the light of day. Ultimately it is the faithfulness of God that makes possible the release of *Giving Wings to the Gospel* at the Golden Anniversary of Mission Aviation Fellowship.

Foreword

Mission Aviation Fellowship is indebted to Dr. Dietrich Buss for the enormous effort he has expended in writing this book. He is a researcher of the highest caliber, a gifted historian with great patience and an amazing ability to gather, read, put into order, and document material representing thirty years in the life of complex organizations like ours.

MAF is somewhat unique—an enterprise in aviation, yet a significant part of the modern-day church of Jesus Christ. We are participants in the historic post-World War II mission movement that extended to hitherto unknown and unreached people the Good News of Jesus. MAF has bridged most major barriers separating millions of people from the knowledge of God. We have been the carriers of love and compassion to the hurting and the needy, the transportation arm of thousands of courageous men and women who responded to the call of God to reach the lost for Christ and nurture and serve the found.

MAF people are unique. They are more at home in the left seat of a small airplane than trying to document the history of the organization to which they were called. Their skills lie more in the area of negotiating their way through the rugged mountains of some faraway place on their missions of love. They battle tough and hostile conditions and methodically work through the disciplined processes of annual airplane inspections. Their rewards come through missions completed, lives saved, churches established, food or medicines delivered. They are good at what they do and take joy in simple words of thanks, grateful eyes, and healthy smiles.

We are not historians like Dietrich Buss, who has applied his remarkable skills to tell the story of this ministry. We are grateful to him for this work.

As you read about the men and women of MAF, may you smell the smells and hear the sounds of faraway jungles or deserts. May you hear the anguished cries of the needy and the low moaning of the hungry. May you sense the joy and freshness of newfound reconciliation with God. Behind the well-known sound of an airplane engine may you hear the clear call of God that brought Mission Aviation Fellowship into being. May you understand that our bottom line is participation in that great invitation to "go and make disciples of all nations, baptizing them in the name of the Father and of the Son and of the Holy Spirit, and teaching them to obey everything I have commanded you" (Matthew 28:19–20).

Surely, he has been with us always.

If you sense him in this book, Dietrich Buss and all of us in MAF will be satisfied.

Max Meyers
President and Chief Executive Officer
MAF-US

1

Birth of a Vision

During the dark days of World War II, the idea of using aviation for evangelical missions took form in the hearts and minds of a number of military fliers. Three of these started what eventually became the worldwide movement of Mission Aviation Fellowship (MAF) organizations. Jim Truxton of the United States, Murray Kendon (a New Zealander) of the United Kingdom, and Edwin "Harry" Hartwig of Australia enlisted other Christian airmen to start their respective agencies. In 1946, the American group was the first to launch an air arm with a 1933 Waco biplane. Since then, the MAF fleet has grown to over 175 aircraft serving in some forty nations. This represents an investment of approximately five hundred families, constituting the pilots and support personnel who do the actual work of MAF.

To date, the larger story of the MAF organizations' origin, growth, and development has not been told. In this history of their early years, you will find a narrative probing their formative experiences and the personalities behind them. Subsequent chapters retain a historical framework, but the story shifts to illuminate significant developments or themes that have come to characterize the ministry of one or more MAF wing.

At first, the three initial MAFs worked in entirely separate spheres. Pilots of the American organization assisted the Summer Institute of Linguistics (SIL) in Mexico. The British flew missionaries in the Anglo-Egyptian Sudan, and the Australians helped the Lutherans in the Territory of New Guinea. Early on, these Christian airmen made contact with one another. In those first

13

struggling years, when financial backing lagged far behind mission vision and reliance was totally on the Almighty, the intercommunication of these three struggling agencies served as fuel to faith—and kept the vision growing. Letters were meant as much to encourage as to inform.

Once field operations commenced and attention turned to equipment and flight standards, communication served to help in more specific ways. This was done in a friendly and effective manner. All communication was on a first-name basis, seasoned with good humor. They took their work, but not themselves, seriously. As the MAF groups planned new flight operations, they duly informed one another, seeking and receiving cooperation. This made for the orderly development of missionary flight service in remote and previously inaccessible parts of the globe.

By the mid-1950s, all three initial organizations had, in the main, settled on the Cessna line of planes and had adopted similar pilot qualifications and safety and flight standards. This made for easy exchange of flight personnel when the need arose. Today, while guarding their separate autonomy and pattern of finance, these three organizations cooperate closely with one another to assist the spread of the gospel by giving wings to evangelical missions and indigenous churches and assisting those who, in the name of Christ, minister to suffering humanity.

Each MAF entity has a uniquely interesting history. Each will be explored in separate chapters illustrating personal faith, shared commitment, dogged perseverance, and the grace of God. This story reveals how visions became realities through triumphs and tragedies. Above all, there is a steady counting on the faithfulness of God. When severe tests of faith came, these people sorrowed but did not despair. In the midst of pressures of all types, they exuded hope and loyalty to one another. As time went by, the separate agencies became entwined. Auxiliary organizations were formed. New Zealand MAF (MAF-NZ) emerged to assist the Australia MAF (AMAF), and South Africa MAF (SA-MAF) helped British MAF (MAF-UK). SA-MAF has since matured and developed its own flight program in South Africa. But we are getting ahead of our story. Let's revisit their separate beginnings.

Forging Deep Friendships

The American MAF story started with a warm friendship between two men who had enlisted for pilot training in the U.S. Navy—James Truxton and James Buyers. These two Jims first met at a Bible study Buyers had started during their preflight boot camp training at Chapel Hill, North Carolina. They soon found that although each had chosen military aviation as a means of serving his country in World War II, both had begun to dream of using the airplane to facilitate missionary service at war's end.

Then Truxton faced a challenge that could have ended his aviation career even before it started: the Navy's very demanding swimming examination. Truxton had nearly drowned when he was nine years old and carried from that experience a fear of deep water. But to enter pilot training he had to conquer his fear and pass the test. By God's grace he succeeded.

Saying their good-byes at Chapel Hill was hard, but Truxton and Buyers were pleasantly surprised to find they had both been assigned to Anacostia in the District of Columbia for their secondary flight training. Due to a brief illness, Truxton was now one training squadron behind Buyers. Even so, they were able to encourage each other in their Christian walk and share their dreams of flying for missions.

After Anacostia, they prayed that they might be sent to the same training station for advanced flight. Providentially, both were given orders to report to the Naval Air Station at Pensacola, Florida.

Here, Truxton faced a very different crisis. In the final stages of their training, students had to pass flight checks with an instructor. If a student flew two down-checks (unsatisfactory flights) in a row, he was washed out unless the captain of his training squadron found grounds to grant what was called captain's time. If granted, the trainee had to fly three up-checks (satisfactory flights) in a row!

On his way to request captain's time, Truxton stopped at the base post office and found a "Dear John" letter from his fiancée calling off their engagement. He was crushed! When he shared the bad news with Jim Buyers, Buyers placed his hands on Truxton's shoulders and said, "Jim, you and I both know that the Lord makes no mistakes. He works all things out for our good." It was just what Truxton needed to hear.

He was granted that captain's time and did fly those three up-checks. Through this helpful encounter, Truxton began to believe that God planned to accomplish something through this developing friendship.

He received orders to join a Kingfisher, single-engine patrol seaplane squadron on the Island of Jamaica—only to find that it was packing up to return to Norfolk, Virginia, and disband. When asked if he had any preference as to a form of Naval air service, Truxton expressed interest in twin-engine flying.

A few weeks later he was amazed when orders came through to join an operating twin-engine Martin "Mariner" seaplane patrol squadron. His squadron was protecting supply convoys heading for Britain from German submarine attack. The supplies made possible Hitler's defeat. Truxton's squadron was based at Floyd Bennett Field, New York, where he knew Buyers was already based with a squadron that ferried military aircraft.

By the fall of 1943, they learned of another Christian airman, Clarence "Soddy" Soderberg, who also had the vision of flying in missionary service. Together they prayed, studied the Bible, and talked much about the role of aviation in missions and how they might participate in such work. Their common interest in Christian ministry brought them in contact with Jack Wyrtzen of the Word of Life Fellowship in New York City. Jack met and prayed with Truxton, Buyers, and Soderberg as they continued to think and pray about their vision of using aircraft in missions.[1]

George Fisk

Before the winter of 1943, Truxton's squadron was transferred to Quonset Point, Rhode Island, for training in using million-candle-power searchlights to seek out German submarines at night. While stationed there, he received a letter from his aunt Virginia Campbell, who had served as a missionary in Egypt and had a profound influence on Truxton's spiritual development. She told Truxton that George Fisk, a missionary with the Christian and Missionary Alliance (C&MA) in Borneo, would be speaking at

Providence Bible Institute (later Barrington College) during Easter break of 1944. The campus was located near the naval base.

With a longing for some good Christian fellowship, the possibility of meeting a fine coed, plus his keen interest in hearing Fisk's story, Truxton made his way to Providence Bible Institute. The meeting had already begun, but he found an empty seat at the back of the auditorium.

"It was noontime," Fisk was saying. "Weary and hungry, we pulled our huge, heavily loaded dugout canoe up to the sandbar at the river's edge to rest and eat. As I stepped from the bow of the canoe to the shore, I looked back down the steep gorge and the rushing rapids. I could hardly believe my eyes. There, at the first bend in the river, I saw our campsite of the previous night! For two weeks we had toiled against the swift currents and portaged around waterfalls, dragging the canoe uphill. That was all the distance we had covered in six hours, and we still had another two weeks ahead of us. Overwhelmed with discouragement, I looked up at the ribbon of blue sky between the high walls of the gorge just as two brilliantly plumed hornbill birds flew lightly across."

"At that instant," Fisk continued, "God used those birds to spark the vision of harnessing the airplane to his work—to redeem all those weeks of precious time and all this spent energy, for my work among the Dyaks of this Apo Kayan District of Borneo [now East Kalimantan, Indonesia]. Right then and there, I invited my Dyak helpers to kneel and join me in prayer for a plane."

Fisk went on to relate how in the weeks and months that followed, the possibilities of how the airplane could help with frontier missions burned itself into his heart and mind. When he returned home on furlough, he shared his vision with a group of businessmen who banded together to purchase a single-engine Beechcraft equipped with floats. Fisk got flight instruction, earned a pilot's license, and then headed back to Borneo as a pilot-missionary. To his delight and amazement, the four-to-six-week overland trek was reduced to one and one-half hours by air.[2]

Fisk closed his presentation to the students with a plea for prayer that God would call out military and civilian pilots to meet this strategic need. Truxton, who had banded together with Buyers and Soderberg to pray about this very thing, met with Fisk

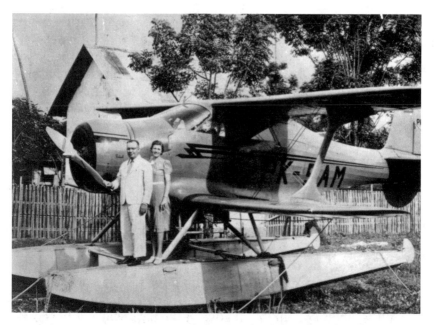

Mr. and Mrs. George Fisk on their amphibious Beechcraft "Sam" in Borneo.

after the service. The two had a long and memorable discussion on the use of aircraft in missions.

This encounter with Fisk was a significant milestone in Truxton's thinking. Here was a man who had tried and proven what had thus far been only an "idea and vision" to him.[3] Furthermore, Truxton and his friends had only thought about what they might do as individuals; Fisk lit a fire under them to get an organization started right away, so that when the war ended they could recruit veterans and others into missionary aviation service.

Christian Airmen's Missionary Fellowship

Following Truxton's transfer back to Floyd Bennett Field in New York in early 1944, Fisk, Buyers, and Truxton met for lunch in a Brooklyn restaurant. The discussion turned into a marathon brainstorming session on getting an organization started. All three felt strongly that they should move ahead before they were again separated. For the present, they decided not to formalize any arrangement but make decisions by consensus, as the Lord led them. This simple arrangement came out of four hours of spirited discussion, while waitresses watched from the sidelines and wondered when these "squatters" would leave. Truxton and Buyers met regularly throughout the spring of 1944. Together they came up with the name Christian Airmen's Missionary Fellowship (CAMF), which was retained until 1946. Just what CAMF was going to do, other than contact like-minded airmen, remained to be seen.

The Brooklyn meeting with Fisk launched CAMF as an organization to encourage and challenge Christian airmen to dedicate their flying skills to the cause of Christian missions. Their purpose was hardly focused. None of the three envisioned a highly specialized flight-service organization. These three men felt that the broad purpose of enlisting airmen to serve Christ was sufficient for the present. As it turned out, another year was to pass before they would be released from military service following the collapse of both Germany and Japan.

The three shared their vision with Jack Wyrtzen, who was holding evangelistic rallies at Times Square during the spring and summer of 1944. The first public announcement of the existence and purpose of CAMF was made at one of these rallies. Although as an organization it hardly existed and did not even have an office, these men had a clear sense of God's calling and direction.

Dawson Trotman

In May 1944, Buyers was transferred to the naval base at San Diego, California. Through his efforts to track down other Christian servicemen, he came upon Dawson Trotman's Navigators. These Christians had a unique program of Scripture memorization and outreach to American servicemen. Since the organization existed almost solely to contact Christians in military service, it proved to be a perfect vehicle for spreading the news of the existence of CAMF. Buyers went to Los Angeles to speak with Dawson Trotman in the middle of June. This well-known Christian leader gave Buyers a warm reception and encouraged him to pursue the vision.

Dawson Trotman, although a native of Arizona, had grown up in Lomita, a small town on the fringes of Los Angeles. While in high school, he became involved in Christian Endeavor and made what seemed to be a serious profession of faith. Even so, after high school his life began to drift; he even had a brush with the law that sobered him. This caused him to resume church attendance, where he was challenged to memorize Scripture. He took up this challenge with remarkable seriousness. Scripture now took hold of Trotman's life and redirected it to the service of his Maker.

Once committed to a cause, Trotman was not one to waste time. As a Christian, he immediately got started organizing a number of Bible memorization and activity clubs. Given his enthusiasm, these proved highly successful in Lomita.

In 1932 Trotman moved to San Pedro, California, for the purpose of reaching sailors with the message of Christ. While running a service station to make a living, he developed the Navigators program of Bible memorization and witnessing. With the outbreak of the Pacific war on December 7, 1941, Trotman expanded the Navigators program and sought to penetrate every battle group and task force of the Navy, then of the Army. By 1944 there were Navigators in 450 Army camps and on 350 Navy vessels. He communicated to the members via his publication *The Log*.[4]

It was strategic that Buyers came to Trotman at a time when the Navigators had contact with many servicemen. Trotman became immediately and unreservedly interested in CAMF. He even offered CAMF office space and part-time secretarial help at his Hope Street headquarters. This was centrally located in downtown Los Angeles in the complex of buildings comprising the Church of the Open Door and the Bible Institute of Los Angeles (the latter is now Biola University).[5]

By this time Truxton knew he would soon be transferred from the East Coast. He had been thinking about opening a CAMF office there before departure. As a result of the good news from Buyers about Trotman's interest, Truxton wrote him a detailed and remarkably frank letter setting forth CAMF's guiding principles, as he saw them then.[6] He was looking for confirmation that the Lord was really leading CAMF to open an office in Los Angeles, since he had been considering other possibilities.

As to CAMF's mission, the two Jims were not interested in simply forming a fellowship or club of "flying missionaries." They and Soderberg envisioned the need of an organization that would "study and develop all the inherent possibilities" in harnessing the airplane to serve missions. They felt keenly the need to begin recruiting aviation technicians of all kinds—pilots, mechanics, engineers, and radiomen—to ready themselves for service in a viable program for missions at war's end. In light of this, Truxton wrote president V. Raymond Edman of Wheaton College, hoping to make contact with some fifty potential recruits from among Wheaton graduates serving in the military.

These CAMF founders believed that time was not to be wasted. The immediate future provided them with an opportune time to secure the cooperation of missionary societies and track down information on "where aircraft can aid their work, what their problems and needs are, and how CAMF can help." They also asked for assistance to "open their eyes to the ways in which CAMF ministries might be extended."[7]

Truxton thought that CAMF's posture toward mission organizations would determine its success or failure. For this reason, CAMF was to be strictly interdenominational. Truxton put this emphatically: "We who are interested in the CAMF want to cooperate with and have the cooperation of every Christian effort whose ministry can be aided and extended by the use of aircraft." The CAMF ideal was to be completely infused with the "purely unselfish motive of doing everything possible to hasten the advance of the Gospel to the ends of the earth." In this connection, Truxton wanted to let it be known from the outset that CAMF should never be known as "so-and-so's work." He felt that "whenever a ministry becomes built around any one person or small group of persons, its ministry, and its ability to cooperate and obtain cooperation, becomes limited."[8]

Truxton was highly appreciative of Trotman's offer of office space and a part-time secretary. He was, in fact, amazed at Trotman's generosity. He hardly expected to run across a Christian organization that was "willing to do so much for others when so little benefit could be expected in return."[9] Despite his awareness that he should not be looking a gift horse in the mouth, Truxton was somewhat troubled by the offer of a secretary. He had some very definite ideas about the qualities of the person who would represent CAMF as secretary.

Trotman was doubtless impressed with Truxton's caution. Significantly, he agreed with Truxton on virtually all his concerns. He generously promised to send a CAMF brochure out "to a host of airmen in all branches" just as soon as the material was ready, and pledged to print information about the organization in *The Log*. As for the fact that CAMF had no office, secretary, or treasury, Trotman counseled: "Thank God for that. It gives CAMF the opportunity to trust God and not men, and I am sure that you will agree with me that there is little of such faith in much Christian work today. Nevertheless, 'GOD'S work done in GOD'S way will never lack GOD'S supply.'"[10] Truxton picked up this phrase of Hudson Taylor and made it his own fund-raising policy as general secretary.[11] Trotman was so enthusiastic about CAMF that he sent off copies of Truxton's letter to the directors of the Navigators centers: Lorne Sanny in Seattle, C. Harold Chrisman in Oakland, John Thorne in San Diego, Richard Hightower in Brooklyn, and Harold DeGroff in Honolulu.

Truxton was grateful for this warm reception from Trotman, despite the fact that the two had never met. His written response was, "I can see, Dawson, that you have really caught the vision behind the CAMF and that a real fire of interest has led you to assist us in working out a way for it to get under way. We praise God for this, and after much thought and prayer feel certain that He has thus led us to the first big step. How I rejoice to see your oneness with us in the CAMF vision."[12]

Trotman assigned Addie Rosenbaum, one of the Navigators secretaries, to handle the correspondence for CAMF. She worked in that position until Betty Greene joined CAMF as secretary in November 1944. In the meantime, Truxton sought Trotman's help on a whole range of issues that concerned him and the new organization: a letterhead, insignias, printing costs, a bank account, personal recommendations, policies, and so forth. Trotman answered all questions in great detail, gave help where he could, and always faithfully discharged the role of "encourager."

Jim Truxton's Priorities

From the outset, Trotman gave Truxton strong personal endorsement. This raised some questions in his inner circle. After all, Trotman knew nothing of Truxton's past. As an afterthought, Trotman asked Truxton for a biographical sketch to reassure his staff. As one who knew that his own background did not entirely commend him, Trotman wrote Truxton: "As far as your background goes, it makes little difference to me. It is your present position, foundation and vision that counts."[13] Truxton gave the following biographical sketch:

> As to my background, I'm twelve years old in the Lord, and twenty-nine in the flesh. I have never been in full-time Christian work, circumstances having prevented me from doing so. My father passed away shortly after graduation from high school making it necessary for me to abandon plans for college, medical, and Bible training. I went to work to help my family until the war drew me into the Naval Air Corps. Christian work has always been a sideline, however. I have participated in mission, church, and street meetings, and served as a council member of the Youth Center at the Philadelphia Gospel Tabernacle. I have had experience in Christian work over these past twelve years, but I am only too conscious of the little growth in grace. I am by no means a trained student of the Bible, though I love God's word, and love to study it on my own. I can't write articles or preach a sermon, and do not have mountains of scripture at my finger tips. All I can do is fly a plane and tell the simple Gospel story of God's love wrapped up in John 3:16. Somehow there just seemed to me to be a connection between the two, and I long to use that one talent for Christ my Savior.[14]

This was a modest self-appraisal, to be sure, but it essentially reflected Truxton's candor in finding himself moved to pursue big goals to do God's will, not to feed his own ego.

For Trotman this was sufficient, which he made very plain to Truxton. "Regardless of anything, I pledge my love to you and all those who shall be connected with CAMF and will count it one of the greatest privileges of my life to give of my time and strength to help you fellows carry out HIS orders" in this great venture.

Looking back at this formative period, Truxton could only speak of Trotman with the warmest affection for "responding with such overwhelming enthusiasm and such immediate generosity."

To round out this picture of the person who had the CAMF vision and became the driving force behind the founding of MAF, it is interesting to note that Jim Truxton was of Scotch Presbyterian ancestry. His father, Joe Truxton, taught at Kingsley School —later named Northeastern Bible Institute—in Essex Fells, New Jersey. Jim was next to the oldest in a family of six children. A good indication of his developing interest in aviation was the time he and his older brother, Joe, built an almost life-size airplane in their backyard, complete with a propeller driven by foot pedals from their toy car. In a make-believe way, they flew all around the world—one as navigator, with flight plan resting on his lap drawn on their geography book maps, and the other as pilot, pedaling to keep that propeller whirling! Some time later, Jim's father died of tobacco-induced cancer, and Jim had to become the family breadwinner.

The event that set Jim's course on a life of Christian service took place when he was sixteen. The Truxtons were a church-going family, but Jim was having doubts about the validity of his childhood faith. A missionary aunt, Virginia Campbell, had come to live in the Truxton home while Jim's mother was recuperating from typhoid fever. This aunt's calm, quiet devotion to God and her love and reverence for Scripture profoundly impacted his life. One of his greatest areas of struggle and doubt had to do with the miracles of Jesus, especially his resurrection.

One day, Jim openly and even a bit antagonistically shared these doubts with his aunt. Her soft-spoken and unruffled response was a bit disarming. She suggested that he read a passage in the New Testament. In the quiet of his room that night, Jim read: "The Spirit searches all things, even the deep things of God. . . . The man without the Spirit does not accept the things that come from the Spirit of God, for they are foolishness to him, and he cannot understand them, because they are spiritually discerned" (1 Cor. 2:10, 14). Jim fell to his knees beside his bed and prayed, "Oh, God, if this is of you, please give to me this spiritual discernment!" Two weeks later he made his public profession of faith in Christ in what was then the nonsectarian tabernacle at Broad and Master Streets in Philadelphia, Pennsylvania. A desire to serve his Lord soon began to grow.

When the United States declared war following Japan's attack on Pearl Harbor, Jim Truxton enlisted in the Naval Air Corps, thinking that one day he might become a flying missionary doctor. The wartime setting, especially his experiences as a pilot, saw him refine his ideas of where he might best give his talents for Christian service. Truxton believed God had planted the same idea in the hearts and minds of many wartime pilots. He viewed himself as a facilitator, bringing these fliers into an organization.

> CAMF is a group of (fliers) . . . who long to put their flying talent to use in reaching those who have never heard and in extending and speeding those works already started. I feel that I, alone, hardly have the right to set down any hard and fast rules either as to organization or administration. I can only try to reflect what I believe through my associations personally and through the mails, to be the convictions, plans and visions of these others as well as myself. We have all of us talked about CAMF long before it ever became known by that name, and it was in our hearts long before we ever met one another.[15]

Had there been an opportunity to call an organizational meeting of prospective CAMF members, Jim Truxton would have been the first to do so, but the all-out war effort of 1944 made this completely impossible. Jim decided to give visibility to, and promote interest in, aviation for missions. His plan was to call a meeting of interested fliers soon after the close of the war and then encourage them to participate in deciding the direction of the organization.

CAMF drew up a statement of faith quite similar to that of the Navigators. Its founders wanted to be in a position to serve all believers throughout the world. They wanted no roadblocks to cooperation. It proved to be a strong statement on the essentials of biblical authority, the deity of Christ, the lostness of unregenerate people, the redemption and new birth through the atonement of Christ, the assurance of eternal life, and the missionary mandate.[16]

Jim Truxton wanted to give interested persons a picture of the nature of CAMF, so he put together a pocket-sized booklet titled

"Speed the Light on Wings of the Wind."[17] To have lift, there must be movement, and Truxton used the imagery of the airplane in flight to illustrate CAMF's aims.

This was the first printed material distributed in the name of CAMF, and Jim wanted it to make a favorable impression. He wrote Dawson Trotman, "I know you realize as fully as I do the importance of this first impression. This is one place where I'm not in favor of skimping, and am willing to pay the bill myself, if necessary [which he did], in order to have neat attractive booklets printed in good taste and in good quality."[18] This introductory booklet detailed the broad purposes and specific activities envisioned for CAMF. It closed with a challenge to airmen. The threefold stated purpose was: "To fulfill Christ's Commission, to hasten the return of our blessed Saviour and Lord, Jesus Christ, and to inspire united, cooperative and coordinated efforts to accomplish these ends."

Given MAF's specialized flight work today, it is surprising to note some of the specific activities Truxton envisioned for CAMF in the summer of 1944. His vision was that the organization must be designed:

1. To serve "as a clearing house of information" for airmen seeking opportunities for service with missions and missions seeking competent pilots
2. To provide a "home missionary base or bases at which missionary aircraft may be housed, assembled, repaired, and where instruction may be given, flight time put in etc., at absolute minimum cost"
3. To aid in "the transportation of missionary personnel and supplies where other adequate transportation or commercial airlines are not available"
4. To provide "flight instruction for missionaries on the field, in their own aircraft, and in the conditions of weather and terrain with which they will actually be faced"
5. To supply "traveling maintenance and repair units to serve all missionary aircraft world wide"
6. To assist, "through all available missionary aircraft, in emergency relief work both at home and abroad"
7. "To publish a periodical bulletin on missionary aviation"

8. "To establish CAMF chapters in other countries for the dissemination of information on an international scale, to inspire and encourage unity, and to study and enlarge missionary activity from a 'world' viewpoint"

The wide range of proposed activities shows that CAMF saw many options for service to missions. At the time this was written, they did not have the experience to know which of these services would really be feasible. The next several years saw them sorting out those activities that were possible and needful. Obviously, much would depend on the level of cooperation achieved between missions in any locale, as well as the evangelical community's financial support.

The above list shows that these pilots had the faith, enthusiasm, and courage of youth. The storms they would encounter in realizing their dreams were not yet on the horizon, but they would come in many forms. There would be competing aviation concepts in missionary circles, skeptical missions, financial pressures, airplane accidents, and less-than-helpful foreign governments. On the other hand, there would also be faithful co-workers, encouraging mission leaders, sacrificial supporters, and, above all, the Lord who had put the vision of missionary aviation into the hearts of these pilots.

All these experiences would refine their program to fit the times. By making necessary adjustments, they found the pattern of missionary service to which they felt called. Much searching of heart and many sharp trials, disappointments, and errors would overtake them during the years ahead, but their faith in God never wavered as they resolutely sought to realize their dreams. Some of the changes that came about are reflected in the name shift from CAMF to Missionary Aviation Fellowship and the dropping (in 1971) of *missionary* in favor of *mission* in the name of the American wing. For the American and British organizations, this shift reflected the indigenization of Christian work that went on in the post–World War II period, especially in the 1960s. On the other hand, Australia MAF, which also adapted to these changes, retained the term *missionary* in its title. Titles may or may not reveal significant changes over time.

Betty Greene

In the summer of 1944, when Jim Truxton was planning to send out his printed material, he keenly felt the need for a CAMF member to head up the work in the office.[19] Trotman had his eyes open for a suitable person, but the position was not filled until Elizabeth Greene opened the CAMF office in mid-November. She also became the first MAF pilot to fly on the field.

Jim Truxton had learned of Betty Greene from an article she had written in InterVarsity's *His* publication in the spring of 1943. At the time, she was serving as a pilot with the Women's Airforce Service Pilots (WASP). After training, she was assigned first to Camp Davis, North Carolina, and then to Wright Field near Dayton, Ohio.

While serving with the WASPs, Betty flew a variety of aircraft, including the Douglas "Dauntless" (A24) and "Helldiver" (A25), both dive bombers. She flew the "Beechcraft" (AT11) for night searchlight practice. Betty made several flights into the stratosphere testing flight equipment and she flew as copilot in a B-17 out of Wright Field. Jim made contact with Betty in the summer of 1944 and arranged to meet her in Washington, D.C. She was interested in CAMF but was not in a position to make any commitments. She was still on active military duty and had no idea when she might be released.

Betty came away from that meeting feeling that serving CAMF was something she really wanted to do. She prayed earnestly to know the Lord's leading. In early October she received a letter from Jim, asking if she could come. She set aside the next day, Sunday, October 4, for prayer. That very afternoon the colonel in charge of personnel asked her to copilot his flight to Florida. When they stopped to refuel in Atlanta, she heard that the WASPs were going to be disbanded. She was copiloting the plane of the man in charge of personnel, so she asked him if she could take advantage of her accumulated leave and be discharged ahead of time. His positive response was how God opened the door for her to work with CAMF.

A day or two before her departure, one of the flight officers telephoned Betty to see if she would pilot a flight to Washington, D.C.

Betty told him she was packing for the train trip home, but if he couldn't find anyone else to go, to let her know. He decided to go himself. On the return flight, shortly after takeoff, the plane exploded and all aboard were killed. Greene was humbled to think that God had spared her. She took this as a confirmation that the Lord had CAMF in her future.[20]

Betty's return home caused her to reflect on where she had been and where she was going. She was born and raised near Seattle. Her father was a metallurgical engineer, and she had three brothers, one her twin. Betty was about four when her oldest brother became interested in flying. While still in high school, she took up flying to the point of soloing. When it was time for her to go to the University of Washington, her parents persuaded her to enroll in nursing, but her heart wasn't in it. After two and one-half years, she dropped out of the university.

Betty longed to do something meaningful and of service to her Maker. She sought advice from an elderly friend who had taken considerable interest in her. This lady asked, "Betty, what would you really like to do?" She instantly replied, "I'd like to pursue flying." Her wise friend's response was, "Then why don't you use flying to help on the mission field?" Betty could hardly believe that something she really loved to do could be used for the Lord's service.

In reflecting on her dilemma and her conversation that day, Betty comments, "I guess we all tend to think that the Lord's service must involve things we really don't want to do. I don't know why we always think that way, because it certainly isn't true."

Betty registered for civil pilot training and went back to the University of Washington to continue her studies as a sociology major. She successfully completed the flight course in May 1941. Her private pilot's license also qualified her to use floats. She continued her studies in sociology and graduated in the spring of 1943. Thereafter, she joined the WASPs and headed for Sweetwater, Texas, for military flight training, receiving her wings in September of that year.

Approximately one thousand women served in this wing over the lifetime of WASP. Betty had the better part of two years of service. By the middle of November 1944, she was in Los Angeles to begin work with CAMF. Truxton rejoiced. He described Betty as "wonderfully qualified" and the "type of Christian who is ready and willing to take a step of faith, leaving good pay, for a position of no guarantee or visible evidence of support."[21]

Immediate Challenges

Another high point of that fall was Truxton's September meeting with Fisk and Buyers in Brooklyn.[22] This took place before Jim Truxton had word from Betty that she would be coming. The three reviewed the content of the promotional material they were about to have printed. They agreed on the twofold designation of active and associate member. It was envisioned that the fliers (active members) and mission representatives (associate members) would cooperate and point the way to new advances in missionary aviation.

The need for leadership was now becoming acute. Even so, Truxton still felt "it unwise to designate any *high* and extensive set of administrative officers at this point." They wanted to wait until the organization had grown sufficiently so that an "intelligent selection of the best-qualified persons" could be made. Since someone had to be in charge, it was decided to make Jim Truxton general secretary. They further agreed that the person in the Los Angeles office should be designated as secretary-treasurer and empowered to write checks. Ground was also laid for the formation of an advisory council of key men drawn from a variety of missions organizations to give guidance to CAMF.

Just then Jim received some unsettling news from George Fisk. The Reverend Paul C. Hartford of Indiana had just decided to incorporate a flying school for missionaries under the name of Victory Sky Pilots. He was a pastor, owned a 1939 Aeronca "Chief," and had done some support flying for Melvin A. Todd, an independent missionary in Mexico.[23] Fisk had written Hartford about CAMF and learned that he was not interested in joining the work. He wanted to start his own organization to train missionaries for flight work on the field.

At the time, CAMF had not yet clarified its objectives sufficiently to object to this particular approach. By the summer of 1945, CAMF decided that flying was a task for specialists and that missionaries should not, as a rule, be trained as pilots. This difference in philosophy took on increasing significance in the immediate postwar years as both CAMF and Hartford tried to influence the direction of missionary aviation.

News of Hartford's plans came as a real disappointment to Jim. He had long hoped to bring all experienced fliers into one organization, pooling their resources and knowledge in the cause of advancing missionary aviation worldwide. His mind was filled with conflicting possibilities. First, there was the news of Hartford's flamboyant plans. Second, there was CAMF's tremendous opportunity to challenge soon-to-be demobilized young airmen with the prospect of service for Christ. Third, the expectation of open doors for Christian work in the postwar era made Jim chafe under the military bonds that made it impossible for him to accomplish anything directly and personally in missions. His heart was truly in turmoil. Jim was transferred to San Diego, then to a series of other posts—Panama, the Galápagos Islands, and Japan—before he was released from military duty. He only found peace when he surrendered himself to his Lord and committed CAMF and missionary aviation to the Lord of the harvest.

Jim Buyers had gone back to New York and continued making contacts for CAMF. The printed materials were just then coming off the press, and Buyers made arrangements to fly the material to San Diego. From there it was mailed to Los Angeles.[24]

With all of this coming together—office space, Betty's positive decision, and CAMF's newly printed pamphlets and letterhead—Truxton and Buyers had "hearts filled with joy and praise." They had worked and prayed, then they were obliged to step back and let God work on their behalf. When he opened doors, they moved forward. These steps finally brought them to the verge of opening an office and sending out the first booklets on CAMF. Just where and how the Lord would lead this venture, they hardly knew. They were filled with eager anticipation as they looked to him for the next move.

In His Time and in His Way

Once arrangements were set for Betty Greene to come to Los Angeles, Dawson Trotman wrote a warm letter of welcome. The Trotmans had an open-door and open-heart policy with half a dozen co-laborers staying with them at their home in South Pasadena.[1]

Betty started work at the CAMF desk in the Navigators office in the middle of November 1944. She considered herself a co-laborer with Truxton. The latter saw no immediate possibility of an early release from the Navy and was still thinking about recruiting a director to work with Betty. She questioned the need for such a move and assured Truxton that she saw herself working closely with him, even though he could not be there in person.[2]

Betty shared her own perspective on this venture of faith. "I am in CAMF as His servant, I want to do it as well as I possibly can. I am not interested in whether or not my feelings are hurt. . . . So I beg you, for His sake, be frank with me on all matters and subjects. It really is wonderful to be co-laborers for our Lord Jesus Christ is it not? When we are absorbed with being well pleasing unto Him we welcome the criticism of others to aid us in that effort." Both recognized the formidable nature of their task, of which Truxton wrote, "Humanly speaking it is impossible, but when we know that the Creator of the universe is our boss everything suddenly becomes so simple."[3]

CAMF's First Year

Practical matters needed attention. Betty opened a California bank account totaling two hundred dollars in donations.[4] Truxton and Buyers got together in New York to discuss financial policy. They decided on a "no-debt policy," not because they lacked faith but because they felt that one "of the tokens of God's will, in the matter of starting out on something, will be His provision for at least its start."[5]

The employee pay policy they decided on was close to that of both C&MA and the Navigators. All employees, regardless of position, would receive fifty dollars a month "plus board and keep." *Keep* included such things as insurance, medical, dental, and other emergency costs. If there were insufficient funds to pay the fifty dollars some months, there would be a reduction across the board, with the understanding that this would not be made up in subsequent months.

Greene and Truxton were continually impressed with the need for prayer, and they encouraged the growing number of prayer partners to set aside Tuesday night to seek God's direction for CAMF. Meanwhile, it was already apparent that they needed another secretary, typewriter, and filing cabinets. Betty's father sent a surplus typewriter that belonged to the family. The Navigators office space was limited, and some alternative location had to be found.

The need for CAMF to actually do the task for which it was established was now on everybody's mind. The purchase of a suitable plane and finding a base for developing expertise in missionary aviation concerned Betty and Truxton.[6] Being confined to terra firma was a discipline that few airmen relished. Truxton, while not entirely thrilled about an impending assignment to the Pacific, was happy to be flying again.

Betty had other opportunities, such as going down to San Diego to challenge airmen about missionary aviation. She was not sure how she would be received as a woman in a largely man's world. She was surprised and pleased by the seriousness with which she was heard and she reported to Truxton that "there are people down there who are actually praying about CAMF."[7]

Betty put all her energies to the task of answering inquiries. She worked six days a week, sometimes as late as 7:00 P.M. Still she could not keep up with the correspondence and found an eager assistant in the person of Selma Bauman, a student at the Bible

Institute of Los Angeles (BIOLA). Selma came to work part-time in January 1945 and subsequently became a full-time secretary. Later she married an MAF communication man, Overton "Red" Brown.

In the meantime, Jim Truxton wrote articles on CAMF that appeared in InterVarsity's *His* magazine, the *Sunday School Times,* the New Tribes Mission's periodical *Brown Gold,* and others. Truxton tried to publicize CAMF as widely as possible. It was his vision to unite Christian airmen heading for missionary service for the purpose of creating an effective international organization.[8]

As 1944 came to a close the priorities that the CAMF team— Truxton, Greene, Fisk, and Buyers—saw were the need for an airplane, an operating base, and CAMF incorporation as a California nonprofit corporation. Truxton, though feeling quite frustrated from not being free to direct the efforts of the organization in Los Angeles, was very affirming to Greene. She kept him fully informed by forwarding copies of significant correspondence and regularly solicited his opinion and advice on a variety of CAMF concerns. Truxton gave close attention to all her comments and praised her for her good judgment.[9]

CAMF ended 1944 with a balance of $335 and no debts. Truxton considered this a miracle, in view of the fact that the organization had only been in existence one and one-half months and had made no appeals for money. Quite a number of servicemen were already sending in their tithes to CAMF.[10] By April, they were in contact with 110 men in military aviation.[11]

CAMF's close working relationship with the Navigators gave them access to the names of eighteen hundred servicemen in various aircraft-related capacities. With the rapidly growing membership in the midst of war, it was inevitable that some would become casualties. In March, Fred McIntosh was killed in combat, flying a B-24 over Germany. His wife, Peggy, requested that friends contribute to a memorial fund for purchase of a suitable plane for Bill Jones, a missionary working in Nicaragua with the Central American Mission.[12] More than seven hundred dollars was raised for this project. Other requests for planes started coming in when Mr. Strong, of the Soldiers Gospel Mission in Chile, sought

Early members of CAMF. *Left to right:* Charlie Mellis, Nate Saint, Larry Montgomery, Jim Truxton, Grady Parrott, Clarence "Soddy" Soderberg, Jim Buyers, Jim Lomheim.

CAMF's help. Greene wished something tangible might be sent in reply, rather than a letter spelling out CAMF's dreams.

By March 1945, a year after Truxton's encounter with Fisk, discussion on incorporation was moving forward, as was the search for more office space. With both the Navigators and CAMF needing larger quarters, Greene surveyed the immediate area for some suitable location. The Park Central Building was promising. In the middle of April, Greene secured a small ninth-floor room for $22.50 a month. Margaret Truxton, Jim's sister, a graduate of the Philadelphia School of the Bible, came to Los Angeles to give welcome help in the office.

A highlight for Betty during the spring of 1945 was the opportunity to address the final missionary conference session of the Church of the Open Door (COD). Since BIOLA took part in the conference, many college students attended. Betty described it as "ten of the best minutes of the entire week of conference at COD."[13] Actually it was much more than ten minutes. She wanted this opportunity because a symposium held during the week simply knocked down the whole idea of missionary aviation. Two of the speakers held biased and uninformed opinions. She wrote Truxton:

> I made, in what I said Sunday night, somewhat of a comeback at what was said previously. Absolutely no names or reference to the other you understand—simply the facts of the case. It was a thrill to sit up there on the platform next to Mr. Fuller, one of the speakers of the evening. There were about 3,000 people in the audience to say nothing of the radio audience. We have the Lord to thank for this, through Mr. Nyman of the Wycliffe Bible Translators who is in charge of these conferences for the Church of the Open Door.

Given the contemporary controversy over the place of women in ministry, it is interesting to note that Betty had already resolved this issue for herself. Before accepting this opportunity to speak, she thoroughly reviewed her position with regard to a woman speaking in a church. After further reflection, she decided, "I shall speak on the basis of witnessing to what He is doing. I am not preaching or occupying any ministerial position over the members of the church by-laws."

Fisk was now engaged as a field representative for CAMF in the East. He stirred up interest in CAMF at the Christian and Missionary Alliance (C&MA) school, Nyack College, and Columbia Bible College in South Carolina. Fisk also continued his own connection with C&MA.

Jim Truxton was slated for transfer to the Far East and wanted to see CAMF become incorporated before his departure in early August.[14] The imponderable in all this was the absence in Los Angeles (except for Betty) of those most able to provide CAMF with qualified leadership. Jim had on several occasions suggested to Betty that they seek another executive head to replace him, but this was hardly possible, inasmuch as he and Greene were the driving forces behind the new organization.[15]

Grady and Maurine Parrott

As these concerns were weighing on the minds of Greene and Truxton, the Lord was preparing Grady Parrott for responsibility in CAMF. Parrott was then serving as an advanced instructor for the Royal Air Force (RAF) on AT-6s at Falcon Field, Phoenix, Arizona. He was an accountant by profession, president of the Gideons in Arizona, and served on the board of the Mexican Gospel Mission. He had been active in the Phoenix Christian Business Men's Committee, of which he was a charter member. He and his wife, Maurine, were members of the First Methodist Church but also attended classes at the Phoenix Bible Institute, which later became Arizona Bible College.

Parrott was a native of northern Virginia and son of an auditor in the post office in Washington, D.C. In the Washington of his day, it was not unusual to see the country's leaders at close range. He remembers walking down the street near the United States Treasury as a youngster. "We started to cross the intersection and there were two men, one a huge man, and he called me and said, 'Hey sonny, come here. Could you tie my shoe?'" Grady looked up and instantly recognized former President William Howard Taft, whom President Harding appointed Chief Justice of the Supreme Court in 1921.

Grady Parrott attended McKinley Technical High School in Washington, where he enjoyed studying art. After graduation from high school, he and a friend had the wanderlust. They headed for England looking for adventure and secured posts working on a freighter. That marked the beginnings of Parrott's consuming interest in other places and people.

In 1929 the family left for Arizona, where his father was advised to move to improve his health. Grady obtained employment with the power company. During these years he met Maurine, who had grown up in Wichita, Kansas, and then had settled in Pueblo, Colorado, with her family. The two were married in 1933. Before going into the military, Grady became the office and credit manager of a wholesale paper company. Aviation was something he had been doing privately since coming to Arizona, and he flew throughout the Rockies in single-engine planes.

In early 1942, he enlisted in the Air Force as flight instructor and then was loaned to the British, who were setting up an RAF flight training base in the American West. Grady was with this program for nearly three years, instructing Royal Air Force pilots in advanced flight, including preliminary aerial combat maneuvers. Much of the flying was done close to the ground. Reflecting on that experience, Grady said, "The benefit of what I had learned, maneuvering in close places, getting out of tight spots, flying blind canyons under restricted navigational conditions all seemed a most helpful orientation for later work with MAF."

As a layman, Grady had become increasingly interested in harnessing the plane for missionary service in underdeveloped countries. He felt like a prophet crying in the wilderness until contacted by Paul Hartford of Victory Sky Pilots. Hartford's vision struck a responsive but uncertain chord in Grady's heart. He began to correspond and think seriously about joining him after the war but increasingly had doubts about Hartford's flamboyant style and emphasis on training missionaries to fly.

In January 1945, Grady called Betty Greene. He had learned about CAMF from Beth Brunemeier, a military nurse serving in California, and had made initial contact by mail. As a result of that conversation, Betty was impressed that "here was someone we should know." Grady promised to look up Betty at the CAMF office the next time he came to Los Angeles.

Grady had been leaning "60–75 percent" toward going with Hartford. Instead, he decided to take a closer look at CAMF.

Grady came in to see Betty at CAMF's Navigators' office at the end of February. She sized him up as a good man who had "done a lot of clear thinking on the problem of flying and its finances." Grady said he was looking at an alternate mission aviation group, about which he wanted more information. The two of them prayed about Grady's future. Apparently the Lord was in all this, for Grady signed up as an active member of CAMF before leaving.[16] At this point in CAMF's development, joining meant that the member was actively interested in the organization and slated to receive updates on news; it did not mean enlisting for full-time service.

Betty wrote Jim Truxton about the meeting with Grady, calling it good news, but she assumed that Grady would join Hartford. "He is very level-headed and could give Hartford the balancing factor he seems to need."[17]

Jim wasted no time following up the contact. In his first letter to Grady, he shared his vision for CAMF "as a strong, sound and

God-directed organization which embodies the united efforts of Christian airmen *the world over*."[18] He recognized that Grady might have some contacts in Britain and indicated his hope of receiving replies from overtures he had made to Dr. Thomas Cochrane of the World Dominion Center in London and a pilot named David Featherstone. At that time, Murray Kendon was hoping to interest Cochrane in the potential of aviation for serving missionaries. Since Jim knew that Grady was initially leaning toward joining Hartford, he explained his vision of CAMF becoming an international air corps for Christ.

Grady was favorably impressed by CAMF. He told his wife, Maurine, "This is it" and cooled his relationship with Hartford. Of course, he wanted to meet Jim Truxton, and when Jim was stationed at San Diego before his departure for the Pacific, the two finally met at Trotman's home. The first night, they talked until two in the morning.

These two men approached aviation differently. Jim had flown Mariner seaplanes, while Grady worked with single-engine craft in canyon country. Jim had visions of a large CAMF operation, while Grady was thinking in more measured terms. In their give-and-take, a fusion in their thought emerged. When they parted, Grady knew that he would be working with Jim Truxton, but he went back to Phoenix without making any commitments. He had to consider Maurine and their two small children. Obviously, the cost of his joining CAMF would be higher than that for Betty or Jim, since both were single. He and Maurine prayed about their future.

Before the end of April, Grady cast his lot with CAMF. He called Betty to let her know that he would be joining at the close of the war. For Jim, Grady's favorable response was heaven-sent. Since he was heading to the Far East, Jim wanted another officer to help Betty. He approached Betty with the idea of making Grady vice president. She agreed, adding, "Don't think of him taking your place (if you don't mind my advice), but rather as supplementing your work."[19] Buyers and Fisk also agreed, but was Grady ready to accept this much responsibility? The incorporation papers were ready to be finalized, and Grady's response was pivotal.

Grady thought it over and then sent this telegram to Betty on June 1, 1945: "WILL ACCEPT CAMF OFFICE PREVIOUSLY DISCUSSED / WITH

UNDERSTANDING WILL DEVOTE TIME AS LORD PERMITS AND RELEASES ME
HERE WHICH AT PRESENT IS INDEFINITE / NOTIFY TRUXTON WILL COOPER-
ATE ON INCORPORATION SIGNATURE AS HE SUGGESTED IF THAT SEEMS
MOST EXPEDIENT UNDER CIRCUMSTANCES / SECOND CORINTHIANS THREE
FIVE." In citing that passage, Grady let it be known he did not feel
presumptuous in accepting the office but trusted God to supply
for the unforeseen future. Grady went from inquirer to vice president in a brief six months. That commitment was bathed in prayer
and Grady moved forward with confidence. He served as vice
president of MAF until 1949, then as its president for twenty-one
years, transforming MAF into a worldwide operation.

In the summer of 1945 Grady's heart was set to work with
CAMF, but the meager resources of this new venture of faith could
not support more than one officer. To support his family, Grady
worked at other jobs for two years while he served CAMF. Grady's
commitment to CAMF was not without cost.

For several months he worked in Beaumont, California, for a
Christian businessman who was opening a manufacturing plant
there. He served him weekdays and joined his family and conferred
with CAMF on weekends—not a very satisfactory arrangement.

The Beaumont enterprise was not successful, and Grady was
uncertain about his next step. Before driving home the day the
plant closed its doors, he fell on his knees and sought the Lord's
guidance. That same day Grady told his pastor his circumstances.
The pastor said, "Let's pray that God will indicate through the
others the need for your service full-time."

When Grady arrived home that weekend, he found word from
the other CAMF officers that he was needed full-time! At that time
CAMF personnel received salaries only as the Lord provided.
When there was a shortage, each person took a cut in that month's
pay. Abandoning all thought of further outside employment took
faith, and this faith commitment to work together full-time forged
strong bonds among the members of the CAMF leadership team.

Incorporation of CAMF

Pressing business brought most of CAMF's leadership to Los
Angeles in June. Truxton, Parrott, and Buyers joined Greene to

work on the incorporation papers with attorney Oscar Elvrum. The by-laws had been circulated and revised three times, but the full purposes of CAMF had not yet been clearly defined. All that the leadership knew was that it would be independent and non-denominational, an agency seeking to serve evangelical missions. What was not at all clear was the most efficient manner of integrating air service into existing mission work. Some thought that missionaries should be trained as pilots and fly their own planes. As a missionary pilot serving C&MA in Borneo, Fisk leaned in this direction. Having begun as a fellowship of airmen interested in missions, CAMF had by mid-1945 begun to consider flight training as a large part of its mission. At the same time, flight training organizations were sprouting up in various quarters. Should CAMF duplicate this activity or tackle some more strategic goals?

Given the formative nature of CAMF's mission, attorney Elvrum sensed the need for flexibility in the charter. Grady Parrott characterized Elvrum's contribution this way: "He was a very sympathetic listener and picked up the generalizations of what we were trying to do, and put it into a framework that would give us a wide scope in which to move." Elvrum drew up a long list of possibilities, including relief work as part of CAMF's mission. Grady recalled that they agreed wholeheartedly with Elvrum's reaching out for all the possibilities.

CAMF saw the airplane as an instrument for Christian service, a vehicle for redeeming time for the missionary instead of trekking over long distances of tortuous terrain. They decided that flying planes was a task for specialists, not novices. Just where the boundaries lay for the plane's contribution to missionary work had yet to be explored. CAMF's leadership was not prepared to set arbitrary limits in this untried field.

Incorporation papers were signed on May 20, 1945. The document was recorded on June 4. The four officers constituting the first board of directors were James C. Truxton, president; J. Grady Parrott, vice president; Elizabeth E. Greene, secretary-treasurer; James W. Buyers, executive secretary. The by-laws recognized that on occasion some of the officers might be in distant places and made provision for flexible leadership. If the president and vice president were away, the executive secretary could assume responsibility. For purposes of decision making, an executive committee consisting of Grady and Betty was empowered to carry forward the business of CAMF.[20]

To fully appreciate this flexible structure, one has to recognize that none of the leaders felt they owned CAMF. They were convinced that God had called them together to carry out this work, although it had yet to begin. The organization was not the creation of one charismatic leader who rallied his followers in support of his goals. As Jim wrote from Okinawa on August 11, 1945, just days away from Japan's surrender, "Please do not delay things in order to hear from me first. No one of us is indispensable to the work, and I feel sure God led Grady into our midst at just the time He did, for a good reason."[21]

Truxton called for continued reliance on the Lord. He summed it up this way. "From the very first day God gave us the vision and call to CAMF, He has never unfolded a complete picture before us, nor removed all obstacles from the path. He has led us step by step."[22] Truxton's reflection on the first two years is also a commentary of how MAF's future unfolded. It continued to be a venture of faith, with many unexpected turns in the road.

Leadership Style

In May 1945 the organization had a balance of three dollars, with all bills paid. Along the way, as Betty pointed out to Jim Truxton, the needs were supplied just in time, so the organization "never had to go in the red one cent." The Lord opened and closed doors for them. At times they had to wait for doors to open, but neither Jim nor Betty wanted to pry open any doors that the Lord had shut.

Decisions were made in extended consultation with one another. Jim encouraged the airing of views and constructive criticism in search of sound decisions based on consensus. A style of collective leadership emerged with submission to one another as the operative principle, together with esteeming the other person better than themselves. This collective leadership continued in the form of the executive committee. As the organization grew and pilots and their families began to serve on fields stretching from

Mexico to New Guinea, it became evident that field personnel could not possibly become involved in top management-level deliberations. Where decisions affected them personally—such as the location and nature of their service—the pilots were consulted.

The resultant openness among the leaders reflected decision making by consensus, which Truxton, Greene, and Parrott fostered. They viewed themselves as responsible servants, not lords of all who were interested in missionary aviation.

All those who joined the CAMF leadership team knew they would sacrifice materially. What they did enjoy was a large measure of Christian fellowship and significant involvement in developing a new agency for advancing the cause of Christ. They encountered much uninformed criticism against the use of airplanes in Christian service. In many circles, this was viewed as an unnecessary expense, a luxury, and a flight of fancy that had little practical value for effective missionary work. Early CAMF pioneers worked to demonstrate the viability of properly selected and effectively used planes as economical and efficient tools for assisting missionaries.

As an independent organization, CAMF was not assured of acceptance or recognition in evangelical mission circles. It had to earn their respect. CAMF had the backing of neither a denomination nor some other influential sending organization. They were wise in seeking the assistance of respected Christian leaders of the stature of Dawson Trotman of the Navigators; V. Raymond Edman, president of Wheaton College; Cameron Townsend, general director of Wycliffe; Stacey Woods of InterVarsity; Jack Wyrtzen of Word of Life; Robert McQuilkin, president of Columbia Bible College—all members of the CAMF advisory council in July 1945.[23] Significantly, it was Townsend of Wycliffe who was the first to call on CAMF's service in Mexico. While Townsend helped CAMF gain experience with flight work in Mexico and Peru, his expectation that CAMF would work exclusively for Wycliffe's Summer Institute of Linguistics (SIL) resulted in CAMF clarifying its mission in favor of planting regional cooperative flight programs.

CAMF also needed advice from people with expertise in various other fields. Attorney Elvrum's excellent help made them realize what a good lawyer could do. Counsel was also needed in aviation, especially when efforts were being made to adapt it to primitive conditions found in many underdeveloped nations throughout the world. Initial members on the technical board were Carl Wooten of Beechcraft and Paul B. Payne, airline pilot from Chicago.[24]

As for Fisk, he had plans for an early departure to Borneo after the war, and these plans precluded him from taking official responsibility on the home front. In recognition of his place and influence in the work of CAMF, Fisk was given the honorary title of foreign secretary.[25]

Truxton hoped to forge links between Christian pilots internationally. To this end he pursued a variety of leads. He contacted Dr. Thomas Cochrane of the World Dominion Center in London, to apprise him of developments in America. Dr. Cochrane kept in touch with Christian work worldwide, and it was through this contact that Truxton opened correspondence with Murray Kendon, an RAF pilot from New Zealand. The zeal for missionary aviation on the part of Kendon led Cochrane to support him in the creation of an air wing under the Movement for World Evangelization, August 1, 1944.[26] This official beginning of British Missionary Aviation Fellowship (now MAF-UK) came some eight and one-half months after Greene opened up the CAMF office in Los Angeles.

Truxton also had his eyes open for the possibility of developing missionary aviation in Australia. Since Fisk's work was among the Dyaks in Borneo, Australia might seem the logical base of support for missionary aviation throughout Southeast Asia. Inasmuch as Fisk was looking forward to returning to Borneo, Truxton wrote him and an Australian airman, Ken Cooper, a CAMF member, about the possibility of exploring contacts there. Cooper was among those who founded Australia's MAF in Melbourne in 1947. The start of British and Australian MAF are subjects of later chapters, but it is interesting to note that, even at this early stage, Truxton was thinking about MAF's global extension.

Prior to Truxton's reassignment to the Pacific, he set in motion CAMF's quarterly publication, *Missionary Aviation*. With a growing membership of 225 active and 175 associate members, Greene and Truxton wanted to keep the members apprised of each other's activities, the developments of CAMF, and the growing opportunities for service. Additionally, the periodical was envisioned as an advertisement for the concept of missionary aviation. The first edition of ten thousand copies was issued on CAMF's first anniversary. The bill came to five hundred dollars. These funds were not in hand when the order was placed, but Jim and Betty launched the first issue as a step of faith bolstered by the fact that the Lord had met all of CAMF's expenses during that first fiscal year. Even so, paying for the publication proved to be a formidable task. For subsequent issues, whenever finances were too tight, CAMF simply skipped publication.

The first issue of *Missionary Aviation* had pictures of CAMF members Jim Truxton, Jim Buyers, Paul Robinson, and Stanley Cain, then a student at Westmont College. Robinson later founded the missionary flight training program at Moody Bible Institute. Truxton anonymously wrote the lead article, "Where There Is No Vision the People Perish." He also included a challenge from Dawson Trotman: "Go Prepared . . . Equipped." Including Trotman in this first issue reveals the close working relationship between CAMF and the Navigators. Betty contributed "The CAMF Story . . . In Brief." She also launched what would become a separate monthly newsletter, "Wings of Praise and Prayer," which appeared as part of this first issue. It is significant that forty-five years later Betty Greene was still on the forefront of promoting prayer for MAF. Indeed, she distinguished herself as MAF's prayer secretary.

Betty Greene's effective work in the office meant that word on CAMF was getting out to the Christian public. At the same time, Betty had a yearning to put feet to CAMF's field operations. In the fall of 1945 the possibility for launching a flight program seemed quite remote. By the following February Betty flew CAMF's first plane to Wycliffe's SIL's Jungle Camp in Mexico. How the Lord made this possible is our next story.

Launching Operations in Mexico

Jim Truxton, in Japan with the Navy, was stationed first at Okinawa and then at Sasebo on Japan's Kyushu Island as part of Gen. Douglas MacArthur's occupying forces. From there he kept up a brisk correspondence with Betty and others.

The periodic typhoons that swept up the Philippine Sea to southern Japan kept Truxton on the move. In mid-October, his wing was evacuated to Shanghai, China, where he promptly investigated the potential for missionary aviation. He had extended talks with China Inland Mission evacuees who had recently been released from internment under the Japanese, inquiring into their appraisal of mission transportation needs within China. From his conversations with American and British missionaries, he became convinced that although mission aviation was not really needed in China, this did not rule out other parts of Southeast Asia. What was needed was a "strong, recognized, and influential international organization" to deal with governments whose permission would be required in order to launch such operations.[1]

Charlie and Claire Mellis

In the middle of August 1945, Betty Greene received a letter of inquiry from Charles J. Mellis. He had briefly been a student at Wheaton College before going off to war. After the war, he learned about CAMF from a bulletin that Wheaton president V. Raymond Edman had sent out to all fliers on the college roster. Charlie Mellis had earned a private license prior to the war. After his induction into the military, he became a B-17 copilot, flying thirty-two missions with the Eighth Air Force over Germany. He was currently a flight instrument instructor at Bryan Field, Texas, and expected to be discharged at the beginning of September. Charlie wrote that he felt drawn to missionary work and, since his training in the Air Force, "felt more and more led toward using the flying experience I have gained to glorify the Lord."

Upon reading the CAMF literature Betty sent him, Charlie wrote, "I was amazed as I read each page and found that practically all your ideas on the subject coincided with ideas I'd had concerning this work. In every way I'm in accord with the policies of the Fellowship. That's why I believe the Lord has definitely answered prayer in leading me to the CAMF."[2]

After his discharge from the Air Force, Mellis immediately made himself available for service. Since no immediate prospect existed for full-time work with CAMF, he and his wife, Claire, headed for St. Louis to spend some time with his parents. His father was a successful independent builder. He had the same love for missions that Charlie picked up when the family made a year's tour of Africa, visiting missionaries in a "Carry-All" in 1937.

Claire Schoolland Mellis attended Calvin College for two years and completed her undergraduate work in education at the University of Colorado at Boulder, where her father was a highly respected member of the faculty. Charlie and Claire had made preparations to go to Wheaton when word arrived that Grady Parrott was heading East following his release from Falcon Field. He stopped by to see the Mellises in Chicago, which proved to be a turning point for Charlie. He was immediately possessed by a strong desire to promote interest in missionary aviation. In response, Parrott and Truxton agreed to have him serve as CAMF's Midwest field representative.

Charlie plunged into this task and gave himself wholly to it until he and Claire, and their six-week-old son John, moved to Los Angeles in May 1946. The intervening months saw him step out in faith. They had no guaranteed income and had to rely on church offerings for support. Without an office, car, or calling card, Charlie began to make contacts, first in the Chicago area, then in St. Louis. The Mellises literally lived out of suitcases, continually on the move. Fortunately, Claire's cousin opened her home to them. After Christmas, they lived in the home of a couple that had gone to California for the winter.

Between speaking engagements, Charlie wrote articles for *His*, *Sunday*, and *Power*. Writing articles came naturally to him. The pace of CAMF's work in Los Angeles had quickened, but good channels for keeping Charlie fully apprised of developments were not yet in place. The biggest problem for him was lack of current information.

One individual with whom he kept in contact was E. W. "Hatch" Hatcher, then attending Wheaton College. Charlie first met Hatch at a Foreign Missions Fellowship (FMF) meeting in January 1946. Hatch did not have the depth of flying experience of some of the MAF men, but in one respect his qualifications were broader than any CAMF officer's to date, inasmuch as he was licensed to maintain and service planes.

The Summer Institute of Linguistics

Uppermost in the minds of Greene, Mellis, and others was the need for CAMF to begin serving on the field. The necessary preparatory work seemed endless. All of them felt that the time had come to put a CAMF airplane into mission service. This was a sure way to acquire the experience necessary for flight operations and find out what planes would be best suited for the various demands of missionary aviation.

The initial opportunity for service lay close at hand. Cameron Townsend, founder and general director of Wycliffe Bible Translators (WBT), needed help in Mexico. Peru invited him to engage in linguistic work among the Indians of its eastern tropical frontier under the name of SIL. To prepare linguists for the rigors of the field, Townsend set up a jungle camp in Mexico, an outgrowth of Wycliffe's SIL Sulphur Springs, Arkansas, program that began training linguists for Mexico in 1934.[3] The very nature of SIL allowed Townsend to bring in Bible translators as education and development workers rather than as Protestant missionaries. The latter sometimes found it difficult to acquire visas to enter Peru and other Latin American countries. SIL's task was to reduce the languages of indigenous peoples to written form and translate the Bible into their tongues, while at the same time retaining excellent relations with the host government. To facilitate SIL's work, Townsend had long contemplated adding an air arm to facilitate the movement of linguists, especially as work expanded into the Amazon basin.

Bill Nyman, the able secretary of Wycliffe's board, approached Grady Parrott to see if he would be interested in starting an air arm for SIL. Naturally, Grady told Nyman that he had committed himself to assist building a missionary aviation program with CAMF.

In September 1945 Townsend called on CAMF to study the feasibility of airplane use in jungle operations in Mexico and Peru. Betty conferred with Truxton and Parrott, and the decision was made for her to depart for Mexico at once. Selma and Peggy were left to manage the office while Betty was gone for what she thought would be just two weeks.

In Mexico City, Betty found herself in a social circle dominated by SIL personnel. Cameron Townsend served as her host. This was exhilarating for Betty, who had been working long days alone in a small office. She was now free to observe SIL work on the field and visit their Jungle Camp near Tuxtla, the capital of the state of Chiapas. She discussed Wycliffe's immediate flight needs with Townsend and agreed that they had need for a pilot and plane in Mexico. Townsend also projected air transport needs for SIL personnel who would soon be arriving in Peru. Betty agreed that the transport requirements in Peru called for a plane, a pilot, and a mechanic.[4]

As it turned out, Betty did not come back to Los Angeles until Christmas, and in January 1946 briefed the CAMF board on SIL's needs. As a result, CAMF decided to start its first operation in Latin America. This involved the purchase of a plane for Mexico.[5]

Who would be the first CAMF pilot to fly in Mexico? It was decided that since Betty had developed such a good working relationship with SIL and was fully qualified as a pilot, there was no better person to start the flight program.

In the meantime Jim Truxton had returned to Los Angeles in December 1945 and was soon discharged from military service.

With Betty slated to depart for Mexico, the question arose as to who would manage the office. Charlie Mellis volunteered to put his talents to use in the home office. However, he continued his work as Midwest field representative until May before coming west with his family.

Operations in Mexico

The big question now was the type of plane needed for SIL's Mexico operation. Mellis felt the job would be best accomplished with a light plane, such as a Piper "Cruiser." Others had been thinking of a larger craft, such as the Waco biplane. Truxton and Parrott weighed the arguments and decided to purchase a Waco. Given the nature of the Mexican work, which entailed moving heavy supplies and many personnel over extended distances, they felt this first plane had to be very versatile and capable of flying over high mountain ranges.

On February 14, 1946, CAMF purchased a newly rebuilt 1933 four-place Waco cabin biplane with a new 220-horsepower Continental engine. At five thousand dollars, the plane was a bargain. It was paid for through large contributions from CAMF's leaders and Wycliffe's friends, but the title was in CAMF's name.[6]

In going to Mexico with SIL, CAMF would be flying supplies and personnel between Tuxtla and Jungle Camp. CAMF entered Mexico as part of SIL's work, as it later did in Peru. At no time did CAMF identify itself by name in either of these programs, since it came to support SIL's work. Of course other trips were made but not with the idea of setting up any form of cooperative flying service for evangelical missions of the type CAMF later promoted in Ecuador. It must be recognized that in launching its first service in Mexico, CAMF began to formulate what its future flight policies should be.

Understanding this reality makes it easier to comprehend why in 1948 Townsend felt he could not go along with CAMF's policy of providing regional cooperative mission flight programs and created Wycliffe's Auxiliary: the Jungle Aviation and Radio Service (JAARS). This was motivated in great part by SIL's need to shield itself from identification with evangelical missions. The governments with whom Townsend carried on linguistic and literacy work in Latin America viewed SIL as a purely humanitarian and development organization. They would not have given Townsend entry if it were known that he planned to evangelize by introducing the indigenous people to the Scriptures. As it turned out, MAF's evolving service policy was to openly assist evanglical missions, and this approach was incompatible with Townsend's design.

Dewey Lockman of La Habra, orange grower and founder of the Lockman Foundation, took an interest in CAMF's work. When it was known that the organization would soon have a plane, Lockman offered to clear a field close to his office so a celebration might mark the acquisition of CAMF's first plane. Truxton later reported the occasion as follows.

On that Saturday at 1:00 P.M. there was a large reception committee including Mr. & Mrs. Lockman, also many of his staff, Mr. & Mrs. Goodner of Santa Ana, patrons of Wycliffe, several photographers, and other spectators waiting for the bright red Waco. . . .

Waco biplane before departure for service in Mexico, 1946. From right to left: Grady Parrott, Jim Truxton, Betty Greene, Ed Goodner, and friends of CAMF.

As you can imagine, my old heart was skipping double time as Grady Parrott brought it down to a perfect landing on the excellent strip Mr. Lockman had prepared.[7]

After familiarization flights, on February 23, Betty Greene and two Wycliffe workers, Lois Schneider and Ethel Lambottee, took off from the Lockman field and headed for SIL's Jungle Camp in Chiapas. This was CAMF's inaugural flight. By noon the second day, Betty reached Brownsville, Texas, where border crossing and weather conditions held them over until eleven o'clock the following day. Betty followed the shoreline on a three-hour flight to Tampico. From there she moved on to Tuxpan, to spend the first night on Mexican soil. Problems with fuel and weather conditions delayed departure for Mexico City. Betty related the events thereafter in colorful detail.

The greeting received in the city was surpassed only by the one waiting at Jungle Camp Sunday morning. For Camp it meant the long anticipated plane had finally arrived. Native Mexicans and Indians had a new surge of faith in these white men. With clouds down on the mountain tops and only valleys and cliffs and small towns as checkpoints (there are no maps accurate enough to navigate by) on the last leg of the journey I was very thankful for my pilot friend, Joe (Urquidi) who guided the way in. Providentially, he had to make a flight that morning which took him right by Camp. It was indeed a thrill to cross the last ridge and see the group of huts by the river quietly lying below. Landing on that 1,800 ft. strip was quite different from the kind you would make on a typical military field in the States. It gives you a funny feeling to creep through a cut in the trees that cover a ridge and then drop to a strip about as wide as your wing spread. The welcome Mr. Townsend, Miss Elaine Mielke (his fiancée) and I received will always be one of my choicest memories. The *abrazos* from the old and new friends, most of them training to go on to Peru this spring, the greetings from Mexicans and Indians, some familiar and others new, the excited exclamations over the plane, the thankful hearts, the dinner and the worship service that evening all contributed to a day of untold rejoicing.[8]

Betty had not come down to celebrate but to facilitate SIL work. She met a score of SIL's workers preparing themselves for Bible translation work in Peru but concerned to complete their applications for passports at Tapachula, some 165 miles distant. The next morning Betty flew Townsend, Gloria Gray, and Culley (the camp doctor) over the jungle, beyond the nearby Lacandone Indian village where Phil Baer had settled and begun the arduous task of language learning and Bible translation. Betty circled a clearing near the camp and Dr. Culley dropped a package of raisins and letters into the clearing. This visit meant a great deal to the isolated linguist.

On the round trip to Tapachula, Betty skirted ten villages where SIL workers were located. Many other flights followed in the next weeks. The Waco proved itself valuable and reliable. The plane climbed easily to thirteen thousand feet when not heavily loaded. Townsend was thrilled with the performance of Betty and the ship and looked forward to an early start in Peru. He was totally sold on the use of the airplane for missions and considered its use "absolutely essential for evangelizing inaccessible areas in this generation."[9]

The Waco Accident

As things stood, Betty was to move down to Peru in March. Plans were to have an amphibian carry forward the work there. George Wiggins, a naval pilot who had been flying off carriers, prepared to replace Betty in Mexico. He came down as scheduled, and Betty took him on familiarization flights for almost a week. Wiggins piloted the craft with perfect confidence. He tried a landing on the El Real strip close to Jungle Camp, and seemed to be fully oriented to his new task.

On March 26, Wiggins was at the controls and Betty was with him when the Waco came in for a second landing at El Real. Wiggins had circled the field and Betty was certain that he had seen the chicle hut[10] just off the strip where it made an elbow. Both the approach and landing were fine, even though the speed at touchdown was a bit fast. Unfortunately, however, Wiggins had apparently forgotten the structure, and the craft's left wings hit it sharply. Both left wings of the biplane, the propeller, and the left landing gear were damaged. Fuel spilled out of the tank as the plane bounced and stopped. It swung around full circle before coming to rest on the strip. Fortunately, there was neither fire nor bodily injury.

Betty's explanation was frank and fair when she wrote Grady Parrott that, "Somehow it didn't seem to be a question of his (Wiggins') handling the ship but an unexplainable failure to see the hut or remember it was there."[11]

Townsend hoped to keep the report of this accident from becoming public. Truxton received the bad news while on a speaking tour. He had just visited the Beech and Cessna factories in Wichita, Kansas, when he received Parrott's letter relating the details. Contrary to Townsend's desire to suppress the news, Truxton recommended that a report be released to CAMF members and prayer partners stating that what had happened was unfortunate but had to be faced and that valuable lessons could be learned from the accident. This openness was in line with the way CAMF had operated right from the start.

Parrott, in the home office, found himself caught between Townsend's and Truxton's recommendations. He counseled Truxton to respect Townsend's sensibilities in the matter, which he did for a brief time. Wycliffe did not lose confidence in CAMF as a result of the accident. It delayed Greene's move to Peru, but plans for CAMF's assistance to SIL remained intact.

Labor of Love

The most pressing immediate problem was to get the Waco repaired. Neither Wiggins nor Betty Greene were capable of doing the repair, and replacement parts were nowhere in sight. Had it not been for Nate Saint's willingness to do the work, the Waco might never have left the jungle.

Betty initially hoped to get spares from another Waco being dismantled at Villahermosa. This proved impossible. Instead, parts had to be shipped from the United States. Greene and Wiggins waited for three months for the parts and mechanic to arrive. It was December before the Waco took to the skies again. This was a very trying time for both CAMF and Wycliffe. Betty found comfort in the realization that God was teaching her patience! She was especially thankful that Nate Saint was willing to come all the way from the East Coast to take on such a complex repair job.

Nate Saint was a native of Huntingdon Valley, Pennsylvania. He enlisted in the military in 1942. Since he had previous flying experience, he was sent off to Santa Monica, California, to learn to fly C-47 transports at Douglas Service School. In this regimented atmosphere, he found that he was the army's "lock, stock, and barrel," but as a Christian, he was the Lord's "heart, soul, and spirit."[12] He was moving up the ladder as a cadet when ill health closed the possibility of his becoming an army pilot.

Nate was still interested in flying and he took special interest in an article his father clipped for him, Truxton's "On Wings of the Wind," which appeared in a January 1945 issue of the *Sunday School Times*. He felt strongly drawn to CAMF. In his initial correspondence, Nate related, "Last New Year's eve in a watch-night service I responded to the missionary challenge. Have been interested in missionary work for some time but the Lord owned only my finances. He now has my life."[13]

Nate's pragmatic technical abilities and his single status suggested that he might be the right person to repair the Waco. Nate's plans were for studies at Wheaton College, but he had kept the door open for a possible change in plans if CAMF did not find the right person to repair the plane.

Jim Truxton made it a point to visit Nate at his Pennsylvania home and managed to get in a little flying in Nate's Piper "Cub." They spent some time together in the plane practicing, shooting slips, cross-wind, wheel, and full stall landings and, of course, discussed the work of CAMF. The next day they had a contest to see who could use the least runway for landing. Jim recorded, "My first one beat his, but he came around again and nosed me out in a way which could only be done by one thoroughly familiar with his own ship." These two days of personal encounter gave Jim a great deal of confidence in Nate's flying ability. Furthermore, he sensed that Nate was a resourceful young man, and Jim let him know that he was needed to repair the Waco. Nate rose to the challenge.[14]

Initially, Betty suggested that the Waco company should be contracted to send down two complete wing panels. Logistical problems led to the decision to repair the existing ones. Had it been realized that Nate would have to be there four months rather than six weeks, the decision would have been made to acquire those replacement panels. By July, all arrangements were made for Nate to head to Mexico. He took the train from Philadelphia to St. Louis and from there to Laredo, Texas. A quick flight to Mexico City brought him in contact with Betty just before she left for Peru. She briefed him on the overall picture and the repair work that was needed. In the meantime, Charlie made arrangements to stockpile the new propeller, fabric, glue, and other essential items in Laredo. George Wiggins took them through customs and brought them to Tuxtla.

Nate had to deal with more than technical problems in this repair work. Joe Urquidi, a pilot who operated his own local air service and had previously supplied SIL with air transport, now realized that getting the Waco back into the air would cut into his business. He put roadblocks into Nate's work that forced him to leave Tuxtla and relocate his repair work in a building near the El Real strip.

The combination of frustration, youthful inexperience, imbalance in diet, and poor sanitation eroded Nate's health. SIL missionary Phil Baer, who earlier had been the recipient of "drops" from the Waco, heard of Nate's plight. He volunteered his help and did the cooking. This was more than a gesture of goodwill; it proved a tremendous encouragement to Nate.

Work progressed slowly but steadily. A seemingly endless amount of glue, caulking, fabric, and paint was needed to complete the job. The moist tropical air prevented prompt drying and further delayed the project. Cost of repairs ran close to a thousand dollars and delays brought much frustration and soul searching for everyone.

In the end, CAMF learned a great deal from this setback. Emphasis on safety was strengthened. The Waco experience led to renewed thinking in the planning of long-term operations under primitive conditions in tropical climates. At Nate's urging, all CAMF pilots were required to have technical qualifications such as an earned airframe and engine rating (A&E; later renamed airframe and power plant, A&P). The accident delayed MAF opera-

Rigged hangar in which Nate Saint mounted the Waco biplane's rebuilt left wings after the accident in Mexico, 1946.

tions for six months, but according to Charlie, the lessons learned advanced CAMF's work by two years.[15] Charlie did not think that the accident, which seemed like such a hard blow at the time, was *"turned* into a blessing," but that the "Lord meant it for a blessing from the very start, even though Satan may have meant it to us for evil." While this development was extremely frustrating to all concerned—not just to the CAMF team but to SIL as well—this experience made for greater reliance on God and brought about higher standards of safety.

Nate was finally able to get the Waco back into ferrying condition, a triumph of faith and determination over difficult circumstances. Other frustrations were the lack of a hangar in which to work on the plane and inadequate financial resources for securing supplies.

George Wiggins was offered the opportunity to pilot the repaired Waco out of jungle camp. He took the offer to regain his confidence. Nate was authorized to repair the plane and check the engine, but George was designated to fly it out of the El Real strip and off to Mexico City the day before Thanksgiving. This was real cause for rejoicing. While the plane was in ferrying condition, Nate judged it in need of additional work to bring it up to Civil Aviation Administration (CAA, later changed to Federal Aviation Administration, FAA) standards. The decision was made to sell it in Mexico but, for lack of bidders, Betty and Jim flew it back to Los Angeles, where it was sold for five hundred dollars.

Nate headed back to Los Angeles, briefed Mellis and others on his work in Mexico, and prepared for studies at Wheaton College in February 1947. He remained there for only one year before resuming service with CAMF. Somehow, despite the difficulties of the Waco repair, his desire to serve the Lord in aviation became a settled conviction. When CAMF extended another call to him, this time to become the pilot for the Ecuador program, he was prepared to move. As a result Nate had a part in opening CAMF's first cooperative flight program.

Clarifying the Mission

In the spring and summer of 1946 Jim Truxton traveled extensively in the Midwest and the East, conferring with mission leaders on the best way to use aircraft in serving missions. In the postwar period, these executives were assessing strategies for the future. They recognized that aviation could play a significant part in helping their expansion into areas yet unreached with the gospel. For instance, there was a highly publicized evacuation of stranded and ill missionaries from the interior of China in a chartered DC-3 (*The St. Paul*) immediately after Japan's defeat. There was also a Norwegian missionary effort involving the purchase of a DC-3 named *The Ansgar* that was used to bring missionaries back from Africa. In those days others were dreaming of using aircraft in mission work. We also know that within the next two years the Assemblies of God purchased a C-46 for that purpose.

Competing Mission Aviation Concepts

By 1948, the World Mission Aviation Council (WMAC), an umbrella group of diverse mission aviation interests led by Paul Hartford, proposed a worldwide air transport network to fly evangelical missions personnel.[1] This grandiose plan, like Jim Voss's vision of a global missionary communication network in the 1960s, did not materialize because it was too expensive.

Truxton's survey of mission leaders came at this propitious time. Questions of feasibility, costs, and overall approach to harnessing the airplane were very much on the minds of mission strategists.

59

Not many mission leaders supported Paul Hartford's approach of turning missionaries into pilots. Most, in fact, advised CAMF to continue to leave mission aviation to specialists, believing there was the danger of making poor pilots out of good missionaries.

Time and again Jim Truxton learned that mission leaders did not wish to tie up missionaries in flying or invest in costly aviation equipment. They did, however, see the advantage of the cooperative use of aircraft for a group of missions working in contiguous areas, provided the pilot was highly skilled. In speaking with Christian Weiss and Don Shidler, president and vice president respectively of the Gospel Missionary Union (GMU), Jim "began to see as never before the advantage in the cooperative use of planes for a group of missions in a particular area."[2] In 1948, CAMF made this concept operational in the Ecuador program. CAMF's growing conviction that this was the preferred way to help missions with aircraft unfortunately created tensions in dealing with Cameron Townsend of Wycliffe, who thought of MAF as working exclusively for SIL.

Further contributions to CAMF's policy development that summer came from various conferences Truxton and other leaders attended. Truxton made a presentation at the Evangelical Foreign Missions Association (EFMA) conference in Minneapolis in May 1946. He proposed three sets of circumstances that would lead CAMF to assist missions. First, where an individual missionary had a proven need for a plane and was himself a well-qualified pilot. Second, where a mission, such as the Sudan Interior Mission in Nigeria, needed one or more planes to maintain its widely scattered and remote stations. Third, the most typical circumstance, in which a group of missions working in a region (such as Ecuador) called on CAMF to supply the flight service for all. These cooperating missions would pay a nonprofit fee based on a basic rate per mile that would cover the operation, maintenance, and depreciation costs of the total aviation operation.[3]

Betty Greene received information on these policy developments but was preoccupied with operational problems and her new Peru assignment. It would have been difficult for anyone far removed from the center of discussion to enter into and fully appreciate the ferment of this period.

Discussions with Clarence Jones of radio station HCJB and Kenneth Pike of Wycliffe also confirmed that, in most cases, it was undesirable to train missionaries to fly. Flying and related aeronautical matters should be in the hands of a competent organization like CAMF with expertise in the field. CAMF's emerging policy might be summed up in Truxton's phrase: "Flying is for skilled fliers—not for already busy missionaries."

Any ideas of training fliers, except for flight orientation in preparation for service on a specific field, disappeared from CAMF's thinking when the Moody Bible Institute accepted Paul Robinson's proposal to train fliers and appointed him to start the Moody flight school. This development led CAMF to conclude that the best course of action was to seek to influence the diverse groups interested in promoting missionary aviation. CAMF favored training Christians to become professionals as pilots serving missions.

The CAMF team brought these perspectives to the discussion at the First Missionary Aviation Conference at Winona Lake, Indiana, in August 1946. Over forty people representing a wide array of mission aviation interests were in attendance. Murray Kendon came from England to contribute and benefit from the interaction.

What resulted from this personal exchange between American and British leaders at Winona Lake was CAMF's decision to adopt the name of their British counterpart: Missionary Aviation Fellowship (MAF). The name change did not become official until the 1946 board meeting in Los Angeles. At that time it was clear that the purpose of both aviation organizations was to serve overseas evangelical missions. Truxton's initial hope for an international organization did not materialize, but the spirit of cooperative endeavor for the purpose of spreading the gospel was furthered as a result of Kendon's coming to Winona Lake.

Clarification of MAF's mission in 1946 tightened the management of the organization. As acting secretary, Charlie Mellis at first followed the earlier pattern: Board members discussed business by mail, and whenever a consensus emerged, it became mission policy. This was an enormously time-consuming process. By late 1946 Charlie recognized that this way of conducting business could no longer be tolerated if MAF was going to become effective. These internal concerns, coming at a time when MAF was clarifying its mission, impacted MAF's dealings with Wycliffe's Cameron Townsend.

Purchase of the Duck

Cameron Townsend had made arrangements with the Peruvian government to start linguistic work among the tribes living in the Oriente, the tropical eastern half of the country that is part of the vast Amazon drainage basin. Townsend laid plans for a series of stations centered at Pucallpa on the Ucayali River. Betty Greene was to provide air transport with an amphibious aircraft.

The search for a suitable plane had been going on for some time. Truxton, Parrott, and Mellis considered lighter craft, such as the Seabee or Trimmer. The payload for these, given the necessity of climbing to an altitude of seventeen thousand feet, fell far short of the transport need in Peru. The work called for shipping large quantities of supplies over the towering Andes into the Amazon basin.

The price of these planes was a major consideration, and MAF extended its search to the United States government's Foreign Liquidation Commission. Truxton visited Washington and traced a U.S. military Grumman "Duck" with a 950-horsepower engine for sale in Peru for thirty-five hundred dollars. The MAF leadership was not thrilled with this, but could locate no better option. Townsend immediately moved on the information and purchased the Duck without any further consultation. The MAF leadership was totally taken aback, for Townsend had failed to ask if MAF was in agreement with the purchase. At that point there was an uneasy feeling that Townsend was taking control of the flight program that MAF had expected to run.

Furthermore, Townsend—in conjunction with the Peruvian ministries of education, health, and aeronautics—worked out an advantageous arrangement whereby the first two Peruvian ministries would pay for half the purchase price and one-half of the major repairs. In return for this favored treatment, the plane had to be made available to the government for transport of medical and educational services. The minister of aeronautics supplied the plane with parachutes and ordered that it be treated as a Peruvian government plane with fuel available at seventeen cents per gallon.[4]

These advantageous terms had all the appearances of a real coup. Nevertheless, MAF's leadership in Los Angeles sensed that all might not be well in their future relationship with Townsend if he pursued this pattern of autonomous action. His unilateral purchase of the Duck and the arrangements he made for its control did not bode well for the same kind of good working relationship that MAF had enjoyed with SIL in the Mexico jungle camp operation. There MAF owned and operated the Waco and was responsible for the flight program. Not so in Peru.

From Townsend's perspective, the entire arrangement for the Duck was heaven-sent. Betty, then in Peru, enthusiastically supported Townsend. However, the MAF leaders in Los Angeles were somewhat hesitant. The Duck was such a high-cost aircraft to maintain. It could prove to be a white elephant in the long run.

Given the reservations of her fellow board members, Betty began to have mixed emotions.[5] She was troubled by the dissatisfaction in Los Angeles over Townsend's purchase of the Duck. Dissatisfaction widened into disagreement when MAF, as part of its policy development, began to define more specifically the type of plane (single engine) that should generally be used for missionary aviation.

Betty Greene and the Duck

Betty Greene arrived in Lima at the end of July and was overwhelmed by the welcome she received from SIL personnel and U.S. Ambassador Cooper. The following week, while making a number of familiarization flights, she discovered that an American military advisor to Peru was "looking very much down his nose at the whole linguistic project," adding "you can imagine what he thinks about a girl pilot."[6] She felt that being a woman pilot was becoming a drawback in Peru. As a result, she wrote

Betty Greene standing in front of the Duck, 1947.

Truxton that she did not think she should continue to be on the forefront of MAF's work in new fields.

By the end of the first week Betty took the Duck to 19,500 feet without any difficulty. She also found that it used less than thirty-five gallons of fuel an hour. The plane was able to take off and land on a stretch of six hundred feet with two passengers and a full load of fuel. All seemed well. However, her initial jubilation over the Duck turned to disappointment when she realized that the engine needed an overhaul. This was done at the Peruvian Air Force Arsenal.[7]

In the meantime Betty went ahead with surveys in the Oriente in a single-engine Faucett, with the help of the Peruvian Air Force. She flew from Lima over the Andes to San Ramon and then north to Pucallpa, which had been earlier designated as the possible base for the Duck. From Pucallpa, she headed overland to Aguaytia, the proposed site for the SIL base. She wrote Charlie Mellis, "Wish you could have shared that glorious drive thru the beautiful, thick jungle under the warm sun. I spent Tuesday looking over the jungle base area, especially the river, for a possible landing place for the Duck."[8]

The next morning missionary Henry Osborn escorted her to visit the town and local officials at Tingo Maria. From there, she drove to Haunuco and headed for Lima over the world's highest highway. This was the first time she had traveled the route she would later be flying. Familiarization with the river and anticipated landing sites was important for safe air service. Greene included a goodwill trip to the local officials in the region, recognizing that the time might come when their influence would be important to flight operations.

As a result of this tour, Greene determined that the river landing at the proposed Aguatia base was hazardous. She recommended against landing there and favored waiting until a government-ordered landing strip was built at another location. She also suggested that the Duck be used only for longer flights north and south and over the Andes. She recommended a smaller plane for local flights.

Growing MAF-SIL Tensions

Back in Los Angeles the MAF leadership continued to be uneasy about an operation that encroached on their area of responsibility. They also began to realize that MAF was being restricted, since the Duck was not available to meet other missionary needs in the region. Consequently, the Duck, while it provided useful service to SIL, was not viewed as a good model for future operations.

Greene was in a position to appreciate both sides. She recognized that the objections raised for operating such a large aircraft were valid but, being in Peru, she also appreciated Townsend's broader strategic intent of cooperating with the Peruvian government, which had underwritten a good part of this operation's costs. He needed the support of the Peruvian government to be able to send linguists into the interior. By cooperating with the government in the use of the plane, SIL earned a great deal of prestige.[9] After all, such air transport arrangements required the initial support of Peruvian cabinet ministers. In effect, Townsend was almost more concerned with the diplomatic ramifications of operating the Duck than he was with its economics. MAF, on the other hand, viewed its viability in terms of its serviceability and cost efficiency. Both perspectives were valid.

As a result, while MAF was concerned about the high operational costs of maintenance and downtime of the Duck, Betty agreed with Townsend that the use of the plane brought about so much prestige with the Peruvian government officials that it was a diplomatic coup for SIL and opened many new doors for them in that country.[10]

Truxton's Initiatives in the East

These troublesome developments, serious though they were, should not be viewed as all-consuming to MAF. Other positive MAF initiatives brought encouragement. As a result of Jim Truxton's contacts with the Sudan Interior Mission (SIM) that summer, SIM decided that a plane was needed to advance their work in Nigeria. At that time SIM had 366 missionaries serving in seventy-four stations in West Africa. This was a classic situation in which the plane would be purchased and operated by the mission. Jim advised SIM to meet their needs with a Piper "Super Cruiser" because of its maneuverability in tight places and the fact that it could fly anywhere in Nigeria and land on short strips. It was an inexpensive plane that was easy to repair. Jim led the meeting with the leaders one day and had a check in hand the next. He went off to Piper headquarters at Lock Haven, Pennsylvania, to place an order for the Cruiser. With a 10 percent discount, the total, with parts and shipping costs to Lagos, Nigeria, totaled four thousand dollars.[11]

Now SIM needed a pilot. Jim contacted Clarence Soderberg and his wife, Alice, a registered nurse, and suggested the possibility of service in Nigeria. They were elated and began to negotiate with SIM and were accepted within a month.

Jim and the Soderbergs joined Jack Wyrtzen for several meetings in August. Clarence was talented musically and was called upon to lead the congregational singing and sing solos. One of these was the MAF theme song: "On Wings of the Wind," which had been written by Jim Buyers' wife, Norah. Truxton later commented, "How I love to hear him sing it!" Jack Wyrtzen also fell in love with it. As leader of the Word of Life rallies, he took great interest in Soddy's plans for Nigeria and had him participate in a key rally on Saturday, August 27, 1946, where the song was printed and handed out for everyone to learn. There was no doubt that Jack Wyrtzen was giving MAF his wholehearted support.

MAF's Reorganization

About the time that Betty Greene was in Peru and Jim Truxton was making arrangements to purchase the Cruiser for SIM, Charlie Mellis pondered the need for streamlining MAF's decision-making process. Charlie frankly stated, and Jim agreed, that the board's way of conducting business by correspondence could no longer be tolerated. The year 1946 marked a shift in policy formation. From the birth of the vision until then, the momentum of growth had carried it forward. The officers were scattered over a wide area, promoting the work. Under these circumstances, not much attention was paid to policy formation or the need to speak with one voice. Until MAF's entrance into Peru, the officers generally saw eye to eye, and where they did not, no major problems had arisen. The policy questions that the Duck raised caught MAF somewhat by surprise. Peru required MAF to take a close look at itself.

Mellis brought forward a reform package that streamlined policy formation and decision making so MAF would not be caught off-guard in the future, as they felt they had been in the Peruvian operation. Charlie argued for a centralized directorship that included an executive director plus a quorum of directors that could be called together on short notice to make policy decisions. As things stood, board meetings just could not be held with members scattered across North and South America. Charlie's plan required a virtual reorganization. He gained support for this from all the directors. The reform package was discussed during the summer and passed at the fall 1946 board meeting, the same time as the name change to MAF—Missionary Aviation Fellowship.

In the reorganization, Charlie was appointed secretary-treasurer. Jim Truxton continued as president and Grady Parrott as vice president. These three formed the executive committee and constituted a quorum for purposes of conducting business. Betty Greene continued on the board, but Jim Buyers, who was then attending Columbia Bible College, resigned.[12]

Policy differences with SIL over the Peru operation had led to soul searching, much prayer, and hard thinking on the most effective role MAF could play in serving missions. MAF leaders felt frustrated that Cameron Townsend had encroached on their aeronautical responsibilities. Fortunately, Ecuador proved to be a new start. Here, MAF launched out on its own and started its first cooperative missionary aviation program. Before its entry into Ecuador, MAF came to amicable terms with Cameron Townsend. This proved to be a difficult and delicate task, but it gave insight to those who had eyes to see God advancing his work amid the tensions that sometimes accompany even the best-intentioned endeavors to serve him.

Agony and Ecstasy

In Peru Greene ended 1946 flying the Duck, which was now named the *Amauta*, an Inca word meaning "a wise man serving his people."[1] Betty made history on December 19 by being the first woman to pilot a plane over the high Andes. Her flight is a chapter in the annals of aviation history.

Leaving Lima at 9:15 A.M., the *Amauta* climbed to nineteen thousand feet before heading east to the Reinos Valley and landing at San Ramon two hours later. Townsend operated the radio and assisted all around, including tying down the craft upon landing. The rainy season had just set in, turning the rain forest into even more luxurious jungle greenery.

The first week of January, Betty made a flight to Atalaya, just over one hundred air miles downstream. The town, located on the forks of the Ucayali River, posed a challenge for amphibious landing because of the swiftness of the river. Greene was especially cautious because of dangers lurking just below the surface. Given the constant menace of logs and other debris floating downstream in the swift current, she had reason to look over the site with extra caution. Everything was running smoothly, and Greene praised God for his care. At times, Cameron Townsend assisted with the radio and generally helped with loading passengers, fuel, or other tasks. Betty enjoyed working with him.

There was need for another pilot who could double as mechanic, and Larry Montgomery arrived in Lima to fill this need. He had served with the U.S. Air Force in Peru before deciding to serve with MAF. He joined Betty in Peru after she had been there for a year. She was looking forward to getting some relief.

Engine Failure

Before Larry had done much familiarization flying with Greene at Iquitos, he had to return to Lima. In his absence, a call came from the Peruvian military to aid in the search for two downed pilots in the Amazon basin near Iquitos. Betty put herself and the plane at Peru's disposal. After a day of air search, Betty noticed vibrations in the engine. She brought this to the attention of the officer in charge, who had a mechanic check it out. She and a Peruvian lieutenant went out again over the endless green canopy of the rain forest, only to have the engine suddenly stall. Rapid loss of altitude forced her to land on a short stretch of river just below. The lieutenant became extremely agitated and shouted in Spanish, "Senorita, why are you so calm?" Betty saw no reason for panic. She knew God had not forsaken them and assured the lieutenant that all was well.

Soon curious natives came by dugout canoe to take a look at the Duck and helped the two tie it securely to the bank without so much as a scratch to the plane. Betty radioed her position to Iquitos. She and the lieutenant accepted a native's invitation to spend the night in a house built on stilts twelve feet off the ground. They began to settle in for the night, but swarms of mosquitoes descended on them, forcing them back into the Duck to wait for morning.

After Betty's rescue, the *Amauta* was taken downstream to Itaya, near Iquitos. There the mechanic gave a bleak assessment: The engine had to be replaced. Supposedly the engine had been given a major overhaul before the Duck was sold to SIL. The nearest reasonably priced replacement engine was in Panama. To bring an engine from there would clearly take some time. At least Montgomery was now back on location to do the work.

Given these developments, Jim Truxton, Grady Parrott, and Charlie Mellis were even more convinced that Cameron Townsend's impulsive decision to purchase the Duck had been a mistake.[2] MAF had reservations about the purchase of the Duck in the first place because of the operating costs; now SIL was faced with another period of waiting.

Cameron Townsend was definitely put out by this breakdown in service and expected MAF to come to his immediate rescue. MAF's inability to respond quickly brought down Townsend's criticism that MAF was discussing surveys for flight needs in distant places when it should be following through on its existing commitment. He suggested that he might have to establish his own air arm.

Back in the U.S., Mellis was conducting missionary aviation conferences in Los Angeles, Dallas, and Wheaton, Illinois, to encourage aviators to serve missions. Discussion with mission heads had established the possibility of MAF serving missionaries in many places. He stressed the MAF viewpoint that included use of simple, single-engine equipment best suited for primitive landing strips. It gave priority to reliability of service, safety, and economy.[3]

Jim Truxton was convinced that MAF's position was sound, both in its thinking about such craft and in its desire to serve a wide variety of missions. But that was the sticking point. Townsend could not afford to have SIL identified with an evangelical mission organization, lest it jeopardize SIL's standing as a purely humanitarian and development organization. Townsend's intent in forming SIL was to introduce the indigenous people to Christ, but he was not at liberty to reveal this in Peru.

Jim tried as best he could to assure Townsend that MAF was working to meet SIL's needs, but he also let it be known that MAF was going to stick to its operating principles. He wrote Charlie, "Perhaps God, knowing the difficulties which we shall continue to have in days ahead, wants us free of the responsibilities in Peru, and able to devote our energies to building a solid foundation elsewhere."[4]

Leaving Peru

This period of mounting frustration on all sides came to an unexpected crescendo with a letter from Betty Greene announcing that she was pulling out of Peru and heading back to Washington to help her ailing parents.

She wrote Parrott and Truxton: "Greetings! You never know what I am going to do next and now it will be the last straw when I tell you I am making plans for going home without getting your permission or okay."[5] This was the most unlikely scenario to both Townsend and Truxton. The former wired Truxton to urge her to stay. Jim, who was in Mexico reinstating the Jungle Camp flight program, made arrangements to meet Betty in Mexico City. Greene's sudden departure from Peru seemed baffling to the MAF men and Townsend. Betty had always submitted her views on MAF business to the others for approval, but this time she took unilateral action.

Through extended discussions with Jim, Betty recognized that she was caught between conflicting expectations. She had gone down to Peru to serve SIL, as she had in Mexico. However, in Peru there had not been the same unanimity between the MAF leadership in Los Angeles and SIL's Townsend over purchase of a plane and its control. The fact that SIL and the Peruvian government jointly owned the Duck muddied the lines of authority. MAF still had responsibility for the operation of the Duck, but there was a growing feeling that Townsend had encroached upon MAF in purchasing the Duck and generally directing the flight work.

James and Marti Hefley's biography, *Uncle Cam*, discussing Townsend's desire for his own air arm, give as a contributing factor that "Betty Greene could only help [SIL] part-time, since MAF asked her to fly their plane for other missions in Peru, too."[6] The fact was that MAF served only SIL in Peru and did so in the SIL-Peru jointly owned Duck.

Townsend needed his own air arm to work with SIL. Frustration over the breakdown of the Duck, plus the differences that had arisen between him and MAF over the operational philosophy of mission aviation, led to his decision to found Jungle Aviation and Radio Service (JAARS).

It is true that MAF was young and lacked resources, but they had capable people and were developing increased technical expertise. Cameron Townsend soon recognized that he needed experienced pilots. Both Townsend and Bill Nyman, secretary of SIL's board, personally asked Betty to join them. She was honored by the invitation but did not think it right to leave MAF. Townsend also invited Betty and Grady Parrott to serve on the JAARS development committee.[7] Grady attended the initial meeting only, to prevent widening the rift between the two organizations. Betty declined. Dawson Trotman, who initially chaired the JAARS development committee, was all for raising funds to support SIL's air transport costs, but when Townsend decided to release MAF from work in Peru and decided to start his own aviation wing, Trotman strongly objected.[8]

As for the work in Peru, Larry Montgomery wanted a smaller plane for local flights, in addition to the *Amauta*, which carried bulk supplies. The Duck did meet a need, but as Montgomery pointed out, "It can't even start to pay its way and about the biggest trouble we have here is finances."[9] SIL's financial situation continued to deteriorate during this period, forcing a reduction of flying time.[10]

Reflections on the SIL-MAF Difficulties

It is important to note that these policy differences between SIL and MAF were very real, had significant fiscal impact on operations, and led to separate paths of service for MAF and JAARS. Cameron Townsend had his board terminate the working agreement between SIL and MAF in Peru. MAF was asked to retain an advisory role, but the responsibility for the flight program now rested with Cameron Townsend.[11]

The whole SIL-MAF relationship is a classic case study illustrating why well-intentioned and good Christian people, and their organizations, sometimes find it necessary to strike out on separate paths. Some would stigmatize this as failure. The history of Christianity, however, is replete with examples of stalwart men and women who took new initiatives in service because of policy differences.

Any judgment as to whether such a separation is worthy or unworthy must be held in abeyance until the motives of the participants are understood and their actions are weighed in the balances of the Almighty. Concern over this separation must be tempered with the recognition that both SIL and MAF prospered in their rapidly expanding work in obedience to the Great Commission.

On the human plane, one might say that the Christian leaders of these organizations should have been able to resolve their problems. The fact is that honest efforts were made, and still the tensions grew. Short of both parties accepting the same operational philosophy, the differences could not be resolved. The only good solution was for each organization to follow its own vision.

On the positive side, development of JAARS speeded Wycliffe's expansion to many lands. MAF initiated its work in Ecuador and went on to provide air service to missionaries in far-flung reaches of the globe. MAF continued working with SIL in Mexico, where Jim Lomheim and later E. W. "Hatch" Hatcher served both SIL and other missions. As it turned out, SIL left it up to each of their fields to decide whether or not they wanted JAARS or MAF. Their personnel in Mexico appreciated MAF's service and rely on it to this day.

It may also be said that the tensions that arose between MAF and SIL made the leadership of both organizations more reflective about themselves and their policies and more open to the wonderful and often unanticipated leading of the Almighty.

Faithfulness in small things, from a Christian perspective, is the prerequisite to larger responsibilities. MAF seemed to have this as a motto in 1947 with "Follow Through," the subject of one of Truxton's articles in *Missionary Aviation*.[12] "Following through" meant that work interrupted in Mexico had to be reestablished before any new projects were undertaken. With funding just covering expenses and salary cuts in summer of 1946, MAF had to wait before replacing the Waco.

A Cruiser for Mexico

In January 1947 Jim Truxton joined Charlie Mellis in placing a bid on a U.S. government surplus Piper "Cruiser" ambulance plane located in the Midwest. They found it to be in excellent condition, with a minimum required bid of $1,200. This was more than they had thought they might have to pay, but Jim felt strongly drawn to offer an additional $5, bringing the bid to $1,205. Imagine the surprise and joy when they found that the only other interested party had offered an even $1,200. This was another sign of God's leading, and Jim rejoiced over this purchase as he ferried the plane west to California.

At that time Betty Greene was still serving in Peru, and Truxton went to Mexico to reestablish service for jungle camp. Jim was set for solo departure at the end of March and proceeded via Brownsville, Texas, Vera Cruz, and Mexico City to Tuxtla in the state of Chiapas. Everything went well. At Tuxtla he made the acquaintance of Fred Tinley, John Kempers, and Joe Urquidi, who operated an independent flight service in Chiapas. Joe gave Jim a

Left to right, front row: Jim Truxton, Grady Parrott, Charlie Mellis; *back row:* Hobey Lowrance, Betty Greene, Jim Lomheim, Hatch Hatcher, 1950.

warm welcome and charged him sixty-two cents a gallon for fuel, a high price. Apparently Joe was not happy about the prospects of losing SIL's business with the reintroduction of the MAF plane. Jim assured Joe that he had no intention of seeking any commercial business. The SIL-MAF operation was much like that of a plane belonging to a business corporation. Joe, somewhat reassured, was kind enough to show Jim the best route to fly through the mountain passes into Jungle Camp. The wreckage of a commercially operated Cruiser in which Townsend had been seriously injured was still sitting on the crash site.

Jim shuttled Dr. Kenneth Pike around to help him with Townsend's insurance papers. He also gave service to two local missionaries, Phil Baer and Phil Mendenhal, the latter in charge of Jungle Camp. Jim transported an SIL expedition out of Tuxtla to a small field to visit a newly found group of Lacandones and explored some old Mayan ruins. Given the terrain, he estimated that the thirty-two-mile flight saved four or five days of overland travel.

In three weeks of work on the field, Truxton gained more insight into missionary aviation than in two years of discussions on the subject. He saw many advantages of the Cruiser: the ability to land on small strips, economy of operation, and ease of repair. Truxton's Mexico experience convinced him that small single-engine craft were tailor-made for missionary aviation.

Truxton's other task before heading back to Los Angeles was to undertake a survey for the Presbyterian mission of their aviation needs in the state of Tabasco, located next to Chiapas on the Gulf of Mexico. The survey was the only way to determine whether air transport could effectively facilitate missionary work in a given area.[13] There is an interesting story behind these developments.

In 1945 the Presbyterian mission opened a small Bible school for training lay leaders in Villahermosa, the state capital of Tabasco. One of the two mission teachers serving there, Fred Tinley, had the vision of using a small plane to shuttle Bible school student teams and several ordained ministers from village to village, to evangelize and teach the Scriptures. Small, isolated, pastorless groups of believers were widely scattered throughout the state. The country was flat and very swampy, making even horseback travel torturously slow, and the unreliable bus service of the region did not meet the students' transport needs.

Fred's vision was innovative and constructive. The difficulty came when he disclosed to his missions committee that he hoped to be the pilot. The committee balked. They saw that this would entail training, fund raising, and possibly misguided diversion from Fred's first calling as teacher and leader at the school. Consequently, Fred's proposal remained frozen in committee until one of the mission's seasoned and respected senior missionaries, John Kempers, brought forward a recommendation. He was well acquainted with MAF's air arm and proposed inviting MAF to implement Fred's plan.

In view of the fact that Jim Truxton was going to turn the Mexico operation over to Jim Lomheim before departing for the Ecuador survey, it was timely for the two Jims to carry out the survey.

This part of Mexico is very swampy, and there was a question about whether a wheel plane or a floatplane should be used. The aerial survey showed that all but three locations out of fifty could be reached with a wheel plane.[14] The survey also revealed that the missionary flight needs in Tabasco and the SIL needs in Chiapas could both be served with one aircraft.[15] This having been settled, Jim Truxton hurried back to Los Angeles for the directors' meeting.

Approvals from the MAF board, the Presbyterian mission, and the Presbyterian church in Tabasco paved the way for the circuit "flying" preacher program known as "Institutes." This flight program became a model for future cooperative ventures that required rapid movement of personnel. Jim Lomheim became the central figure in giving wings to the Institutes until Hatch Hatcher joined him.

Lomheim was single, a native of South Dakota, and the second of five children. He grew up in the church and made a profession of faith at summer camp. He had a long-standing interest in planes and attended Parks Air College, now East St. Louis University, in Missouri. He was drafted into the Navy six months short of graduation. While in training, he came down with scarlet fever and, after eighteen months of convalescence, was discharged as "disabled." This was a severe blow, not unlike what Nate Saint had experienced. While Lomheim was on his back recovering, he first made contact with Mellis.

The discharging medic suggested to Lomheim that he get an easy job to prolong his life. Jim felt he was cut out for better things. While he did not regain his former stamina, Jim went back to Parks and completed his course of study. During this time his interest in serving the Lord through MAF had grown to the point that he made application for service. Charlie Mellis counseled Jim to get training in the Bible and suggested The Bible Institute of Los Angeles (BIOLA). Lomheim enrolled there in the spring of 1947.

While Truxton was at jungle camp, Lomheim studied and went to work on projects at the MAF headquarters. This was the extent of candidate school in those early years. It was very much a matter of personal interaction with the leadership and being informally evaluated for spiritual, emotional, technical, and dispositional fitness to serve on the field. Jim Lomheim passed muster and was accepted for service, thus paving the way for him to work with Jim Truxton on the Tabasco survey. Thereafter he took over MAF's Mexico program and freed Jim Truxton to conduct a survey in Ecuador.

Launching the Ecuador Program

The other big encouraging breakthrough for MAF in 1947 came in Ecuador. This is where MAF realized its vision and developed the classical MAF operation. Jim Truxton laid the groundwork for a full-scale cooperative missionary flight program, using a small plane and a field committee to advise the pilot. This is also the field where Nate Saint later served as pilot and where he and four other missionaries gave their lives in efforts to befriend the Aucas in order to share the Good News with them.

There is an interesting story with a pointed message behind these events that goes back to Jim Truxton's meeting with Christian Weiss, Director of the Gospel Missionary Union (GMU) at the Moody Aviation Conference in 1946. Weiss left there encouraged about the possibility of involving the other evangelical missions in Ecuador in a cooperative flight program. The desire to get started right away led GMU to buy its own single-engine Stinson. Paul Hartford of Victory Sky Pilots provided training for Bob Hart, the pilot.

In this way, service was started to four jungle stations even before Truxton made the MAF survey. This might have worked out well, had the Stinson been properly serviced. Hart's inattention to plane maintenance was noticed by many, including Shell Oil personnel who warned that the plane was no longer airworthy. Bob Hart flew the plane until it crashed as a result of engine failure. Fortunately, he escaped unhurt and trekked out for help. George Poole of HCJB, his passenger, suffered major injuries.

Jim Truxton's coming to Ecuador shortly after the crash was most timely because the missionaries who had a taste of air service wanted it restored as soon as possible. The missionaries were happy to see a reputable organization such as MAF, with its disciplined approach to aviation, come in and take over the work.

Others had also seen the possibilities of missionary air service in the Ecuadorian jungle. Clarence Jones of HCJB, a member of MAF's advisory council, had wanted to establish an air service and had even been offered a plane. He wisely turned it down until a survey could be made of the regional needs.

At the same time, George Poole, who worked with Clarence Jones, wanted MAF to take responsibility for HCJB's aviation needs, but he had hopes of becoming the pilot. George Poole believed a plane could be based at Quito and flown down to the Amazon basin to serve the missionaries. This was totally impractical, because the mountain passes were often locked in cloud cover. Besides, a relatively good, though hazardous, road ran from Quito to Shell Mera, the main Shell Oil Company base for oil exploration in the Oriente.

The time was ripe for MAF to step onto the scene and make a proposal for meeting the Ecuadorian missionary flight needs. Jim Truxton proceeded by plotting the location of all the missionary stations on the map. He made detailed studies of the potential flight needs of every station that wanted air service, noting whether it planned further expansion into the interior. Special help came from Dr. Wilfred Tidmarsh, an Englishman educated in the sciences and senior missionary of the Plymouth Brethren Mission, who had accumulated considerable information on proposed future mission stations throughout the region.

It was from Dr. Tidmarsh that Jim Truxton first heard of the fierce Aucas (who today call themselves the Waorani[16]) as the two traveled in a dugout canoe on a river survey journey. At one location they rounded a bend and faced small rapids, where all passengers had to get out of the canoe and drag it over the rocks. Dr. Tidmarsh related how the Aucas had ambushed a small party of travelers at that very spot not long before. The thought sent a chill up Jim's spine as he looked into the dense jungle foliage on each side of the small river and realized how vulnerable they would all be to the barbed Auca spears. He even thought that he heard some rustling in the bushes—was it his imagination, or a wild pig? Dr. Tidmarsh believed that the Aucas could only be reached by helicopter because "one of the great difficulties is that rubber hunters in past years have used their contact to mistreat, enslave and kill them. Hence, the Aucas are afraid to place trust in any outsider, however friendly he might initially appear to be."[17]

Jim conducted the survey with a view to serving the existing stations and assist their reaching out to plant new ones. The plane, it was hoped, would become the means to achieve this expansion of mission work. In visiting the stations, Jim found unexpected help from the Shell Oil Company, which transported him, free of charge, from Shell Mera to strips located near mission stations. Still, some had to be reached on foot. Two located among the Jivaro Indians were five- to six-day treks over jungle trails. Tidmarsh accompanied Jim on several of these exploratory trips.

In Quito there was much talk of the proposed MAF service. Since a single-engine plane had earlier crashed in the jungle, many argued for the safety of twin-engine craft. MAF-UK had purchased the Miles "Gemini," a twin-engine plane, for the African survey. Jim Truxton was confronted with the problem of convincing the future users of the MAF service that it was not the single-engine plane that was the problem but lack of maintenance. He stressed that aviation safety depended on qualified, disciplined pilots who maintained the highest aviation safety standards, including uncompromising engine maintenance. Jim Truxton recognized the importance of a successful operation in Mexico and wrote Jim Lomheim the following homily.

> You may serve as a very needed object lesson for yours truly one of these days soon. By all means don't take any chances. The success of operations in Mexico will affect the success of missionary aviation in Ecuador, Peru, and wherever we go next. I hasten to add, though, don't get burdened under the responsibility of it all— I know this can wear a fella down to a frazzle. Just do the best you can and leave all the burden with the Burden-Bearer.[18]

Jim Truxton was wondering about getting in a reliable supply of fuel for this program, since it would be located on the edge of the rain forest. Shell came forward to offer them all the aviation fuel they needed at Shell Mera.[19] Shell was extending this help to maintain good relations, but it solved a bothersome logistical problem for MAF. Jim was actually surprised that Shell did not link this offer with the stipulation that MAF bring in a twin-engine craft, since the American embassy had just come out with a statement that "no single-engine plane has any business flying over the jungle."[20] Prospects looked good to Jim as he completed his survey. He wished that he could be the pilot to start the Ecuador program.

When Truxton began to give serious attention to finding the right person to serve as pilot, Nate Saint kept coming to mind. If there was ever one who could make a case for a single-engine plane, it was Nate. Jim wrote Mellis, "If we recommend and send a single-engine ship down here, and any time within several years, it too goes into the jungle—you can put it into your little black book that the repercussions will be tremendous! We need someone with lots of practical experience, and a man who has proven himself as a qualified mechanic."[21]

Even before a pilot was named, an airplane was donated from a wholly unexpected source. Betty Greene was back in Washington studying Spanish at the University of Washington. She was in contact with Dave Weyerhaeuser, of the lumber empire. He wanted to know if MAF might have use for his Stinson 150. As it turned out, the Stinson was ideal for Ecuador. Here was another answer to prayer.

As Jim Truxton sat down to write up his survey recommendations, he was more sold on missionary aviation than ever before. He was also sure of the absolute necessity of doing thorough field

MAF pilot Jim Lomheim talks with John and Elaine Beekman of Wycliffe Bible Translators in Mexico. The Chol Indians observe.

surveys before entering any region. He drew up an agreement between MAF and the users, carefully delineating the relationship to prevent any misunderstandings.

A number of the clauses in his report are notable. MAF would provide the plane and pilot-mechanic. The plane would be operated at a nonprofit, per-mile fee that covered depreciation, insurance, and costs for fuel, repair, and maintenance. All monies received from the program were to be deposited in a plane fund that would make the program self-sustaining and self-perpetuating. As for the plane, the Stinson 150 that had been donated would be upgraded with a 165-horsepower engine. In case the fear of a single-engine plane still bothered the users, Jim quoted the costs of a twin to sober his readers. He also included an operational chart that listed the performance data for several representative plane types, including comparative takeoff characteristics. This gave the Ecuadorian missionaries information on the increased cost and the length of the runways needed for takeoff and landing. Interstation radio communication with the plane was mandatory.

Furthermore, the need for a field aviation committee representing the users was recognized. Its responsibility was to monitor equity in scheduling the plane so the greatest possible benefit could be received by all. Finally, MAF promised to supervise the pilot and pledged not to discontinue the Ecuador program without giving six months notice.[22]

This proposal, dated December 24, was a fitting Christmas gift for both the Ecuadorian missions and MAF's home office. It was an encouraging end to a year of difficulties in Peru. More important, the forward-looking agreement of a shared flight program among the missionaries in Ecuador brought 1947 to a satisfying close. A mood of ecstasy prevailed. The Lord was good to give sunshine after the rain. The skies were now clear, and MAF looked forward to navigating into the new year with less turbulence.

These positive developments for MAF-US found an echo in the United Kingdom, where MAF-UK literally got off the ground that same year with the purchase of the Miles "Gemini," a twin-engine plane. The beginnings of this venture among World War II pilots stationed there brings us to another story of extraordinary faith, enterprise, and perseverance.

Founding of MAF
in the United Kingdom

Unbeknown to the Americans forming CAMF, a group of ex-Royal Air Force (RAF) fliers stationed in the United Kingdom were also organizing to use the plane in support of missionaries. There, the Missionary Aviation Fellowship (MAF-UK) began under the auspices of the Movement for World Evangelization (MWE). This evangelical organization was started by Dr. Thomas Cochrane to promote and research mission work. He was the founder of MWE's London Mildmay Center, named after the section of London in which it was located.

Through its missionary surveys, the Mildmay Center had its fingers on the pulse of missionary activity around the globe. Dr. Cochrane, founder of Union Medical College in China in 1911, first made a survey of the penetration of Christianity in that country. This survey was the start of later world surveys and the World Dominion Movement.[1] Their creed consisted of "Three Loyalties": "Loyalty to the Lord Jesus Christ, and the centrality of His Cross; loyalty to the Bible as the final authority in faith and practice; and loyalty to our Lord's command to witness to every creature."[2]

Late in 1944 Murray Kendon, a World War II pilot in the Royal New Zealand Air Force, approached Cochrane about the use of aircraft in missions.[3] Cochrane immediately supported the idea of missionary aviation, asking Kendon in August 1945 to assume the position of organizing secretary and develop this idea under a Missionary Aviation wing of Mildmay. This was less than a year after Betty Greene set up the Los Angeles CAMF office. Unlike its American counterpart, which was seeking grassroots support prior to organizing, MAF-UK began as part of an existing Christian organization, although it later became independent. The Australians, under Harry Hartwig, followed the pattern of the Americans in getting an independent organization started in Melbourne in 1947.

From the outset, Murray Kendon felt that MAF-UK should begin service in Central and Eastern Africa. A letter of inquiry sent to the Congo Protestant Council in the summer of 1945 brought a positive response to the idea of initiating a survey of the aviation needs of that region.[4]

Murray Kendon already had clear objectives for an independent missionary flight service that would meet all the aviation needs of cooperating societies in a particular area. He explained it this way: "We firmly believe that the only way we can be of real and practical service in the speeding of world evangelization is to undertake to organize the flying and maintenance side completely, handling all details, and giving the service as a whole to the missionaries who are 'doing the job.'"[5]

It was Murray's vision that Christians at home should raise the total capital expenditure to get a flight program started. By *capital* he meant "the money necessary to buy aircraft and equipment, complete the training of the personnel and send them to the field."[6] The missionary societies on the field would absorb "the running costs, maintenance costs, and depreciation of the aircraft, plus the salaries of the flying and technical staff" through "an equitable system of cooperative levy on all the missionaries or societies concerned." The Americans planned for the salaries of the aviation personnel to be underwritten by friends and churches at home. Truxton considered the pilots missionaries who are fliers. This would cut down the costs to the missionary societies and make the American program more financially attractive to its users.

Murray Kendon's plans called for an annual fee for service, whereas MAF-US's proposal was to charge a flat fee based on use. On the whole, MAF-US's planned service was geared to minimizing the costs to the user, which meant subsidizing the program to a much greater degree than envisioned in London.

At the outset, MAF-US felt that the air service would have to be attractive to missions, especially to those on meager travel budgets. The argument that the plane would save enormous travel time was appealing. The question was, would the potential users be convinced that there was an effective savings in the cost of travel? These differing views made for lively discussion when Murray Kendon came to America for the Missionary Aviation Conference in August 1946. Plans for a joint African survey were discussed, but when the project turned out not to be feasible for MAF-US, MAF-UK planned and carried it out on its own.[7]

About that time Jack Hemmings, a Royal Air Force pilot, joined Murray Kendon. He helped plan the African survey, select the plane to be used, and hold promotional meetings. After extensive flight testing and evaluation of comparative performance, Kendon and Hemmings decided on a twin-engine Gemini.

News of the MAF-UK decision to purchase the Gemini surprised Jim Truxton. He was astounded that the British were prepared to invest $15,000 in a plane that might prove unsuitable for service after the survey. Truxton suggested that they reconsider and take a look at the single-engine Stinson 150. They could purchase two of them for $10,500. After the Waco experience, Jim felt it would be wise to have two identical planes working side by side. If one broke down, they could fall back on the second plane to continue the work or, if necessary, use it for parts. Jim considered the Stinson "a topnotch survey aircraft, its short landing, takeoff, and climb characteristics being almost unbelievable for a four-place ship."[8] The British decided to purchase the Gemini.

Central African Survey

In preparation for the survey Murray Kendon mounted a huge map of Central and East Africa in the office. On it he plotted all the mission stations of the region. He contacted the mission societies working in the area, and over forty missions eventually responded. Kendon and Hemmings then set in motion plans to visit one hundred stations. They plotted these on the wall map to plan their flight path and set up a schedule.

As these plans were going forward, Kendon wrote Truxton about an inquiry from the Baptists and Presbyterians in Brazil for MAF-UK's help, suggesting that the British and American MAF wings consider separate regions for service. Truxton immediately picked up on this idea and replied that it would be good if the British worked in Africa and the Americans expanded service in Latin America. Kendon advised the Gospel Missionary Union (GMU), which desired flight support in Peru and Ecuador, to contact Los Angeles. The concept of regional service was significant. Still, the Australian and U.K. organizations had limited resources and many urgent mission calls for service. Hence they called on MAF-US to assist. MAF-US was willing to stretch its limited resources to help AMAF in New Guinea and MAF-UK in Africa. Given these realities, MAF-US assisted and carried forward some programs in regions beyond the Americas.

The British survey team included pilot Jack Hemmings, engineer Stuart King, and navigator and survey coordinator Tom Banham. The latter two joined MAF-UK in the summer of 1947. Banham served with the Royal Navy and only stayed for the survey. Stuart King, an ex-RAF technical officer, went on the survey and then devoted his energies to building MAF-UK's work in Africa.

Stuart's decision to cast his lot with MAF-UK was not an easy one. In 1946, he was one of the few RAF volunteer reserve officers offered a permanent commission. An attractive career was his for the taking. Many Christian friends advised him not to resign but to serve Christ in the Air Force. Their attitude was, "This MAF thing is just a dream, a bunch of wartime pilots trying to perpetuate their flying."

Stuart knew that he had to find God's will for himself and wrestled with what he ought to do. In view of the unexpected opportunity to stay in the RAF, he felt that this was most likely God's plan for him. Consequently, he decided to accept the RAF offer. He attempted to telephone the RAF office three times to let them know of his decision, but each time he called he was unable to make connections. Stuart perceived the Lord's guidance in this and decided not to pursue the offer.

In addition to the RAF offer, Stuart also had the opportunity to enter into postgraduate studies in aeronautics, financed by a government grant—a childhood dream that remained with him. However, when it came right down to making a decision, uppermost in Stuart's mind was his desire to follow God's will. He struggled in prayer for God's direction, and the Lord gave him Hebrews 11:8

to ponder: "Abraham . . . went, even though he did not know where he was going." Stuart remembers the Lord saying to him, "That's what I want you to do; you do not know where this is going." In the process, God gave Stuart a settled conviction that he should serve with MAF-UK. That call stretched into a lifetime of challenging and fruitful ministry in flight work on the continent of Africa.

While trying to decide which offer to accept, Stuart was also training for a civilian pilot's license and a civil aviation aircraft maintenance engineer's license. He received both of these prior to departure for the African survey. Jack Hemmings worked on a civil radio operator's license and was likewise certified prior to leaving.

The Gemini aircraft did not come with air-to-ground communication equipment, and none was available in England. Kendon called on Grady Parrott, who found exactly what was needed in Los Angeles.[9]

Dedication of the Gemini was set for September 6, 1947, and in anticipation, the *Mildmay Outlook*, the organ of the Movement for World Evangelization, sponsored a contest for a suitable name for the plane. Miss A. Allison of Borough, South London, suggested the winning name of *Mildmay Pathfinder*. Mrs. Thomas Cochrane announced the winner at the dedication services at the Broxbourne Aerodrome in London.

The Mildmay Center wanted to raise the aviation awareness of Christian missions and made a special point of using the upcoming African survey to interest the Christian public. They sent the *Pathfinder* on a tour of thirty-three towns and cities throughout England, Scotland, Wales, and Ireland. Some twenty thousand people heard about the venture, and some fifteen hundred visited the various airfields where the plane was exhibited. One of the great benefits of this tour was the opportunity it gave to correct defects in the plane prior to departure. The plane was fully paid for before leaving for Africa. MWE contributed three thousand of the total cost of fifty-five hundred British pounds; the balance was raised from supporters and prayer partners.[10]

Tom Banham prepared the way for the *Pathfinder's* work in Africa. He left for Nairobi, Kenya, on Christmas Day to set up an office to handle the myriad details of the eight-month survey. Much new interest resulted from his presence there.

On Tuesday, January 13, 1948, Jack Hemmings and Stuart King took off on their five-thousand-mile trip to Central Africa. They left Croydon field and immediately hit a 100-mile-an-hour gale over the Channel. Bad weather accompanied them until they crossed the Mediterranean three days later. Crossing North Africa called for clearances at Tunis, Tripoli, and Cairo. En route to the Sudan, Jack and Stuart stopped at Luxor, three hours flying time south of Cairo. Always alert for ways to save money, the two looked for a ride from the airport to the city. They took a Shell Oil Company lorry and left the taxi drivers puzzled about why people "owning" an airplane couldn't afford a taxi.[11]

The Nile led them from Luxor to Khartoum, Sudan. There they made contact with the American mission consisting of Presbyterian and Reformed missionaries, the Sudan Interior Mission, and the Church of England's Church Mission Society. At the time, there was no thought of MAF-UK doing work in the Sudan, but two years later Stuart King would be back in that country, initiating MAF-UK flight service.

There were signs of future problems when the *Pathfinder* headed east toward Addis Ababa, Ethiopia. After landing at Asmara at an elevation of eight thousand feet, the fully fueled plane failed to gain altitude upon takeoff, landing in a plowed field just beyond the runway. This was the first evidence that the 200-horsepower engine was insufficient for flying at high altitude. Actually, a 300-horsepower engine was standard for the craft, but the bigger engines were not available, due to postwar production shortages. Given this advance warning, the crew canceled the planned flight to Addis Ababa. Instead, the *Pathfinder* headed for the lowlands of Malakal in South Sudan.

After linking up with Banham in Nairobi, the survey officially commenced in Kenya. From there the team proceeded to the Congo, Uganda, Equatorial Africa, and Rwanda, a region the size of eastern and western Europe combined. The Congo Protestant Council met at the end of February 1948 and reiterated its support for an MAF-UK survey of its entire field. The recent vote of confidence registered support for the manner in which the survey was being conducted.

The actual field work began in March. Banham wrote, "The great survey is on!"[12] Four days later, on their way back to Nairobi, the crew reported, "We arrived over Kijabe after one quarter of an hour's flying and did dummy runs over the proposed strip. Even on a dummy run—at low speed—the climb away from the strip was such that we only just cleared the trees."[13] They dared not land there. An additional 100 horsepower might have done wonders.

It was soon obvious that the plane was not only good for conducting the survey but was also a spectacular means for attracting crowds. At Kitui, about seventy miles east of Nairobi, the local Christians took the opportunity to share the gospel with the curiosity seekers. Hemmings and King each gave a word of testimony; all spoke from the top of the plane's wing.[14]

Tom Banham watched his two associates driving themselves very hard and praised the Lord for the good health all three of them were enjoying.

> It is difficult to realize just how great this blessing is, especially where Jack and Stuart are concerned. They have maintained a very strenuous programme of travel both by road and by air with a wide range of climatic changes. They have frequently changed their conditions of food and water and sleeping accommodations. It has been a strain on them as on their periodic returns to Nairobi they have been obviously the worse for wear in spite of their irrepressible spirits. They have not spared themselves and I know from having talked with missionaries coming into town that their pressure of work has been remarked-on by the Lord's people. So let us thank God for their continued health and strength.[15]

From surveys of North Congo, they flew to French Equatorial Africa, which the fliers described as "A land flowing with red tape and bureaucracy."[16] On Saturday, June 12, the *Pathfinder* broke its own flight record in the North Congo survey. They left Bangassou in a hurry to avoid an oncoming storm and headed for Arua, Uganda. En route, they skirted other storms, but a tail wind helped them cover 570 miles in five hours. The following week they worked in Uganda.

Loss of the Gemini

With the survey almost completed in Rwanda and Burundi, King and Hemmings left Usumbura, Burundi, on July 10 and headed for Nairobi, Kenya. The last stage of the survey was Tanganyika (Tanzania), and it was important for them to get back before the weekend because of the itinerary that Banham had arranged. For that reason, they chose to make it a nonstop flight and fueled up to capacity. Given the equipment they were carrying, this brought them up to the maximum permissible weight of three thousand pounds.[17]

Takeoff from Usumbura's runway at an elevation of three thousand feet was normal. Since they had to cross a series of high mountains, Hemmings circled over the city to gain altitude and found that the rate of climb to sixty-five hundred feet went as expected. To conserve fuel, Hemmings decided to head eastward and gain further altitude by flying up the mountain valleys. This, however, proved to be a mistake. As they approached the final crest of the mountains, the plane headed into down currents that prevented it from gaining altitude and actually forced its descent at the rate of three hundred feet per minute, even at full throttle.

The only alternative for the crew was to fly back down the valley and try to cross the small transverse ridges they had safely cleared during the ascent. The currents, however, were unrelenting, and the plane continued to lose altitude. After a close call crossing the first transverse ridge, where they brushed against banana plants, Hemmings tried in vain to bring the *Pathfinder* over the next saddle. Hitting the crest of the hill, the plane immediately broke up, with the tail and wing sections tearing off behind the cockpit. Miraculously, there was no fire, and the angle of impact was such that the cockpit slid down the slope and came to rest intact, its wooden construction absorbing the shock. King and Hemmings, though bruised and in a daze, walked away from the wreckage without serious injury.

Despite this devastating setback, Hemmings and King continued the survey, traveling overland to Tanganyika to complete their itinerary. From there they returned to London.

Lessons of the Survey

The accident, though unfortunate, yielded a number of pointed lessons. The attempt to reach Addis Ababa from the Sudan had revealed that an underpowered aircraft was dangerous. High temperatures, altitude, and relative humidity in tropical climates require additional power for "climb-out" performance. This aeronautical reality had not been appreciated until the *Pathfinder* flew across central Africa.

The crew also learned that grueling schedules and working under the pressure of deadlines was dangerous because it tempted the pilot to reduce margins of safety. The crew constantly needed to be on guard not to compromise the plane's safety.

Then there was the recognition that mountain flying was hazardous due to illusions that distort perception of space relations. Even more dangerous were the unseen downdrafts that could override safety margins with very little warning. Nate Saint would experience this on takeoff from Quito, Ecuador. In some situations, flying up the center of a valley could be the worst possible approach. The ascending air is often closer to the valley walls, but flying too close to these can be hazardous. These lessons and more were fully absorbed and appreciated on both sides of the Atlantic.

The loss of the *Pathfinder* had a sobering effect on MAF-UK, just as the Waco accident had on its American counterpart. Fortunately, Lloyd's of London absorbed the MAF-UK financial losses. The monies recovered were used to buy a de Havilland "Rapide" that initiated service in the Sudan in 1950. However, a few hurdles had to be crossed before that program was started.

As for the results of the African survey, the crew brought together all the statistical information and came up with a cost analysis that showed that no economic gains would be achieved through MAF-UK flight service. A fairly good road transportation network existed throughout most of Central Africa. In parts of the Congo, missionaries could drive at seventy miles an hour for long distances. What was not recognized at the time and could not be foreseen without experience, were the many nonfiscal advantages to be gained in using a plane. Time savings, emergency service, accessibility to remote areas, more productive use of time, to name a few, were not sufficiently appreciated, especially in the aftermath of the accident. More immediate concerns of insurance coverage and accident reports occupied the organization's attention.

Stuart King and Jack Hemmings resumed their work for MAF-UK in London, but they were emotionally in the doldrums. The strenuous survey and complications resulting from the crash were draining. A ray of light in all of this was that the two were asked to serve on the board of the MWE. Before the end of 1949, Kendon left on an evangelistic tour for MWE and promoted MAF-UK in his native New Zealand and Australia.

Call to Serve in the Sudan

About the same time, letters began to arrive from the Sudan—especially from Dr. Don McClure of the American Presbyterian Mission and the Sudan Interior Mission—asking MAF-UK to consider service in that country. McClure fully appreciated what an airplane could do for the Sudan, since he held a private pilot's license. He would have been happy to fly, had it not been for the stringent requirements of the Sudan colonial government. The requirements included a twin-engine or powerful single-engine plane with radio and a licensed Morse code operator. Pilots needed commercial and navigator's licenses and there had to be a licensed aircraft engineer with access to a hangar and workshop. For McClure, these requirements were impossible. He had confidence in the Lord and kept on praying that he would send MAF-UK to the Sudan to meet the mission's various transportation needs.

Hemmings and King felt strongly moved to respond favorably, but the other members of the board were extremely reluctant to act after the loss of the *Pathfinder*. Under these circumstances, the two "Young Turks" proposed that if MWE wasn't going to do anything more with missionary aviation, they should frankly say so. This the board was not willing to do. Lindsay Glegg, chairman of the board, one of the great evangelical leaders of his time, broke the impasse by suggesting that if MAF-UK really felt the Lord leading them to initiate work in the Sudan, then the board should start a flight program there. For King, the really amazing thing was that no one said no. Up to then, not one voice had been raised in support of such an initiative. Looking back at that meeting, King recognized that "the hand of God worked through one of his." The result was a new lease on life for MAF-UK and the start of plans for a new program.

To meet the requirements of the Sudan government's civil aviation department, MAF-UK bought a twin-engine de Havilland "Rapide." It seemed to be the only sane thing to do, since southern Sudan was one giant swamp during the May to November rainy season.

As preparations for the Sudan flight program were progressing, a new threat appeared. MWE found itself in financial difficulty, and Dr. Cochrane informed King and Hemmings that the Rapide would have to be sold to keep the organization solvent. "Well, fair enough," the fliers replied. "But if we sell the plane, we must stop missionary aviation. We're not going to keep talking to the British public about this thing which doesn't have an operation overseas." Dr. Cochrane replied, "All right, I'll let you go, but remember we may have to sell the plane at any time." With that threat hanging over their heads, Hemmings and King headed for the Sudan. God was in the venture, and the plane was never recalled for sale.

The *Mildmay Pathfinder II* left Croydon airport on March 11, 1950, with Jack and Helen Hemmings and Stuart King on board. Eight days later, they arrived safely at Khartoum. This time they were not just passing through; they had come to stay and serve in the Sudan. Two years earlier, they had been thankful to leave this hot, arid plain with its scrub forest for the lush greenness of the Congo. Not in their wildest dreams did they imagine they would be coming back to Khartoum to initiate the first MAF-UK program.

Realities of the Sudan

What forced recognition that there was a need for year-round aviation service in the Sudan were the widely scattered stations of the American Mission and the Sudan Interior Mission. These stations were isolated during the flood season from May to November. In addition to the flood problem, the lack of an adequate road network gave MAF-UK the opportunity to provide a lifeline to the missionaries.

MAF-UK's second aircraft, a de Havilland "Rapide," prior to departure for Africa in 1950.

The Sudan was under British control until 1956 and was known as the Anglo-Egyptian Sudan. This one-million-square-mile nation sits astride the upper course of the Nile. The Blue Nile flows down from the Ethiopian highlands to the east and merges with the White Nile at Khartoum, the capital of the Sudan. The city is located in the geographical center of the country. During the rainy season, the nearly half-million square miles of southern Sudan are flooded when the White Nile's tributaries overflow their banks. This annual cycle isolates scattered elevated island settlements that, before MAF-UK's arrival, were cut off from the outside world for months at a time. The government forbade missionary penetration of these areas unless year-round outside contact could be maintained.

As things stood in 1951, the Sudan Interior Mission was working among the Dinka, Mabaan, and Uduk tribes in the central section of the country east of the Nile. The coming of the *Pathfinder II* and construction of airstrips gave much greater accessibility to the tribes. The various mission organizations had earlier been assigned geographical areas. The Presbyterians worked to the south of SIM territory in the region from Malakal to the Ethiopian border, where they worked among the Shilluk, Nuer, and Anuak peoples and were receptive to MAF-UK transportation. By locating the Protestant missions among the tribal non-Moslem people of the South, the British were fostering a policy of separating the Arabic-speaking people of the North from the Christian and non-Christian tribes of the South. The latter had more in common with the people of Uganda.[18]

Hemmings and King's initial task was to survey the fourteen stations of these two missions. They concluded that there was a need for lifeline air service for stations separated by an average of more than one hundred miles. This support was not only desirable, but absolutely essential for the well-being of the missionaries.

Unfortunately, Hemmings did not qualify for a commercial pilot's license due to an eye problem. This was a severe blow to the program, since government regulations required both a pilot and a communication man on each flight. This need was filled by Steve Stevens, a South African Air Force (SAAF) pilot. During World War II Stevens had flown the Cape-to-Cairo route many times and was familiar with the region.

In joining MAF-UK, Stevens initially left his wife, Kay, and two children behind in South Africa. While arrangements were being made for Stevens to come, Stuart King practiced Morse code in the torturing heat of Khartoum. He had a difficult time working up to twenty words a minute. The Morse code is a slow, cumbersome, and obsolete way of carrying on air-to-ground communication but, at that time, there was no other system in use in the Sudan. Paradoxically, mission stations were allowed to install radio communication equipment to keep in contact with one another but were prohibited from communicating with aircraft.[19] The regime feared subversive activities among the restive non-Muslim peoples in the South and prevented the missionaries from making use of the communication equipment that made for accessibility to MAF-UK aircraft.

By the middle of July Stuart passed the Morse code certification. The Rapide was already equipped with a two-hundred-pound Marconi wartime transmitter and, of course, both pilot and communication engineer had to fly together. These requirements meant that a single-engine two-passenger plane could not adequately service the region. The Rapide was the right choice of craft, at least for the time being.

Since the British colonial government laid down the technical requirements to MAF-UK, King and Stevens assumed that once they met these requirements, service would be allowed to begin. They were badly mistaken. The projected timing for starting the service coincided with a visit of the Presbyterian's mission leaders to the field. They wanted to see the entire field by plane. Stuart filed for permission to begin flights, not anticipating any objections from Khartoum. He was very surprised to receive the reply: "The decision for this is out of our hands. The Political Department has final say as to whether you are given a charter to operate."[20]

The next step was to see the Political Department. The Political Secretary seemed to have grave reservations about the application. When asked why this was a problem, the answer was, "Your proposals are going to set a precedent, and we have to consider the matter very carefully." Then came a series of questions. When all these were satisfactorily answered, Stuart King ventured, "How long will it be before a decision is made?"

"About three weeks," came the reply. This delay was cause for much prayer.

Just six days after the meeting with the Political Department, a letter arrived from the government with the welcome news that the program had been approved. Instead of waiting for three weeks, the MAF-UK program was now up and flying!

Adjusting Service to the Sudan

The *Pathfinder II* was initially based at Akobo, a police post five hundred miles due south of Khartoum, where Don McClure served. There was no hangar for the plane. The feeling was that it would be good to have the pilot in touch with the day-to-day concerns of the missionaries and base the Rapide at a mission outpost. This would be less expensive than being based at a town.

The flight service finally got underway in November, and by February 1951, Steve and Stuart had flown 8,700 miles, carried ninety-five missionaries and thirty-five children. While these statistics may not be very impressive, they did signal that a whole new era in Sudan mission work had begun.

To extend the service in 1951 new landing strips were built at Nasir, Pibor, and Pochalla. In the SIM territory to the north, year-round flight service was possible at five remote mission stations. These landing strips required a great deal of labor to get them above flood stage and provide proper drainage during the rains. The most recently constructed strip at that time was at Doro in SIM territory, near the Ethiopian border. It took fifteen hundred Africans eight weeks to construct it. Completion of this strip allowed the Majors family to stay on their station year-round.

This was a wholly different kind of life for the pilots. Their first Christmas in the Sudan proved to be unlike anything they had ever known. They shared this time with the missionaries and the Anuak people at Akobo. The day started with a 5:00 A.M. shooting of a bull to be roasted for dinner. Then at 8:00 A.M. there was a Christmas service, which was followed by sports at 9:00. The 1:00 P.M. dinner consisted of bull meat and Kaffir corn, both of which the fliers "smelled and tasted" for days afterward. More sports followed at 3:00 P.M. at the police post. After 4:00 P.M., preparation got started for the next day's flight. For these Englishmen, the missing ingredients were a Christmas tree, mince pie, and caroling under colorful lights. Making up for this loss of amenities was an added measure of praise to the Savior and love for each other.[21]

To get the Sudan program started, MAF-UK made adjustments in its charges to the users. This brought the flight costs to the user closer to that of the American program. It was well and good to say that the missions served should absorb all operating costs, including the cost of the pilot and the plane's depreciation. The reality of financial restraints made this impossible, so MAF-UK decided that the mission agencies should absorb only the operating costs. This meant that MAF-UK had to subsidize the work to keep it going. Distances between stations averaged nearly one hundred miles. This meant that on many occasions the pilot had to ferry an empty plane. Rather than charging the customer for these empty runs, MAF-UK absorbed these costs. In the process, transport charges to the customer came to twenty-five cents a mile. Everything possible was done to keep user costs at a bare minimum. It is not surprising that the mission stations found that ground transportation could not compete with the low MAF-UK air fares.[22]

This policy shifted costs to the MAF-UK home office in London. This might not have been a problem if the Christian public had been able and willing to support the work. Unfortunately, this was not the case, in part because the missionaries serving in the Sudan were largely Americans rather than British. The supporting constituency that appeared most responsible for this burden was the Americans, but MAF-UK did not ask the American Christian public for financial support. The financial picture turned ever bleaker. In the first months of 1951 operating costs were fifteen hundred pounds sterling; total income was barely five hundred. This situation could not continue indefinitely. Nevertheless, with the runways at Pibor and Pochalla completed, service was extended that spring. Such advances in the face of financial limitations seemed improbable. What must be said about these British fliers is that their faith in God's provision continued, even in the face of financial stringency.

In March the *Pathfinder II* was flown to Nairobi for its annual engine overhaul and renewal of Certificate of Airworthiness. Due to financial constraints, London could not immediately pay the bills. This necessitated an extended stay of three additional weeks. Despite this, Stevens arranged to have his family come up by boat to Mombasa, but that had to be canceled when his three-year-old became violently ill. The delay turned into a blessing when Stevens took the extended stay to make a quick trip to South Africa to pick up Kay and his children. He returned ferrying a fully loaded Navion aircraft for a commercial operator, thereby eliminating all costs of their own transportation.

When the Rapide was finally released, all flew back to Akobo. The Stevens family must have felt a bit like Job when, in their first night as a family at Akobo, they were chased out of bed by an army ant invasion. On the fourth night their house caught on fire and burned to the ground, reducing all their personal belongings to ashes. Stevens wrote Grady Parrott, "The Lord giveth and the Lord taketh, blessed be the name of the Lord." Steve and Kay were happy to be alive and well after these harrowing events. The trying circumstances made their lives more difficult but did not break their spirits; they saw it as an opportunity to recognize the fleeting nature of possessions and rejoiced in the gift of life. Besides, their tour of service had just begun, and they were looking to the Lord to sustain MAF-UK in the Sudan.

Ecuador: The First Year

In January 1948 the MAF-US program in Ecuador was still in need of an experienced pilot. Nate Saint was studying at Wheaton College. He received a letter from MAF spelling out how ideally suited he was to meet the need. After much prayer and weighing his desire to finish college, he wrote, "I have decided to toss my lot in with you fellows." From then on, his commitment was total.

Marjorie Farris, Nate's fiancée and a registered nurse, was in hearty agreement. The two were married on February 14. Truxton was delighted with the decision of this gifted and enthusiastic couple.[1]

When Nate and Marj were ready to start the new MAF work, there was no field administration or home waiting for them. The judgment was that Nate's work would be "plenty rough and nerve wracking." Truxton recommended that a suitable home be built at Shell Mera, so the Saints might do the best possible job of serving the missionaries. Upon inquiry, the Shell Oil Company was willing to sell MAF land for a house and a hangar adjacent to the runway.

Before the Ecuador program got started that summer, Truxton headed back to the United States for a whirlwind of activity that included marrying Betty Clarke, attending the Winona Lake Aviation Conference, and heading back to Los Angeles to prepare for the September flight to Ecuador with Nate Saint.

Truxton's wife, Betty, grew up in Washington, D.C. She graduated from the University of Maryland with a bachelor of science degree and, as a registered nurse, joined the Army Nurse Corps during World War II and was based in England and France. While overseas, attending a Bible study for service personnel in Marseilles, Betty came to a place of deeper commitment to Christ and missionary service. Upon returning home at war's end, she entered Eastern Baptist Seminary in Philadelphia and graduated with a master's degree in religious education.

At the seminary she met Truxton's brother Addison, who soon began writing Jim that he had found the girl "who has everything you've been looking for." The two first met when Jim came to speak to a Student Foreign Missions Fellowship meeting, and it was really love at first sight. Due to his travels to Mexico, Ecuador, and Peru, their courtship was mainly by mail. They were married on June 19, 1948.

Hobey Lowrance

Truxton first met Hobert "Hobey" Lowrance at the 1948 Winona Lake World Missionary Aviation Conference. Lowrance was a native of Tulsa, Oklahoma. He attended the University of Tulsa and became an American Airlines pilot at the age of twenty-one. During the war, he flew military transports as a civilian. Through the influence of other Christian pilots, he became a believer, and following the war felt called to overseas Christian service. To this end, he was studying at Wheaton College in the spring of 1948. During those years, Wheaton students had a missionary aviation club, and it is not surprising that some of its stalwart members—Nate Saint, Hatch Hatcher, Don Berry, and Hobey—were serving with MAF-US by 1950.

Nate Saint joined Hobey Lowrance and Jim Truxton at the Winona Lake Aviation Conference. The three took part in debates on an issue that had arisen two years earlier at the 1946 conference. The supporters of Paul Hartford stressed equipping missionaries to do their own flying. Jim and the MAF-US representatives believed that specialists should do the flying and wanted to see cooperative regional mission aviation programs come into being. Hobey spoke up for the latter, and Jim recognized him as a person blessed with a clear, analytical mind.

Hobey had been thinking about service with MAF, and Jim's encouragement did much to help him settle the issue. At the end of August, Hobey turned in his resignation to American Airlines, effective September 1. He wrote Charlie Mellis, "It was a big step, but I have the peace of heart that I am doing the right thing. . . . My hesitation and concern has not been due to worldly attraction or fear of loss of security. I have been perfectly willing to step out of my job if God so willed, and the decision was not as to whether I could give up something, but whether God was telling me to give it up."[2] The caliber of the people already in MAF strongly influenced Hobey to join. Besides Nate Saint and Jim Truxton, he had also met Jim Lomheim, of the Chiapas-Tabasco program, and had helped him service a plane in Dallas.

Jim Truxton wanted to groom Hobey to work with him on field surveys, but first he wanted Hobey to work with Lomheim in Mexico and go to Ecuador to help Nate before joining him on surveys of Colombia, Venezuela, and Brazil.[3]

Truxton and Saint Depart for Ecuador

The first week of September 1948 Jim Truxton and Nate Saint headed for Ecuador in the MAF Stinson while their wives flew to Ecuador by commercial airline. On the second evening of their ferry flight to Ecuador, Jim and Nate reached San Jose, Costa Rica. Overhead was a dark, threatening cloud buildup. As they cautiously approached a local mountain pass, there was a great deal of turbulence. A storm set in. They spotted what looked like an abandoned airstrip down in the valley below the city. Since darkness was approaching, they considered it best to spend the night there, even though it meant spreading their sleeping bags over top of their cargo and sleeping inside the plane.

Just before dark on the following day, they landed at a small strip near the Colombia-Ecuador border. There was no town—just a couple of radio operators and several Colombian workers. The radiomen graciously had their cook fix dinner for the two gringo pilots, who made valiant attempts at speaking Spanish. Again, they spent the night in the plane.

Early the next morning, they warmed up with hot coffee as they watched the sun light up the majestic Andes. Then they were off to Quito. It was one of those perfectly clear days. To cross the mountains, they climbed to 14,400 feet. "It was wonderful," wrote Truxton, "to see Quito burst into view in the valley below, and what a royal welcome we received."[4] By mid-morning they landed at Shell Mera. The Humphries, George Poole, and "Dad" Mellis were there to greet them.

Charles J. Mellis Sr., Charlie's dad, had volunteered to construct a house for the Saints at Shell Mera as a short-term missions project, one of a long line of his mission projects. He celebrated his seventieth birthday in a canvas tent on the edge of the Amazon rain forest, supervising Saint, Truxton, and others in the building of the needed house.

Dad Mellis made a wager with Mr. Humphries, the head of Shell Ecuador, that he would have the roof on the house in thirty days. Whoever won the bet would take the other out to dinner. Truxton and Saint came to wish this wager had never been made. They found themselves hammering nails in the rain because their boss would not let them take shelter from the daily tropical downpour. It rains close to eighty inches a year in the Amazonian rain forest of eastern Ecuador, and over one hundred inches at Shell Mera.

Building the Shell Mera house (from left to right) Charles J. Mellis Sr., Jim Truxton, George Poole, and Nate Saint.

Dad Mellis's tight schedule called for putting up the Saints' house by October 1. He needed to get back to St. Louis and did not want to lose the wager with Humphries! This meant that all hands had to be there, full-time, to speed along the construction. Given the setting, all supplies had to be shipped in for some distance. The locals marveled at the drive of this slender, aging man, but the heat and humidity sapped his energies. Dad Mellis got the roof up but had to leave the project before it was completed. His labor of love was much appreciated, and the home he built continues to provide shelter to MAF families.

Founding of *Alas de Socorro*

Uppermost in Jim Truxton's mind was the need for MAF to obtain permanent status in Ecuador, which meant gaining approval from the National Legislature.

When MAF worked for Wycliffe, they relied on Townsend to pave the way diplomatically. Now on its own, MAF had to pass inspection on its own merits. This was an entirely new situation, one fraught with many uncertainties and much waiting.

Clarence Jones, of station HCJB, advised Jim Truxton to seek the advice of attorney Dr. Antonio Quevedo, a highly respected professional who later became Ecuador's ambassador to the United Nations. When Quevedo learned that the organization's name was Missionary Aviation Fellowship, he felt that the word *missionary* would stir up needless opposition.

A Spanish name with a humane touch was more likely to gain ready acceptance. One night, Truxton specifically asked for God's direction regarding a name. He awoke the next morning with the words "Wings of Help" running through his mind. He asked how this would best be stated in Spanish, and the name *Alas de Socorro* was born. *Socorro* is a strong term for help, aid, relief, or assistance of any kind. This name would tie in well with missions and leave open the door to helping the government.

Back in Los Angeles, Grady Parrott and Charlie Mellis pondered how they might best deal with this new identity. They decided that they should contact attorney Elvrum for legal advice. He drew up incorporation papers for *Alas de Socorro,* a California-based corporation designed to assist various types of organizations or individuals working in education, medicine, and relief, particularly those of "Christian persuasion." By stressing the philanthropic nature of *Alas de Socorro* yet stating its broad Christian commitment, MAF, like Wycliffe's SIL, found ready acceptance in many Latin American countries.

When Quevedo saw the name *Alas de Socorro* and the documents describing its purpose, he said, "With this I can go anywhere," and he did. Not only did *Alas de Socorro* gain government approval, it received a ten-year contract that was automatically renewable unless one side canceled it. The contract prevented *Alas de Socorro* (ADS) from doing any commercial flying to prevent competition with Ateca airlines, a private carrier serving Ecuador's Oriente.

ADS was viewed favorably at the highest levels of government. The president of Ecuador, Galo Plaza Lasso, received Jim and Betty Truxton for a short interview on November 5. Both the president and Betty were alumni of the University of Maryland. Truxton only had time to pay his respects and make a gesture of friendliness. The president did raise a number of questions about the operation, but overall, Truxton was delighted by his positive response.

The Ecuador program finally got started the first week of September. Nate Saint touched down at Tena, the station of Dave and Grace Cooper, missionaries of the Christian and Missionary Alliance. Next he flew up into the mountains to Ambato, the site of the lumber mill that supplied them with the building material for the house, then was back down to Macuma to deliver fresh vegetables to missionaries. In Nate's hands, the MAF flight program literally took off. By the first week of November, he had logged thirty-five hours, flown thirty-three hundred miles, moved thirteen people and over twelve thousand pounds of cargo. Jim Truxton estimated that this saved at least thirty-five hundred hours on the trail. During this time, a student at the mission school at Dos Rios suffered a serious leg injury and was taken out for proper care at Quito. It was doubtful that he could have come out over the trail.[5]

Nate was ideally suited for the program, given his talent for improvisation. He had the ability to find solutions where others saw only problems, whether it was generating power, providing soft water, or finding a landing strip. His gift came into play in an unexpected development as a result of C&MA's opening of a new station on the Napo River. Detractors spread the word that MAF's promise of plane service there was not going to be fulfilled any time soon. They did not count on Saint's ingenuity in finding and landing on a long sandbar on the river, just across from the station. Truxton wrote, "The words were no more than out of the critic's mouth than our plane came buzzing in with all kinds of supplies, equipment, and food."

Then a smallpox epidemic broke out a short distance upriver. Saint flew vaccine in from Shell Mera and enabled completion of injections before anyone hardly knew what had happened. These events had a dramatic impact on the population, inasmuch as it boosted the credibility of the evangelicals. All the able-bodied Indians went to work building a permanent landing strip to assure continuous service. The effective use of the plane opened doors for expanded mission work among the indigenous people.

By Christmas Nate and Marj Saint were back in Quito, expecting their first child. The crisp, cold Quito air added to the festive season. Jim and Betty Truxton were down at Shell Mera working on the house and celebrating the wonder of Christmas with a tree decorated with Christmas cards. Their Christmas letter was addressed from "Jungle's Edge," Ecuador. Their letter spoke of the joy of celebrating the Savior's birth "on the edge of a vast territory into which the Christmas Story has not yet come." The Cofane Indians in the northeastern jungles and the Jivaros, Quichuas, and Aucas had not yet received the Good News.

Nate's Quito Crash

Joyous commitment to God's work and careful planning are not guarantees that there will be no heartaches along the way. Shortly after 12:00 noon on December 30, Nate Saint took off from the Quito Airport for Shell Mera. Gwen Tidmarsh, who was several months pregnant, and her young son Robbie were on board. It was a cloudy day, but visibility was generally good. The wind was gusty. The fully loaded plane climbed to two hundred feet, then hit a severe downdraft, stalling and crashing in a plowed field. As it struck the ground and rolled over, fuel poured out of the tank, but mercifully, no fire broke out.[6] The Stinson was totaled. Nate suffered a back injury, fractured vertebrae, and an ankle injury. The passengers had minor lacerations. Both Nate and Gwen Tidmarsh were hospitalized.

Assistance could not have been more immediate. The Truxtons made a night trip up the road from Shell Mera to Quito to see the injured travelers and learn what had gone wrong. Betty wanted to be with Marj Saint, who was soon to have her first child.

Saint was unable to explain the stall and crash. Hobey Lowrance, having recently arrived from Mexico, proved to be most helpful. His wide experience in flying was important for an accurate analysis. Since this was the second single-engine missionary plane that had crashed in Ecuador, it was feared that the use of a single-engine plane would be blamed.

Hobey's analysis showed that it was not a matter of inadequate equipment but the pilot's inexperience in handling sudden downdrafts that led to the crash. Hobey concluded that "Nate hit a downdraft at marginal airspeed, was frightened by the descent, lifted the nose up and stalled."[7] By turning the plane into a sharp left turn to get out of the downdraft, Nate exacerbated the stall. Had he allowed the plane to proceed on course, the chances of landing safely beyond the runway would have been much better. Nate came to see this and learned a valuable lesson as a pilot of limited flying experience in the Andean region. The lesson that was driven home to MAF as a result of this accident was the need for a highly specialized flight orientation program prior to field assignment.

In view of the findings, Nate offered his resignation. Grady Parrott looked beyond the accident. He saw that the way MAF personnel emerged from it could make for an even more effective team. He quoted Kenneth Pike of Wycliffe, who had commented that "if MAF succeeds it will not be because the Lord brought together several fellows who just clicked, but . . . because the fellows who were brought together by the Lord determined that despite personality differences and (other) minor differences in viewpoint, they would pull together to get the job done."[8] This accident did have the effect of pulling MAF people together, and out of their deliberations came constructive safety measures.

Shoulder harnesses and nets for cargo became standard equipment. Serious thought was given to formalizing a flight orientation program that would simulate the hazardous conditions inherent in mission field flying and teach pilots corrective responses and preventative measures.

Flight Safety

Until then, MAF pilots met flight qualifications when they had the required ratings and a certain number of hours of logged flight time. That is not to say that pilots went straight to the field without being checked out. Grady Parrott had a great deal of experience with canyon flying and incorporated many features of this military experience (including the famous "canyon turn") into the orientation program. Now, however, it was deemed necessary to give the pilots the type of terrain flying experience that they could expect on the field. Given the widening circle of talent on the MAF team, Lowrance was best equipped to give close attention to developing the MAF flight-safety program.

Hobey recognized that mission aviation was qualitatively different from commercial flying. His flight observation from the MAF fields brought him to the conclusion that "proficiency cannot replace experience." He explained it this way:

> Those of us who have considerable time are not safer pilots necessarily because we can maneuver an airplane better, but because we have flown through so many different situations that our reflexes have become trained so as to take care of most any situation that may arise, as far as is humanly possible. If we do get into a strange situation, we have a lot of past experiences to draw from. I was scared stiff on my first forced landing, the first time I barreled into a thunderstorm, the first time I picked up ice—but after that, I knew what to do when I encountered each.[9]

Lowrance developed the areas of accident investigation and flight safety for MAF. On furlough in 1953, he expanded the flight orientation program that subjected the licensed pilot to many of the rigorous conditions likely to be encountered while flying in unfriendly terrain and weather conditions.

Effects of the Plane's Loss

The loss of the plane in Ecuador once again threw the isolated GMU, Brethren, and C&MA frontier missionaries onto their own resources. This occurred only a few months following inauguration of the air arm and before the two-way radio network between the MAF base and the stations had been established. The GMU Macuma station, some sixty miles into the rain forest from Shell Mera, was the most vulnerable.[10]

Marie Drown, wife of Frank Drown, the mission station's manager, was expecting Nate to fly her out in ample time for her baby's safe delivery. It was now that time, but the air arm was shut down. Before MAF's coming, standard procedure was for a missionary's wife to leave the station early in her pregnancy, but it was too late for that now.

Nate remembered the arrangements he had made with the Drowns, felt grave concern over the dilemma, and notified Jim Truxton. Jim relayed the concern to Hobey Lowrance at Shell Mera, who lined up a local commercial operator and worked out a plan for Marie.

The landing strip at Macuma was so marginal that Hobey hesitated risking a landing there. Instead, he had a Shell Company plane fly over and drop a message explaining the circumstances and requesting Marie (and any others needing evacuation) to trek the relatively short distance to a more suitable strip, Ayui. Hobey and the local flier would be there within a few days to fly them out. The plan worked, and Marie was out in good time.

Before these plans were settled, Frank Drown assembled a trekking party and started out over the treacherously difficult trail for help. He had no way of knowing that MAF was making its own plans to fly his wife out.

Frank and the other trekkers spent six harrowing days struggling over a muddy trail. On the way, they crossed one turbulent river on a raft that went out of control and resulted in the loss of all their equipment, money, and nearly their lives. The senior missionary among them became ill, his legs and feet swelling so badly that he could hardly walk. The party arrived at Shell Mera in a state of total exhaustion. Marie's flight, by contrast, lasted about thirty minutes; she arrived at Shell Mera almost at the same time as the weary trekkers. On this mission frontier, the plane was sorely missed![11]

As for Nate Saint, he was in a cast from neck to toe. He couldn't do much, but he laid plans for the future. For one, he and Marj decided that they had to slow down if they were going to retain their sanity. In their first months of service, they had worked themselves to the bone. Nate wrote Jim Truxton, "When I get wound down I'm like a wind-up type phonograph when it gets below governor speed. Everything sounds wrong. Even the proverbial molehills become Andes and seem to block the way." The answer to this, Nate and Marj decided, was to "commit to God the million-and-one things that need to be done until we are able to do them."[12] This was very good advice, and it freed them to take time out to relax even when all their work was not done.

Nate had other immediate problems to think about during his enforced rest. The potential of a plane having engine failure over the wide expanse of rain forest due to water or impurities in the fuel got him thinking about an alternate fuel system. He proposed mounting an additional fuel tank that would feed the fuel directly into the intake manifold.[13] Nate got the idea from watching Ecuadorian truck drivers do this to keep their vehicles running. As a safety feature, all planes already came factory equipped with a dual ignition system, but this did not guarantee that there would be fuel flowing into the engine. By supplying an alternate fuel system, the safety feature of twin engines could be approximated.

Grady Parrott considered the biggest hazard of such a system was a potential carburetor fire. He believed this hazard might be even more serious than a controlled landing in the treetops. Nevertheless, Grady took Saint's suggestion seriously and discussed it with Civil Aviation Administration officials in Los Angeles. Nate turned to perfecting this system during his furlough. As a result, Saint's alternate fuel system was approved and installed on MAF-US planes in 1953.

Resuming Flight Operations

To get the Ecuador program back on track, Grady Parrott flew a second Stinson down in April 1949, stopping in Mexico to confer with Jim Lomheim on the projected Oaxaca and Yucatán surveys.

The first flight of the Stinson in Ecuador was a mission of mercy to help C&MA missionary Morey Fuller, stationed on the Napo River. He was running low on medical supplies, so Grady and Hobey Lowrance prepared a parachute drop of an emergency supply of penicillin. Grady visited all seven Ecuador stations while there and became acutely aware of the much-feared Auca people of the upper Napo region. Just before then, C&MA missionary Dave Cooper had traveled with an adventure-seeking party that was ambushed by a group of Aucas. They managed to escape by diving into the swirling waters. Fortunately, the Auca's spears did not find their mark, and Cooper's party managed to elude them. Grady later flew out the Auca spears that Dave had retrieved from the river and agreed with Nate's prediction that the plane would someday play an important part in reaching these people.[14]

Grady remained at Shell Mera for a week to confer with Hobey Lowrance, Nate's stand-in, and got a good taste of the pressures that pilots face on the job. Out at Tena, both Grace Cooper and Dr. Tidmarsh had been waiting for days to be flown out. Persistent bad weather was preventing the flight. Grace needed to come out for reasons of poor health; Dr. Tidmarsh wanted to leave because his wife was in Quito, due to give birth. The plane would have to carry three persons plus baggage. Assessing the load, Grady was fairly certain that the runway was long enough for a safe clearing. However, since this was his first flight out of Tena and the short strip was very wet, he wanted to give himself an ample safety margin. He decided Tidmarsh should remain behind and be picked up the next morning. Tidmarsh cornered Grady and started putting on the heat. He argued that he just had to get out of there on that flight. It was the first clear day in five, and he was certain that if he were left behind the weather would close in for another week.

Grady wavered for a moment under Tidmarsh's persuasive plea but decided that safety had to come first. He turned to Tidmarsh and asked him if he would join him in prayer that the Lord would provide good weather for a return flight to Tena the next day. Tidmarsh rose to this challenge and turned to Grady with a grin. Sure enough, the Lord heard that prayer, provided clear skies the next day, and Grady was able to fly Tidmarsh out without further delay.[15] These types of decisions are a routine part of every MAF pilot's day. One misjudgment can hazard the flight.

Hobey Lowrance became pilot in charge of the Ecuador operation following Nate's accident. The seven-station circuit of the C&MA, GMU, and Brethren was now being well served.

At the end of July, eight-year-old Bobbie Fuller, son of missionary Morey Fuller, accidently slipped into a power saw that severely cut his arm. The radio network allowed communication with the tower at Shell Mera, which alerted Lowrance to the emergency just as he was taking off from Tena. Lowrance immediately headed for Ajuano, Fuller's station, which was only twelve minutes away by air (four days on foot). Hobey contacted Marj Saint for emergency instructions on treating Bobbie. Within half an hour, they had Bobbie at the Shell hospital, and the next morning flew him to Quito for skin grafting. Recalling that time, Lowrance still remembers how Mrs. Fuller, so thankful for the quick response, with tears in her eyes, said to him, "Praise God for MAF."[16]

The radio network making this kind of communication possible was put in place by HCJB radio technicians Bob Remington and P. K. Mhyre. Later, MAF was to have its own radioman, Overton "Red" Brown, a World War II Marine. Remington and Mhyre installed surplus military equipment that they and other Ecuador-bound missionaries had picked up in Los Angeles. The system, though cumbersome by today's standards, proved its worth in many respects, as Grady Parrott detailed to Charlie Mellis. "It has facilitated inter- and intra-mission committee meetings, closer cooperation among the stations, better disposition of national workers, increased prestige for the gospel, opportunities to do favors for the government and small towns near the stations." In addition, radio communication made possible a well-coordinated flow of fresh vegetables into the widely separated mission stations.

By the end of July Nate Saint was ready to fly again, and Hobey Lowrance checked him out. Nate was willing to be put through whatever paces Hobey saw fit. The latter took Nate out to some of the marginal fields, to see how he would perform. Hobey noted that Nate flew the plane with not a sign of nervousness or tension and surprisingly well from the start.

Marj Saint on radio in Shall Mera, Ecuador. The Stinson is in the background, 1949.

Nate's attitude was much more upbeat, now that work at Shell Mera was well along. Carving a home and a new life out of the Amazonian wilderness was no easy task; it took persistence and willingness to live without the many creature comforts of life.

Although much has been said about Nate's accident and his complete recovery, it should be noted that much greater tragedies struck Ecuador in 1949. The Shell Oil Company lost three planes in five months. One in August took thirty-six lives. A devastating earthquake centered near the Andean city of Ambato took the lives of four thousand people the same month.[17]

Thankfully there was also joy. During his stay in Ecuador Hobey Lowrance met and became engaged to Olivia Scott, a C&MA missionary running a clinic among the Otavalo Indians. The two were married in Quito's English Fellowship Church shortly after the quake. Lowrance's visitor's visa was about to expire, so he and his bride left for Medellín, Colombia, where the Truxtons were located in preparation for the Colombia and Venezuela MAF surveys.[18] Jim and Hobey were scheduled to team up for this effort.

In 1949, MAF stood on the brink of further expansion. The exuberance of laying plans had given way to the realism of establishing the first MAF-US cooperative missionary flight program in Ecuador. It filled a dire need. Despite well-laid plans, unforeseen terrain and air-mass conditions threatened the safety of flights on perfectly clear days. Nate's accident led to a more comprehensive flight orientation program to give fliers the skills to anticipate and deal with very real dangers. Like the Waco accident in Mexico, the Quito crash served to strengthen the MAF flight program.

In the coming years new initiatives came in the form of expanded surveys and programs in Central and South America as well as halfway around the globe, where MAF-US joined hands with Harry Hartwig of the Australian MAF to launch operations in the Territory of New Guinea. The 1950s saw the "takeoff" of MAF in a way that had scarcely been imagined in earlier years. MAF earned increasing respect and confidence among mission leaders. It also received the Christian public's financial support. Given these heartening results, MAF felt confident in going on the offensive in presenting its arguments on the best way to use the airplane in missions.

A Quickening Pace

Launching the Ecuador program gave MAF-US a much-needed boost. The next four years saw a quickening pace at home and abroad. At home, MAF challenged and interacted constructively with competing ideas in mission aviation. Grady Parrott emerged as president, to help lead the organization into the future. Abroad, new surveys were undertaken in Colombia and Venezuela, and the work in Mexico was expanded. Overall progress was made in the area of flight safety. Given these developments, MAF needed an enlarged home base.

The World Mission Aviation Council

In mission aviation circles of the immediate postwar years, MAF's specialist approach was neither universally applauded nor widely accepted. MAF's aviation philosophy was mainly challenged by a segment of what had emerged in 1948 as the World Mission Aviation Council (WMAC), an attempted umbrella organization of diverse (and in some ways incompatible) mission aviation interests. MAF was a participating nonmember largely because it wanted to check the influence of those who, like Paul Hartford, were promoting the idea that missionaries should seek to become pilots.[1]

The divergence in approach between WMAC and MAF first surfaced at the 1946 Winona Lake Conference, formalized at the two 1948 WMAC conferences, and finally reached its crescendo at the 1949 Chicago convention. These years saw much discussion on the best way to integrate aviation into mission field work.

The MAF philosophy basically saw mission aviation as a specialized service carried out by aviation experts. MAF was flexible in providing services. In Nigeria, it supplied SIM with a plane and pilot to launch its air arm. In Mexico, MAF purchased a plane and provided a pilot for logistical support to SIL. It sent pilot Betty Greene to Peru. In the meantime, MAF began air support for the Institutes of the Presbyterians in Tabasco. Then, in Ecuador, MAF started its first cooperative program, bringing in both the plane and pilot. In Venezuela, MAF undertook a demographic survey pinpointing the location of native peoples at the request of the Orinoco River Mission (ORM). In Brazil, MAF set up an airplane overhaul and maintenance center at Anápolis for the benefit of independent missionary fliers. The record demonstrates MAF's flexibility in providing services, but in each of these approaches, MAF stressed servanthood, technical competence, and cost effectiveness.

Jim Truxton had become disillusioned with some of the lines of interest represented at the 1948 Washington conference. He felt that some there were "obsessed with the grandeur and glamour of missionary aviation."[2] The thrill seekers among the WMAC were referred to by the MAF leadership as the "flyboys." In 1949 this group organized a "fly-in" to Mexico City for December 31 to January 1. The affair grew spontaneously when several WMAC members decided to visit Melvin Todd and George King, independent missionaries in Mexico. Those pushing this public-relations winter outing advertised it as "the winter thrill flight vacation of a life time."[3]

Just prior to the flight, the group was sobered by the tragic news that Todd and King, operating their own plane, were killed in a crash near a village located at sixty-five hundred feet in the state of Guerrero. Although WMAC had pictured itself as the forward wave of missionary aviation, this calamity pointed out its lack of experience and technical maturity.

After the successful inauguration of the Ecuador program, MAF had sufficient self-confidence to divorce itself from WMAC in 1949. MAF went on the offensive, selling its approach as the best one for missionary aviation. Grady, Jim, and Charlie launched an assertive campaign. Grady traveled East in the fall of 1949, presenting the MAF message to various mission leaders who showed interest. He let mission organizations know, in unmistakable terms, that WMAC did not represent MAF and that MAF had a tried-and-tested program that effectively facilitated frontier missions. Its Ecuadorian program was beyond the experimental stage. The government had granted a ten-year renewable contract which, in effect, signaled its stamp of approval.

As Grady put it, "Nothing succeeds like success. And most of the mission leaders are smart enough to recognize that."[4] The strategy was simply to let missions know what MAF was doing and continue to expand field operations on an invitational basis. Parrott felt that the Lord had guided its philosophy, raised up the essential "missions structure," confirmed its direction, and set it on course. Furthermore, its critics were diminishing. There was work to be done in the Lord's harvest, and MAF found itself committed to a ministry of service in the frontline of postwar mission advances.

Home Office Developments

At the August 1949 board meeting, Grady Parrott exchanged leadership roles with Jim Truxton, largely at the urging of Jim. Besides having technical experience, Grady was even tempered, had broad sympathies, and possessed the skills of a diplomat. He handled the crisis over the differences with Townsend with grace. He was exactly the type of person MAF needed at the helm at that juncture for working with Wycliffe and diverse mission organizations that ranged from Presbyterians and Lutherans to Assemblies of God and Anglicans. Grady served as MAF's president for the next twenty-one years.

The change in leadership titles allowed both officers to exercise their respective gifts most advantageously. Betty Greene expressed it this way to Jim Truxton:

> The Lord has been good to bring you and Grady and Charlie together to lead MAF. You complement, balance and supplement each other remarkably. If Grady is to be president for a time, I am sure it is our prayer that the Lord will give him the same grace

He has so wonderfully given you. You each have parts to play of
such importance that a change in office name cannot effect their
actuality.[5]

Charlie Mellis had organizational ability and a sharp eye for
detail. As secretary-treasurer, he worked out the administrative
details with skill and dedication. The publications *Missionary Aviation* and "Wings of Praise and Prayer" bore Charlie's imprint. He
was able to reduce complex ideas in such a way as to gain reader
interest without becoming sensational. In addition, he was the
office manager until his departure for New Guinea in 1952. Along
with the others, he devoted his time, talents, and energies to building MAF. These pioneers gave generously of themselves not only
to further MAF-US's work, but to advise, cooperate with, and
encourage the leaders of MAF sister organizations.

As for Betty Greene, her heart was solidly with MAF, but she
had suffered burnout in the Peru experience. She continued to
serve effectively on the board, maintaining meaningful correspondence with the officers. In addition she contributed helpful
advice from the Northwest. Her retreat to academia at the University of Washington—studying, meditating, and waiting on the
Lord—brought about healing. This gave her a needed sense of
well-being and direction for her future, which included further
service with MAF. In two years, she was in Nigeria, flying the
Evangel, a Cessna 170, for the Sudan Interior Mission during
Clarence Soderberg's furlough.

By the fall of 1949, MAF was out of its infancy and moving
toward adolescence. As an organization, it had a good foundation
with policies that had been clearly thought out, tested on the field,
and found to be successful. The number of committed personnel
in the organization had grown from the initial officers to four additional pilots: Hatch Hatcher flew in Tabasco while Jim Lomheim
was on furlough; Nate and Marj Saint were in Ecuador; Hobey and
Olivia Lowrance worked with the Truxtons on surveys in Colombia and Venezuela. The organization had the energy of youth and
the will to take on new challenges. MAF was poised for expansion.

The growth that subsequently took place did not come in isolation from its sister MAF organizations, but in concert with them.

This international cooperative spirit allowed each of the MAF wings to develop its own program with support from one another. Despite limited resources, MAF-US loaned personnel overseas in the 1950s to mission aviation service in New Guinea, Nigeria, and the Sudan. A constant flow of communication kept each wing informed of technical developments and progress.

Hatch and Penny Hatcher

Closer to home, Hatch Hatcher and his wife, Doris, known as Penny, departed for Mexico with son Rodney the first week of January 1949. They were moving down to take over for Jim Lomheim in Chiapas when he left for furlough.

Jim had been flying for SIL in Chiapas and had done pioneering work in Tabasco in facilitating the Presbyterian "Institutes," Fred Tinley's airlift version of the circuit-riding preacher. In this swampy region the airplane was used to place two-man teams in isolated villages where there were small congregations. These teams, consisting of a pastor and a layman or Bible school teacher, would visit each church for three days, holding Bible classes during the day and evangelistic services at night. Films and slides were frequently shown. Five such teams kept Jim Lomheim busy shuttling people from location to location. The airplane was very strategic in meeting the transportation needs of those who worked with the 110 congregations thriving in this swampy region in 1949. Eighty-three of these could be reached from fifty-five landing strips, many of which had been built by churches eager to be included in the Institute program.[6]

Hatch Hatcher was a licensed aviation mechanic, and both he and Penny had studied Spanish. Hatch took over Jim's work and the SIL flight program in Chiapas when Jim left on furlough. Once oriented to the field, the Hatchers based the plane at Ixtapa, an Indian village in Chiapas. By moving the plane's base from Tuxtla to a rural location, the MAF operation had less visibility and correspondingly reduced the chances of offending the commercial fliers who saw MAF as threatening to their businesses. From Ixtapa it was possible for Hatch to serve other SIL workers in the mountainous region of the state of Oaxaca, 250 air miles to the west.

Hatcher flew in Mexico for more than twenty years. His congeniality, wit, and warm smile became trademarks of his work. The Mexican people affectionately called him Don Elias since Hatch was too difficult for them to pronounce.

Jim and Darlene Lomheim

Jim Lomheim's furlough in 1949 took him to his native South Dakota and back in contact with longtime friends, among them Darlene Hofer. She was of Mennonite Brethren background. The two had met when Lomheim sang in a quartet and traveled with the American Sunday School Union. Over the years they saw each other summers at Camp Byran, a Christian camp. When Jim headed to St. Louis to get his A&E ratings and pilot's license and then to serve in Mexico for two years, Darlene was teaching school and studying at Grace Bible Institute in Omaha. Jim and Darlene renewed their friendship and quickly fell in love. They were married shortly after Christmas. Though Darlene had had no intention of serving in foreign missions, she and Jim headed for Mexico the following year, and Jim flew for the Presbyterians in Tabasco province.

Their arrival set the stage for wider MAF service in Mexico, particularly Oaxaca, the Pacific province, and expansion of the Tabasco program into the Yucatán peninsula on the Caribbean. Jim Lomheim and Grady Parrott had earlier conducted surveys in these regions. It should be noted that the Piper "Clipper" was first introduced here.[7]

By 1953 the growth of the Chiapas program and increasing requests for service in mountainous Oaxaca led to a division of the two programs.[8] Jim Lomheim continued to fly in Chiapas and Tabasco with the Pacer.

Yucatán Survey

The First Presbyterian Church of Berkeley, California, underwrote the Yucatán survey costs. A good many of its members were of Hispanic background and took a personal interest in reaching their own people. Fred Passler, their missionary working among the Mayan of the Yucatán, accompanied Parrott on this survey and took advantage of the opportunity to visit and minister to the scattered Christians who were the descendants of the ancient Maya people.

Fred took along a generator, projector, screen, and slides to introduce the young people to the training possibilities available at the Xocenpich Bible School. At these meetings, Fred, though fluent in Spanish, took along an interpreter who could speak Mayan. It was quite a sensation to the Mayan Christians to have a visitor fly in and set up an evening program. Good attendance was always assured.

Grady Parrott was fascinated to note a Christian chief in one of these villages who listened attentively to the message and, under his breath, gave audible support to the preaching. The village was located on a well-traveled trail. As an outreach to anyone who passed through, the Christians invited travelers to spend some time with them, providing simple guest quarters under a thatched roof. After serving refreshments or a meal, the villagers would ask the visitor if he knew the Lord. This opened the door to Christian witness. When the traveler was about to depart, these believers gave out provisions for the trail. Such was the uniqueness of the Yucatán setting in which the MAF plane was introduced.

The Yucatán interior was practically void of settlements. Except for the frontier city of Chetumal, the people lived in small villages scattered along the coast. Fred saw the plane as a vehicle for evangelistic thrusts rather than the type of Institutes inaugurated in Tabasco.

Colombian Survey

Parallel to these 1949 developments, Jim Truxton and Hobey Lowrance, who were now in Medellín, Colombia, worked out a strategy for surveying that country. This was in line with the goal to survey the mission needs of Latin America country by country. When they first arrived in Colombia, they had no plane. It did not take long for them to conclude that a plane was essential. For instance, the Pacific coastal region stretching some four hundred miles from Tumaco to Buena Ventura was the C&MA field. Mission work in such an extended area evolved into itinerant work up the rivers and coastal channels and would virtually demand the service of a seaplane.

The Mennonites worked inland from the coast, eastward to the Andes. They wanted to know about the people groups living in the mountainous areas. Overland travel was one way to find them, but an aerial survey could pinpoint them quickly. The need for a plane for the survey became obvious.

While Hobey traveled throughout the "Llanos" or grasslands of eastern Colombia surveying the travel needs of several small missions, Jim went to the coast for a close-up view of the Alliance's efforts to reach the people along the river estuaries. Oscar Jacobson of C&MA took Truxton into the region in a twenty-foot dugout canoe powered by a 22-horsepower outboard. The natural hazards, though formidable, paled in comparison to the human booby traps. This region had elements strongly opposed to evangelical work. On the Guapi River, a fuel dealer sold the pair gasoline spiked with silt. This was not discovered until a clogged fuel line forced the engine to sputter and stall. Oscar Jacobson and Jim Truxton poled and paddled their way to Charo, a two-day journey. If their canoe had been a plane, the outcome could have been more serious.

Unfortunately the political situation in Colombia hindered a proper survey. Calls soon arrived from the Moravians in Honduras and the Orinoco River Mission (ORM) in Venezuela. Prospects for working in Brazil also appeared on the horizon as a result of Jim Truxton's interaction with the leadership of the Latin American Council of Presbyterian Missions USA during their conference at Medellín in August 1949.

Hobey Lowrance purchased a slightly used Piper "Clipper" for twenty-seven hundred dollars for these surveys. Before moving on to survey work with Jim in Venezuela, Hobey undertook an operational five-month flight needs study in Honduras. This laid the groundwork for Don and Phyllis Berry, who would soon follow. From there, the Lowrances joined the Truxtons, who made their headquarters at the ORM center at Ciudad Bolivar, Venezuela.

Venezuelan Survey

The Venezuela survey was unique in that its purpose was not to explore possibilities for an air arm for existing mission stations but to pioneer missionary advances into unmapped native settlements. ORM sought information on the location and number of tribal people living south of the Orinoco River, and this required surveys to obtain topographic and demographic data. Therefore, plans were laid for a blanket survey of great stretches of virtually uncharted territory. The plane was equipped with an additional fuel tank and emergency supplies in case of a downing. Concern for safety was routine, but the June 9 crash of a New Tribes Mission DC-3 with sixteen persons aboard heightened awareness of aviation's hazards.[9]

For the first Venezuela flight, the Piper "Clipper" from the Honduras survey was used. Jim and Hobey flew up the Orinoco River to Caicara. Their aeronautical charts were accurate up to this point but not for the region beyond, among the river's tributaries. Alvin Lewis and Chuck Olvey of the Orinoco River Mission (now merged into TEAM) were impressed with the ease with which next-to-river settlements, otherwise hidden to the river traveler, could be spotted from the air. These villages were all duly plotted on maps. The survey found that most of the Indians lived in the headwaters of these rivers, far from the white man. The population centers of six known Indian tribes and other unidentified peoples were mapped. Hobey did the piloting while Jim recorded the information.

To assure safety for the 115 hours of flying over a 110,000-square-mile territory in southern and eastern Venezuela, Hobey developed a system of safety checks that had parallels to a baseball diamond. Since each seven- to eight-hour flight was a round-trip, checkpoints were set up to correspond to the three bases. The flight went up a river valley to the tributary to be explored. This was dubbed first base. Only if everything was clear did they proceed to second base, the range of mountains between the major river systems. They would not proceed up into the upper regions, third base, unless visibility was good ahead and behind. From there it was off to home base in the afternoon, with a planned two hours of reserve fuel still in the tanks upon landing.[10]

The Venezuela survey was in advance of mission penetration. In this respect, it was different from any previous MAF undertaking because it was not geared to establish an MAF program but provide up-to-date demographic information on which missions could make intelligent decisions for new advances. In doing this survey, Truxton explained:

> Careful attention was being given to all that might effect future efforts. How could they best be reached: by river, or by air? If by air, by seaplane or by land plane? What were the weather characteristics at different seasons of the year? Significant topographical factors were noted. Rapids and waterfall breaks along the river arteries were indicated. All open or semi-open areas were marked on the survey charts in case of future forced landing, or the need to construct landing strips. Often it was possible to observe certain characteristics such as: type and style of houses and gardens, whether the people were clothed or naked, had painted bodies, or specific reactions to seeing the plane—things which might help in determining tribal affiliations, and hostile or friendly intentions. Thus the way for the first translator-missionary was being paved.[11]

Jim Truxton was anxious for Wycliffe to receive the information. Bill Nyman Jr. was just then gaining entrée for SIL into Venezuela. Jim suggested that all the information they gathered be turned over to SIL as well as ORM, so both might benefit.

The information proved to be of great value to ORM and Baptist Mid-Missions, as well as SIL.[12] Jim was gratified with the work and felt certain that the Lord would honor these efforts in speeding the gospel to these "hidden people." Appropriately the aerial survey ended on Thanksgiving Day, and Hobey and Jim returned to Ciudad Bolivar to join their wives for Thanksgiving dinner. With work completed in Venezuela, Jim headed back to the United States. Hobey flew to Honduras to launch a new MAF program with Don and Phyllis Berry.

Don and Phyllis Berry

Don Berry grew up in Loveland, Colorado, and joined the Air Force during World War II. While on a solo flight out of Tex Rankin Field in Tulare, California, Don realized that the airplane could be used for missionary transport. He and his wife, Phyllis, had been in correspondence with converted Catholic priest Walter Montano, who had been exiled from Colombia. Together, they envisioned using the airplane to assist Christian mission work in Colombia.

Don and Phyllis graduated from Wheaton College in 1948. Don was a good friend of Hatch Hatcher, and together they formed the flying club that promoted interest in missionary aviation. When Paul Robinson launched Moody Bible Institute's Mechanical Training Course, Don was the only one in the first class.

In 1949 the Berrys headed for Los Angeles, where Don enrolled in California Fliers to finalize his A&E mechanics rating. He taught swimming for a living at the downtown YMCA. As time permitted, he helped Charlie Mellis at the MAF office. In 1950, the Berrys were accepted into MAF. They spent the summer studying Spanish in Mexico City and returned in the fall for deputation, then Don joined Hobey in Honduras for flight familiarization.

When MAF started in Honduras the chief flight responsibilities were in connection with the Central American Mission hospital at Siguatepeque and logistical service to Moravian missionaries located some 250 miles to the east. The plane was used as an air ambulance, bringing in the injured and sick. At an elevation of thirty-four hundred feet, this location had a healthful climate. There was already a little-used but quite adequate airstrip close to the hospital, and MAF purchased a home adjacent to the runway. Don only had to taxi through the banana-plant-enclosed yard to get to the runway. Red Brown set up a missionary radio network for Honduras. Strategically located Siguatepeque proved to be an ideal base for a MAF program. It was also perfect as a communication center. Even Hatcher, who was stationed in Ixtapa, Mexico, some 365 air miles away, could pick up Berry with clarity on the aircraft radio.

Red Brown had served with the Marines as a radio technician in the South Pacific during World War II. He joined MAF in 1950 and gave valuable service as new fields were opened in Latin America. Red endeared himself to the missionaries and also found a warm response from Selma Bauman, the secretary who had started in MAF's first office. The two were married in 1952 and continued to serve MAF.

Refining Flight Orientation

Out of the experiences in Ecuador, Venezuela, Honduras, and Mexico, Hobey Lowrance refined many of the MAF flight orientation techniques. There are an endless number of things a pilot must be aware of and be prepared to respond to when flying over varied terrain and changing climatic or weather conditions. It is normal for MAF pilots to have to take off and land on short, narrow, rough strips. Hobey developed techniques for precise approaches and pinpoint landings. He had worked on these while flying DC-3s and now adapted them for single-engine planes.

The landing approach was made by maintaining a set angle of descent and controlling the rate of descent by adjusting power with the throttle. Using this technique, the pilot could visually control the point of touchdown with a high degree of accuracy. This accuracy was most essential when landing on short, uphill, one-way strips where a second attempt was not possible.

The second phase of this technique was to make a wheel landing. The pilot made a tail-low runway touchdown at the planned point, instantly rocked the tail up to a level position, then applied brakes, preventing a nose-over by applying a coordinated back pressure to the control wheel. It was found that this type of landing not only gave a high degree of accuracy but also prevented bouncing and allowed much better braking action. Hobey had developed this procedure for landing and had been using it for twelve years when he read about it in the Navy safety magazine, *Naval Approach*.[13] It was standard practice for aircraft-carrier landings.

Hobey perfected many other MAF flight techniques. He promoted safe landings under a wide variety of conditions: narrow strips, dogleg strips, soft or rough fields, beach landings. For unproven landing sites, he developed safe procedures for "dragging" the field to determine hidden hazards that might spoil a safe landing. Pilots have been killed assessing a primitive runway's condition. A pilot might drop down and fly close to the ground to inspect a field only to find obstructions at the end of the strip in attempting a climb-out. This is especially tricky if the airstrip is located on an incline with the strip running uphill.

Landing on an uphill airstrip can be especially dangerous. There often is a point on the landing approach where the pilot is committed to land because the terrain is too steep to abort the landing and climb out for another try. If, after that point of committal, an animal or vehicle should move onto the strip or a strong updraft should occur, the pilot must make an instantaneous decision, which generally is to continue the landing. Many pilots have been killed by attempting an impossible go-around and not being able to out-climb the terrain.[14]

Hobey also developed skill in flying over varied terrain. These locations all have deceptive air currents, and it is important for pilots to recognize their potential existence if they are to navigate safely. Some places have updrafts, others have dangerous downdrafts or special conditions of turbulence. Pilots have to recognize deceptive illusions of gradual rise or fall in ground elevation or incline. Valley flying can lead into traps, as the *Mildmay Pathfinder* learned in East Africa. So could flying through mountain passes, where turbulent winds prevail.

To cope with these and many other conditions, in 1953 Hobey started to work on an expanded flight orientation program designed to sharpen MAF pilots' skills and orient them to the distinctive terrain and climatic conditions encountered in frontier mission situations. The program was also designed to teach MAF pilots the personal discipline required for long-term safe field operations. Fatigue, pressure, and presumption are the three everpresent deadly enemies over which the pilot has to exercise vigilance. If he should let his guard down while flying, one or all three might conspire to jeopardize his safety. Hobey's flight orientation program was designed to keep the pilot alert and aware of all the contingencies that could spell disaster. Grady Parrott had an apt phrase for the fliers: "Knowledge," he would say, "reduces vulnerability." Next to knowledge is the need for flight experience that makes correct responses second nature to the pilot.

Flight orientation, safety, and accident investigation were areas in which Hobey contributed much to MAF. His high standards enhanced MAF's reputation the world over. As a member of the MAF board from 1953 to 1974, Hobey's contributions touched all areas of the work. His role on the MAF executive committee from 1958 until the reorganization in the late 1960s meant that Hobey worked closely with the other members on decisions affecting the work of MAF in its far-flung fields around the globe.

As for the pilot performance standards that MAF set, these became the standard for which students at Moody Aviation strove. Paul Robinson, who pioneered the Moody program, was the link to MAF. Over the years, close to 70 percent of all MAF-US personnel came from the Moody flight training course. In the late 1950s and for most of the next decade, each senior class flew cross-country to the MAF Fullerton base to get a taste of MAF's flight orientation program. This also gave MAF officers opportunity to see the caliber and skill of Moody students and appraise prospective MAF candidates.[15]

The influx of many new candidates in 1952 and the years that followed made it imperative that Lowrance launch an expanded flight orientation program. The Hatchers, serving in Mexico, went on furlough in 1952. His meticulous work on the field and the need to standardize procedures led Parrott to assign Hatch the task of putting together a manual of "Standard Operational Procedures."[16] This facilitated the orientation of new pilots and served to complement Hobey's specialized flight program for candidates. The manual has been refined over the years and remains central to reinforcing the disciplined MAF approach to mission aviation.

The summer of 1952 saw a much-cherished homecoming celebration in Los Angeles. Current and former MAF members and their families met for a June 19 banquet planned as a farewell for the Mellis family, who were about to leave for New Guinea. Pilot families present were Soderbergs (SIM, Nigeria), Saints (Ecuador), Montgomerys (SIL, Peru), Buyers (Presbyterian, Brazil), Lomheims (Mexico), Truxtons (Venezuela), Don Kennedy (SIL's JAARS), and Parrotts (New Guinea, where Grady had just spent four months).[17] Nate Saint showed his movie *Conquering Jungle Barriers*, depicting MAF's work in Ecuador. The movie was shown around the country with great effect as the Saints traveled during furlough, and many people learned about mission advance into the upper Amazon basin through their presentation.

Search for a New Home Base

Over the previous year expanding MAF work demanded more adequate facilities beyond those provided by their flight base arrangement at Hawthorne Airport. With Hobey Lowrance ready to set up a more formalized flight orientation program, there was additional reason to look elsewhere. What forced the issue in 1952 was Hawthorne Airport's decision to encourage MAF to construct its own hangar on airport property. At the time serious thought was given to whether MAF should also start a commercial airplane engine overhaul shop to provide hands-on experience to those freshly out of A&E schooling. To determine the best course, Grady Parrott called a conference of his "North American brain trust," a group of technical experts working at North American Aviation who advised MAF.[18] The meeting proved to be significant. From it flowed MAF's decision not to start a commercial venture because the cost and possible liabilities of such an undertaking were "out of proportion to the gains which could be counted on for testing and training purposes." With that conclusion, MAF began the search for a better airport location.

The 1953 search included Big Bear, Whitman Airport in the San Fernando Valley, Torrance, and Fullerton airports. On a tip from Nate Saint, Jim Truxton looked over the prospects of the Fullerton airport. The same drawbacks they faced in building at Hawthorne faced them at Fullerton. MAF could build a hangar, but after ten years, ownership would revert to the airport. This arrangement was not satisfactory. Torrance seemed like the best option.

Grady called a board meeting to review the entire question. After looking at the pros and cons, the board unanimously decided that Torrance held the best prospects. However, at the close of that meeting, Grady asked the board, "Would you feel that I am less than spiritual if I go out to Fullerton to take one more look at it?" No one objected.

On the next Sunday Grady and Maurine Parrott drove to Fullerton. Grady stopped at a real estate agency and told the realtor what he wanted. He responded by referring to a Mr. Cobb's property that had recently gone off the listing and promised to call Grady on Monday. Grady had a feeling that the property was close by and drove down the street just east of the airport. Sure enough, they found a house marked "For sale by owner." The Parrotts stopped, met the owner, and saw the house. Cobb quoted a price of thirty thousand dollars for the house and six acres. Grady said that he was interested and would be back in touch with him shortly.

As the Parrotts were about to leave, Jim and Betty Truxton unexpectedly drove up. The Truxtons were eager to learn what Grady had found out. The four drove to the nearby airport restaurant to talk about this turn of events. The property was a six-acre site with land extending north from Commonwealth Avenue. That led to talking about rumors that the city of Fullerton planned to extend the runway eastward. Grady noted, "If we get this six acre orange grove, three of these acres are going to be needed by the city." A plan crystallized in their minds, and they decided to call a board meeting to reconsider the Fullerton location as soon as it was confirmed that the property for sale intersected with the proposed runway extension. They were aware that another parcel lay between the airport and the Cobb property. If that owner refused to sell, Fullerton airport expansion might be delayed, and with it MAF's hope for access to the airport. In that case, the city could invoke the right of eminent domain to obtain the property.

Despite these contingencies and the uncertainties of the rumored runway extension, the board sensed a strong leading of the Lord and agreed to move ahead on the purchase of the Cobb property. Before MAF's offer to purchase, a doctor had offered to buy the front three acres. The Cobbs had turned down the offer, fearing that the back three would prove unsalable.

Within two weeks of going into escrow, the City of Fullerton made contact with Mr. Cobb to let him know that it wanted to buy the back portion of his property. Cobb told them that the property was in escrow and that he was selling it to MAF. It seemed to Truxton that "God was surely holding this land in order to answer MAF's prayers."

On November 25, Grady signed final papers for the Fullerton property. Sometime later, MAF sold the back three acres to the city, provided that MAF had permanent access and egress to and from the proposed runway. Initially, the city objected, saying that would be a bad precedent. Grady countered that the city should take into consideration that MAF was a philanthropic flight organization. Any privileges conferred on MAF would not have to be transferred to a future commercial owner, should MAF sell. On that basis, the City of Fullerton accepted MAF's condition. This was an unheard-of concession that cost neither MAF nor its supporters a penny.

For the time being, MAF planes that needed major modifications had to have their wings taken off and be towed a short block to MAF's shop. Then in 1958 the city extended the runway and opened the fence to give MAF the direct access it had negotiated.[19]

These developments were striking evidence that when God is in a matter, obstacles melt away. A friend of MAF, C. Luke Boughter Jr. wrote MAF that he believed God was blessing their endeavors because, as part of their service to him, the organization was continuing "the struggle to keep spiritual and technical standards high."[20] Indeed, this was the reason expansion was necessary. MAF was determined to train its pilots better and serve the Lord more effectively in all its overseas operations.

At that time, commitments had been made in Honduras and were about to be made in New Guinea and Brazil. This required growing financial support from the Lord's people. In 1946, total receipts were $16,102. By 1952, this had climbed to $72,751, and in 1953, $121,680. Giving made possible a growing work, but money was always tight and kept MAF constantly "on its knees."

The pace of MAF's work was quickening. Surveys in Mexico, Honduras, and Venezuela led to the need for new flight programs. South of the border, the Lomheims, Hatchers, and Weirs (the most recent additions) comprised a growing Mexico team. The Berrys were flying in Honduras, and the Mellises were now enlarging MAF's role in assisting Australia MAF in New Guinea. Betty Greene had served two years in Nigeria (1950–52) and traveled in the United States as a MAF representative. Grady had warned her before her return from Nigeria that she would hardly recognize MAF because of the organization's enlarged responsibilities and the many new faces in the office. This was doubly true in 1954, when MAF moved onto the Fullerton location.

Australia Launches MAF

Publicity on CAMF reached former servicemen in distant parts of the globe. Ken Cooper and Edwin "Harry" Hartwig, both Australians attending the Melbourne Bible Institute (MBI) in 1946 were two such men. Cooper had heard about CAMF as an RAAF trainee in Canada. On his way back to Australia he stopped by the Los Angeles office, took out membership, and became the first CAMF "card carrying" Australian. He corresponded with Truxton and had already begun to meet with others interested in missionary aviation when Hartwig joined him at MBI.[1] It was Hartwig who built on this interest and organized the Australian MAF (AMAF).

Hartwig, like Truxton and Kendon, was a wartime pilot. He received his initial RAAF training in Australia. At the height of the war in 1943, he and Vic Ambrose, a Tasmanian, along with a host of other Aussies, left Sydney aboard American troop carriers. Their destination was Brantford, Ontario, Canada, where they received advanced training. Later they were stationed in Britain.

Hartwig flew as captain on B-24s and saw service with the English Coastal Command in 1944–45 doing anti-submarine patrols. Ambrose served in the Bomber Command, carrying out night raids over Germany. In the plans of Providence, both men were to play important roles in the development of AMAF.

At MBI, Hartwig was enrolled in a missionary preparation program and was moved by the possibilities of using aircraft for advancing the gospel in the Australian outback and the South Pacific. Hartwig himself would fly the first survey. Later he went to the northern section of New Guinea to assist the Lutheran missionaries in reestablishing the flight program that World War II had interrupted.

In the spring of 1946 Hartwig made contact with CAMF. Truxton gave him an exuberant reply, encouraging him to keep his eyes open for the many opportunities that were just around the corner in using aircraft in remote areas in mission.[2] Hartwig's imagination was stirred. He wrote to Charlie Mellis to get a list of CAMF members and friends living in Australia and contacted MAF-UK to see about affiliating with the London group.

With the encouragement of MBI principal John Searle, Hartwig generated interest that led to the June 30, 1947, organizational meeting. Leonard Buck chaired the session, at which it was decided that "M.A.F. Australia (should) be an autonomous body affiliated with Mildmay Movement Australia and also affiliated with M.A.F. America and England."[3] The charter officers chosen at a follow-up meeting were John Nimmo, president, Bruce Morton, treasurer, and Harry Hartwig, secretary. It is interesting to note that Morton and Ken Cooper later teamed up to introduce aviation to the Borneo Evangelical Mission. That organization is now part of the Overseas Missionary Fellowship. AMAF took over its aviation program in the mid-1970s.

AMAF officers were men of action. At the very next meeting they decided to form a technical committee to study aeronautical questions that would have to be answered before they purchased a plane. No strategy had been worked out for effectively placing planes into service for Christian missions, but Hartwig was optimistic when he wrote to Charlie Mellis that they expected "great possibilities and also great trials ahead."[4] Little did he realize the prophetic nature of his own statement.

Contacts with MAF-US

Australia MAF looked to London for guidance in getting started. They literally adopted London's doctrinal statement as their own. Nevertheless, it was Mellis, Truxton, and Parrott who immediately entered into long correspondence with Hartwig. They advised and encouraged him on the whole range of concerns that he and his fledgling organization were facing. Mellis sent Hartwig a copy of the summer 1947 Missionary Aviation Conference report detailing the main lessons they had learned.[5] In the meantime the MAF men in Melbourne had begun to think strategically of the area they should serve.

Hartwig wanted to know if the Americans had any plans for surveys in the South Pacific. Mellis answered that MAF-US had given some attention to this area, based on its continuing contact with the American Baptists for World Evangelization (ABWE), and the Christian and Missionary Alliance (C&MA). Both had definite plans to send missionaries to Dutch New Guinea at the earliest possible date. Neither had received the necessary permits, so no concrete steps had, as yet, been taken. Mellis advised Hartwig that the promise to assist C&MA was alive and that their office was also in contact with that denomination over its work in Borneo. Much of the discussion was merely of an advisory nature, as C&MA was considering plans to purchase and send its own plane to that island.[6] The C&MA later sent Al Lewis to fly a Sealand in Borneo and Dutch New Guinea (West Irian).

Apparently this unexpected news of the Americans' plans for work in the South Pacific spurred the Australians on. They were incorporated as an Australian nonprofit corporation in April 1948. They purchased a twin-engine Avro "Anson" and planned to use it for survey work in New Guinea and Borneo. The Department of Civil Aviation, however, would not grant it a certificate of airworthiness, given the deteriorating wooden framing of one of its wings.[7]

While this was disappointing, the circumstances forced Melbourne to take a closer look at flight needs. The result was the purchase of a de Havilland "Tiger Moth" in 1949 for the initial Australian survey. Alex Freind, a pilot-engineer who accompanied Hartwig on the first survey, overhauled the engine and prepared the plane for departure.

In view of Hartwig's proposed field surveys, Parrott suggested that the two organizations team up for their mutual benefit. The Americans could give them the benefit of their experience in survey work and operations. MAF-US could profit by learning the problems peculiar to the Australian desert and island environment. Parrott's expressed hope for such a joint venture could not be realized. MAF-US's initiatives in Central and South America completely tied up its meager resources.

In the fall of 1948, AMAF was negotiating with missions working with the aborigines and other peoples in Australia's Northern Territory and Queensland.[8] Jim Truxton, stationed in Ecuador, followed these developments with great interest. He noted some of the painful lessons that MAF-US had learned through the Waco experience and pointed out the benefits of cooperative work such as MAF was developing in Ecuador.

The Australians appreciated the encouragement and advice of their American counterparts. They were already looking beyond the survey to initiating service, and Hartwig hoped to purchase an Auster.[9] He did not have money available and was giving much thought to communicating more effectively with the Christian public about their needs. Parrott sent him a set of slides of MAF's work in Mexico to help him with publicity.[10]

Hartwig hoped to begin his survey in Australia's Northern Territory and Queensland by May 1949. He also planned to travel by commercial carrier to the Territory of New Guinea, to carry out the survey for Lutherans in the central highlands. In this connection he sought advice from Truxton. The latter gave a lengthy, helpful reply detailing his experience in Ecuador. At the time Nate Saint's December crash at Quito airport was very much on Truxton's mind, and he underscored the need for safety.

The Australian Survey

Groups that had shown interest in aerial assistance in the arid Northern Territory were the Aborigines Inland Mission, Methodists, Anglican Church Missionary Society, Brethren, and Presbyterians. Within the Territory of New Guinea, the greatest interest came from the American Lutheran Mission (affiliated with the Australians), Unevangelized Fields Mission, South Sea Evangelical Mission, and Kwato Mission.[11]

Dedication of the Tiger Moth, personnel, and mission took place on May 7, at the Anglican St. John's Church of Toorak in Melbourne. John Searle, principal of the Melbourne Bible Institute, gave the address.[12]

Complications and delays prevented Harry Hartwig and Alex Freind from leaving until the last week in July. They flew north along the coast to Brisbane and then west through Queensland and the heart of the arid Northern Territory. From there they headed back east to Cairns on the Pacific. Hartwig then flew north by regular airline to Lae in the Territory of New Guinea to conduct that field survey. Freind piloted the Tiger Moth back to Melbourne.[13]

It was evident that there were plenty of opportunities to make good use of the plane to advance the gospel on this open frontier. The trouble was that there were isolated groups of aborigines scattered over vast expanses. Lack of transportation was the major drawback. Another problem was the power of the ranchers over the aborigines. Ranchers who were not sympathetic to the gospel could effectively bar ministers from access to their hired hands. In this way, all missionary effort could be thwarted.

These MAF fliers were encouraged by contact with Vic Pederson, an evangelist of the Salvation Army who was witnessing considerable gospel response among ranchers and their hired hands in the Darwin area. Pederson was a circuit-flying preacher who moved about by air from Monday to Friday and was back home on weekends for services at Darwin. He flew his own plane and carried a projector, films, a folding bicycle, and literature with him as he made the rounds.

In his preliminary report of September 11, 1949, Hartwig summarized his conclusions. From his discussions with Pederson, Hartwig learned that the cultural and racial prejudices of the local whites could be neutralized by an outsider who flew in to minister to them. Hartwig noted that a plane would make the missionary more productive because it allowed him to be centrally based. He could move from station to station quickly, without long stretches of overland travel.[14]

New Guinea Survey

Hartwig then took a commercial carrier to New Guinea. Lutheran work in the Territory of New Guinea included an air arm in the period before World War II. In the pre–World War I era, the Territory was under German control. The entire western half of the island, Dutch New Guinea, continued in the hands of the Netherlands until the 1960s. Papua, the southeastern quarter of the island, was a British colony until after World War I, when it became a mandated territory by action of the League of Nations.

Before World War I, German Lutherans made their headquarters at Madang and penetrated into the highlands as far as Mt. Hagen in 1934. Accessibility was a major problem, so mission leaders brought in a single-engine Junkers F13 passenger plane that they named *Papua*. Their initial plan was to conduct regular flights into the interior. They hired a professional pilot, Fritz Loose, who started flight operations in February 1935. This lifeline was essential for continuing the mission's work in the highlands, yet it was interrupted in 1939 by the outbreak of World War II.[15] Having had an air arm in the past, the Lutherans were naturally eager to have it reestablished. During the interwar period, the American Lutherans of the Missouri Synod joined the ranks of the German Lutherans. Their influence after World War II was decisive in setting the agenda for the New Guinea work. This connection between the Lutherans from Germany and the United States proved vital to the later development of an overall Lutheran flight program that served all Papua.

Hartwig conducted the survey for the Lutherans on airline and charter flights. The Lutheran mission contracted for flights to their interior highland stations from Lae, Finschhafen, and Madang. The survey revealed that a need existed for a joint missionary air service that could assist a variety of denominations throughout the Territory of New Guinea. It did not take the dominant Lutheran groups long to decide in favor of AMAF. Furthermore, they were willing to underwrite the cost of the plane. Hartwig was delighted, but not really surprised, because the Lutherans were already paying charter companies for transportation service. His observation was that these commercial carriers were overcharging while rendering inferior service.

Time and again, missionaries from inland stations found it necessary to charter additional flights or another plane from the coast because the freight companies made no provision for carrying passengers on their highland circuit and back to the coast. What Hartwig set out to do was prove that AMAF could give better service at a reduced cost and allow the missions to put more of their money into expanding their work.[16]

The Program at Madang

For the Madang-based program, the Australians were attracted to the Auster "Avis," a high-winged monoplane with a 145-horse-power engine. AMAF looked at the American-made Beechcraft single-engine "Bonanza" but saw two drawbacks: the difficulty in obtaining dollars for purchase and the distance and consequent time-lapse in obtaining parts from the manufacturer.

Parrott, now president of MAF-US, spared no pains corresponding in detail about the pros and cons of various plane types. While he did not know exactly what the main work of the plane would be, he pointed out that it was a common misconception that a larger two-engine plane such as the Beechcraft "Twin-Bonanza" was more effective than a smaller single-engine craft. Parrott explained:

> One of the most important things that the Lord has shown us is the manner in which the job can be done efficiently, economically and effectively without going overboard in the matter of big equipment. Costly operations may discourage mission societies from considering the use of aviation as a tool to reach the unevangelized. The principal thing in using the lighter aircraft is for the pilot to know his ship, its performance and its limitations, as well as the importance of being thoroughly familiar with small plane techniques under limiting circumstances. I do not say that there are no places where the terrain will call for a larger, more powerful ship, necessitating more costly equipment. But I do feel that the problem should be analyzed objectively and the lighter four-place, single engine ships conscientiously eliminated before going to the heavy costly equipment.[17]

Hartwig didn't need anyone to convince him that light craft were preferable. After comparing British and American models, Melbourne decided on an Auster "Avis." Hartwig was aware that New Guinea had airstrips with short runways (four hundred to five hundred yards), many located near six thousand feet elevation. Since these strips were located in rugged terrain, forced landings would be unforgiving. All things considered, Hartwig believed the Avis was the most suitable plane. Equally important was the fact that they could call on Auster parts from Sydney and have them in New Guinea within twenty-four hours. Without a reliable supply of spare parts, dependable service could not be maintained.

Parrott still had misgivings about the Auster's maximum ceiling of 10,000 feet when loaded to capacity. The Pacer 125's ceiling at full load was 14,250 feet. He cautioned Hartwig, "You are going to be operating in mountainous terrain. That means that much of the time you are going to be flying with marginal performance in terrain which encourages turbulence and air mass disturbances. Are you not putting yourself into a vulnerable position?" Parrott was also concerned about the Auster's limited rate of climb at 6,000 feet, especially with a full load. While the Auster climbed about 300 feet a minute, under the same conditions the Pacer could climb 500 feet a minute. Parrott again cautioned: "The difference between the two performances might be the difference between a safe program and otherwise. . . . If you are maneuvering around ridges and find yourself in a mass of air settling at three hundred to four hundred feet per minute, your very best climb won't pull you out of it. Remember the experience of the MAF England boys with their first *Pathfinder* in Africa."[18]

With a prewar background of flying in the Rockies, Parrott was genuinely concerned about Hartwig's safety in the New Guinea environment. Knowing that many dangers lurked in the terrain and were compounded by the unpredictable weather mix of New Guinea, Parrott challenged Hartwig to take another look at his choice of equipment.

Hartwig thanked Parrott for his "prayerful and practical interest." He did address Parrott's concern on the rate of climb for the Auster, but felt "that the greatest safeguard against accident is that the pilot should know his aircraft well, and we intend concentrating upon this point."[19] Hartwig had discussed the Auster's performance with New Guinea pilots on his survey and observed that "all assured me that the Auster was an excellent aircraft for that country."

Having decided on the Auster, the next question related to personnel. Melbourne wanted a two-man team for this assignment: a commercially licensed pilot who would do most of the flying and an engineer who was qualified to work on airframe and engine. The latter also had to have the possibility of obtaining an Australian commercial pilot's license. The plan was to place the engineer into apprenticeship with Auster service to get firsthand experience with the Gypsy Major engine. Hartwig asked if there were any Americans who might fit these requirements and would be willing to serve with AMAF. Hartwig had already indicated that he would be the pilot, so Parrott turned his attention to finding an engineer.

These years of steady communication between Parrott and Hartwig forged a close working relationship between the two. They agreed on the need for the highest standards and the best technically trained and spiritually qualified men in their respective organizations. By May 1950 Hartwig had even insisted, "We must standardize our programs."[20]

Parrott had earlier mentioned several potential individuals to Hartwig, then finally settled on Bob Hutchins (as yet unassigned) "as an even better man for you."[21] Hutchins had grown up in a warm Christian home as the son of the pastor of the missionary-minded Lake Avenue Congregational Church in Pasadena, California. He and his fiancée, Betty Hansen, were both graduates of Wheaton College. At twenty-four, Hutchins already had his American A&E rating. He had 150 hours of flying experience and expected to have his commercial pilot rating before his September wedding.

Parrott was exuberant about Bob. He characterized Bob "as a prince of a fellow who has a fine winning personality, is aggressive and well liked." Since Australian Civil Aviation Standards require retirement from commercial aviation at the age of forty-five, Hutchins was an excellent choice because of the potentially long years of service he could render to AMAF. Hutchins gave his affirmative to this challenge.

The recommendation of Hutchins received hearty approval in Melbourne.[22] The terms of service were set for five years with a full year of furlough and passage money to be paid by the Lutheran Mission.

The main question now was, how soon could Bob and Betty come to Australia? Since Bob was to be enrolled in eight weeks of technical training with the Auster firm in Sydney, the sooner the couple arrived, the sooner the program in New Guinea could get started. Even after completing this apprenticeship with Auster, Bob had to qualify for commercial flight ratings in Australia.

Bob and Betty departed from Los Angeles for Sydney on December 3, 1950. They were warmly received and immediately had the opportunity to speak at the Upway Convention at Melbourne over Christmas. Bob then commenced work on his Australian commercial license. The difference between American and Australian requirements was a matter of ten hours of instrument flying. Hutchins flew Tiger Moths to obtain the rating.

Everything seemed to be coming together. The Auster "Autocar" (rather than Avis) was en route from England. When it arrived, Bob assembled it, and the Christian Radio Missionary Fellowship installed the radio.

In mid-December Murray Kendon arrived in Australia and met the Hutchinses. He had been in New Zealand, drumming up support for an MAF organization there. Having recently been in Singapore and the Dutch East Indies, Kendon felt MAF air service could be developed for the Philippines, Sarawak (Borneo), and the Dutch East Indies. He anticipated that an emerging New Zealand MAF would begin work in Sarawak in 1951. The New Zealand MAF had become active as a support arm of AMAF's New Guinea work, but did not initiate any flight programs on its own.

The farewell service for Harry Hartwig and Bob Hutchins took place at Bankstown aerodrome. They took to the sky on April 12 and made their way north along the coast. Their wives left Sydney for New Guinea a week later on board the *Malaita*.

As Harry and Bob headed north out of Newcastle, the plane suddenly had a magneto problem that required immediate attention. Providentially, the Nabiac airstrip was close at hand, and Kingsford Smith Aviation Service was able to supply them with a replacement the very next day. At Cairns they enjoyed the hospitality of the Unevangelized Fields Mission.

Through radio contact in the vicinity of Thursday Island in the Gulf of Carpenteria, they learned of an emergency situation

MAF-Australia's Auster on the day it was dedicated at Bankstown, New South Wales, in April 1951. Harry Hartwig is standing at far right.

involving a native woman who was near death's door. The nearest Flying Doctor Service was one thousand miles away. This was a perfect opportunity to give help, and Hartwig and Hutchins turned the craft in the direction of Weipa Mission, where they landed in thirty minutes. In another fifty-five minutes, they were on their way to Horn Island, from where the patient was taken to the hospital at Thursday Island. This was baptism into the service of Jesus Christ for the plane and the crew.[23]

The Auster headed across the open sea and arrived dead on course at Daru. Harry and Bob proceeded on to Port Moresby on the southern Papua coast. Two days of discussions with the men of the Department of Civil Aviation (DCA) opened the door for them to head for Lae over the Kuku-Kuku Mountains. This region had many unidentified native tribes that the Lutheran Mission hoped to contact through the use of the Auster.

Harry and Bob immediately initiated familiarization flights to locate the fifteen mission stations they were assigned to serve, learn the location of mountains and passes, and observe weather patterns. New Guinea's tropical climate and the towering mountains of its interior highlands made it a veritable weather machine. Even if the day was perfectly clear at sunrise, heavy cumulus clouds could soon build up in the interior. All flights through seven- to ten-thousand-foot mountain passes had to be made early in the day, before weather conditions turned turbulent.

Harry reported that in the first three weeks of this operation, he logged fifty hours in the air, carrying three tons of cargo and ten passengers (both native evangelists and missionaries). The stretcher attachment had come in handy in bringing out Mrs. Young, the wife of a Methodist missionary working in the highlands.

The weather was unusually turbulent in May and June of 1951. Hartwig considered this the chief hazard in air service. To compound difficulties, the Auster had severe ignition problems that Hutchins traced to the faulty assembly of its magnetos. Despite these adverse circumstances, Harry and Bob logged 170 hours of flying time during the first two months. This was an unusually heavy schedule, when compared to the other single-plane MAF programs operating at that time.[24]

Harry and Bob were able to carry out a strenuous program because they alternated pilot responsibilities. This reduced the danger of pilot fatigue, the indirect cause of many accidents.[25] The Aussie-Yankie team worked well together. Harry had nothing but praise for Bob and Betty, whom he characterized as a grand couple. As for Bob's technical abilities, Harry praised him as an excellent pilot, adding, "I have no anxious moments while he is flying."

The two fliers worked out a regular schedule for serving mission stations and began to look for ways to make their air service more convenient. For example, the people at Omkalai had to walk eleven miles through rugged country to reach the nearest strip. Missionaries of the East and West Indies Bible Mission at Pabarabuk had to trek twenty miles to the airstrip at Mt. Hagen. Constructing new strips at these two stations would greatly improve access. Of course, they had to seek permission from the Department of Civil Aviation.

By the beginning of July 1951, construction had begun at Madang on a steel hangar measuring forty by fifty feet, designed for two single-engine planes. While this was good news, the performance of the Auster was less satisfactory than hoped. The craft did not measure up to Hartwig's expectations. By fitting it with a metal propeller, he was able to get better performance out of the 130-horsepower engine. The plane could carry a 650-pound payload with a service ceiling of 11,000 feet. This was barely adequate for New Guinea. Hartwig was most concerned about the meager 350-feet-per-minute climb. True, it was better than that of the de Havilland "Dragon," a plane used extensively in New Guinea, but it was still not good enough.

Word was out that a replacement engine for the Auster, a 155-horsepower Cirrus "Major," would greatly improve the plane's performance. Hartwig was looking forward to making this early conversion. New Guinea service required a plane with a rapid climb and the power to carry it through turbulence. Given their eighty-five hours of flying a month, the anticipated improved performance would also prove to be a time saver. For the long range, Hartwig was looking for a plane with even better performance. He inquired into the Cessna 190.

The time was quickly approaching when a second plane would be needed for the Madang program. With three months of service behind them, Harry compiled a report in which he noted that reliance on only one plane was a mistake because it would take twelve months to obtain a replacement craft. Even then, the program had to be shut down four to six weeks for its annual overhaul. If they developed engine trouble on an inland strip, they had to rely on chartered service to bring in a mechanic and spare parts. Prudence dictated that another plane be purchased.[26]

Harry also made an evaluation of AMAF economic performance. He had initially projected a conservative 10 percent savings to the Lutherans, but the actual savings came to between 25 and 30 percent. The Lutherans were well satisfied. Furthermore, AMAF was winning the respect of the Department of Civil Aviation. In short, AMAF in New Guinea had gotten off to a good—even a great—start. Hartwig noted: "There is a tremendous missionary aviation program here and we are doing about 50% of the work." In an equally forthright manner, he reflected, "We have much to praise the Lord for and we are endeavoring to walk cautiously and quietly before Him."[27]

Harry Hartwig's Fatal Crash

This was the last letter Hartwig wrote to Grady Parrott. On August 6, Hartwig was killed when his Auster crashed while attempting to cross the Asaroka Pass in the Central Highlands. He was returning home alone on his second flight of the day.[28] A native teacher from the Asaroka Mission Station saw the plane circling in the pass overhead and heard it crash into the mountain. A ground party was organized to find the plane. They and a government search unit moved up to the area of the crash, hoping to find Hartwig alive. But a group of natives shouted across the gorge that they had found the wreckage and the dead pilot.

When rescue teams reached the site, they found Hartwig with his hands still on the controls and all switches on, indicating that he had died instantly. His body was removed from the wreckage, wrapped in blankets and canvas, carried by natives to the Asaroka Mission, then flown to Madang and interred at Graged Island cemetery. He was survived by his wife, Margaret, and his infant daughter, Beth.

Hartwig died even as he lived—serving the Lord. This was not to be the end of AMAF. Harry was a seed planted in fertile ground, and from his death would sprout vigorous new life. The Lord had resurrected mission aviation in New Guinea through Harry, and it would flourish.

Foremost on Grady Parrott's mind was the personal loss to this missionary aviation pioneering family. Grady sent words of comfort to Margaret Hartwig. He had carried on a lively correspondence with Harry, and although they had not met face-to-face, he felt he knew him well. Parrott wrote Margaret, "We had come to feel the close bonds of Christian fellowship in this ministry of Gospel work. I have long looked forward to an opportunity to know him personally, but now still have the glorious hope of one day being with him in Glory. The prayers of us all over here are that God's strength and rich blessings be yours."[29]

The cause of the crash was closely analyzed on both sides of the Atlantic. To Stuart King it was due to "an aircraft unable to produce sufficient reserve of power at high altitude, and a lack of realization of the danger of this situation." He saw shades of the *Mildmay Pathfinder* mishap.[30]

The Airplane Advisory Committee, chaired by Lutheran Acting Superintendent Albert Frerichs, met to discuss the new realities. Their recommendations were to resume the flight program
as soon as possible and purchase a plane with additional reserve
horsepower and higher ceiling. They advised against purchasing
another Auster and recommended either a Cessna 170 or 190, since
these planes had been recommended by both Harry and Bob.
Finally the committee felt it was essential that if AMAF was going
to send another pilot, this replacement be "another pilot-mechanic
with really first class qualifications and with a maximum of experience in flying small craft."[31]

Melbourne would have been happy to send a qualified person
to Madang, had someone been available. Unfortunately there was
no one. The American Lutheran Mission then looked to MAF-US
for a qualified airman-mechanic to replace Hartwig, requesting
their supervision.[32] Grady Parrott recognized that direct correspondence with him could jeopardize the good relations existing
between Melbourne and Los Angeles. He informed the Lutheran
Board that MAF-US had qualified pilot-mechanics preparing
themselves for service with MAF. He did not want to enter into
further discussion on the question of personnel until he had some
clarification from Melbourne.[33]

Grady was certain of the potential growth of the New Guinea
program and knew there were American pilots ready to step into
the work. However, something else weighed on Grady's mind.
The pilots preparing for service were looking to MAF-US headquarters to give the "technically qualified assistance of the home
front to guide and supplement the experienced men out on the
field." These pilots appreciated the vital technical link with the
Los Angeles home office, and they might hesitate to serve under
a less-established organization. This was not the type of news that
buoyed Melbourne's sagging spirits.

Grady then made a bold and generous proposal. MAF-US was
prepared to carry the New Guinea program forward with U.S.
personnel and administration. This meant MAF-US would take
over the Australian work, but only on a temporary basis. Grady
had in mind that MAF-US would run the program for an indefi-

nite time until Australia was again in a position to resume full responsibilities.

Grady was aware that this proposal could be easily misconstrued. He found it hard to write Charles Rout, general secretary of AMAF. He suggested that he was willing to send this "frank proposal, believing that it will be the means of *continuing* our joyous co-laborship until Jesus comes."[34]

Even before Grady's proposal arrived in Melbourne, the Lutheran Mission advised AMAF that it was going to purchase a Cessna 170 as a replacement for the Auster. To effect speedy purchase, conversion, shipping, and supplying of spare parts, they had decided to ask MAF-US to direct their program.

This announcement from the Lutherans came as a big disappointment, inasmuch as Melbourne would not be able to continue the work that it had pioneered at such cost. Yet they could understand the reason for this decision. They also recognized that since the Lutherans were mostly American missionaries and the remaining pilot, Bob Hutchins, was an American, the decision to look to the United States was almost inevitable. If the letter was difficult for Parrott to write, Rout assured him, it was also very, very difficult to receive.

Since the decision was really out of their hands, Rout offered Parrott his wholehearted cooperation. At the same time Rout indicated that AMAF was not pulling out of pioneering work in Dutch New Guinea. He requested that Parrott not announce that MAF-US would be working with the Lutherans at Madang until AMAF had the opportunity to "announce the work which we are opening." Rout sensed that support for AMAF would suffer a setback if there was an untimely announcement of AMAF's intention not to engage in further service in the Territory of New Guinea. He wanted a simultaneous announcement of this and their intended advance into Dutch New Guinea.[35]

The loss of Harry and the Madang program was bound to lead to a loss of Australian support unless something good could be shown to come out of it. Rout saw Australia's proximity to New Guinea as a prior claim to service in the area. After all, this had been Harry's vision. Rout wanted to hold out the promise of future service.

At that time, Grady was unable to fully appreciate AMAF's sense of ownership of the planned advance into Dutch New Guinea. AMAF was not about to walk away from this commitment. Perhaps Grady was unable to appreciate Rout's position because his focus was on the interrupted flight program and how to get it reestablished. Indeed, this was an all-absorbing task. Nevertheless MAF-US eventually had to come to terms with AMAF's expectation of future service in Dutch New Guinea.

Advance into Dutch New Guinea

The New Guinea Lutheran Mission's call to MAF-US made it imperative that Grady Parrott see the New Guinea field firsthand. However, the immediate flight needs in the Territory were not the only MAF-US interest in that Pacific island.

MAF-US had viewed Dutch New Guinea (now Indonesia's Irian Jaya) as the unrivaled missionary aviation frontier. Grady was interested in making a survey of the region while reestablishing the flight work for the Lutherans in the Territory. When he expressed interest in extending his New Guinea survey to include Dutch New Guinea, Leonard Buck, then serving on the AMAF board and secretary of the Unevangelized Fields Mission, volunteered to pay his passage so he could do this for Melbourne. Grady appreciated their assistance but did not immediately recognize Melbourne's intent. They were determined to open up Dutch New Guinea as *their* program. He carried out the Dutch New Guinea survey for reasons related to MAF-US's objectives.

The Americans' interest in Dutch New Guinea emerged during World War II and was strengthened by the American presence there during the war. The earliest attention-riveting information coming out of that part of the world was the 1938 Richard Archbold Expedition, an American undertaking officially known as the Indies-American Expedition. The Archbold Expedition fascinated American readers with news of the discovery of the hidden Baliem River Valley located deep in New Guinea and encircled by a towering ring of peaks.[1] The "Grand Valley" of the Baliem, as

149

Archbold named it, was a twenty- by forty-mile area populated by the Dani people.

Fascination with this "Shangri-la," as it became known in the United States, grew during the World War II occupation of New Guinea. In May 1945, a U.S. military plane crashed there, leading to a glider snatch of three survivors by a C-46.[2] Military pilots were all familiar with this operation. Truxton had so much interest in the prospects of using a plane to reach the Baliem Valley with the gospel that he visited the American Natural History Museum to personally read the logs of the Archbold Expedition. While in Philadelphia he also visited with nine men and women, including Jerry Rose of the American Baptists for World Evangelization (ABWE), who were preparing themselves to serve as missionaries in Dutch New Guinea. Truxton talked to them about the possibility of cooperative use of a plane that would serve C&MA, ABWE, and the Dutch missionaries.

In those days there was the expectation that C&MA, already flying in Dutch-held Borneo, would be the first to receive flight permission in Dutch New Guinea. The Evangelical Alliance Mission (TEAM) was also poised to send in missionaries. Walter Erikson of TEAM traveled to Hollandia in 1951 with the hope of receiving permission to go inland. It was a near miracle that Erikson made it there, inasmuch as Domine Kline, the representative of the Dutch state church, dismissed all visa applications for American missionaries applying for service in Dutch New Guinea.

These interests lay behind MAF-US's desire to open up Dutch New Guinea to missions and provide them with air transport where needed. Grady made arrangements to head for Melbourne in January 1952 to meet with the AMAF council about reestablishing the Lutheran flight program at Madang. He also hoped to make a survey of Dutch New Guinea for MAF-US. At that time, funds were so depleted that Grady considered the cost of the flight a huge sum and suggested that Melbourne pray as he stepped out "entirely on faith and in complete dependence upon God's faithfulness."[3]

Three days of fruitful discussion in Melbourne led to a series of decisions. Grady would confer with Albert Frerichs of the Lutheran Mission in Madang and survey the needs there. Then, time permitting, he would survey the vast Fly River region of

Papua New Guinea, the southern region facing Australia. Following this, Grady planned to cross over to Dutch New Guinea and conduct a survey there. He believed he was doing this for MAF-US with the approval and financial support of AMAF. On the other hand, AMAF viewed Grady as conducting the survey entirely for their benefit.

The AMAF board volunteered to underwrite the cost of Grady's survey of Dutch New Guinea. Leonard Buck, a member of the AMAF board and general secretary of the Unevangelized Fields Mission (UFM), indicated that UFM was going to be sending missionaries into the region. Even as he spoke, UFM's Fred Dawson, an Australian, and Russell Bond, a New Zealander, had been waiting in Dutch New Guinea for over a year, hoping to find transportation to take them inland. Fred Dawson had earlier made direct contact with Grady in Los Angeles, asking for his assistance in entering the Dutch New Guinea hinterland. By the time Grady arrived for the interior survey, these missionaries, plus Val Jones (an Australian) and Hans Veldhuis (an American) were building a forward base at Sengge.[4] They were all straining at the opportunity to move inland. What they lacked was information about the location of people groups in the interior and the means to reach them. A series of inaccessible rugged mountain ranges held off all who would reach the interior. Finally the approval of Dutch officials was needed to move inland, and that had not yet been secured.

The Makings of a Misunderstanding

Leonard Buck and Grady Parrott had common reasons for conducting this survey of Dutch New Guinea, but the latter did not understand Buck to mean that he was to conduct this survey solely as AMAF's agent. Both sides looked toward the penetration of New Guinea and each assumed that the other recognized and supported its aim for leading the work into Dutch New Guinea. The good spirit of Christian fellowship in Melbourne may have kept the participants from raising potentially divisive questions. It is true that AMAF asked Grady if he could return via Melbourne to give a complete report on his survey. This he was happy to do.

Both sides were oblivious of, or simply downplayed, the others' commitment to develop an aviation operation in Dutch New Guinea. It would have been helpful had the AMAF board come right out and told Grady they were determined to have sole control of the flight program in Dutch New Guinea. Actually AMAF expressed this specific intention to Bill Knights of MAF-UK while Grady was carrying out his Dutch New Guinea survey.[5]

Other jurisdictional questions were not discussed while Grady was in Melbourne. He assumed that AMAF was in no position to make an advance there and was thinking entirely of the entrance of an American air arm into the region.

Bruce Lumsden, the new president of AMAF, was highly impressed with Grady's breadth of experience and his "spirit of humility as a servant of Christ." Lumsden felt that Grady was the person to give leadership to the entire missionary aviation work in the area.[6]

Dutch New Guinea Survey

Grady was in the Territory for six weeks, surveying air transport needs and conferring with the Lutherans at Madang. He promised that MAF-US would assist them with their program but, at the same time, said MAF-US felt called to "promote and cooperate in Gospel *advance* into unevangelized areas."[7] He then sought a way to go west to Hollandia, located on the Dutch New Guinea side of the island. Missionaries Fred Dawson and Walter Erikson got wind of Grady's plans and sent him a telegraph urging him to come over, but there were no regularly scheduled flights from Madang to that particular region.

Then Grady learned that an American had chartered a DC-3 in Australia for a private flight direct to Hollandia. Radio contact with the pilot led to the good news that the DC-3 would obligingly divert to Madang and pick up Grady. While Grady was waiting, word came that the pilot had changed his mind and radioed his regrets; he had filed his flight plan directly to Hollandia and would not divert to Madang. Grady's heart sank. Then, within minutes, the pilot radioed back that he would land at Madang.

When the crew disembarked, the copilot explained that after they sent the message canceling their promised landing, an electrical short had developed in the radio. Since all flights into Dutch New Guinea had to maintain radio contact, the plane was forced to return to Madang, the nearest field. Within one hour, the faulty radio was repaired and Grady was on his way to Dutch New Guinea.

There Grady met with Fred Dawson and Russell Bond of UFM, Jerry Rose (now with C&MA), Walter Erikson of TEAM, and the Dutch mission. He met with the governor, the head of the Dutch Department of Civil Aviation, and military officials. Grady also received permission to bring in a chartered survey plane, a Norseman from Wewak.

This flight was targeted to survey the Dani population in the Baliem Valley. The above-mentioned representatives from TEAM, C&MA, and UFM were on board. Dutch officials and a top commander of the Dutch military also went along.[8] The flight was the first civilian entry into the interior since the 1938 Archbold exploratory flight, for which a Crown Governor had given permission.

For three hours the Norseman flew inland and westward over awe-inspiring territory. The river courses pointed the way inland. Beyond the flooded Idenberg River, the flight took the path of the Hablifoerie that drops down into Lake Archbold. From that landmark, the plane crossed the Dinggun Ridge to even more rugged and forbidding terrain. Suddenly and surprisingly vistas of settlements appeared. Shirley Horne, veteran missionary to the Danis, described the scene:

> Round mushroom-like houses surrounded by extensive cultivation clung to slopes and crowded the valley floors. Hundreds and hundreds of them in valley after valley. They indicated people, a teeming population made up of individuals—man and woman with a personal need. It was for them that the eyes from the airplane windows were searching.
>
> The Norseman negotiated the rugged pass and flew straight down the main Baliem Valley to pyramid-shaped rocks rising steeply out of the flat valley. All along the way were houses, gardens, and people—150,000 Stone Age people waiting for eternal life![9]

Individuals on board snapped pictures of this breathtaking scene of Dani settlements, their well-cultivated sweet potato gardens, and their herds of pigs. During the flight, the civil authorities wondered aloud how they were going to subdue these people. The missionaries were giving thought to how they might move in to begin work here. This was an entirely new frontier. The challenge to reach these people was real and compelling; all realized that the plane would have to play an important role.

On their way out, the plane followed the Baliem River to the far northern end of the valley. Here the wide river abruptly disappeared and became an underground stream as it cut through layers of limestone. The Norseman swung into the Swart Valley to the north but, seeing threatening cloud cover just ahead, turned and headed back to Hollandia.

Grady made a full oral report of their findings to the governor. He also called a conference of representatives of the three missions to lay plans for their future air service. As things stood, the Dutch government serviced its sole interior outpost, located in the Wissel Lakes region, from their military base at Biak, an island just north of New Guinea's Bird's Head. They were not about to increase air transportation for missions. However, it should be noted that Grady received Dutch military assistance to fly into the Wissel Lakes region as part of the survey. As a result of this initial contact, the governor gave MAF permission to conduct additional surveys that opened the door for MAF to establish air support throughout Dutch New Guinea.

Charlie Mellis in New Guinea

Given the decision to have MAF-US reestablish the work in the Territory of New Guinea and cooperate with Dutch officials to penetrate into Dutch New Guinea, it was imperative that a senior MAF-US officer go to the field to initiate and coordinate these efforts. Charles J. Mellis was chosen for this strategic task.

Charlie had served in the Los Angeles office since the summer of 1946. As field experience was entirely new to the Mellises, Charlie brushed up on his flying skills by taking his family on a cross-country flight in a Cessna.[10]

By the end of June 1952, Charlie, Claire, and their family were in Sydney, Australia, conferring with the Melbourne Council. The new Cessna 170 had already arrived at Madang, and Bob Hutchins had put his skills to use assembling the plane.[11] Its design and power made it easy to climb over mountain passes.

Mellis's first priority was to secure the proper Australian permits and gain the confidence of the men in the Department of Civil Aviation. Fortunately, Hutchins was already knowledgeable about the area and was able to show Mellis the ropes. Most of the summer was taken up with reestablishing their two-man flying team for the Lutherans at Madang. The next objective was to get a flight program started in Dutch New Guinea.

MAF-US's Bid for a Flight Program

From the standpoint of MAF-US, many uncertainties lay in the way of starting work in Dutch New Guinea, inasmuch as the missions made no prior commitment to use the service. Much depended on the speed and reliability with which MAF advanced its program in the country. No prior loyalties had been established, so it was a matter of seeing who would be the first to provide transportation. If C&MA could supply the flight needs, these missions would be happy to rely on their flight support.

C&MA had the biggest stake in the expansion of missionary aviation into the Wissel Lakes region of Dutch New Guinea. By the summer of 1952 they already had twelve missionaries operating there, and more recruits were on the way. The Dutch Navy supplied their military post by air and brought in limited supplies for the mission via a Catalina amphibian stationed on the island of Biak. This limited service was inadequate for C&MA's growing transport needs. Furthermore, the Dutch were in the process of limiting the Catalina service to the lakes. This meant that their vital lifeline was precariously secured.

It was not surprising that Al Lewis, veteran C&MA pilot, was interested in establishing an amphibian service in Dutch New Guinea. He had pioneered the C&MA flight program in Borneo and Indonesia following George Fisk's introduction of the plane. The Sealand he had brought over for service in the region had been destroyed, fortunately without loss of life. Insurance coverage made its replacement feasible. However, C&MA mission leaders had yet to determine if they wanted Lewis to launch such a program in Dutch New Guinea. A decision from the C&MA board was expected that summer.

In June 1952 when Grady Parrott met with the C&MA board in Atlanta, it looked like C&MA, UFM, and TEAM would all call on MAF to supply their flight needs in Dutch New Guinea.[12] However, in Atlanta the C&MA board was divided as to whether to go with MAF-US or follow Al Lewis's advice and use larger twin-engine equipment. The question of safety was very much on their minds. Dr. Alfred Snead leaned toward using MAF. After an evening meeting, Snead asked Grady to meet again with the board, since some members still had questions. The concern was whether a single-engine craft could provide the necessary margin of safety. Al Lewis had raised the issue in advocating the twin-engine Sealand for use in New Guinea.

Grady pointed out that C&MA had taken some risks in sending missionaries to Borneo before they had any flight service. At one point Grady said, the mission had put "faith along side of practicality" in making decisions. Snead interrupted Grady with shouts of "Hallelujah, Hallelujah," underscoring what Grady had voiced: It was a mistake to place reliance solely on machines in this work for the Lord. Admittedly the need was for prudence in the selection of planes, but also for faith in God's protection and enablement. This encounter, though dramatic, did not completely settle the issue for C&MA.

Al Lewis continued to argue persuasively that he could transport bulk supplies to the Baliem Valley more easily than MAF using the larger twin-engine Sealand. This caused C&MA to back away from MAF. Since MAF was going to continue to rely on light single-engine craft, C&MA finally opted for the Sealand.[13] Given the rapid anticipated influx of missionaries, MAF did not feel it should abandon the field. Less than three years later, with the crash of the Sealand, C&MA called on MAF for help, eventually turning over their entire Dutch New Guinea flight program.

Snead knew that C&MA had to move quickly to lay claim to mission work in the Baliem. Other missions were right on their heels and were pressing to get in—TEAM, UFM, and ABWE. Snead let it be known that C&MA intended to move quickly to start work in the Baliem and that they had the resources to begin at once.

On April 20, 1954, Al Lewis made his maiden flight from Sentani. On board were his copilot Ed Ulrich, two missionaries, Kapauku pastor Elisa Govai, and his family.[14]

This was only the third time a plane had landed there. Both earlier incursions into the valley had led to withdrawals. This time when Lewis brought down the ship for a perfect landing on the broad Baliem River at 8:40 A.M. it was to pave the way for a permanent missionary presence among the Dani people. Shouts of "Praise the Lord, glory to God, hallelujah!" went up as the plane came to rest on the river. Just six years later, in one of the most remarkable "people movements" on record, the Danis would embrace the gospel.

Al Lewis's success did not end MAF-US plans to penetrate Dutch New Guinea. Any advance there had to wait until Mellis had a replacement at Madang, since he was carrying a heavy flying load there. Charles and Dorothy Rasmussen supplied the need in November 1952. Rasmussen had been a flying instructor at the Kingsford Smith Flying School at Bankstown Airport, New South Wales, prior to his joining AMAF. Now he teamed up with Bob Hutchins.

It soon became apparent that Melbourne was concerned that AMAF be a full partner in the new Dutch New Guinea venture. Plans were afoot to have Ray Jaensch, a Lutheran pilot, join Rasmussen at Madang, thus enabling both Mellis and Rasmussen to devote full-time to the Dutch New Guinea advance.[15]

As these preparations were going forward, Grady received the unwelcome news that UFM would not be relying on MAF-US service. They wanted AMAF to serve them. Leonard Buck's strategic leadership position in both of these Australian organizations had much to do with this decision.[16] When both C&MA and UFM backed out of seeking MAF-US service in Dutch New Guinea, Grady was bewildered.

The UFM's direct invitation to AMAF for air support in Dutch New Guinea reflected Melbourne's determination to develop the flight program there as *their* project. Melbourne wanted MAF-US to be the junior partner in opening missionary aviation in Dutch New Guinea.[17]

To further their point Melbourne appointed Vic Ambrose, AMAF's recently appointed deputation secretary, to oversee advance into Dutch New Guinea. Ambrose was a bright young ex-Royal Australian Air Force wartime pilot with administrative experience in the retail business. Bruce Lumsden described him to Charlie Mellis as being "possessed of business capacity, organizing ability and initiative of a high order." Ambrose's immediate task was to become acquainted with Mellis's plans for an MAF advance into Dutch New Guinea and see how AMAF might gain control over it.[18]

When Melbourne's intention became clear, both Grady and Charlie responded with surprise and understanding. Mellis wrote:

> I've naturally felt stunned—especially by the *extent* to which these misunderstandings have grown. . . . But as I've read and reread your letters, the Lord has also caused me to *rejoice* that you've *expressed* these misgivings, before Satan swelled them to a proportion that might destroy our joint efforts for the Lord. Like you, I feel confident that as we discuss these problems with a mutual recognition that we've made mistakes, the Lord will give us a solution that will be readily acceptable to both, and will honor and glorify His Name.[19]

Melbourne had full appreciation for the generous way in which MAF-US had come in to reestablish the flight program in the Territory of New Guinea. They felt they had even asked Grady to make the survey of Dutch New Guinea *for them,* and did not want the Americans to "go ahead and spearhead the advance." This they considered to be their mission.[20] All of this came as quite a surprise to Grady and Charlie, who had not viewed their New Guinea efforts in this light.

Despite these misunderstandings, the Lord's hand in the matter was confirmed for Charlie when he met Vic Ambrose in January. Vic represented Melbourne's interests, but he came to learn all he could from Charlie. The two immediately hit it off well. Their similar background was no doubt a factor. Both had come from entrepreneurial families, Vic's father in retail and Charlie's in construction. Both had served in Europe during World War II with their respective country's Air Force. Both were married, and each had three young children in 1952.

Later, Vic wrote to Grady of the significance of this encounter, both personally and for their respective organizations: "It was the one thing above all others that was needed to get me oriented. Something like Aquilla and Priscilla getting hold of Apollos and teaching him the way of the Lord more perfectly."[21] Vic also reported that as a result of his discussions with Charlie "things have turned out beautifully." He was convinced that the two organizations could and should work closely together in the future.

Reflecting on the tensions that had arisen between the two MAF's, Vic observed, "As we approach the problems that arise out of such an association, heeding the exhortation that each consider the other better than themselves, the Lord will use the very things that could have been hindrances to further the plan He has given us." A key to the resolution of the problems was both leaders' attitude of cheerful service to one another under the Lord and a clarification of their respective jurisdiction in Dutch New Guinea.[22]

Charlie Mellis and Vic Ambrose

Significant new directions for the MAF work in New Guinea emerged as a result of the Mellis-Ambrose meeting. These two men were kindred spirits who formed a faithful partnership. Charlie Mellis had been struggling with the projected MAF advance to Sentani in Dutch New Guinea. Concurrently, there was need for air support down south in the Fly River region of Papua New Guinea. The Sepik River basin was also beckoning for air support. Ever since Hartwig initiated the Madang program, discussion had centered on Sentani as the next base. Moving to Sentani, however, would put the plane into Dutch territory beyond the reach of these Australia-controlled areas of the Territory and Papua.

Strategic questions faced Charlie and Vic as they sought to stretch their limited resources to serve the growing number of mission stations scattered over a vast area. A review of what they accomplished is a study in Christian leadership at its finest. The courage of these two is truly amazing in view of the enormity of their task. Very few would even have tried to tackle the daunting obstacles they faced. Not only was the task immense, but the conditions on this frontier were exceedingly primitive. Both men were willing to subject themselves and their families to protracted hardships for the sake of God's work. Amid discussions of strategies for the most effective use of their aircraft, there prevailed a willingness on the part of these pioneers and their families to endure great hardship to fulfill their mission.

Charlie had planned to establish their next base at Sentani in Dutch New Guinea, but immediate need called for expanding the transportation network in the Territory and Papua. Ambrose came

160

in with a fresh eye to the logistical problem dogging Charlie. He suggested that an intermediate base be established at Wewak, halfway between Madang and Sentani. Charlie was immediately taken with the idea, and the more they considered this plan, the more merit both saw in it.[1]

The advantages in moving to Wewak were numerous. The program could be considered an extension of the Madang base, under Australian authority. By contrast, the Sentani location entailed dealing with the Dutch government and the many uncertainties that existed in dealing with this government. Furthermore, commercial airline service was not available at Wewak, and as missionaries kept penetrating into the Sepik River basin and the highlands beyond, the MAF link at Wewak would become increasingly strategic.

In early 1953 four groups were already in need of air support there: the South Sea Evangelical Mission, Brethren, Baptists, and the Assemblies of God. It was estimated that these alone would call for two hundred hours of flight time a month, to say nothing of serving new bases that were being opened in the Central Highlands.[2] Wewak could be considered a stepping-stone to Dutch New Guinea. From there Charlie could continue to supervise the Madang program, check out pilots for the Wewak region, and implement plans for an MAF base at Sentani.

With these considerations in view Vic and Charlie made a recommendation for this Wewak projection in January 1953. The council heartily approved. Further confirmation of the wisdom of this move came when Ken Griffiths, of the South Sea Evangelical Mission, gave AMAF a large block of land in Wewak for a base site. The understanding was that Los Angeles and Melbourne would develop the program jointly, with Melbourne eventually taking all responsibility.

The commitment to develop the Wewak base required readjustment in a number of areas, including the purchase of a plane to initially serve both Wewak and Sentani. On the surface this plan seemed to be a good solution, but it was soon complicated by other considerations. In late 1952 two Columbia Bible College alumni, Walter Erikson and Edward Tritt, both TEAM missionaries, were murdered by natives in Dutch New Guinea. In response, Columbia's Student Foreign Missions Fellowship immediately launched a memorial fund drive to raise five thousand dollars for the purchase of a MAF plane that would open up the interior of Dutch New Guinea.[3] The MAF-Columbia College connection went back to the days when Jim Buyers was a student there and R. C. McQuilkin became a member of the MAF advisory council. Grady's concern was that the student drive was to raise money for a plane based in Dutch New Guinea, while the more recent field decision called for it to be based at Wewak in the Territory of New Guinea. Charlie saw a silver lining in this dilemma. He suggested that the plane be named the Dutch New Guinea *Pathfinder*, temporarily based at Wewak. Putting it that way would be an advantage for Melbourne, inasmuch as they could apprise their constituency of the coming need for a new plane of their own, permanently based at Wewak.

For the entire month of April 1953 Charlie was in Wewak coordinating efforts to build the MAF base. Claire and the children moved to Wau in the highlands for that month to escape the heat.

Seeing a need to get the Wewak base built, Kay Liddle, a New Zealander serving with Christian Missions in Many Lands, came down from Lumi to do the actual building. This was a wonderful provision, for Liddle had an accounting and construction background. He had been in Madang when Vic and Charlie first conferred about starting a base at Wewak and volunteered to help with construction when the decision was made to begin the work.[4]

As these plans progressed at Wewak, a Piper "Pacer" selected to be the Dutch New Guinea *Pathfinder* was modified for use with either wheels or floats. Vic felt the Pacer was definitely the right choice of equipment. He believed that MAF work in New Guinea was capable of vast expansion and hardly anyone realized its possibilities for future growth. He was absolutely right. Given the advances in American light plane equipment, Vic also felt that AMAF should continue to look to MAF-US for equipment for a long time to come.[5]

Wewak was a frontier outpost far removed from the support services at Madang. Building materials shipped from Australia had to be stockpiled at Madang, transshipped by boat to Wewak, then transported ashore by small boats. They were then labori-

ously hauled to the construction site by Jeep. Logistics were difficult and time consuming. To compound matters, Charlie was not
feeling well, having come down with malaria. Fortunately, Liddle
and the crew of local people made good progress on the two missionary workers' homes and storage shed.

Given Charlie's push to get things done, it is not surprising that
he began to be bothered by "continuous spinning in his head."
The problem persisted even after he got back to Madang and
backed away from heavy physical work. Since adequate medical
diagnosis and treatment were not available in New Guinea, Mellis made a trip to Melbourne. Even then, the exact cause of his
problem proved elusive. Charlie took time for extended discussions with Vic and the council about the future of New Guinea's
flight program.

Tari Valley Survey

Before leaving Madang to settle in Wewak with his family in
January 1954, Charlie launched several major survey flights. A
memorable one was into the Tari Valley, located two hours inland
through the Rentoul Gap. The object was to assist Len Twyman of
UFM in surveying the ridge and borders on the south side of the
valley. Twyman was a missionary pioneer who had pushed relentlessly into new frontiers and had just recently arrived from work
in the Fly River region in Papua.

The trip to Tari was always touch-and-go because of its almost
incessant cloud cover. On December 29 Charlie navigated through
the Rentoul Gap and then climbed to twelve thousand feet, where
he overlooked a blanket of clouds. From that vantage point, he
found a hole in the clouds, slipped down to overlook the Tari River,
and came in for a landing. This frontier location witnessed tribal
life in its variegated forms. On this occasion Charlie Mellis and
Ray Jaensch, a pilot with the Lutheran mission at Madang, were
spectators to an intertribal war involving some eight hundred
people. A government patrol had to be called in to quell the fighting. They soon brought the situation under control by arresting
two of the leaders.[6]

The next day the long-awaited Wewak Pacer arrived aboard the

S.S. Malekula. Unloading took place on New Year's Day, 1954. All the plans for opening the Wewak base were now in place, and the Mellis family made the transfer to their new home at the end of January in the Wewak Pacer. This *Pathfinder* was later used to survey great stretches of unexplored territory in Dutch New Guinea. Reports of previously unsighted concentrations of people came in monthly, as in the case of the Strickland River region in Papua New Guinea, where an estimated hundred thousand people were located in June 1954.[7]

These exhilarating pioneering efforts of missionary aviation were not accomplished without pain or frustration. With the push to get the Dutch New Guinea program on its feet, not enough time was allowed to get the families settled in their new homes and surroundings before the men undertook new survey flights. At Wewak the Mellises had moved into their new home before its interior was completed. Claire recounts being kept awake at night by the sound of rats scampering across rafters in their ceilingless bedroom.

Even more poignant is her tale of entertaining guests in a house that had virtually no cupboards, in which she was carrying on school for her children while trying to type up reports for her husband. The dedication and longsuffering of these missionary wives must not be forgotten. Their frustrations and pains were a large part of the price that was paid to make these frontier advances for the gospel possible.[8]

Overwork and the tropical climate sapped Charlie's energy and took their toll on his health, but these dedicated missionaries did not shrink from the task to which they had set their sights, even when difficulties arose. They found joy in giving themselves unreservedly to the task to which the Lord called them, and the benefits of their labors continue to this day.

While the costs in hardship were great, the benefits were numerous. Wewak opened up the entire Sepik River region that divided the coastal range from the interior highlands. Crossing this barrier on foot was a hazardous and time-consuming task. The following table gives some idea of the travel time inland from Wewak by land and by air. Without missionary aviation, the advance of the gospel into this interior region would have been much slower, and the cost in lives lost probably much higher.[9]

Claire and Charlie Mellis, with their three boys, John, Jim, and Gordon, leave Madang for Wewak, 1954.

Destination	By Land	By Air
Yangoru	1 day	15 minutes
Hayfields	12 days	25 minutes
Maprik	10 days	25 minutes
Lumi	3 weeks	1 hour
Green River	5 weeks	1.5 hours
Telefomin	3 months	2 hours

The Missions Frontier

Vic and Joan Ambrose and their four children arrived at Madang in early March 1954 on their way to Wewak. Recognizing that there was no one on the horizon to fill the chief pilot position in New Guinea when Charlie eventually returned to the United States, Vic decided he would get his pilot ratings before coming to New Guinea. Ambrose joined Charlie at Wewak in preparation for taking over that program when Charlie moved to Sentani. Ambrose held only a private license and had done no serious flying since his military service. He had to take all four subject examinations. He was able to get all this done before departure for New Guinea.

At Wewak, the Mellises and Ambroses lived under one roof. Vic vividly recounts that the "impecuniosity as an organization meant that the walls were not lined and there were no ceilings in the house." Consequently these families really got to know each other! Vic's description of life on the edge of the New Guinea wilderness is educational.

> The cooking stoves which had kerosene wicks as burners, had a tendency to smoke and thus transfer a taste of kerosene to the food. Washing machines were non-existent. Our one small water tank was filled to only the second rung, and water for washing was obtained in 44 gallon drums from the creek at the Catholic Mission a mile away.
> It was thought that the soft pine floor of the main house would be protected from white ants if it was painted with sump oil. But the oil picked up the dirt from many feet, and was quickly transferred to children's clothes, sheets and mattresses! Frequent washing of the floor with petrol, turps, and soap finally alleviated the situation, but it was years before it could be sealed with a varnish.[10]

From this rugged beginning, the MAF base at Wewak rapidly developed into Melbourne's base for New Guinea flight operations. From the outset, the Australians supplied all the buildings and the U.S. provided the aircraft.[11] A spacious hangar and the Hartwig house, together with the other residences, made this location the logical place for the annual conference of pilots and their families. The first such conclave in July 1958 saw the Mortons, Dinsdales, Flavels, Hutchinses, Ray Jaensch, Bruce Lindsay, and Vic Ambrose converging to discuss plans for the future. They also gathered to have their families enjoy much needed Christian fellowship and inspiration.

When Wewak opened, it served forty missionaries working in the interior. By 1958 that had increased to seventy. This shows how rapidly the Australian work expanded on the Territory side of New Guinea. Rapid MAF growth in the 1950s came as a result of its response to the missions that were poised to reach further inland. Tropical climate and terrain conditions ruled out ground transportation. MAF moved to meet this logistical need and worked hand-in-glove with missions as they opened new areas. This was true with respect to TEAM's spearheading the work in the far western Dutch New Guinea's Bird's Head, the UFM presence in the Papuan Fly River region, and UFM and Australian Baptists in the areas between. It is also true that once MAF began flight service to these missions, advances into the interior were greatly facilitated through the population and terrain surveys that MAF provided.

In response to TEAM's penetration into the Bird's Head, Charlie and Vic launched a survey for that mission from Noemfor Island, using an abandoned World War II airstrip. To do the survey, Mellis ordered fuel shipped up the coast to Manokwari, TEAM's coastal base of operations west of Noemfor Island. From there the fuel had to be transshipped to Noemfor. Once all the pieces were in place, the survey party flew from Wewak up the coast to Sentani, and then across the Strait of Japan to Noemfor. The survey was a success and brought the goodwill of the Dutch officials, as had Parrott's initial penetration. This goodwill was important for getting approval for an MAF base at Sentani the following year.

Territorial Division for Service

The maturing MAF program in New Guinea led to a division of work into Australian and American spheres. Under the agreement that Vic and Charlie drew up, Melbourne took over MAF work on the Territory side of New Guinea in December 1954. The Americans continued to have responsibility for MAF operations in Dutch New Guinea.[12] Given the growth of personnel, Australia felt that it was desirable to appoint an Australian field leader. In taking over the operation on the Territory side of the island, they willingly obliged themselves to pay for their own Wewak Pacer.

MAF-US was now clearly committed to work on the Dutch New Guinea side. This was not what AMAF had hoped for when the issue of control first surfaced as a problem in 1952. But now that the Territory side of the program was developing, Australia had all it could do to supply the needs there. It became apparent that they would do well to consolidate their flight operations throughout the region under Australian political control. The Americans were prepared to work under Dutch colonial government restraints to develop aviation service for missions throughout all of Dutch New Guinea.

This strategic decision proved to be sound. It gave area responsibility to each of the MAF wings yet kept them in close proximity for reciprocal help. At that juncture Vic became the chief pilot of the Australian program; Charlie directed the work in Dutch New Guinea. When he left, Charlie turned his supervisory responsibility over to Vic for one year, until Dave Steiger worked himself into the position of program director for MAF-US's Dutch New Guinea work.

Unfortunately Vic had an accident with the Pacer on his first operational solo flight. Right after the plane had been issued a certificate of airworthiness, the battery of the Pacer gave out at Hayfields. Vic decided to start the engine by hand cranking the propeller. Since there were four other men there at the time, two of them natives, he enlisted them to restrain the plane (two on each wheel) as he cranked the propeller. When the engine fired up, the natives ran; the plane immediately turned and began to roll into a ditch. Vic jumped into the plane to grab the controls, but it was too late. Even the minor damage proved troublesome, as parts had to come from the United States, and the Department of Civil Aviation had to inspect the repairs.

MAF-US Beachhead in Dutch New Guinea

Charlie Mellis had wanted to get an MAF beachhead into Dutch New Guinea ever since his arrival at Madang. Back in early 1952 Grady Parrott had flown over the Baliem Valley with the hope that MAF would soon be able to assist missionaries in reaching these interior populations. The demands of the work on the Territory side and the delay in releasing the Dutch New Guinea *Pathfinder* for Sentani basing had made Charlie wonder if his dream would ever be realized. Charlie wanted very much to be able to initiate this service, and although regular Dutch New Guinea MAF flights were not started until after his departure for America, he was able to lay the groundwork for this operation.

By 1954, the Wewak Pacer had made a number of surveys into the Dutch New Guinea region. Meanwhile, C&MA pilot Al Lewis was flying the amphibious Sealand into the Baliem Valley. These realities made it appear that MAF could only make a limited contribution, given its commitment to smaller single-engine planes. Charlie nevertheless moved forward with plans for a coastal base at Sentani, expecting that the scattered non-C&MA mission stations would be looking for flight service. In any case, regular operations could not be started without the Dutch governor's approval. C&MA had received permission, so there seemed to be every reason to believe that MAF, with its good safety record on the Australian side, would also be able to qualify.

Yet when Vic flew the Mellises to Sentani in June 1954, they had neither a Sentani-based plane nor government permission to start a flight program in Dutch New Guinea. They were really starting an entirely new work. The linguistic and cultural mix was very different in Sentani, too. Here the Malay language was the vernacular, although the officials spoke Dutch and English. Furthermore, Charlie felt less initial welcome about the start at Sentani compared to MAF's beginnings at Wewak. At Wewak they were the only ones launching a missionary aviation program. At Sentani they were following on the heels of C&MA's Sealand. Consequently they felt less needed.

Still, Charlie was not easily discouraged. He was committed to getting the necessary clearances from the Dutch and getting started with a Sentani-based program. In the meantime, he had the opportunity to assess the needs for MAF at the October Dutch New Guinea missionary conference held on Japen Island. He found out that the air transport needs were many and growing.

Shortly thereafter their prefabricated Kingstrand house arrived from England. Ambrose and Hutchins came over and gave a week of their time to erect it. Local Regions Beyond Missionary Union (RBMU) men Bill Widbin and Paul Gesswein also pitched in. This made it possible for the Mellis family to move into their own four-room house just two weeks after it arrived in a crate! The rainy season was on its way, but heaven held up the downpour until the house was ready for occupancy.

Start of the Dutch New Guinea Flight Program

The arrival of the Dutch New Guinea Pacer at Christmas made it a joyous season for Charlie. All he needed now was the approval of the governor. The governor was supportive of MAF's work. He had seen how effectively the Pacer had operated in an emergency evacuation situation in which the Pacer had rescued an injured Dutch official from Sengge.[13]

The first condition to the governor's approval was that MAF had to become a Dutch corporation in order to work in Dutch territory. The second restricted MAF from making "*normal* mission runs" over routes that were served by local government services. The latter could be complied with easily enough; the former required approval from Fullerton, a Dutch name for MAF, and filing of all legal papers in Dutch. By March, all of this had come together and MAF-US in Dutch New Guinea emerged as *Zendings Luchtvaart Vereniging* (ZLV), which translates into English as Mission Aviation Society.

This was the third time MAF-US had taken an indigenous name, having done so previously in Ecuador and in Honduras. Later, in Portuguese-speaking Brazil, MAF was known as *Asas de Socorro*, and in Suriname, South America, MAF was incorporated as a Dutch company but retained its American name.

As soon as it was known locally that the Dutch New Guinea Pacer could be used with either wheels or floats, a call came from the UFM for assistance at Lake Archbold. This small lake, located between Sentani and the Baliem Valley, had been the landing site of the 1938 Archbold expedition. The UFM missionaries had come from the Baliem to the lake and begun building a camp there with the aid of supplies Al Lewis dropped from the Sealand.

Preparations to get the Pacer on floats coincided with Dave and Janet Steiger's arrival in March 1955. Dave had served as a World War II B-26 bomber pilot and had broad mechanical training that suited him well for this pioneer effort. Dave was immediately drawn into helping Bob Hutchins and Charlie Mellis get the Pacer on floats to operate off Lake Sentani.[14] Al Lewis, pilot of the Sealand, was on hand to give Bob and Charlie practice with float takeoffs and landings. Two days with his help and a week of practice on their own got them ready for Lewis's checkout.

Lake Archbold was too small for the Sealand, and with the need to bring out an injured Hans Veldhuis of UFM, Charlie came to the rescue. While he was in the area, he also located a place further inland for a landing strip at Bokondini. Floats, weighing some 250 pounds as compared to 80 pounds for the wheels, severely cut down the Pacer's payload. Nevertheless, the rescue operation was a success.

Al Lewis's Fatal Crash

Then, out of the blue, on April 29, 1955, came news that Al Lewis and his Sealand were missing on an interior flight. He had left Sentani for the Baliem Valley the day before but failed to arrive at his destination. The Dutch authorities immediately started a search with a twin-engine Catalina, but they found no trace of the plane. Mellis and Steiger put the Pacer back on floats to assist with the search and prepare for supplying the Baliem Valley. Strips had not been built in the valley, as the Sealand landed on the river. Fortunately, the valley was well stocked. It was accessible only by air, and should resupply prove too difficult, the Dutch authorities would order an evacuation of all missionaries.

After a month of search, the Sealand's wreckage was found at ten thousand feet, about five miles east of the Baliem Gap. The ship had insufficient altitude and crashed straight into the mountain, instantly killing Lewis.[15] His pioneering work and labor of love would long be remembered.

With the Sealand gone, C&MA had no way to resupply the Baliem and Wissel Lakes outposts. MAF came forward with the solution. Rather than resupply the Baliem from Sentani, Steiger and Ambrose decided to ship the supplies via boat to coastal Nabire, located on the lower neck of the Bird's Head, then fly the supplies inland, using air drops. A strategically built Japanese World War II runway at Nabire made transshipment from the boat to the plane relatively easy. The runway had not been in use since the war and had to be cleared of brush and debris. In just two days, the Pacer made ten round trips and dropped five thousand pounds of cargo in the Baliem Valley. The resupply work proved effective and was a good demonstration of what a small MAF plane could do when strategically placed and innovatively used.[16]

Toward the end of July, C&MA personnel completed their first landing strip in the Baliem Valley. Vic flew in a few days earlier to inspect it. He said it was the steepest one he had ever seen. Steiger and Ambrose flew in with 250 pounds of supplies in each Pacer. The Danis had never seen a plane land on the ground; they had only seen Al Lewis bring his ship down on water. Ambrose related the following Danis apocalyptic prediction. A story circulated that when the plane touched down, there would be an earthquake and all the trees would fall. Mellis's tongue-in-cheek response was, "I don't as a rule do such heavy landings." As it turned out, the plane landed safely, without an earthquake! Nevertheless, the Danis saw something special in the plane's mission. One native asked, "Is Jesus in the plane?" In his understanding of MAF's spiritual task, this young man could not have been more on target.

Before he returned to Fullerton, Charlie oriented Dave Steiger to MAF operations at Sentani. He was slated to be the next manager of the MAF-US Dutch New Guinea program. Given the short period of overlap, Vic was placed in charge of the Dutch New Guinea side of the work for one year, though he remained based at Wewak. This meant that he was field leader of the joint Australian and American MAF work in New Guinea for twelve months.[17] Vic Ambrose did for the Americans what Charlie Mellis initially was called on to do for the Australian fliers at Wewak. Both did their work professionally and with hearts motivated to serve.

Charlie was justifiably pleased with what had been accomplished in New Guinea missionary aviation in just three years. True, he had driven himself relentlessly. This was characteristic of Charlie. Consequently, he experienced symptoms of stress for much of the time he was in New Guinea. Despite the strain, Charlie praised the Lord for the opportunity of expanding the work of MAF in the territory and establishing a sound air service for missions in Dutch New Guinea. The work was very rewarding, and Charlie and Claire were at peace as they made their way back to Los Angeles in June 1955. Charlie was aware that Papua New Guinea would be the next missionary aviation frontier and felt confident that under Vic's able leadership this would develop well.

It must be remembered that the pioneering efforts in mission aviation launched from Wekak and Sentani opened regions over which the government claimed jurisdiction but had yet to occupy. Unlike in Mexico or the Sudan, where MAF came in to help existing work, in New Guinea, MAF paved the way for missions to find tribes no one from the outside had ever seen before. This was frontier missions indeed.

Ecuador's "Operation Auca" and Its Legacy

In Ecuador the mutual support of MAF and HCJB opened the way for building the Vozandes Hospital at Shell Mera. This development grew out of Dr. M. Everett Fuller's assistance in upgrading HCJB's clinic at Shell to more adequately serve the people of the Ecuadorian rain forest. In April 1950 when Dr. Fuller came to Quito to see how this might be realized, Nate Saint gave him a tour of the HCJB clinic. Dr. Fuller saw how inadequate it was for the growing health-care needs of the region, decided to serve at Shell Mera, and laid plans for the hospital. To help make this a reality, MAF donated five of the sixteen acres it had purchased from Shell Oil Company.[1]

Developments at Shell Mera

From there Dr. Fuller took the initiative. Dr. Ralph Eichenberger of Wycliffe, Nate Saint, and missionaries of the Gospel Missionary Union, among others, gave much-needed help. Theodore Epp of the *Back to the Bible* broadcasts in Lincoln, Nebraska, contributed significant funding.

Over the years various MAF pilots and their wives assisted in this medical work. When Dr. Fuller performed the first surgery at the facility, Nate rigged up photo floodlights above the operating table. When Bob and Keita Wittig came to Shell Mera, Keita took the job of driving a truck bringing in building supplies. Bob took on a major engineering project in erecting a water tower. Dr. Fuller purchased a steel water tank from an American road construction firm on the coast and personally trucked it over the Andes. The trouble was he had no way of getting it mounted. A wooden tower was not going to work. No steel was immediately available until Bob told Dr. Fuller that Shell had left behind a good amount of structural steel at Arajuno, one of their drilling sites. The trick was to retrieve it. Wittig then flew out to cut up the steel, employed Indians to lengthen the Arajuno strip, and had an Ecuadorian pilot friend, Gonzalo Ruales, who owned a German tri-motor Junker, haul it to Shell Mera. Bob took the steel and welded it into a forty-foot structure that still supports the hospital water tank.[2]

Bob's many talents made him in demand. In 1955 HCJB was in need of a diesel engine maintenance expert. Bob filled this need. The station had installed several new engines to run the generators, but qualified mechanics were not available. At first Bob divided his time between MAF and HCJB, but when it was clear that SIL would not be calling on MAF for logistical support, Bob worked full time for HCJB. John and Ruth Keenan then joined the Saints in Ecuador.

This was also the period when Nate perfected his "bucket drop,"[3] the technique that made it possible for a plane to render service even when there was no landing strip. By tying a ballasted bucket to a rope and lowering it into a clearing while the airplane circled five hundred feet overhead, a container could be lowered to people on the ground. By the summer of 1954 Saint had refined the maneuver and installed a telephone hookup from the pilot to the bucket. The device proved itself when Nate was called on to meet a medical need among the Arapajos. On reaching the village, he lowered the tethered bucket into the hands of Frank Mathis. The missionary picked up the telephone and described the patient's symptoms. Nate relayed the information via radio to the hospital in Quito. Within minutes Nate received a diagnosis and a prescription that he was able to have filled.[4]

Another of Nate's ingenious devices was the paddle-wheel generator that he hooked up in a stream to provide his house with electrical power. One of the last things Nate did for Dr. Fuller was to repair an opthalmoscope. To do this, he had to use a hand lens. It was really a microscopic repair job that Nate managed to do with very simple equipment. There seemed to be no limits to his inventive genius. His role in MAF's development of an alternate fuel system for the plane has already been discussed. One of the projects on which he experimented in 1955 was a new biplane configuration. He got carried away with it, overstepping regulations on flight safety in the process.[5]

Launching "Operation Auca"

Assistance to frontier missions was an MAF priority, so it was natural that Nate Saint was involved with three Brethren missionaries and one from Gospel Missionary Union (GMU) in "Operation Auca," a secret mission to reach the fierce Auca (now known as the Waorani)[6] Indians living in the Oriente.

The veil of secrecy was suddenly torn from this mission when on January 8, 1956, as a result of Keenan's reconnaisance flight, word spread that Auca Indians had destroyed a MAF plane and possibly killed five missionaries. Within days the grim reality of this murderous attack at "Palm Beach" on the Curaray River was confirmed. The world learned that Roger Youdarian (GMU), Pete Fleming, Ed McCully, and Jim Elliot (Brethren), and Nate Saint had given their lives to reach a Stone Age people in the jungles of Ecuador. That story has been fully told in *Through Gates of Splendor*[7] and will be recounted here to relate MAF's role.

All the missionaries in the Oriente had been aware of the fierce Aucas. It was their burning desire to share God's love with these violence-prone people that set "Operation Auca" in motion. These missionaries looked forward to the day they could establish friendly contacts and share the gospel message with this people. This single-minded motive led to the joint venture of the five missionary families—Ed and Marilou McCully, Pete and Olive Fleming, Jim and Elisabeth Elliot, Roger and Barbara Youdarian—as well as Nate and Marj Saint. Their plan relied on the use of the plane and Saint's bucket-drop technique to establish initial contact with the Aucas.

Recent Auca attacks had led the government to consider military reprisals; hence the need for secrecy. The government might have moved faster against the Aucas, had they known of the missionaries' initiatives and that they had located their villages. As the project's pilot, Nate knew how to counsel the group on logistics, but it was because of joint planning that "Operation Auca" moved forward.[8]

The general region of the Aucas' homeland adjacent to the Curaray River was well known. They tolerated no intruders, and missionaries in the region, including SIL personnel, initially took care not to trespass. However, by 1955 the Oriente missionaries felt the time had come to attempt friendly overtures. On September 19 Nate Saint and Ed McCully spotted one of their jungle clearings with huts. Ten days later the two found yet another site.

The use of the bucket drop to contact the Aucas met with immediate success. Thirteen weekly contacts were made this way at what was later dubbed "Terminal City." The Aucas even cleared trees and built a platform to make it easier for Nate to aim the bucket so they could access it easily. Gifts of various types, including machetes, were lowered and received with apparent approval from the villagers, who reciprocated with hand-crafted objects.

Nate Saint by his Piper Cruiser, holding a gift from the Aucas in his left hand and his bucket-drop invention in his right hand, 1955.

These friendly exchanges led to a search for closer contact and a landing site. The only feasible place was the strip of beach along the Curaray River. Nate considered the risk in landing there alone and decided to carry a concealed .22 automatic. He felt justified in having a means of scaring off any hostile attack. He also let it be known that "more important than any precaution we take, we are anxious to operate within the will and providence of God."[9]

The new year saw the operation come to a critical phase—face-to-face contact with the Aucas on the ground. Supplies, gifts, and a prefabricated tree house were flown to "Palm Beach" on Wednesday, January 3. The house was mounted high up in a large tree; it would provide a safe place to sleep at night. All five men stayed on the beach during the day, but Nate flew the plane out for the night as a precaution against a rising river, should heavy rains set in.

On Friday, January 5, three naked Aucas stepped out of the jungle and appeared across the river from the beach—an older lady, a younger man, and a teenage girl. Jim took the initiative, crossed the river, and gestured for them to come over, which they did. They called the young man George and the teenage girl, Delilah. There was tension in the air until the visitors joined in eating; then the mood changed. George wanted a plane ride, so Nate took him out over his village, where George shouted to the people below. This first contact seemed to be a resounding success. Anticipation of future friendly meetings was high.

Next day all was quiet; no Auca visitors made their appearance. Sunday came, and all was quiet that morning. Nate called Marj promptly at 12:30 P.M., as had been agreed. He told her he would call again at 4:30. That call never came. Sometime after 3:00 P.M., the men were attacked. When Nate did not show up with the plane that afternoon, Marj knew something was wrong.

Early the next morning Johnny Keenan flew due east, down the Curaray, to investigate. At "Palm Beach" he found the plane stripped of its fabric but no one in sight. Many intervening flights followed. Not until Wednesday, when Keenan again flew down the river, did he spot a man's body floating in the water. His worst fears were confirmed. Perhaps all five were murdered. He relayed the numbing news.

Given this confirmation, Frank Drown organized an overland expedition at Arajuno. Missionaries, soldiers, and Indians made preparations for the long trek into the Auca territory. Some glimmer of hope remained, but all five men were confirmed dead, slain by Auca lances.

We know now that George played a big part in convincing the Aucas to kill the missionaries. After his reception on the beach on Friday, he spread word that the five missionaries were plotting to kill them. He urged a preemptive attack. His treachery bore fruit in the murderous strike that Sunday. Despite the fact that they had two guns among them for protection, the missionaries by pre-agreement offered no resistance. Exactly how the event unfolded is unknown.

The slain were buried in a mass grave under the jungle canopy next to "Palm Beach" during a rainstorm. It was as though the very heavens were weeping for these five brave missionary families, now left without husbands or fathers.

The risks inherent in this mission had been weighed carefully. Well before this, Jim Elliot had concluded, "He is no fool who gives what he cannot keep to gain what he cannot lose." The possibility of such a turn of events had been considered. Given the carefully laid steps to become progressively acquainted with the Aucas, including a bucket drop of photos of the five men, the probability of tragedy seemed very remote. However, the five had no inkling of George's duplicity.

Their wives gathered at Shell Mera to give one another support during the vigil. Having committed the outcome of their husbands' best-laid plans to the Lord, they also accepted the sad news as from his hand. Despite their shared sorrow, they sang, "Be Still My Soul" in recognition that the Lord had given and the Lord had taken.

Word of the savage attack on the five missionaries stirred news-gathering organizations into action. *Life* magazine sent out photographer Cornell Capa, who arrived at Shell Mera a day after Grady Parrott. Capa's interest in Saint's work had been whetted by contact with Nate's brother Sam, an American Airlines captain.[10] Capa wanted everything he could get his hands on for the story. There was some hesitation at first. Would *Life* accurately disclose or distort what motivated these men and their wives to risk their lives? If this message would come through clearly, Nate's diary and all the documentary material, including an undeveloped film, should be made available to Capa. *Life* was given exclusive rights to use the documents for one publication, with the requirement that all these items be returned.[11]

Abe Van Der Puy of station HCJB came down to Shell Mera to be of immediate help to the widows and their families. He saw to it that the news release from HCJB detailed the spadework that the missionaries had done in "Operation Auca." The moving portrait he drew of the dedication of these missionaries led the widows to ask Van Der Puy to write a book-length version to challenge young people to give themselves and their talents to serve their Maker.[12] Van Der Puy diligently gathered information, much of which later appeared in Clarence Hall's August 1956 *Reader's Digest* article "Mid-Century Martyrs." Ultimately the widows directed one of their number, Elisabeth Elliot, to write a more complete account of their labors. This resulted in *Through Gates of Splendor.*

Grady Parrott volunteered MAF as the place to keep Nate Saint's photos and films. A fund for the widows and their families was started, as was the MAF Nate Saint Memorial Fund for a replacement plane. A great outpouring of support came from many quarters.[13]

The Ecuadorian government took note of the efforts and sacrifice of these families. The president "decorated" the evangelical missions on February 16, in a ceremony at which Abe Van Der Puy represented the missionary community. The president saluted the missionaries and conferred on them the National Medal of Merit in the Order of Commander. The citation recognized the missions' "unceasing, unselfish and sacrificial service."[14] On the tenth anniversary, Ecuador issued a commemorative stamp picturing each of the slain.

Back in Fullerton word of the slayings greatly distressed Jim Truxton. The MAF Fullerton office had been kept fully abreast of the planning, and each step of the operation was followed closely. Nevertheless, Jim felt a heavy responsibility. He and Betty had come through Shell Mera just a month earlier on their way home on furlough from Brazil, and Nate had briefed Jim on all the details of "Operation Auca." He had spoken of the Aucas' positive response

The Piper Cruiser that replaced the one destroyed by the Aucas.

to the bucket drops, their building a platform to reach the bucket, and the reciprocation of gifts. For Jim these events confirmed God's hand in the matter, yet he spent a sleepless night weighing the risks involved in the planned "Palm Beach" encounter with the Aucas. Had he judged the operation too risky, he could have convinced the MAF officers to call off the operation. Despite some misgivings, he felt God was in it and let it proceed.

Understandably, a planned MAF banquet drew a larger than expected crowd. Indeed, many had to be turned away. An after service was included so more could hear the tape HCJB's Abe Van Der Puy and Clarence Jones had produced, detailing the plans for "Operation Auca." The first news of the slaying confounded many. The tape gave full details of the operation and silenced blind criticism. It concluded with the positive challenge to all who heard it to become fully committed to God.

Marj Saint gave attention to her future. Staying at Shell Mera was out of the question. She had an offer from Van Der Puy to become host of HCJB's guest house in Quito. Although Parrott encouraged her not to make any hasty decisions, she accepted Van Der Puy's offer.[15]

This was a poignant time for Marj and her three children. Their lives had been touched by eternity and would never be the same again. What would their future hold? For the present, it was enough to pack up their belongings at Shell Mera and move from the base home—the home Nate had transformed into a refuge from tropical downpours and a place for joyous romping with the growing family. Parrott entered into the anguish of her crisis and loss and penned the following touching note:

> For several days I have thought of writing a separate letter about your stepping out of your "home" in SM, and leaving MAF for HCJB. But for some reason I haven't been able to bring myself to it as it just doesn't seem as though you are actually leaving. It seems emphatically that you are still just as much in the MAF picture as before though moving to lend a hand in Quito. Probably this is because we have always felt so close to HCJB and because we have channeled so much through them in accepting their generosities in the past. Possibly because we have always felt a closer affinity with the various sister missions in Ecuador than in other areas that it still seems you will be in the same big "family" and just as close. I wonder if you feel that way about it. Although we will naturally expect you to have the new allegiances and loyalties which always tie in with new responsibilities. And we expect that even though the present arrangement is on an assignment to HCJB that all of us are actually thinking of that in a more permanent way—as apparently indicated by the Lord. But we don't want you to feel that you have actually "left" MAF. Possibly we should say that you belong to us both. We'd like it best that way, and that goes for Stevie, Kathy and Phillip as well![16]

These families did not wallow in self-pity, nor were they intimidated by fear of the future. Thirty-three years after the Auca massacre, Olive Fleming Liefeld, now the wife of Dr. Walter Liefeld at Trinity Evangelical Divinity School in Deerfield, Illinois, looked back at her husband's slaying with the eye of faith. "I have learned through the years," she said, "that even in hard things God can bring good out of those bad experiences."[17] As for the children who were left fatherless, their parents gave them a strong legacy of faith. Stephen Saint became involved in development work in Mali, West Africa, in 1986. He not only knew that God had used his dad's death for good, but that his mother, Marj, had passed on the torch of faith to her children. As a result, Stephen celebrated the sharing of his faith with Nouh Ag Infa Yatara, a young believer living among Moslems in Timbuktu. *Guideposts* (January 1991) tells how the living example of his parents' walk with God gave Stephen a faith that he could pass on.[18]

One of the unforeseen and unexpected complications of the publicity that the Auca story generated was the question of media, publication, and distribution rights. MAF saw potential for challenging Christians via a film message. Sam Saint, Nate's brother, sought and received power of attorney for media rights from the five widows.[19]

Grady had hoped to enter into negotiation with Westminster Films on a limited presentation of "Operation Auca" based on Nate's actual footage, but he backed away from any claims to that film once Sam negotiated power of attorney for the widows. The door closed to MAF for making a film on the Auca story that would have been a sequel to Nate's film *Conquering Jungle Barriers*.

Grady recognized Sam Saint's right to all that Nate had written and produced in connection with "Operation Auca." Furthermore, he felt it was more important to retain harmony and goodwill with all those touched by the Auca slayings than for MAF to struggle to gain access to Nate's films. Consequently MAF was not able to produce a film on "Operation Auca." They did produce a sound filmstrip version based on still shots that was released under the title *Mid-Century Martyrs*.

Mourning and Transition

Right on the heels of the Auca murders came news of Violet Derr's death in Tabasco, Mexico, on January 17, shortly after the birth of her daughter, Marilyn. Dan and Violet were with MAF's Oaxaca program, working with the Hatchers. While the birth was normal, a coronary condition developed that was complicated by hemorrhaging.[20]

Within a span of ten days two MAF members—Nate and Violet—had passed on. Since its founding, no one in the immediate MAF-US family had died, although they had lost others who were close to the organization: Australian Harry Hartwig and Al Lewis of C&MA. In the summer of 1956 Dawson Trotman, so helpful in MAF's early days, suffered cardiac arrest while rescuing a swimmer at The Navigators Conference. Trotman and all the above gave their lives in service to others.

After the death of his wife, Danny Derr's sense of call to mission aviation and to MAF remained, but he felt it necessary to withdraw from frontline service for a time. As a result it was decided that Danny would return to Fullerton to fill the spot vacated by Hobey when he and his wife, Olivia, headed for Shell Mera to carry on the work of the Saints. Hobey Lowrance was developing a first-rate flight orientation program for MAF candidates at Fullerton at the time. He had met Olivia in Ecuador while filling in for Nate seven years earlier. It was only fitting for these two to serve in this field. Hobey and Olivia's qualifications perfectly fit the needs at Shell Mera at that point. They served there until July 1958 when Danny Derr, now married to Elsie Schneider, took Hobey's place as pilot in Ecuador.

Sequel to "Operation Auca"

"Operation Auca" did not end with the missionary slayings. The bucket drop to Terminal City continued, though reduced to a monthly visit. Attempts were made to encourage the Aucas to visit nearby stations. In August 1957 Lowrance took Parrott and Dr. Tidmarsh on a visit to witness a gift drop.[21] Rachel Saint, sister of Nate Saint, who was affiliated with SIL, had by then befriended Dayuma, an Auca girl who escaped from her people. At the same time Dr. Tidmarsh continued his efforts to befriend this people. He planted a frontier outpost, a simple shelter from the rain some miles closer to them than Arajuno. This move brought him to their very doorstep. To show their displeasure, the Aucas sacked his outpost in October 1957, leaving two lances in the doorway of the shelter to register their displeasure.[22]

Without any warning, two Auca women—Mintaka and

Mangamu—ventured to the Quichua village on the Curaray not far from Arajuno. They came when Dr. Tidmarsh was away and met Betty Elliot and Rachel Saint, who were staying at Arajuno at the time. The two considered this a sign that the Lord wanted them to visit the Aucas at Terminal City, especially when they learned that these Auca women had promised their people they would be back "when the kapok is ripe." Betty seriously considered going back with them. Those around her, however, naturally feared for her and her daughter Valerie's safety.

In line with this desire, Betty made contact with Danny Derr, hoping to arrange for future supply drops at Terminal City. Danny referred the request to Grady Parrott and Grady demurred. He was unwilling to support any move that might endanger Betty or her daughter. Although he was convinced that the loss of the five men should not detract from future efforts to make contact with the Aucas, he believed that the Aucas should take the initiative and establish contact with mission stations.[23]

Betty's request caused Grady to reflect on MAF's established policy vis-à-vis the missions they served. In this case he took the position that while MAF was not going to tell missions what they could or could not do, given the "circumstances of the history of the entire Auca project, we have become in a sense a part and parcel of it and therefore feel that we should be given ear in determining the Lord's will with respect to any part which would call us into participation."[24] Grady realized that MAF service to missionaries placed a measure of responsibility on their shoulders for the safety of those they dropped off at the doorstep of people like the Aucas.

However, Grady was not content just to turn down Betty. He made a point to visit her when he was in Ecuador in August 1958. His observations were that Betty had not accepted the counsel of her family, whom she described as being "beside themselves" about her plans to go to the Aucas.[25] She then made it clear to Grady that the Lord had shown her she would be one who would make contact with the Aucas. Grady accepted this as a valid conviction but questioned her on the timing of the proposed visit, pointing out that he did not think the situation was opportune for her to make such an entry.[26] Betty decided to hold off on the visit.

On September 25 seven Auca women, including Mintaka, Mankamu, and Dayuma, and three boys arrived at the Quichua village. By then Betty had come to live with the Quichua, made friends with their women, and learned as much as she could about the Aucas. After discussion and prayer it was agreed that Betty, Valerie, and Rachel Saint would go back to the Auca village with the women and six well-armed Quichua men.[27] This time the contact was friendly. The women's stay there necessitated a steady flow of supplies that were dropped by MAF.

This advance into the heart of Auca territory must be appreciated in the context of the three mission agencies that were involved in "Operation Auca" in one way or another: MAF (Saint, Lowrance, Keenan, Derr), Brethren (Betty Elliot), Wycliffe's SIL (Rachel Saint). Given the prospect of a flood of newsmen, anthropologists, frontier adventurers, and thrill seekers descending on the Ecuadorian rain forest following the news of the Auca visits, the MAF executive committee proposed a cooperative agreement between MAF and SIL assuring a coordinated approach to persons seeking contact with the Aucas and the women missionaries.

Since these two organizations possessed the only private air fleet in that remote region, it was well within their power to protect the Aucas from outside pressures. This agreement identified four areas of mutual concern: the need to recognize that the Lord had allowed three groups to spring up who were seeking cooperatively to contact and evangelize the Aucas; the need to receive and respect Betty and Rachel's assessment as to whether or not bringing other planes near Terminal City would jeopardize their safety; that SIL refrain from bringing Roman Catholic priests into Auca territory; that publicity on the current contacts with the Aucas be kept at a minimum so as not to attract outsiders into the region.[28]

Despite good intentions all around, news of the women's life among the Aucas spread like wildfire to the news services. Danny Derr found himself inundated with requests for transportation to the Auca frontier. All were turned down except for Sam Saint, who held publicity rights for the widows. The upshot was that Cornell Capa came in to do a sequel for *Life*.

Continuing flight support for Betty and Rachel eventually gave them the opportunity to share the gospel with this people. Conversions resulted, and today a church has been planted among the Aucas who, as a total people group, number no more than five hundred. Christianization among them has not been as dramatic as among the Quichua, living nearby descendants of the Incas, whose Christian community numbers nearly 150,000.[29]

What has been remarkable about the continuing Auca story is not only the conversion of those who murdered the missionaries but the reconciliation between the attackers and the families of the slain. A more striking scene depicting forgiveness could not be drawn than what transpired on the banks of the Curaray River in 1966, the tenth anniversary of the attack. Two of those responsible for killing the missionaries baptized Nate Saint's children Steve and Kathy on the spot where their father had been struck down.[30]

The genuineness of that forgiveness and reconciliation was witnessed again thirty-six years after the slaying on June 13, 1992, when the translation of the entire New Testament into Waorani (the Auca tongue) was dedicated at Shell Mera.[31] On that occasion all three of the Saints' adult children—Steve, Kathy, and Phil—were present, as was Nate's sister, Rachel. Three Auca men involved in the attack approached the Saints and asked them, "Please tell your children that we're sorry that we killed their grandfather. Please ask them to forgive us." The influence of the gospel is all the more striking when one considers that neither the Auca language nor their culture contains a concept that might be translated as "forgiveness."[32]

The Role of Pilots in Mission Strategy

The unfolding events in Ecuador show the complicated nature of MAF's work. Not only did they coordinate work among the missions, but they did it under the national policies of their host country. Large diplomatic implications exist in such an undertaking as "Operation Auca." With the Auca killings there were questions of responsibility. To what extent had MAF taken the lead, even though Nate had been careful to plan the operation with the other four missionaries? All decisions had been made together. To be sure, Nate advised them on logistics. In this respect this was

Ten years after Nate Saint was killed on January 8, 1956, his son, Steve, awaits his turn to be baptized. His father's slayers baptize his sister, Kathy (now Kathy Drown).

not an MAF operation, even though the airplane made it possible to move the project forward.

We have also seen how Grady Parrott handled Betty Elliot's request for air support to venture into the Auca region. MAF had been operating with the philosophy of "a servant of missions," but it had to reserve its right to independent judgment on any specific request for flight support.

The outcome in Ecuador led to review of the role of pilots in the field. They were there to serve missions, but Grady wanted to make it clear that pilots were not to "assume the prerogatives of leadership." Initiatives for field expansion were only to come from the missions. He did not want pilots to even insist on an equal vote on these committees. In this same spirit, pilots were to participate in but not dominate committee discussion. While Grady discouraged pilots from exercising leadership within the constituency they served, he did not want pilots to withhold counsel or suggestions that might conceivably move forward the business at hand. The pilot's perspective as specialist was to be part of the dialogue, to lead to sound decisions. In other words, MAF was not going to be setting field objectives but was to provide safe and efficient means through its flight service. This involved no repudiation of what had been done in Ecuador, only prudent reassessment of MAF policy.

Mission aviation required constant reevaluation, not only in Ecuador but elsewhere. In the Sudan MAF-UK likewise found itself having to rethink how it ought to exist as an organization.

Placed in the larger context of Christian mission, "Operation Auca" and the slaying of the five missionaries gives meaning to the often repeated truth that the "blood of martyrs is the seed of the church." While the Aucas did not specifically murder these five because of their Christian faith (any intruders might have suffered the same fate), the five likely did not put up a fight because they sought to bring these people to a knowledge of the Prince of Peace. The understanding that their lives were *given*, not *taken*, stirred a generation of young men and women to dedicate themselves to cross-cultural Christian ministry. There was a tremendous upsurge in mission volunteers in the following decade. MAF saw a parallel increase in the number of applicants, which made for rapid expansion of flight programs.

MAF-UK in the Sudan

Getting the Anglo-Egyptian MAF-UK Sudan operation off and running was one thing; keeping a dependable service going was quite another matter. In the early years, the need for adequate financial support was one of the most pressing concerns facing the organization. To operate longterm, Stuart King knew that MAF-UK had to become an independent mission organization that could directly reach the Christian public for support, rather than rely totally on assistance from the Movement for World Evangelization (MWE). MAF-UK needed to become self-supporting, as were its American and Australian counterparts.

Given the weak postwar financial support base in England, it is a miracle that the operation didn't simply collapse. In Africa, particularly in the Anglo-Egyptian Sudan, there were equally difficult challenges. King and Stevens had to learn how to keep a year-round lifeline service going in the swampy "Sudd" that became one vast waterlogged region during the May to November rainy season. Then there was the problem of a dependable plane and gaining approval for air-to-ground communication with the mission stations, to say nothing of caring for MAF personnel and health concerns, housing, and hangar needs that were constant and pressing.

For King and his team this was a period of difficulties parallel to what MAF-US and Australia MAF had experienced. In all these trying circumstances, the leadership gave no thought to quitting. Their commitment to following through on the vision that first moved them remained undiminished, although they were often perplexed. These trials of faith were a heavy burden from a purely human standpoint, but also the prelude to God's provision and enablement.

By 1957 each of these obstacles had been cleared away. Their motto, "Praise, Pray and Press On" as expressed by their Home Secretary Bill Knights, characterized the work.[1] The Lord supplied the needs of the organization in various ways that included the grit and determination of these men and their wives to "press on." Then there was the generous assistance of friends. MAF-US leaders came alongside for support. Betty Greene joined the Sudan team as their pilot.

Basing the Plane at Doro

Lack of finances dictated that MAF-UK base its plane at a mission station. While this was not ideal from a logistical standpoint, it had the merit of being economical. In the process, King and Stevens experienced firsthand the problems and frustrations of the missionaries, which provided invaluable insights.

In June 1951 Steve Stevens and Stuart King prepared to base the plane at Doro, a SIM station. This was a better location for the plane than Akobo, located southeast of Malakal. The village sat on higher ground and was not subject to seasonal flooding. Stevens built a pilot's home and improved the airstrip while the plane was being overhauled in Khartoum.

Another benefit to Stuart in basing there was the opportunity to fly to Abaiyat, another SIM station ninety miles westward, where he became acquainted with Phyllis Bapple, whom he had earlier met at Khartoum. She was working among the Dinka people. Phyllis had previously served as secretary to the SIM superintendent in Khartoum. She was a native Californian and a graduate of The Bible Institute of Los Angeles, now Biola University.

Their courtship moved along when Stuart and Steve found themselves on an enforced eighteen-day stay at Abaiyat repairing the plane, which had sustained a nose-over while taxiing on a soft strip. The day the repairs on the Rapide were completed, King proposed to Phyllis. The men left the following morning and were unable to return to Abaiyat for several months. No mail got through between Phyllis and Stuart during that time because of the isolation of their locations. When at last the plane was able to return, they became officially engaged and were married in Khartoum in February 1952. Phyllis's many talents complemented Stuart's, and she soon became the accountant for the program.

Bill Knights promoted the work of MAF-UK in London. The task proved to be exhausting, and he was forced to take a leave to regain his strength. In the process he visited the Sudan in the summer of 1952. Seeing and feeling the field proved to be a life-changing experience for Bill.

One day he and Steve Stevens traveled to the village of Abaiyat, one hundred miles north of Malakal on the White Nile and twenty-six miles across the Dinka plain. Unfortunately the trek across the open plain under the blazing sun sapped Bill's energy. His legs were so sore that he could not make it to Abaiyat. He stayed behind in a Dinka village while Steve pressed ahead in the hope of coming back with transportation. While Bill sat there in the twilight, he witnessed a sight that changed his life.

He saw Dinkas begin to sacrifice to the devil and various totems, snakes, and hyenas. The powers of darkness seemed to envelope the scene. The need to spread God's light so gripped Bill that by the time Steve returned with a vehicle to pick him up, he had pledged his life to the Lord for service among the Dinka.[2]

While visiting the Sudan, Knights met Marie Anderson, a missionary from Saskatchewan, Canada. She had been serving among the Dinka for eight years in association with the SIM. Bill and Marie's relationship blossomed and the two were married in Saskatchewan the following summer. The Knights studied for two years at the Two Rivers Bible Institute in Alberta, in preparation for their joint service with SIM.[3]

Gordon Marshall

In the meantime Steve developed a serious eye problem that would not go away and later was diagnosed as a detached retina. This prevented him from flying. Fortunately he had contact with Gordon Marshall, a friend from South Africa who had been called by God to serve in the Sudan. Gordon was the son of a Baptist minister and chaplain in the South African military.[4] In 1945 Gordon joined the South African Air Force (SAAF) as a pilot trainee, earned his wings, and was commissioned the following year. For the next six years he served as a pilot and qualified as a flight instructor. At the opening of the Korean War in 1950, Gordon volunteered to serve there. During the course of his one hundred missions over Korea, he was decorated with the Distinguished Flying Cross for bravery in the line of duty. But God had something even better in store for him.

One day while flying, he was separated from his squadron. He recounts,

> I was perfectly safe and heading south along a railway line. Then I saw refugees walking down the line. There was snow everywhere. I was flying low and as far as I could see both ways these were fleeing refugees, four or five deep. They had no shoes and so few possessions. I had this overwhelming experience, and said to myself: Why am I using this aeroplane in the military when there are people like this?[5]

On completing his tour in 1951, Gordon returned to his native South Africa. The question of serving never left him, and he responded to the call two months later when he received a letter from Steve Stevens. Steve asked Gordon to come to the Sudan to replace him in the MAF-UK program that he had to leave due to his loss of sight in one eye. Gordon gave an immediate affirmative.[6] From that day forward, he has given of himself to serve with MAF.

In preparation for flying in the Sudan, Gordon gained his senior commercial pilot's license with instrument rating. In March 1952, he hitchhiked to Khartoum by air. The day after his arrival, Stevens enlisted Gordon in flying missionaries in the Sudan while he gave him flight orientation to the new setting.

For Gordon, seeing the Stevenses again had a deeper meaning. Steve and Kay had exercised a deep influence on Gordon, leading to his dedicating his life in service to God, even before they left for the Sudan. While Gordon was in Korea, he pondered the work of MAF-UK, and now he stepped into Christian service.

Purchase of the Second Rapide

In the spring of 1952 the Rapide was in need of engine and air-frame work to qualify for a certificate of airworthiness. This wood and glue plane had taken a terrific beating. The three-month over-haul dragged into a nine-month operation, and the end was not yet in sight when it was discovered that there were splits in the main wing spars. That sealed the plane's fate. King initially cast about for a set of replacement wings. When no reasonably priced ones could be found, it was decided to abandon the Rapide.[7]

Stuart had earlier placed a low bid on a Rapide offered for sale in Lebanon. The time for receiving word on his offer was long past, and he assumed that the plane went to another bidder. However, a few days after the decision to look for another plane, he received a cable saying that the highest bidder on the Rapide had been unable to transfer the money to Lebanon. Was King still interested? By this time MAF-UK thoughts had turned to securing an all-metal plane, but they didn't have sufficient funds. Given this sudden open door and the acceptance of their low bid of six hundred pounds (eighteen hundred dollars), they decided to investigate further. They learned that the plane was in excellent condition but would need an engine overhaul in four months.

They decided to convene a special day of prayer to seek God's will. Stuart and Gordon emerged from this exercise with a sense of God's peace that freed them to go ahead with the purchase. They took an airline to Lebanon and found the plane in wonder-ful condition. The owner had spared no pains in keeping it almost like new. It had two new mainplanes, and the exterior had been completely refurbished two years earlier. The previous overhaul had also been extensive. They were satisfied with the plane and purchased it and spare parts with their own money.[8]

Founding a Freestanding MAF-UK

The purchase of the second Rapide was another reminder that the two years of MAF-UK operations in the Sudan had been costly. Although MWE was sympathetic to MAF's subsidy needs, it was in no position to fund the operation. As the problems of financing the work mounted, Stuart King became convinced that MAF-UK must become a freestanding organization able to make direct appeals to Christian friends and supporters. MAF-UK became an independent corporation in September 1952.[9]

Setting up an independent MAF-UK was no easy task. All the questions that MAF-US had faced had to be answered. The nature of MAF-UK's work in the Sudan was already clearly defined. They had also thought through many flight policy questions. However, they had no headquarters in the United Kingdom and almost no support base. They needed to review all aspects of their organization and build a firm foundation so their field operations would be sustained by the prayers and financial support of committed Christians in Britain.

To accomplish this goal the entire Sudan team—the Kings, Stevenses, and Gordon Marshall—packed into the plane and flew back to England. While the overhaul of the Rapide was going forward at Cambrian Air Services in Cardiff, Wales, Stuart and his team decided that Steve and Kay Stevens should stay in London, establish a MAF-UK headquarters there, and begin to build a support constituency. The rest of the team returned to the Sudan in January 1954.

Steve's immediate need was for eye surgery. His month in the hospital stood out as "one of the greatest experiences" in his life. This may seem strange, since the operation proved to be a failure. Stevens explained his reaction this way: "Fortunately, Kay and I did not feel the operation was as important as the opportunity for service in the ward, so it was not a disappointment to us. In any case, there should be no disappointments when we are His. I doubt if I will fly again and I am quite at rest about that. He has other things in store for me."[10] Steve plunged into the task of home secretary of MAF-UK, giving visibility to the ongoing work through his many deputation trips.

Alistair and Margaret Macdonald

Alistair and Margaret Macdonald were also part of the Sudan team. Alistair worked briefly with Stuart and Steve in Khartoum in 1952. He had served as a World War II Royal Navy Aircraft Engineer Officer, then spent two years in Southeast Asia, where he met Margaret Alldridge, an American national working in Thailand.[11] They married and headed for Borneo for service with the Borneo Evangelical Mission, using a Piper "Pacer" that an American missionary doctor had donated. In 1954 the Macdonalds flew the Pacer to the Sudan for service there.

In the Sudan, many emergency medical flights were carried out in mid-April 1954. Flights were frequent and unpredictable. One run was to Akobo to assist a missionary wife who needed hospitalization at Malakal. A few days later a missionary wife at Doro had to be taken to Khartoum, some five hundred miles distant, for a blood transfusion.

Just when they were exceptionally busy carrying out vital transport work, calamity struck. A freak wind and rainstorm hit Malakal on April 20, ripping the Pacer and Rapide off their tie-downs and sending them crashing nearby. The Pacer was blown over onto its back, its tubular steel structure broken and bent. Marshall's report on the twin-engine Rapide is remarkable:

> The Rapide was literally lifted into the air about seven feet and carried by the wind about 150 yards from the parking area towards the old control tower. As suddenly as the plane was lifted by the wind so it was dropped, still in the flying attitude, and neither wing tips had touched the ground. The real damage was caused by the impact when the plane dropped to the ground very close to the control tower. The two heavy engines mounted forward of the wings tore the rear engine mountings right out of the rear spars and also damaged the main spars.[12]

The Rapide was repaired and Alistair Macdonald flew it to Uganda, where it was sold. MAF-UK was now out of operation until a replacement could be found for at least one of the planes. SIM was particularly hard hit by this turn of events. It was the onset of the rainy season, and their need for transportation was especially acute. Mission leaders quickly extended a loan to MAF-UK for purchase of a replacement. In a short while SIM canceled the debt, making the plane an outright gift—a frank recognition of the fact that air service assisted their missionaries significantly.[13]

Insurance coverage on the Pacer helped pay for the Rapide's replacement. Some additional income came when the company that sold MAF-UK the third Rapide also purchased the damaged planes. Within three months, MAF-UK was back in the air.

This latest experience demonstrated that getting a hangar as soon as possible was a must. This meant establishing a permanent operational base with office and shop facilities. All signs pointed to Malakal, the communication and transport hub of southern Sudan, as the logical place to base the aircraft.

Alistair located a hangar that was for sale at Wadi Halfa, an RAF "Blister" type. It was purchased, dismantled, and sent by rail and river steamer some eight hundred miles to Malakal. Home sites were purchased, and Stuart King was instrumental in ordering prefabricated "Kingstrand" metal homes from England.

Stuart put together two films, *Operation Sudan* and *The Struggle Against the Swamps*, which Steve Stevens used to win friends and prayer partners for MAF-UK.[14]

The American Connection

Gordon Marshall's life was moving forward in good MAF fashion. He was the last to remain a bachelor—but not for long. On the field he met a talented second-generation Sudan missionary, Jean Maxwell, whose parents served with the American Mission. She was a Wheaton College graduate and a nurse who had served in the Sudan since 1947.[15] The two were married in 1954. This meant that three MAF-UK men—King, Macdonald, and Marshall—were married to American missionaries.

When MAF-UK cut its ties with the Movement for World Evangelization, much discussion ensued on the possibilities of their merging with MAF-US.[16] Steve Stevens proposed that joining forces would avoid unnecessary duplication, bring about standardization, and centralize planning for surveys and service.

Grady Parrott was cautious about any such merger. Bringing two organizations of differing national and cultural outlook into one operation could prove difficult. Grady believed that even if the British and American MAFs merged, there would still be the need for regionally managed programs.

Standardization of equipment might be easier to achieve than uniform operating policies. Grady felt the question of differences in philosophy should be considered first, to see if there was a sufficient basis for harmony. Without full agreement, he foresaw the risk of disaffection and disharmony. While he was not opposed to an eventual merger, Grady certainly did not want any part in a move that might be construed as MAF-US aggrandizement.

Murray Kendon, who had not been in touch with the thinking of the British but had met Grady in Melbourne, now entered the discussion on merger. Murray contended that the existing separate branches should continue to operate autonomously but be linked by a coordinating council to determine common flight and operating policies. He believed "God had raised up the work simultaneously to guard against only an American headquarters."[17] He felt that such a merger would be detrimental to MAF as a whole because there would be a lessening of interest in the other countries, where an attitude of "let the Americans do it" might prevail. Further official merger talks were held in abeyance until the Kings took their furlough in California the summer of 1954.

By that summer the Parrotts had moved to the newly acquired but by no means completed headquarters complex in Fullerton. The Truxtons were surveying the flight needs of Brazil, and the Mellises were in New Guinea, expanding the work into what today is Irian Jaya, Indonesia. Betty Greene assisted at MAF's Fullerton office. She had served two years with SIM in Nigeria and would be leaving for the Sudan in 1956. Given this global exchange of personnel, it was only fitting that the Kings should visit Fullerton.

During this visit, Grady and Stuart took measure of each other. They were kindred spirits who shared the same vision. The difficulties of financing the work in the Sudan prompted Stuart to press the proposed merger of the two transatlantic organizations. Grady gave it a warm but cautious reception. The extended discussions proved to be important in cementing relations between the sister organizations and led to the standardization of equipment but not of their flight policies. The encounter opened the way for the flow of American equipment, personnel, and money to assist MAF-UK in Africa. Since MAF-UK served mostly American missionaries, Grady encouraged American missions to support MAF-UK. These

Stuart and Phyllis King with their children, John and Rebecca, stand in front of MAF-UK's first Cessna 180, in which they flew to Malakal, Sudan, 1957.

missionaries appreciated MAF-UK and encouraged their constituencies at home to make donations to MAF-UK. This financial strategy brought in needed revenue and substantially reduced the pressure for merger.[18]

Since the MAF-US/MAF-UK connection led to standardization of equipment in 1956, MAF-UK ordered its first single-engine Cessna 180 from Fullerton at a 20 percent discount. For all-around performance in the Sudan, this plane was superior to anything available in Britain at the time.

Service in Ethiopia

Opportunities for wider service now loomed on the horizon. The Rapide received permission to make its first cross-border flight to an Ethiopian mission station in March 1954.[19] The Ethiopian government extended most generous terms. There were absolutely no restrictions on frequency of flight or need for prior approval. MAF-UK could fly to selected airfields as often as desired, the only requirement being the clearing of customs. Some twenty-five missionaries were flown across the border in the first three months.[20]

This was a significant development because of the geographic realities involved. Southwestern Ethiopia was much more accessible from the valley of the White Nile than from the Ethiopian interior. Rugged terrain and totally inadequate surface transportation made western Ethiopia virtually inaccessible overland. Opening the southwestern border to allow air transport to new mission stations was an important breakthrough.

Harvey and Lavina Hoekstra were then working with the American Mission in the Sudan at Akobo as Bible translators among the Anuak. In those days, only very poor surface travel existed in the Ethiopia-Sudan border region. To reach the Abyssinian highlands, one had to detour hundreds of miles to catch a ferry across a tributary of the White Nile. The country was filled with thorny bushes that punctured automobile tires. To repair a flat tire once, Harvey and his fellow missionary shot a zebra and used its hide in place of an inner tube.

At Akobo, where four missionary families were serving, Harvey calculated that the plane had saved them travel time equivalent to one missionary's lifetime of field service. Many qualitative aspects of life were enhanced as well. The arrival of the plane broke long periods of isolation for those living on remote mission stations. Mail service improved, to say nothing of having regular contact with the pilot, who was in touch with the outside world and other mission stations. If there was a medical emergency, help could be obtained quickly.

The plane helped transport missionary children, who first attended school in Alexandria, Egypt, and later at SIM's Bingham Academy in Addis Ababa. In the pre-MAF days travel to or from school in Egypt was a two-week adventure. This meant that missionaries were separated from their school-age children for nine months each year. Once MAF service was established, travel time was greatly reduced, which made it possible for children and parents to be reunited for Christmas.

As a result of flying with Gordon Marshall, Betty Greene, and Ernie Krenzin, young Denny Hoekstra was inspired to pursue flight training to serve with MAF. In 1967 Marshall checked out Denny in preparation for his flight work in Ethiopia. Denny proved himself a skilled and dedicated MAF flier who went on to become the MAF-US manager of flight training.

Lemuel Tew, an Ethiopian Airlines captain, first learned of MAF when the pilots occasionally requested him to relay their position to Khartoum or Addis Ababa when the aircraft was scheduled to be at one of the Ethiopian towns near the border.

One day on a flight to Asosa, he learned that Macdonald and Marshall would be touching down there. Tew decided to meet them and waited for the Rapide to touch down. He left this recollection:

The airport at Asosa was grass surface, but very rough and crisscrossed by several trails eroded by the feet of sheep, goats, cattle, etc. as they crossed the strip. Landing there in the DC-3 was a bone-jarring experience, and I always felt that the plane was taking a terrible beating. When the Rapide landed it crossed one of these animal trails soon after touchdown, and the tail-skid was broken completely off by the impact. The pilot taxied in to park the plane while dragging the rear of the fuselage on the ground.

I was concerned that they might be stuck there for several days waiting to be rescued, but I remember Alistair saying that if he just had a saw, hammer and two-by-four he could make a temporary repair in just a short time. The Greek merchant who had a store in the village sent a runner who returned in a few minutes with a handsaw, hammer, and a two-by-four, just what Alistair requested for making the temporary repair.[21]

We may assume that this was not a daily experience. One does, however, get the picture that these pilots were rather ingenious and knew how to cope with the unexpected.

Betty Greene in the Sudan

In 1955 Stuart King's immediate need in the Sudan was for additional pilots. Grady Parrott suggested Betty Greene. She seemed to be a logical choice from the standpoint of experience. She had flown in Mexico, Peru, and Nigeria. Her executive committee and board experience qualified her to share insights that might be useful to MAF-UK. Grady asked Betty how she felt about service in the Sudan. She expressed definite interest.

It must be remembered that the Sudan was a Muslim country in the process of gaining independence. For MAF-UK to seek approval for a woman pilot seemed the height of folly. Beryl Markham of England and probably other women pilots in the 1930s had to receive legislative approval just to fly through the Sudan en route to England. A request for a woman to be given standing as a pilot in the Sudan, even in the 1950s, flew in the face of long-established Muslim roles for men and women. Given the alternative of having a woman pilot or not having one at all, Stuart King bit the bullet.[22]

Placing Betty's application for a license before the Civil Aviation Department was no routine matter. The law stating that no woman shall fly over Sudan had stood for decades. It required an act of Parliament to receive permission.

After a considerable lapse of time, Stuart visited the department office to find out the status of the application. The director met him and, with a big smile, announced, "The permission for the lady pilot is granted!"[23] This was a direct and wonderful answer to prayer.

Circumstances were also favorable. Stuart said that he did not know all the factors the Lord had used in moving the government to grant this permission. He did know that there was an emergency in the country with uprisings in the South against the government in Khartoum. He surmised that the government wanted as many pilots as possible available during this period of instability. The Sudan had very few pilots at the time, so each person who could fly was considered an asset. What was interesting to Stuart was that the government had moved away from its conservative stance that had persisted for so many years.[24]

Civil unrest in the South led to the suspension of all MAF flights in the fall. Betty's entry into the Sudan was delayed several months until the spring of 1956, not only because of Sudan's internal problem but because of the increased load at Fullerton due to the Auca slayings. In the meantime, Betty asked Stuart to send her a Rapide operational manual so she could study how this flying machine worked. Then she wanted to be sure that MAF-UK was not going to inconvenience their personnel in order to cushion her against any unpleasant field realities. In her words, "When you think of me fitting into the life and program there in the Sudan remember that I want to be one with you in your way of doing things. I don't want any 'special' treatment. It will be pure joy to be there working with you under the Lord's gracious leading—the outworking of His will is the only 'special' treatment I want."[25]

With the new year an independent Sudan took its place among the nations. The first day of 1956, a new flag rose over the banks of the White Nile in Malakal. Instead of the British Union Jack and the Egyptian flag fluttering side by side as symbols of joint control, there was a single flag of blue, yellow, and green. The colors symbolized blue for the Nile, yellow for the arid lands, and green for the forested uplands to the south and east, as well as the extensive agricultural irrigation project at Gezira.

Betty arrived in Khartoum the first week of May. Gordon Marshall took her on familiarization flights to nearby mission stations. In the meantime, she prepared herself for flight qualifying exams. She only needed to pass the aviation law and technical exams. When she had crossed these hurdles, she quickly worked herself into flying the Rapide.

What was it like to fly in this new setting? It was no picnic, but Betty loved the vast open spaces of the semiarid landscape. One full day's work for her, as recorded in her journal, looked like this:

Took off from Malakal at 6:30 a.m. with the Webb children—full load. A huge storm lined our course as we flew East to the Mission Station of Nasir . . . in rain a short while. Radio worked perfectly. Gordon Marshall looked over the Nasir airstrip carefully and decided it was dry enough for safe landing . . . landed. Webbs were glad to see their children [back from boarding school. Surface travel for them used to take three weeks—now a matter of hours by air]. On taxying out at the turn-around point, the Rapide sank into the "dry mud" of cotton soil. I was especially glad to see what could happen . . . wouldn't have believed it otherwise. Five of us finally got away. Flew to Gambela . . . took off and crossed into Ethiopia

and landed in tall grass at Dembidollo. . . . Picked up passengers—
customs inspected luggage. When we were ready for take-off we
saw a herd of cattle meander across the airstrip. Missionary Ken
Radach chased them in his jeep. Landed at Doro. . . . canceled return
flight to Malakal that day due to slight engine trouble.[26]

The Sudanese government's more liberal flight policies and
MAF's proven safety record led to the lifting of restrictions on use
of single-engine planes. Permission to use transceivers for air-to-
ground and station-to-station communication was also forth-
coming. Both of these were extremely important. The twin-engine
Rapide consumed a great deal of fuel, and without ground-to-air
contact, many futile trips were made when preplanned flights later
proved unnecessary or weather conditions at certain stations made
landings unsafe. The lifting of these flight restrictions greatly
improved the efficiency of the MAF-UK Sudan operation.[27]

Back in London Steve Stevens determined that the Holiday Crusade in Yorkshire, held in the middle of September 1956, was a
great opportunity to inform his countrymen about the missionary
sacrifices in Ecuador through a photographic display. Although
the story of the five slain Ecuadorian missionaries had been well
publicized in the United States, the British public was only faintly
aware of these events. Truxton saw to it that Steve received enlarge-
ments of Nate Saint's shots taken on "Palm Beach" on that fateful
weekend.[28]

For MAF-UK, 1956 was a turning point. They had seen years of
almost unbearable hardships but did not abandon the vision. In
becoming an independent organization and then developing a
close working relationship with MAF-US, they were able to gain
much-needed support in personnel and equipment. Betty Greene
joined the work as pilot. She carried over her American financial
support. In December MAF-UK received an unexpected Christmas gift. Sudan missionary Harvey Hoekstra, who served with
the American Mission and had close ties with friends in the
Reformed Church, was on furlough in Michigan. One of these
friends was vitally interested in MAF-UK maintaining continuous service in the Sudan. He was aware that having only one plane
made the lifeline in the Sudan vulnerable. On December 15, while

King was in London assembling the first Cessna 180 from Fullerton, he received a telephone call from Harvey saying that a friend of MAF had donated a 1954 Cessna 180.[29] When Harvey asked who should be designated the receiving and sending agent, Stuart immediately volunteered MAF-US. Stuart then wrote Grady, "I hope this is O.K.?" Mellis replied in the affirmative and added, "We can't get over rejoicing about this wonderful provision."[30]

As an independent agency, MAF-UK had many organizational and financial hurdles yet to cross, but they were not alone. The walk of faith led them to greater reliance on MAF-US. This relationship opened many doors to future collaboration and support that proved to be extremely strategic in the turbulent 1960s, when independence movements swept through Africa and Asia.

The Challenge of Brazil

The country of Brazil was Jim and Betty Truxton's challenge from 1954 to 1960. The possibilities of MAF-US assisting with frontier missions there, similar to what it was doing in New Guinea, appeared excellent. However, a series of unexpected diplomatic and political problems unfolded that turned this missions dream into a nightmare.

Prospects for MAF-US taking a close look at this field first appeared as a result of Truxton's interaction with the leadership of the Latin American Council of Presbyterian Missions USA during their conference at Medellín in August 1949. Truxton and Lowrance were working on the Colombia survey then. The Presbyterian USA leaders were satisfied with MAF's operation in Tabasco and recommended bringing MAF to Brazil for a flight survey.[1]

This vast country, larger than the continental United States, turned out to be difficult to assess. A single survey could not encompass the whole of Brazil. The Truxtons therefore moved from region to region, feeling the pulse of missions, conferring with Christian leaders, meeting with missionaries at their annual meetings wherever possible, and then making an assessment of what MAF-US could offer. Almost two years were consumed in this process. By the time the Truxtons finished the survey, they had visited all the areas served by the Unevangelized Fields Mission, Conservative Baptist Foreign Mission Society, Baptist Mid-Missions, American Baptists for World Evangelization, Presbyterians (USA), and the South American Indian Mission.

206

Jim found no single plan to meet Brazil's varied aviation needs. Instead, a number of plans were implemented to address varied circumstances. Jim found that a few forward-looking missionaries had their own planes. Given this reality, a cooperative MAF program hardly seemed the wave of the future. These pilot missionaries suggested the idea of a maintenance center where planes could be given major overhauls and pilots instructed in proper maintenance and flight safety. Anápolis in Goias province, a moderate-sized city near Brasília, was chosen as the site for the MAF maintenance center. It was suitable because of its central location and accessibility. It had air transport from the north, south, and west and also had connections by railroad. Anápolis was also the home of a Bible Institute and college sponsored by several denominations, including the United Evangelical Brethren and Evangelical Union of South America. The city's elevation of three thousand feet gave it a healthful climate.[2]

Harold and Elsie Berk went to Brazil in 1955 to get the Anápolis maintenance center started. They were joined by Paul and Jackie Lewis in 1957. Over the years that work became part of Brazil's indigenous MAF operating under the name *Asas de Socorro*, meaning "Wings of Mercy" in Portuguese. The work has expanded to two other locations: Eirunepe in Amazonas province and Boa Vista in Roraima.

Directly to the west of Goias province lay the frontier province of Mato Grosso, plateau country that stretches north to the rain forest of the Amazon basin. Here the South American Indian Mission (SAIM) and Presbyterian Church (USA) carried on their work. Jim and Darlene Lomheim came from Mexico in 1957 to meet the flight needs there.

The SAIM wanted an air arm to facilitate its work among the Indians. It so happened that Jack Wyrtzen and a St. Louis businessman promised the money for an aerial survey on condition that MAF carried it out.[3] This left Ernie Lubkeman and their other leaders very little choice, but they fortunately warmed to both the idea of an MAF survey and Jim Truxton.

Jim recognized the need for a communication network and made strategic contact with government officials upon getting back to Rio and São Paulo. At that time Brasília, the new capital, was not yet fully operational. Getting certification for MAF pilots and permission to set up a communication network were difficult problems that took some years to resolve.

There were also calls from the extreme northern Rio Branco province (now Roraima), where Baptist Mid-Missions and UFM were open to cooperation with MAF. Neill Hawkins of the Unevangelized Fields Mission (UFM) made a strong case in his bid to secure MAF's help. The mission was just starting work among the Wai-Wai people across the border in Guyana (then British Guiana) and had purchased a tract of land in Brazil west of Lethem, in the upper reaches of the Rio Branco River.[4]

Since the Wai-Wai lived on both sides of the Brazil-Guyana boundary, Hawkins crossed the boundary freely. Kaneshen, the main Wai-Wai center, was in Guyana, but the advance UFM base, Bon Fim, which eventually became the MAF base, was just across the border in Brazil. There was an international boundary separating the two locations, but the geographic proximity of Kaneshen and Bon Fim led the missions to underestimate the possibility of a diplomatic crisis.

Cross-Border Flights

In the process of developing this work, Hawkins had moved supplies and equipment, including a Jeep, across to Brazil without having them registered in Brazil.[5] This was not only the case with the UFM but also for the Pilgrim Holiness mission that flew an American registered Tri-Pacer across the border into Brazil on a regular basis.

Neill Hawkins urged Jim Truxton to do the same for the PA-14 so it could be used for survey purposes.[6] Sargento Pessoa, agent of the Department of Aeronautics in Boa Vista, a Christian, approved cross-border flights of American-registered mission-owned planes, provided he was fully informed beforehand. Jim had some misgivings about the practice and requested that Pessoa gain clearance from Rio, which came in the form of a telegram. Any question about the advisability of cross-border flights appeared to be cleared up.

In the meantime the survey of the upper reaches of the Rio

Branco got underway. Jim Truxton, Jim Lomheim, and Harold Berk used the Brazil-registered Tri-Pacer that Lomheim and Berk had rebuilt at Campinas while studying Portuguese. Even though no planes could be imported, they had one in hand. The Tri-Pacer was outfitted with an auxiliary gas tank that gave the plane a maximum range of nine hundred miles. These surveys were conducted for both the UFM and Baptist Mid-Missions.

The "Lost" Wai-Wai

This survey was unusual in that Wai-Wai Christians were included as active participants. They were eager to reach out to their own people. Their chief, Elka, was the first to become a Christian and his turning to Christ led to the conversion of the entire tribe. This is one of the most remarkable stories in the annals of frontier missions and parallels what took place among the Dani people of Dutch New Guinea two years later.

Elka told of a situation some twenty years earlier when it was found that the surrounding region could not support the growing Wai-Wai population. The elders decided that half of the village should move to another location. In the course of time Elka's people at Kaneshen were unable to locate these dispersed relatives. He realized that the airplane might be able to spot them, even though his ground parties had not been able to. Neill Hawkins agreed to have UFM pay for several search flights to locate this "lost tribe."

During the first flight in Guyana up the headwaters of the New River, Hobey Lowrance and Jim Truxton found overgrown clearings that gave mute testimony of a previous Wai-Wai settlement. This was disappointing, and Elka thought his people might have been attacked and dispersed or struck down by disease.[7]

On the second flight they reached the headwaters of the Cafuine. There they spotted a village with smoke curling into the sky. The Wai-Wai leader who accompanied them became very excited when he saw the familiar village settlement pattern and recognized the distinctive Wai-Wai house types. The plane circled over the village and made gift drops.

For the return flight Jim prepared jars of paint to be hurled onto the rocks in the river to serve as markers for future overland expeditions. These became the means whereby the Wai-Wai were later located.

As things were then, the Indians camouflaged the trail junction with the river to protect themselves against possible enemy attack. As planned, Jim dropped a quart jar of yellow paint on the rocks one mile below the trail-head to guide the ground party. At each tributary he and Hobey repeated this procedure. Hobey would swoop down and Jim would toss the paint jars onto the rocks below.

When the Wai-Wai organized an overland expedition to find their long-lost cousins, they followed these signposts all the way to the village. As they approached the village the dogs began barking. The villagers, fearing a hostile attack, scattered in all directions. When the visitors called out in the Wai-Wai tongue, the fleeing tribesmen recognized their own and returned to the village. The result was a joyous reunion. The visitors invited their Wai-Wai cousins to come to Kaneshen (which means "God loves you") to celebrate there together. Many heard the message of God's love that their relatives shared freely, and many became Christians.

Jim and Hobey considered the Wai-Wai search one of their most rewarding experiences. As a Christian chief, Elka was able to show his people the way to God. "Being found" had a profound impact on these people and made for an unforgettable Wai-Wai family reunion.

Opening the Rio Branco Missions Frontier

In the next five survey flights, Jim Truxton flew out of Boa Vista, Brazil, where he stayed with Harold Burns. These surveys with Burns and Neill Hawkins yielded significant new information on Indian settlements. In the survey flights with Burns to the headwaters of the Mucajai and Parima rivers, they located Indians who built their homes on the ridge tops and planted gardens on steep mountain slopes. Jim took Neill up the Caura, where they found houses of the Maquiritari people that Hobey and he had seen on the earlier Venezuela survey. Jim described the scene this way:

These houses are exceptionally well built, and even have a venti-
lation flap that can open and close upon the roof for letting out
smoke. Some houses had as many as ten entrances. Explorers who
have passed through here in previous days reported that each door
enters into the part of the house used by one family. Some are ten
family houses. The Indians usually came out and waved at us in a
very friendly manner. Wherever we saw people we dropped gifts
of fish hooks on the end of a long streamer—dropped into one of
their large garden clearings.[8]

Both Burns and Neill Hawkins now had the information they
needed to plan expeditions north and west on the Rio Branco's
tributaries.

Eldon and Sylvia Larson were the next MAF-US family to move
to Brazil. They helped launch UFM expeditions in the upper tributaries of the Rio Branco to reach the people who had been located
in aerial surveys. The couple had their initial field experience
working with the Hatchers in Chiapas.

With the Larsons' arrival, a major advance was launched up the
Uraricoera River. The PA-14 enabled a motorboat expedition to ply
its way upstream without carrying everything needed to settle in
the wilderness. Heretofore, upriver parties had loaded down their
canoes, but Larson's air drops solved this problem. He flew ahead
of the river party, dropping tin cans of fuel into the stream. Since
gasoline is lighter than water, the cans floated and could be plucked
from the river. Food and other supplies were likewise flown to the
advance party. The plane revolutionized the work of frontier missions in South America, as it did in New Guinea and Ethiopia.

The matter of plane importation weighed heavily on Jim Truxton's mind because without additional planes, progress would be
slow. Fortunately he found out that it was possible to import a
plane directly as a nonprofit organization.[9] This made it possible
for the existing mission organizations to import planes but not for
MAF to hold them as a corporation. Jim did not consider this
arrangement satisfactory for the long run and worked to bring
about the incorporation of *Asas de Socorro*. Jim Lomheim was put
in charge of the project and retained a Brazilian attorney to seek
incorporation. The project was bogged down in the requirement

that at least two-thirds of the directors had to be Brazilian citizens. Jim could not, at that stage of development, turn over the entire MAF Brazilian operation to untried hands.

A Series of Setbacks

As for the ongoing Guyana-Brazil cross-border flights, as long as a sympathetic official held the civil aviation post at Boa Vista, everything was fine. That lasted until the coming of Mr. Naronha in early 1959, who, to begin with, was unhappy with his assignment to this frontier outpost. Naronha enforced the letter of the Brazilian law. Cross-border flights of U.S. registered planes from Lethem, Guyana, to Bon Fim or Boa Vista were suddenly prohibited. The UFM mission station at Bon Fim itself was now considered illegal because it violated an old statute forbidding foreigners from living within eighteen miles of the border.[10]

This sudden enforcement of an old statute proved troublesome to MAF because the Northern Brazil program was premised on developing Bon Fim as a strategic base that could serve the Wai-Wai in Guyana as well as in Brazil. If this could not be achieved, then two planes and two pilots had to be assembled for separate basing or the program in one of these countries discontinued.

By this time, the base had been developed substantially, with a landing strip, hangar, and apartment in place. Plans were also in preparation to have Drs. Frank Davis and Charles Patton serve the missionary and Indian medical needs on the bases to which MAF gave logistical support.

Neill Hawkins and Jim Truxton were not fully aware of the possible legal and political fallout of their desire to retain one central base to serve both sides of the border. They misjudged the consequences of bringing the PA-14 to Bon Fim for overnight hangarage.

The third week of April 1959, when Berk made a cross-border flight to Boa Vista and flew the plane to Bon Fim (meaning "good end") for hangarage, the Brazilian authorities grounded the plane and suspended flights to UFM stations.[11] The hangarage of the plane at Bon Fim was the reason given for the grounding. Berk hoped the plane would be released in a few days, but the orders were for an indefinite suspension.

Norm Olson refueling in northeast Brazil, 1960.

This action was only a prelude to a campaign to malign the broader missionary effort in Brazil. Unfortunately Neill Hawkins and Jim Truxton had been virtually oblivious to the potential seriousness of continued cross-border flying. When the grounding took place, Neill was on the field, so he had direct access to the government. Truxton was in Fullerton and did not have the same sense of impending trouble.

This situation meant that new stations in the upper reaches of the Rio Branco were left without resupply. Weeks passed without any indication that the suspension would be lifted. Hawkins and Lomheim went to Rio to speak with authorities and see what needed to be done to reinstate the flights. They were totally helpless in the face of this government order.

Not until eight weeks after the grounding were Harold Berk and Norm Olson of MAF able to fly north in the Brazilian-registered Pacer to see the missionaries in the highland stations. Their supplies were low, but all were well. Meanwhile, the PA-14 remained in official custody.

Failure to resolve this dilemma brought uncertainty about the future of MAF-US plans for Brazil. The beginning of a round of what Mary Hawkins, Neill's wife, called "journalistic persecution" showed that it was not simply a question of cross-border flights. The newspapers began printing charges that the cross-border flights were part of clandestine mission mining operations in the jungles. Accusations were made that the missionaries were really there to despoil the country of its resources.[12]

Truxton found that this was not just radical journalism. The Department of Civil Aeronautics had, in fact, stated these charges in grounding the plane. This put an entirely different light on the episode. The papers continued to scream accusations. For instance, a Forteleza city newspaper published a picture of a twin-engine plane (not the MAF PA-14) that allegedly was used for illegal cross-border runs. Another of the Bon Fim base depicted it as the alleged center of the foreigners' conspiracy. These photos were held up as *prima facie* evidence of illegal mining operations and contraband running.[13]

Given this serious state of affairs, the Truxtons returned to Brazil to see how the truth might best be brought to light. Neill and Mary Hawkins and Jim and Betty Truxton moved to Rio where they rented an apartment to facilitate contact with congressmen, officials in the Department of Civil Aviation and the Indian Protective Service. The latter had control over all outside contacts with Brazil's indigenous peoples.

Jim's perspective was that the picture was "as ugly and black as it could be—but for God!" His assessment was that MAF could be thankful that the opposition had "so extravagantly overplayed its hand that fair-minded, liberal thinking Brazilians were bound to see this."[14] Neill and Jim's efforts began to pay dividends as they got to know some of the Christian congressmen.

Worst of all, the plane incident closed down progress on many fronts. The move to incorporate *Asas de Socorro* came to a full stop, and permission for opening new mission stations and setting up a radio communication network for MAF service seemed impossible to secure.

Assistance from members of Brazil's House of Representatives (Camara) led to Brazil's Security Council making a full-fledged investigation. Even as this was going forward, left-leaning papers such as Rio de Janeiro's *O Seminario* churned out fabrications about the "Yankee invasion."[15] There were allegations of illegal border runs that lent color to the notion that MAF violated Brazil's interests. This venomous editorial caused Jim Truxton to reflect that perhaps the missionaries and MAF personnel were not identifying as closely with the people as they should.

Jim did not shrug off the recent trials in Brazil but wanted to know what the Lord was teaching him and the entire MAF-US organization through this crisis. As a barometer of how he and other MAF personnel were relating to the local population, he wrote: "Maybe it would be a bit of a shock to some of us if we asked ourselves when we last ate in the home of a national, or did more than simply greet him with a passing word or smile on the street. When did we last seek out his counsel on some needed matter of understanding about his country or customs, pray with him, or seek him to pray with us over some problem or concern?" He ended by saying, "*O Seminario* has at least given us much food for thought and self-examination as to our actual relationship to the people to whom we have gone with the Gospel of our Lord."[16]

In the meantime MAF personnel had to drink from the bitter cup of uncertainty about the future of the Brazilian program. Even while waiting for the outcome of the investigation, Jim Truxton and Neill Hawkins took immediate steps to close down Bon Fim and moved the base of operation inland to Boa Vista. They separated the British Guyana and Brazilian operations to eliminate any further charges of illegal cross-border runs.

A Fair Review

This diplomatic nightmare dragged on for nine months. In early 1960 Jim received word of the results of the Security Council investigation. To get to the bottom of the allegations, high Rio officials went to see the Indian mission stations firsthand. Here they saw dedicated UFM missionaries in Rio Branco province and recognized that the rumors of large planes landing on jungle airstrips were patently false. These strips could not land planes larger than MAF's single-engine craft. The good work that the missionaries did with the natives also came to light, as did the need for radio communication between MAF planes and the jungle stations.

In the end, MAF-US was totally and completely exonerated. That was sweet vindication, indeed, especially for the Truxtons, Berks, and Hawkinses, whose integrity had been questioned. Equally encouraging was the fact that the new Rio Branco territorial governor came to see the need for shortwave radio transmission in order for isolated native settlements to be able to call for emergency help. The governor's support was instrumental in Jim getting what he had long hoped for—permission to operate a frontier communication network. Before it was all over, even Mr. Naronha, who had ordered the grounding of the PA-14, became a Christian.

Thus the Lord used these very trying experiences to further his work. It was clear that no one but God could take credit for the resurrection of the MAF Brazil program. As a result of this experience all the missionaries and MAF personnel were made much more aware that they were dependent upon the Lord to shield them, and that missionaries were guests in a foreign land.

As for the separation of the Brazil and Guyana work, it was decided to move Roy and Katie Parsons to Guyana, although they were flying in Ecuador with the Derrs and Keenans.

Jim wrote Roy, "I would not blame you at all for being quite discouraged with what awaits you in Lethem—principally in that almost nothing awaits you, materially speaking." Since they would be serving the Wai-Wai center at Kaneshen, Jim could only encourage them with the prospect of meeting a remarkable people: "You'll be thrilled when you see the thriving native church," he wrote, "and meet the fine Christian chief, Elka, and the Wai-Wai deacons!"[17]

This Guyana operation was fairly limited at the outset but had potential for growth, especially if the Pilgrim Holiness group turned over their flight work to MAF. The Parsons did not have to be concerned about prejudice against MAF, inasmuch as Neill and Bob Hawkins had built bridges of goodwill to the British administration. MAF was coming on the coattails of this work and only needed to maintain this good reputation for hearty cooperation.

Flight Policy Reassessment

The diplomatic problems that MAF-US faced in Brazil led Trux-ton and Neill Hawkins to review the entire subject of diplomacy and mission service. Several recent incidents showed that MAF pilots routinely encountered diplomatic problems.

Earlier that summer Jim Lomheim received a request from one of President Kubitschek's pilots to fly him to Waica, an interior UFM station. The captain explained that he was on a secret mission for the Department of Justice and could not get a regular taxi plane to fly him. The question was whether Lomheim should fly the pilot. The request was fraught with difficulty because if Lomheim flew him without verifying his identity, he could be transporting a criminal and become an accessory to a crime.

Lomheim called the governor of the province to verify the captain's credentials. The governor had no knowledge of the pilot or any secret government mission and was surprised that a foreign organization would be called on to carry out such a request. That was enough information for Lomheim. He turned down the pilot's request.

The captain was outraged on being refused transport and having his credibility questioned. He contacted Naronha, the Department of Civil Aeronautics official at Boa Vista who had grounded the MAF plane and gave orders to harass Lomheim. This came at a time when the PA-14 was still grounded and the problems were still mounting.

Hawkins felt that had Lomheim not asked so many questions, there would have been an earlier resolution of the grounding. On the other hand, if the captain had turned out to be an imposter, there might have been even greater repercussions. MAF pilots had to be as wise as serpents but harmless as doves!

Another concern arose in the mining district of Rio Branco province. Prospectors made their way into the frontier and, on occasion, asked to be flown out. Harold Berk, who had to deal with this reality, routinely refused them transportation unless there was illness or injury.

On one occasion Berk flew Flo Reedley, a missionary nurse, to Mucajai. Immediately he was confronted by a man named Isaias who claimed to be ill and wanted to be flown out. Berk asked him to see the nurse for medical help. With that, Isaias's companion walked up to the plane twirling a pistol and, with that implied threat, ordered Berk to fly out Isaias. In this case, Berk complied, but under duress. The question was whether MAF pilots should, as a matter of principle, refuse transportation to such men. The fear was that if it became known that the pilots gave such persons free transportation, they would not be able to refuse anyone. The assumption was that the pilots would find themselves taken advantage of once they opened the door. Hawkins countered by arguing that MAF should not adopt this stance until there was a history of such abuse. It would appear that MAF was callous in flying out empty when the plane had plenty of space.

Jim Truxton thought it would be worth the risk to give rides to individuals who were in serious need of transportation. If abuse resulted, future service could be restricted.[18]

These situations point out the complexity and variety of circumstances that MAF faced in routine flight work. The diplomatic and legal entanglements that MAF-US faced in Brazil were unusual, but the introduction of MAF service generally created some uneasiness in nearly all foreign countries. To have foreigners criss-crossing the sky in planes and operating their own communication equipment might be expected to raise questions in the minds of a country's leaders. Since MAF had no hidden agenda, it was usually only a matter of time until such fears were allayed.

Ultimately trust in MAF reflected on the trustworthiness of its message. As UFM and MAF demonstrated in reaching out to the Wai-Wai, this message was at the heart of the missionary enterprise. The legal difficulties that developed in Brazil could be attributed in part to the zeal of frontier missions. To be sure, there were mixed signals on the part of Brazilian officials. Not to be forgotten in such retrospective reflection is the work of Satan, who is always there to exploit difficult circumstances, regardless of how they came about. He invariably exacerbates difficult situations to discredit God's work. A lesson from the unfolding story in Brazil is that Satan's fiery darts hit his target, and people do get hurt. At such times, it is important that believers don't turn against one another in recrimination but join hands in support of each other.

Joining Hands to Reach
New Guinea's Interior

Our story to this point has followed the work of the separate MAF wings, acquainting us with the early history and distinctives of each organization. However, as we observe the character of MAF, its bent toward cooperative efforts is evident. We
have already delved into the close collaboration between Americans and Australians and traced a parallel good relationship
between MAF-UK and MAF-US. To appreciate this spirit of
mutual support and other characteristics of the MAF organizations, we must transcend geographic boundaries and look at their
joint accomplishments. This chapter will focus on MAF's cooperative efforts in the entire New Guinea theater of operations.

In their service to missions, MAF provided a lifeline for stations
"built in advance" of air transport, such as in the Ecuadorian rain
forest. Flight service also opened up virgin territory in New
Guinea, as in the case of Bokondini and Tari. Bokondini initially
was made accessible to missionaries as a result of floatplane landings on Lake Archbold. No one lived here, but the lake landing
allowed access to the populated Bokondini valley. To get a strip
built at Bokondini, the Pacer air-dropped tools, including dismantled wheelbarrows, to the missionaries. The nationals were
willing to work in exchange for seashells and colored beads—their
going currency. Similarly, at Tari, MAF worked with Len Twyman
of UFM to develop a new outpost. On the Green River in the Sepik
basin, MAF helped Kay Liddle open up new territory. Such mission advances were repeated time and again.

Once a series of stations had been planted, they continued to be in need of air transport, since the ruggedness of the terrain and the general tropical conditions of the country prevented road networks from being built. Given the limited resources of mission organizations, the cooperation and support of MAF was virtually essential for any advance into this virgin territory and keeping the stations supplied.

Founding of Missionary Air Service

By mid-1954 over a dozen mission stations were strung out on an east-west axis in the Territory of New Guinea highlands. Since an ever-increasing number of inland stations needed transportation from Madang and Wewak, new strategies for greater efficiency were devised. Large commercial aircraft operated out of Madang, so an inland base was developed as a central distribution center for the highlands. The obvious advantage of an interior central base led to 1953 discussions about a cooperatively operated missionary air service to the western and southern highlands.[1] The Lutherans took the lead and sent pilot Ray Jaensch to Banz with one of the Madang planes to ship freight to surrounding strips three days a week. Within a year Bob Hutchins brought a Cessna full time to Banz. Banz proved to be a good location for predicting weather patterns, and it was much more centrally located than the Baiyer River station.

By the summer of 1954 the value of this operation proved itself, and an agreement was reached among the Lutheran Mission of New Guinea (U.S.), the New Guinea Lutheran Mission (Australia), the Australian Baptist Foreign Missions, and AMAF for a transport consortium under American supervision. Under the agreement, each of the parties supplied part of the needs for the highlands base. The Lutherans provided the plane; the Baptists the hangar, house, and store; MAF the furnishings for both the house and hangar and staffing for the service.

Vic Ambrose worked with the committee establishing the service and became the pilot for the program. He moved to Banz in September 1955, and from there expanded the service to the following missions: Baptists (Baiyer River), Methodists (Mendi, Tari),

A welcoming committee at Banz in the Territory of New Guinea. The gold lip shell around the neck indicates wealth.

UFM (Tari, Lake Kutubu, Erave), and East and West Indies Bible Mission (Pabrabruk). He had a Cessna 170 to cover the territory.[2]

After five months of operating this program, Ambrose was satisfied that the central base was "sound in conception and operation."[3] During this period there was a continuous rise in demand for the plane. He wrote Mellis:

> I have flown 330 hours in these five months and what is the situation as of this writing? In the shed are 8 loads for the valley here, 6 for Tari, and in addition two loads at Ogelbeng and 4 for Mendi. Trips are booked to Wau for Saturday, Mendi and Wewak on Tuesday; Erave, Kutubu and Tari tomorrow, all of which involve personnel, which means I do not reduce the cargo backlog.[4]

Ambrose was not complaining, nor was he worried about the backlog, but he did want to point out a trend that was likely to continue, since the missions were pouring additional personnel into the interior.

One of the inevitable by-products of the air service and other MAF operations was increased personal contact between missionaries of different denominations. Given the regional division of the work among mission agencies and denominations, each group normally worked independently. The air service committees representing MAF users brought together representatives of all the denominations being served, which opened channels of communication. Invariably, it led to the breaking down of barriers, as in Honduras, Sudan, and Ethiopia, that simply sprouted up in the absence of contact. Real and perceived differences sometimes kept denominations from participating in MAF. Mellis felt it was a most worthwhile goal to use the air service to get all the Protestant denominations to pull together.[5]

Cooperation led to the appreciation of the variety of Christian traditions. Vic Ambrose, for instance, was of the Plymouth Brethren, and Doug McCraw, AMAF's secretary, was an Anglican. Their backgrounds colored the way they viewed good management. Ambrose and Mellis stressed collegial relations and decisions by consensus. McCraw believed well-run organizations should have decisions handed down from the top. In this case, management style and honest differences with field personnel led to McCraw's resignation as secretary in June 1956. He later served effectively in New Guinea as a pilot. Whereas personality and denominational differences sometimes increased friction between individuals, the MAF cooperative flight service generally had the opposite effect. The quality of the MAF pilots had an elevating effect on the missionaries. Some of the denominations were more formal—their tradition did not embrace the evangelical fervor that characterized MAF leadership—and day-to-day contact led to greater all-around spiritual fervor.

Introducing the Cessna 180

The big news for the pilots in the summer of 1956 was the coming of the Cessna 180s. Compared to the 170s with their 145 horsepower, the 180s had 230 horsepower. The 180 could make rapid steep climbs into the highlands, which reduced flight time and increased load capacity. C&MA replaced their downed Sealand with two 180s; the Catholic Mission in Wewak also purchased one. Bob and Betty Hutchins, upon returning from their furlough at the end of September, found that Lake Avenue Congregational Church in Pasadena, their home church where Bob's father served as senior pastor, had decided to purchase a 180 for Bob. This single-engine hardworking plane, according to Ambrose, proved to be one of the most successful ever put into service in the Territory of New Guinea.

Reaching into the Fly River Region

As Ambrose was developing the highlands base, to the south in Papua, UFM was planting new mission stations in the lower reaches of the Fly River and its tributary, the Strickland. Mellis and Ambrose made a preliminary foray into the area in 1954. Two years later, with continued UFM expansion, that mission called on Ambrose for air service. In early October 1956, Ambrose, Charles Horne, and other UFM personnel launched a full-fledged survey.[6]

The day of the survey the skies were clear until about halfway between the mountains and the Strickland. The area showed evidence of scattered settlements with cultivated fields. As Ambrose and Horne approached the Strickland, they ran into rain clouds that forced them to drop to thirteen hundred feet. Heading south, they were in a region where "aircraft never fly." To add to their sense of isolation, their radio was almost useless at that altitude. Ambrose described the area as "flat and swampy and covered with dense jungle growth with not one solitary landing place between the Strickland and Lake Murray."[7] Lake Murray was a welcome sight. Proof that they were right on target came when they flew over the mission landing strip then under construction. Ambrose made contact with the UFM missionaries by dropping mail and a head of cabbage he had picked up at Tari. This was, literally, the "firstfruits" of the coming air service.

Ambrose navigated north from Lake Murray along the Strickland to take a look at the native population centers UFM planned to reach. Given the very dense jungle growth and poor radio contact, he thought it the better part of wisdom to stay near the Strickland. The region reminded Ambrose of the Sepik basin, both in its appearance (the cloud cover had a base of two thousand feet) and the unobstructed visibility of the totally flat country.

The survey showed that operations were feasible, provided that a pilot coming from the highlands was prepared to stay at Tari overnight. Later in the day, cloud cover obstructed visibility of the mountain passes and closed the possibility of returning. The overnight stay at Tari gave Ambrose further opportunity to discuss future moves for air service in Papua with Horne.

Melbourne waited to get Ambrose's recommendations for the Papuan work. In his "Papua Plan," Ambrose gave primary consideration to the UFM push to reach the tribes north and northeast of Lake Murray, seeing a natural air link between this region and Tari to the north. Interestingly, Ambrose pointed to the possibility of a transport link between the coastal base of Wasua and Lake Murray. If this southern approach to the region were developed, supplies and personnel could be funneled from Australia via Thursday Island. This would be much more direct and cheaper than shipping goods from Australia via Wewak and Madang, the existing port of entry. While this made good geographic sense, limited MAF resources did not make this a feasible option in 1956. At that time, flight resources were stretched to the limit. The logical step seemed to be to station another 180 at Banz and begin service to Papua from there.

Ambrose oriented Bob Hutchins to these plans, since he was scheduled to come up from Madang to take over at Banz while Ambrose left on furlough. Prior to his departure Ambrose took Hutchins south on a familiarization flight to Wasua. Ambrose found that the UFM missionaries, spurred on by news of the soon-to-be-initiated air transport, were building other landing sites. The local people were enlisted en masse to help build these strips and were willing to work hard for wages of one or two Giti shells a day—a good wage in their currency.[8]

The region was opening up with breathtaking speed. Areas totally inaccessible ten years earlier were coming into the mainstream. Ambrose wrote Mellis, "The Papuan work is developing rapidly. We are barely keeping up as the Lord opens the doors, and it is a thrill."[9]

Marj Saint's Visit

The big news among New Zealand and Australian MAF friends and supporters was word of Marj Saint's three-week speaking tour. The story of the five "Operation Auca" martyrs had made a deep impression on the Christian public. Elisabeth Elliot's *Through Gates of Spendor* (which also appeared in a condensed version in *Reader's Digest*), as well as MAF's sound filmstrips *Mid-Century Martyrs* and *Unforgettable Friday* had heightened interest in Saint's personal appearance.

Her tour was sponsored by radio station HCJB, "Voice of the Andes," of Quito, Ecuador, whose leadership had a close relationship with the Saints when they served with MAF. Since her husband's death, Marj had been living in Quito and serving as host at the mission's guest house. Clarence Jones of HCJB handled all her bookings, and when he received word through Grady Parrott that MAF leaders in Melbourne wished to sponsor her speaking engagement in Melbourne and Sydney, Jones obliged. Given the good relations between the two organizations, Jones wrote, "anything we have is 'yours to command.'"[10] The result was that MAF sponsored two of Marj's Australia and New Zealand appearances.

After a two-week tour in New Zealand, Marj and her friend Nancy Woolnough came to Australia, where they made seventeen appearances, three on radio and television. On March 14, she joined Ambrose and MAF leaders at the annual meeting held at Collins Street Baptist Church in Melbourne. Large crowds gathered for many of these sessions. Even denominational pulpits of Baptist, Congregational, and Anglican churches were opened to Marj.

Her message challenged young and old alike to respond to Christ's claims on their lives. She was well received. Ian Stacy, who was beginning his flight training, fondly recalls meeting Marj. For the MAF family there was an additional plus, as Alex Jardine, secretary of the New Zealand organization, expressed it. "We feel now that we have a personal link with the work of American MAF and that helps a tremendous lot in bringing us all closer together and develops the essential fellowship of MAF."[11]

Through Marj Saint's story of "Operation Auca" and other MAF media, the work was becoming better known. The 1957 production *Of Wings and Missions* walked the viewer through a forty-five-minute film of a couple joining MAF-US. It opened with candidates Hatch and Penny Hatcher's initial contact with MAF, the board's acceptance of them, their flight orientation, the move to the field in Mexico, and the challenges they faced there.[12] Since 1952 Nate Saint's film *Conquering Jungle Barriers* had been one of the most popular. Australia came out with its own version of *Conquering Jungle Barriers* that captured the spirit of MAF work in New Guinea. In connection with the Honduran work, MAF-US produced *More Than an Ambulance*.

Of all the media presentations, *Mid-Century Martyrs* made the deepest impression, worldwide. When Marj went on a speaking tour in Britain in 1960, that presentation had been shown over three thousand times. As a result she was already well-known to her audience when she arrived. The Nate Saint story also appeared in popularized form in 1959 when Russell T. Hitt's *Jungle Pilot* appeared. The missionary slayings and publicity that followed brought a tremendous outpouring of support to MAF, which translated into rapid growth of the work over the next decade.[13]

New Zealand's Support

The expanding Papuan mission endeavors and their transport needs were very much on Ambrose's mind when he traveled to Auckland, New Zealand, in mid-June of 1957. MAF-New Zealand's work under Murray Kendon, Alex Jardine, and Frank Glen had done much to encourage a strong support group for the forty-two Methodist, Baptist, and Brethren "Kiwis" who were missionaries in the New Guinea highlands.[14] New Zealand also had shown a keen interest in the Papuan work and by April raised one thousand pounds (one-fifth of the money needed) for purchase of the Papuan plane.[15]

New Zealand's increasing financial assistance led Ambrose to suggest that they take greater direct responsibility for the Papuan work. He expected to have a flight service committee in Papua soon and proposed that MAF-New Zealand work with the committee on the use of the funds that they would provide. Under this plan, Melbourne would still plan overall strategy and place fliers, but Auckland would have a more direct line to the field and its needs. Ambrose felt that direct communication with the field would give MAF-New Zealand a sense of ownership in the program that would motivate greater prayer and financial support. To his delight, Auckland accepted the challenge.

Initially New Zealand committed itself to underwrite support for the Tari base and its personnel in the highlands of Papua. By covering the cost of the pilot, AMAF was able to cut user costs 20 percent.

Volunteers from New Zealand followed. Lew Shepherd and Ashley Tuck and his wife came to Wewak to build "Hartwig House," a hangar for three planes, workshop, storeroom, office, and quarters for native help. Tuck and Shepherd were accomplished builders.

While the Tucks made the finishing touches on Hartwig House, named in honor of AMAF's pioneer pilot Harry Hartwig, Lew Shepherd moved on to Tari to turn that into a first-class Papua base. Shepherd's task was to build a one-plane hangar of native timber, iron roof, and aluminum walls. Len Twyman and Fred Snowdon of UFM, as well as Harold Morton who—together with his wife, Hope, and three children—would live in the home, helped build it out of prefabricated aluminum.

Much of the impetus for a larger New Zealand involvement came from Alex Jardine, MAF-NZ's secretary. Jardine was a son of missionaries to India and an immigrant to New Zealand from Britain. He was a highly qualified aeronautical engineer who had worked for the British Overseas Airways Corporation (BOAC) before World War II. He then served as chief planning engineer with Tasman Empire Airways Ltd. (TEAL) at Auckland and was a fellow of the Royal Aeronautical Society. His stature and experience in aviation was important to the development of Australia's MAF-Air Ltd., the technical support wing of the organization.

AMAF-Air Ltd.

Unlike MAF-US, which had decided not to develop a primary flight training and motor overhaul shop (although they did have an excellent prefield flight orientation program), AMAF gave special attention to this area. Australia MAF's technical division experienced a series of transformations over the years. It started as Aerial Missions in 1958 and emerged as MAF-Air when Alex Jardine took responsibility for its management at Ballarat.

This story begins with Colin Le Couteur, Manager of Airspread, a crop-dusting firm.[16] Le Couteur entertained hopes of flying with AMAF until a serious plane accident closed that possibility. He retained the vision of assisting AMAF, however, and determined in consultation with the council to start an auxiliary enterprise to assist Melbourne. Pilots gained flying experience by crop dusting, and profits from the operation were plowed back into the program.

Le Couteur set up a shop where engines were rebuilt and airframes overhauled. Ken Weaver, a fully licensed pilot-engineer from Western Australia, joined Le Couteur as chief engineer, and Aerial Missions began its training program.

While Aerial Missions served a useful purpose over the next few years, it became increasingly less compatible with AMAF's program. There was the need for expanded flight training and aircraft maintenance, all housed under one roof. Alex Jardine and Bill Clack, president of AMAF, had been impressed with the American home office and shop-hangar complex at Fullerton. They believed Australia needed such an integrated operation.[17]

In 1960 the AMAF council considered a possible move from Moorabbin to Ballarat, where the Department of Civil Aviation owned a hangar. They were interested in purchasing a lot adjacent to the runway that might give AMAF access to the field, a situation similar to what MAF-US enjoyed at Fullerton. Ambrose and Clack were taken aback when the department suggested they might be able to buy an even more strategically located lot. In Bill Clack's words, "We would hardly have had the cheek to ask them for it!"[18] This was a good omen, but Ambrose and Clack could hardly have dreamed of the developments that led to the formation of MAF-Air Services, an entirely new AMAF subsidiary.[19]

Hardly had these negotiations begun when RAAF made an independent decision to close down its Ballarat station. While this might have signaled the collapse of AMAF's hopes, instead it opened the door for more favorable access. The Ballarat city council applied to take over the aerodrome and all its facilities and asked the department to recommend suitable potential tenants. The department recommended AMAF.[20]

As Vic Ambrose explained it, "Just at the time when we felt we must move to provide training opportunities in conjunction with expanded worship facilities at a cost of many thousands of pounds, we have an invitation to occupy houses, hangar, workshop and other buildings, with no capital outlay, and at a rental which is a bare minimum."[21] Here was a whole training complex, with everything AMAF needed, ready for occupancy. Adjacent to this property were a number of three-bedroom houses with electricity and hot and cold running water. In addition, there were married couples' quarters and other buildings available for storage. Actually, even the hangar workshop was ready for overhauling engines as soon as AMAF brought in its own equipment.

Besides these physical facilities, there was also the provision of highly qualified personnel. Alex Jardine became manager of MAF-Air and assembled a capable team that initially included Ken Weaver, Albert Waters, Ray Chapman, and Phil Harness.

Even though Aerial Missions appeared to be defunct, the AMAF council retained this commercial crop-spraying enterprise. The man who developed this flight training program under the new name Aerial Enterprises was Dick Robertson, a New Zealander from Kaukapakapa. Robertson, a very energetic person, had been a Royal New Zealand Air Force pilot. He took to farming, got married, and was raising a family of four when his wife died. This severe blow led Robertson to reconsider his future. He decided to leave the farm and devote himself to Christian service as a pilot. Since he needed commercial flying experience, he decided to work for Aerial Missions. He gained additional flying time with the Aboriginal Missions in the Northern Territory.

Given Robertson's experience, commitment, and temperament, the AMAF council thought he was the right person to direct Aerial Enterprises as a commercial venture where trained pilots could gain at least one thousand hours of flight experience. This worked out very well. Through his Christian character, the force of his personality, and the number of men he trained, Robertson made a singular contribution to AMAF.

The celebration of the opening of the new headquarters at Ballarat was held March 31, 1962. The full name of this subsidiary was MAF-Air Services Proprietary Ltd., a separate but wholly AMAF owned corporation. Its purpose had broadened from the concept of pilot training and motor overhaul to a full-service licensed aircraft maintenance organization. This meant that AMAF would compete in the commercial market to operate for profit that would help finance the mission air service.[22] Not only has MAF-Air proven to be economically successful, but the staff has been and continues to be a Christian witness in the industry.

A single gift from a New Zealand couple helped make MAF-Air possible. Trevor and Helen Bryant, from New Zealand's North Island, had a deep love for the Lord's work. They owned 224 acres of grazing land for sheep and cattle. Back in 1960 they donated their entire estate of 13,500 pounds to AMAF for use in a "special project," rather than as a contribution to the general fund. At the time, they were unaware of the nature of AMAF's needs. The insolvency of Aerial Missions and the availability of the RAAF Ballarat flight facility had just then come to the attention of AMAF.[23] Ken Knobbs, a member of the MAF New Zealand Council, was on a speaking tour and stayed at the Bryants' home one night when the couple stated their clear intention to donate their property to this missionary work. The Lord spoke in a very specific way to both Trevor and Helen, and by morning they knew what the Lord wanted them to do.

AMAF's concern was that this was too great a sacrifice for a young couple with children and suggested putting part of the funds into a trust account for the Bryants, should they need it while their children were still dependent on them. The Bryants maintained that this was quite unnecessary. The Lord had asked them to give all, and he would provide. This proved to be true when the Lord led Trevor into the insurance business, where he prospered.

In their new life the Lord placed the Bryants into the stream of life where they had much contact with people and constant opportunities for Christian witness—precisely what they had desired. As they had cast their bread upon the waters (Eccles. 11:1), the Lord used it to launch AMAF-Air and returned it to the Bryants in multiple ways.

Alex Jardine (left) and Vic Ambrose. Vic preceded Max Meyers as head of MAF Australia. Alex was head of Ballarat Maintenance Training Center.

New Zealanders showed such interest in the New Guinea work that by August 1962 three of their candidates were training at Ballarat and over sixty inquiries were on file in the office.[24]

By contrast, MAF-US did not have to start its own flight training program because of the variety of aviation training schools already existing in America. The Moody School of Aviation was fast becoming the school of choice. In the absence of such possibilities, the Australian and New Zealand MAF had to provide their own training. Once this was established and operating, AMAF made a special point of keeping the Christian public apprised through special Field Days.

The Ballarat Field Day of March 1962 brought out some six hundred people. The timely arrival of the first Cessna 185 and the retired 170 from the highlands, plus furloughed veterans Ron Robertson and Bruce Lindsay supplied much information on the New Guinea work. The AMAF Interstate Conference held simultaneously with the Field Day added significantly to the atmosphere of celebration. This event brought together AMAF supporters from the states of Victoria, Tasmania, New South Wales, Queensland, South Australia, and as far away as West Australia.[25]

Through combined and coordinated efforts, the New Guinea interior, like the distant jungles of Ecuador, was becoming accessible to missions as Christian friends joined hands to support the work. Individuals with vision, such as Ambrose and Jardine, laid plans the Christian public could support. Organizations such as MAF-Air provided the technical assistance to make the missionary advance possible. All these spiritual, financial, and organizational resources had to come together in order to send well-trained and dedicated Christian ambassadors to distant outposts such as Tari or Bokondini.

Attracting Gifted Recruits

The quality of AMAF leaders had much to do with attracting gifted mission aviation recruits. We have noted that Ian Stacy was impressed with Marj Saint when she made her Australian tour. Max Meyers witnessed Harry Hartwig and Bob Hutchins's departure for New Guinea a decade earlier and determined to prepare himself for this type of Christian service. A native of Sydney, Meyers joined the Air Force and gained flight and administrative experience. Max and Jo Meyers were initially stationed at Wewak, while Max Flavel was field leader.[26] They moved to Wasua on the lower Fly River in 1963, where they served UFM for eighteen months. Then came an equal period of service for the Lutherans in the highlands at Wapenemenda before returning to Wewak in 1966 to assume responsibility as chief pilot. Meyers' sterling qualities of

Max Meyers, current president of MAF-US, as an MAF-Australia pilot at Wewak in 1962. He stands with his wife, Jo, by a Cessna 180, with their children, Michael and Timothy.

leadership were recognized all along, and in 1970 the council called him to serve in Melbourne as administrative officer to assist Vic Ambrose, the general secretary.

Four years later Meyers became general director of AMAF's far-flung work, which by then included New Guinea, Central and North Australia, Borneo, and Bougainville. The American wing called Meyers to serve on its board of directors in 1984; later he accepted a 1985 call to become MAF-US president and chief executive officer, a position he still holds today. Despite these honors, Max Meyers carries his titles lightly. He is the first to say that leadership is there to enlarge MAF's service for Christ. When Meyers joined AMAF, that service meant reaching unreached indigenous people.

Reaching Indigenous People

The story of what happened in the Swart Valley in Dutch New Guinea is a thrilling example of cooperative frontier missions. Here the Dani Christians from the Ilaga Valley met with the people of the Swart Valley in September 1959. Missionaries Gordon Larson (C&MA), Bill Mallon and Dave Martin (RBMU), and Don and Eunice Richter (Gospel Recordings) wanted to speed up sending the gospel to these people. Since the Swart-Dani dialect is closely related to the Ilaga language, it was felt that these people would be able to communicate easily. How welcome these strangers would be remained to be seen.[27]

When Paul Pontier flew two Dani Christians, Jimbitu and Mijamakame, from Sentani into the Swart Valley on September 9, 1959, nearly three hundred Danis were waiting for them. The Swart headmen and the Danis then sat down in a circle, and the latter immediately told them their mission. "We've come to tell you the way of eternalness," they said. "We in the Ilaga have burned our fetishes and weapons of war. We have ceased our fighting and have turned to the Lord. It is this message we have brought to you."

The Swart chief and headmen were impressed and asked them to share this good news with their people. For the next two days, these two Danis related the biblical account of creation; man's fall; Christ's birth, life, death, and resurrection; and the plan of salvation. The people responded enthusiastically to this message of hope and asked if they could burn their charms and weapons of war. After some discussion, they agreed that they were not ready for such a big step.

On the third day, September 11, a crowd of three hundred people gathered on the airstrip for a service. This time Jimbitu spoke about repentance and turning from their way to God's way. Since the chief of the Swarts had been present and appeared to take in the substance of the messages of the last three days, Jimbitu was so impressed by the chief's keen interest that he asked him to respond.

With a crowd of three hundred of his own people around him, he addressed the Lord and the people: "Greetings Lord!" he said,

"I want to follow you and your eternal way. We here of the different clans in the Swart (and he named them) want to burn our charms and fetishes and put away war. We want to follow your words. Help me to teach my people what I've learned."[28]

This turning to God was no light commitment. Their enemies shortly thereafter attacked and destroyed one of their villages, but the Swart did not retaliate. Instead, each Sunday one thousand of their people gathered for worship. The message was initially a rerun of the recorded words of Jimbitu, as captured by Gospel Recordings. This was the only way they could be reached for the time being.

What happened among the Swart is evidence of what God can accomplish through the loving cooperation of committed Christians. Bill Mallon and Dave Martin, two young, relatively inexperienced missionaries, had been burdened to reach the Swart. Gordon Larson, a gifted linguist, shared that zeal. The work of Gospel Recordings made it possible to take the taped message and repeat it to the Swart, even after the evangelists had returned home. Finally there was MAF's Paul Pontier to handle logistics and provide the plane to reach the Swart. Without the mobility of the plane all these elements could not have been brought together. With these members of Christ's body cooperating in the mission enterprise, it was possible for the Swart people to hear the gospel in a language they could understand.

On a much larger scale the cooperation of MAF with missions was the key to the rapid expansion of the gospel into the highlands and the interior of New Guinea.

Recognition of Excellence

While we have been exploring the spiritual service dimension of MAF's work in New Guinea, the growing flight operations were also a large economic enterprise for AMAF and MAF-US. The latter was now working exclusively in Dutch New Guinea out of two coastal bases, Sentani and Nabire. Total flying time in 1958 was twenty-four hundred hours, which was up 20 percent in 1959. These mushrooming responsibilities led Grady Parrott to direct Dave Steiger, the program manager, to give his efforts full-time to

C180 on one of the interior Wissel lakes in Dutch New Guinea, 1962.

managerial tasks such as scheduling planes and pilots and handling relations with the government. This was no small task, inasmuch as it involved placing applications for visas, negotiating for
new airstrips, on occasion assisting the government with flights
and being the MAF liaison field officer to the government.

At that time, Paul Pontier was due for furlough. To fill in, Betty
Greene came to Sentani for what she thought would be a year of
service beginning in June 1960.[29] Her stay stretched into twenty
months of New Guinea flying. The Dutch governor appreciated
MAF-US's large role in opening the interior so much that on Dave
and Janet Steiger's return to New Guinea, the governor conferred
on Dave the "Order of Orange-Nassau" from Queen Juliana of the
Netherlands. The Governor gave the following commendation to
all the assembled MAF members.

> I know that you do not strive to earn fame, but that the glory of
> God is your sole aim. However, the work done on earth in humil-
> ity and with sincerity for God's Kingdom will also be highly ben-
> eficial to life on earth. Thus your work has not only been of direct
> support to the Mission in the performance of its duty, but also added

greatly to the development of the territory. You have done a great deal of pioneer work in determining the position of and in constructing airfields, and in the areas where these activities were displayed the government has used them as a basis for its own work.

The government and MAF have always cooperated in a very pleasant atmosphere. You and your organization have been willing to render assistance whenever and wherever this was required. Thus you deserve well of the government of Netherlands New Guinea and I am happy to be given the opportunity to present you Mr. Steiger with the Royal distinction.[30]

The Dutch government usually gives out this high honor only to Dutch citizens. That an American organization was so recognized was most unusual and fully appreciated. Dutch rule in Dutch New Guinea ended in 1963, but MAF continued to fly there when the region became Irian Jaya under Indonesian rule.

Indonesia was open to having MAF-US continue the good work there, but may not have accepted AMAF. This has nothing to do with the flight organizations per se, but everything to do with international relations between Australia and Indonesia in the era following World War II.

In part, the genius of MAF was its international character, which opened doors for service to one wing even though another might not be welcome in a particular country.

A Christian Response to Changing Times

Profound changes marked the 1960s. In Africa and Asia, people who had been colonized demanded independence. This period also saw subtle shifts in the way MAF responded to needs in the countries it served. Some of these changes came as a result of taking advantage of ministry opportunities, as in the case of the MAF Medical Wing. In other cases, individual pilots took initiatives that supported various ministries and services or strengthened the outreach of the indigenous churches.

The spirit of empowering the nationals, an outgrowth of post–World War II decolonization, had its most profound effect in Africa, where dozens of independent countries emerged. The counterpart for MAF may be seen as a shift in its vision and perspective. Instead of serving only missions and their personnel, as it had done from the beginning, MAF started giving more attention to serving national churches. The spirit of Christians serving one another in love, regardless of nationality or race—an obligation stressed by Christ and implemented by the apostle Paul—was now finding greater expression in missions circles in the wake of an era when colonial domination was being toppled.

It will be recalled that in Latin America, MAF-US personnel were eager to be identified with the common people. MAF's problems in Brazil were to some extent fueled by those who wanted to affix the label of "colonial exploiter" on MAF. Grady Parrott and Charlie Mellis embraced the impulse toward indigenization, and Chuck Bennett's rise to MAF-US presidency in 1973 was a confirmation of this policy that provided further impetus in that direction. This chapter will look at some of the developments that characterized this period of transition for MAF-US.

Medical Work

For MAF-US the beginning of regular medical assistance goes back to the work in Honduras. Before 1950 Dr. Sam Marx, brother of Werner, both of whom were with the Moravian Mission of Bethlehem, Pennsylvania, had established a hospital in Bilhuascarma, Nicaragua, across the Coco River from Honduras. Werner Marx was field superintendent of the Moravian work in Honduras. The latter's concern for the welfare of the missionaries led to the Moravian board's request that MAF-US consider service in Honduras, which set the stage for Hobey Lowrance's initial survey there. Confronted with the projected flight costs, the Moravian Mission initially hesitated, but when Grady Parrott suggested that a cooperative flight program would speed up evangelization while reducing long-term costs, the Mission agreed to accept MAF service.

When Don Berry began the cooperative MAF flight program there in 1951, Dr. Marion McKinney of the Central American Mission was operating a hospital at Siguatepeque. At first this was not much more than a clinic. Once a full-fledged hospital had become a reality, however, Dr. McKinney believed that the plane could serve as an ambulance to bring in sick and injured people from afar. Dr. McKinney had already developed a program of village medical care in which he took several nurses to outlying settlements for treatment of the sick.

Don Berry was an enthusiastic supporter of this work throughout the decade (1951–61) he served in Honduras. His flight program and Hatch Hatcher's in Mexico provided newly inducted MAF-US pilots with their first big taste of MAF flying. While Berry was in Honduras, he helped five other pilots become seasoned for the work: Paul Weir, Art Snider, Don Roberson, Windsor Vick, and Hank Worthington. Berry's flight service extended health care to nearly seventy strips. His identification with the people drew him to strongly advocate MAF's involvement in medical work for nationals.

In this country where sugar cane is a staple, Berry saw a critical need for dental care. The prospect of having mobile dental care grew out of this thinking. Strong advocacy on the part of Jim Truxton led to the formation of a Medical Committee in 1958.[1] Dr. Kenneth Cole and his wife, Ruth, caught the vision and volunteered to serve. Cole leased out his successful California dental practice and came to Honduras in 1962. He started the dental work in Honduras and later transferred to West Irian, where he served the Lord and the people for another twelve years with MAF. Dr. John Lundgren, also a dentist and a close friend of Dr. Cole, continued the work in Honduras. This was a significant ministry that directly involved MAF in meeting the needs of nationals.

Behind the Medical Wing stood the Medical Committee consisting of Dr. Bernard Voss, Jim Truxton, Dr. Verne Reimer, and Grady Parrott. From the good results of the Honduras mobile dental clinic, the concept was extended to consider meeting medical needs in Guyana and Brazil. Dr. Frank Davis and his wife, Harriet, went to Guyana to start this experimental program and issued a series of reports in the fall of 1962. On the basis of these, the committee decided that MAF should seek to provide medical service to missions that were in a position to administer the work on the ground. In this way MAF could bring health care to areas far removed from any hospital.

While Dr. Davis remained in Guyana, Dr. Charles Patton and his wife, Louise, headed for Brazil. He needed certification from Brazil and took up residence at the mission hospital at Anápolis. Truxton hoped this hospital would take the initiative and launch an airborne service to outlying areas; however, the hospital did not commit itself to this.[2] The program in Brazil did not materialize.

Another couple volunteering to serve the Medical Wing consisted of Ted and Dr. Nancy Lepper. The Leppers went to Guyana when Dr. Davis came home on furlough. Ted's alma mater was Northwestern Bible College in Minneapolis, where he had graduated from the course in missionary medicine in 1953. He then sought pilot training in New York and his mechanics rating through the Quaker City School of Aeronautics in Philadelphia. His wife, Nancy, was a graduate of Houghton College in upstate New York. She received her M.D. from the University of Rochester

School of Medicine, then secured formal Christian training at Prairie Bible Institute in Alberta, Canada. The Leppers had worked in Suriname as pilot and doctor with the Door to Life Mission prior to joining MAF.[3] In the mid-1960s the Leppers went to Nigeria to operate a MAF flight program for the Lutherans, only to find themselves halted in their tracks by the exploding Biafran conflict. Their anticipated flight program was to operate in the very area where the hostilities developed.

Other locations where MAF-US assisted with air-ambulance programs were Zaire and Zimbabwe, but in Latin America, the most successful medical assistance was carried out in Honduras.

Building Bridges

In Don Berry's Honduras work, one sees more than a flier helping medical missions. Berry used the plane as an agent of goodwill and change. The dental service was an aspect of this, but there was more. He used the mobility of the plane to bring together Christian ministries that had been working in isolation from one another. Each mission group had initially carved out a geographic area for its labors, then had a "gentleman's agreement" with missions in contiguous areas and pledged to respect these geographic divisions. In this scheme of things, each mission carried on independently from all other missions in the region. For example, in the pre-1950 Honduran setting, the agreed-upon territorial arrangement had been adhered to by the Moravians, the Central American Mission, World Gospel Mission, Friends Mission, and the work of the Evangelical Reformed Church. The system did not lend itself to friendly contact or missions giving mutual aid and support.

In the post–World War II era the foreign missions' prior claim to work in a territory lost its earlier legitimacy. The spirit of nationalism gave indigenous church work higher standing than that of foreign missions. Furthermore, the arbitrary geographic boundaries set by expatriate missions often made no sense to national church leaders.

All this was altered in the next decade of mushrooming evangelical work. By 1961 there were fifteen different missions in Honduras. The older missions were on the defensive, and the new ones disliked the territorial limits that curtailed their activities. The work of MAF introduced new perspectives when Berry's MAF plane cut across the old boundaries and opened transport and communication lines between formerly isolated mission personnel.

The new missions found a source of support in Berry. He brought together people of differing views and helped break down the barriers of competition and suspicion. The manner in which Berry accomplished this as a MAF pilot reveals the trust he gained from those he served. The same thing can be said about Bob Hutchins's MAF-UK flight work in Ethiopia (see chap. 18). While missions gave lip service to cooperation, Bob found they made no effort to see how they could join hands. Invariably they scheduled their annual missionary field conference, linguistics programs, and other activities without consulting or informing one another. Only when MAF established a cooperative flight program in Ethiopia that necessitated coordination of flight demands did the field personnel recognize that they had not taken positive steps to learn what others were doing and thinking, nor had they sought actively to assist and complement fellow missionaries.

The role of ambassador of goodwill was inherent in the ministry of all MAF pilots. Anyone who had the maturity to recognize the opportunity and was willing to seize it could do so. Grady Parrott recounts one of the Methodist missions leaders telling him in New York, "You think God called you to fly airplanes; actually he called you to be a bridge." This reality points out how far Christian ministries had earlier moved from the biblical teaching that all those who serve Christ are part of his body; all parts are to complement one another in serving him. The excessive independence of missions working geographically side by side in countries such as Honduras and Ethiopia points out MAF's opportunity to encourage fellowship and cooperation.

Helping Nationals

In the case of Chuck Bennett in the state of Tabasco, Mexico, we find an individual whose vision of MAF's future embraced assistance to the nationals over against that extended to expatriate missionaries. Chuck Bennett took over the Villahermosa-based flight program from Danny Derr in 1965. The work in Tabasco had been planted and nurtured by Presbyterian missionaries. By 1960 the Tabasco churches had their own pastors who had been educated in their own Bible school. In this setting, teams of Bible school students and ordained lay pastors did the work of the ministry. The airplane was the taxi that shuttled these Christian workers from village to village.[4] Bennett immersed himself in the local culture; he went weeks on end without speaking English. In ten years of service he witnessed the number of churches grow from 150 to 250. This convinced him that MAF should not be primarily devoting its energies to transporting missionaries and their paraphernalia. If the Mexican people could be mobilized by the Holy Spirit to reach their own, why not offer them air service as a tool?

In 1965, his last year in Tabasco, Bennett researched the history of the evangelical church there. This study grew out of his contact with Dr. Donald A. McGavran of Fuller Theological Seminary, noted for his pioneering studies in church growth, who visited Costa Rica in 1961. At that time Bennett was puzzled about the cultural nexus he observed in the dynamics of Tabascan church growth. He saw the native church growing in ways that were inexplicable to him. Dr. McGavran had no knowledge of Tabasco, but his insights from India kindled Bennett's interest in studying the history of Tabasco's evangelical church. Before long, Bennett found himself engaged in furlough study at the Institute of Church Growth under Dr. McGavran's tutelage. Further research led him to the Presbyterian Church archives in New York City and the production of a significant study of church growth on Mexico's state of Tabasco titled *Tinder in Tabasco* (1968).

Upon examining church growth in Tabasco, Bennett learned that Mexican Christian leaders had largely evangelized their own people. The church did not grow because of outside support; it developed as laypeople became spiritual leaders who led their relatives, friends, and neighbors to the knowledge of Christ.

Applying this understanding to MAF's work, Bennett observed that while MAF had come to Tabasco to help the church multiply the effectiveness of its lay preachers, the local churches had become increasingly dependent on MAF. In the mid-1950s before oil was discovered in the state, no road network existed in this land of endless swamps. Ten years later the region was criss-crossed by a network of highways that brought roads to almost all the villages. These geographic realities made it possible for lay pastors to reach out without MAF assistance. Given these developments, Bennett recommended that MAF terminate the Tabasco flight program. This was the first time that MAF deliberately ended a flight service to encourage indigenous initiatives for evangelization.

In retrospect, Chuck Bennett's thinking, like that of Berry's on the question of indigenization, had a marked influence in shaping MAF's future approach to service. Grady Parrott and his successor, Charlie Mellis, recognized Bennett's missiological insight and drew him into the circle of MAF's policy makers. In time, Bennett succeeded Mellis as president and shaped MAF's policy from 1973–85. Mellis and Bennett, while working toward indigenization, shifted the organizational emphasis from being predominantly a servant of expatriate missions to assisting national churches.

Indigenous MAF Corporations

A parallel MAF-US goal during this period had its roots in MAF-US's entry into Ecuador in 1948. This was the incorporation of MAF as *Alas de Socorro* for both Ecuador and Honduras.

MAF's entry into Mexico came under the arm of Wycliffe. This continued until the incorporation of *Alas de Socorro* in Mexico in 1961.[5] In Dutch New Guinea, Mellis had to file for local incorporation of *Zendings Luchtvaart Vereniging* (Mission Aviation Society) in order to get MAF officially registered there. This same concept was extended to Brazil, where Lomheim worked and founded *Asas de Socorro* (Portuguese for "Wings of Help"). Later in Suriname, MAF retained its American name but had to incorporate in the country.

The Mexican, Brazilian, Dutch New Guinea, and Suriname flight corporations were indigenous. They differed from the Ecuadorian and Honduran wings in that the latter were California-based corporations. In Mexico and Brazil, the question that MAF-US faced was which Christian nationals were adequately prepared to become trustees. This concern was heightened when it was recognized that such deliberations pointed in the direction of Fullerton losing control of MAF's assets in Mexico and Brazil. These assets hung in the balance, including the Anápolis Maintenance Center. It took some time to determine who should be entrusted with such responsibilities. In any case, by the mid-1960s, the expanded role of the national Christians in all overseas mission work, including that of MAF, was well recognized.

Improving Communication

The advances that MAF-US made in the area of communication were very important to safe and efficient field operations. From the beginning of the cooperative MAF Ecuador program in 1948, it was recognized that station-to-station and ground-to-air communication services were essential for the most effective use of the plane. At that time, military surplus transmitter-receivers were used. These were purchased with the help of the Christian Radio League, an ad-hoc group of Los Angeles-based ex-servicemen who had banded together to help missions with communication equipment.

These military units were first used in MAF's jungle network in Ecuador, but a need for equipment with less battery drain for remote jungle stations became immediately apparent. Even though the military units had a battery-saving feature of hand-cranking to generate power, this heavy cranking was arduous. Almost from the start there was a search for lighter, low-power equipment with long-distance transmission capacity. "Red" Brown, Charlie White (one of MAF's technical advisors), and Grady Parrott were on the forefront of that search at the home base. In the end, however, it was other MAF personnel on the field, working independently of each other—Hank Worthington in Honduras and Tom Gilmer in Dutch New Guinea—who came up with a transistorized design that was a great improvement over the initial equipment.[6]

Along the way, the team at Fullerton came across the name of Earl "Pete" Peterman, a Christian electronic designer living in Palo Alto, California. Grady Parrott followed up this lead, but before anything further could be done, Grady was off to Dutch New

Guinea. In his contact with the Lutherans at Madang, Grady met their radio technician, Carl Spehr, who was also concerned with equipment improvement. Spehr stated that he had seen an article telling of a new marine band transceiver being brought out by Bendix (their model 202A) intended for small-boat use. He thought it might be the very thing MAF needed, but it was designed to operate in the frequency band allocated for marine use and would require modifications. Grady passed word back to Fullerton.

When Grady got back to California, Charlie White handed him a brochure describing the Bendix model. Both recognized that by using an off-the-shelf Bendix model, MAF would find itself in the business of making tedious modifications, something Grady definitely wanted to avoid.

In following up with Peterman, it turned out that he had designed the Bendix model 202A. Peterman was eager to design a radio to MAF specifications at no cost to MAF beyond his out-of-pocket expenses. A prototype of the redesign was assembled and shipped to Worthington in Honduras for field testing. The strong signal made for remarkably clear voice transmission.

At this point the MAF story intersects with Missionary Electronics, a firm Jim Vaus of Los Angeles had started as Missionary Communication Service. Vaus was a converted underworld figure who was known for his electronic communication wizardry. He had dreams of a transcontinental missionary communication network that was visionary but too costly and impractical.[7] Missionary Communication Service was reorganized in the hands of Gordon Sanders, a Michigan-based Baptist pastor, and the organization emerged as Missionary Electronics (ME). Under Sanders, ME turned to more immediate needs, producing single-channel transistorized transceivers they leased to missions. Its own field men would service them.

When Gordon Sanders and his team saw what the MAF men had developed, they immediately recognized the superiority of the Peterman design and proposed a merger with MAF. In the process, MAF committed itself to setting up and maintaining communication networks for missions in isolated places. It also agreed to absorb ME's personnel: Kenton and Margaret Schlehr, Ray and Kay Isbell, and Tom and Carol Albright.[8] The Albrights joined

Charlie White and the Fullerton team, the Schlehrs continued their service in East Africa, and the Isbells moved to Honduras in 1963.

As for manufacturing the transceivers, the MAF-US board did not want to encumber the organization with an ancillary enterprise. Grady Parrott set up a separate firm to manufacture these "Missavias," so named after MAF's cable name. Peterman continued as project consultant. Parrott said that this relationship worked out extremely well because while Peterman was a near genius, he was wide open to suggestions that White, Brown, Worthington, and Parrott gave.[9]

Despite the availability of these sets, using them in the field was another problem. Government restrictions on communication gear or high tariffs slowed the flow of radios. In 1962, when Grady Parrott visited Ethiopia, six of these sets were being held up in customs because their low declared value raised the suspicions of officials. Fortunately, Bob Hutchins had Grady speak to the agents to clear up the matter. Grady made little progress until he pointed out that the sets were designed by and manufactured for MAF. What clinched the argument was that Grady could point to the name of the set, "Missavia," as derived from MAF's own name. That piece of evidence finally overcame the officials' justified skepticism.[10] By March 1963 there were 116 of these sets scattered over MAF-serviced fields and over sixty more requests were being filled.[11]

The significance of a communication network can hardly be overestimated. Take, for instance, the importance of linkage between mission stations as well as between stations and pilots in the Sudan in 1959.[12] Before the network was in place, some stations had to send runners up to sixty miles to the nearest telegraph office to call for the plane. This radio network dissolved the isolation that otherwise was a constant reality. With the radio, news from the outside could be transmitted instantly to all the stations. If there was an emergency, the plane could be on its way in minutes rather than weeks.

At times the transceivers also brought news of tragedy. Harvey and Lavina Hoekstra of the American Mission at Akobo vividly remember Al and Ruth Roode's visit. At that time, Dr. Lowrie Anderson came on and said, "I have the most difficult message to give over the radio that I've ever given in my life."

The Hoekstras immediately thought that a tragedy had befallen their son Denny. Then Dr. Anderson announced that Joe Roode had been killed the previous day in Alexandria, Egypt. Joe's mother, Ruth, was standing right beside the Hoekstras, but her husband Al was out on a trek. They immediately discussed how Al might be reached. The MAF-UK plane was contacted and within two hours the search for Al was in progress. Harvey had prepared a note with the sad news, which he air-dropped to Al. In it he asked him for a signal to indicate the location where he would meet the plane. Al indicated he would walk to Boma. Harvey met Al there and gave him the details of Joe's death. The next morning Al was with his wife.[14]

Another example of the range of service the planes rendered both missionaries and nationals because of the communication system involved the dreaded disease of Kalazar that was sweeping the Sudan countryside in 1959. The disease led to weight loss and a slow death, but distribution of medicine was assisted and accelerated by MAF aircraft.

Bill and Marie Knights, who worked among the Dinka at Abaiyat, witnessed this dreaded disease take its toll. Many came for help when they were totally debilitated and in the last stages before death. Bill himself came down with it and had to be flown to England for emergency treatment.[14] He would not have survived had it not been for the MAF-UK plane and the communication link it provided.

Going the Extra Mile

Willingness to explore new areas of service became a hallmark of MAF-US. In coming to Brazil, they were even willing to "wash the disciples feet" by providing those missionaries with planes a maintenance center. Grady Parrott recognized that MAF could not discharge its mission if it continued to ignore assistance to the growing number of dedicated missionary fliers being encountered in Brazil and Mexico. They were serious—anything but thrill-seeking "flyboys."

Grady asked himself, "What should we do to help these pilots sharpen their skills so that they can become skyworthy?" This question was difficult to face, but the executive committee decided to assist individual pilots where appropriate.

Fred Tinley, the Presbyterian missionary in Mexico whose ideas inspired MAF's launching of the "Institutes" in Tabasco, received advanced flight instruction at Fullerton in the fall of 1955. Hobey Lowrance gave him fifteen hours of flight training. Tinley's receptivity and all-around good attitude won him high marks from MAF staff. Not satisfied that he be the only recipient of MAF's expertise, Tinley lobbied MAF to give the same treatment to Fred Passler and Floyd Grady, two other missionary friends.[15]

Along the same line, Dean Blackwelder, a Brazil missionary with the Conservative Baptist Foreign Mission Society (CBFMS), wanted to take a plane to the field. His board was not favorably disposed, but Blackwelder was adamant. He was prepared to leave the mission if they refused him permission. Given these circumstances and the fact that the mission did not want to lose this key man—their field chairman—the board decided that they would permit Blackwelder to bring a plane to the field if MAF gave him flight certification and checked him out.

Under these conditions Blackwelder took commercial flight instruction and came to Grady Parrott for flight evaluation. Grady found that Blackwelder did not come anywhere near meeting MAF's standards. Blackwelder then turned to the CBFMS board and argued that inasmuch as he already had a commercial license, he should not be required to obtain any other certification. Grady countered that Blackwelder had only met minimal standards and that MAF had much higher requirements for their pilots.

Blackwelder came back to Grady and asked him, "How can I get the type of instruction that will bring me up to MAF standards?" Grady advised him to work with a crop duster supportive of missions who lived in Nevada. Blackwelder agreed to follow-up with this suggestion, but he did not want to risk having Grady turn him down a second time. Grady told him that when he was ready to be checked out, Blackwelder should come back for an unofficial checkout. If he did not make it then, no record would be kept. If he performed up to MAF standards, Grady would consider it an official flight and give a positive recommendation to his board. As it turned out, the crop-dusting work gave Blackwelder the experience he needed, and Grady was able to give him a very positive recommendation.

These and other similar cases show that MAF-US was flexible enough to weigh the merits of special cases. They were even willing to assist individual missionaries who were fliers, if circumstances warranted.

Amid Danger: Zaire and Laos

The revolt of the Congo Army on July 5, 1960, signaled the collapse of Belgian rule in what is now the nation of Zaire, located in the heart of tropical Africa. On the heels of that revolt, tribal warfare ignited; anarchy and general chaos prevailed. The situation deteriorated so rapidly that by the middle of July all embassies were advising missionaries and foreigners to leave the country. Evacuation took place by every available means, including convoys, planes, boats, and helicopters.[1] Many fled for haven in Leopoldville (now Kinshasa) or Brazzaville. Others pushed north across the border to the Central African Republic. Many a harrowing tale came from those who took this route.

Some refugees ended up in Accra, Ghana, where a group of evacuated doctors met in mid-July to discuss a medical relief program for Zaire. Word of a similar committee meeting in Kinshasa led the Accra group to send a delegation there to discuss relief efforts.

A week later doctors Glen Tuttle and David Wilson, representing an ad hoc group of doctors, met with Mr. Kamanga, the Minister of Health of Zaire, to offer the assistance of the Congo Christian Medical Relief Committee they had recently formed. Kamanga spoke of the desperate situation in Kasai Province of central Zaire. Medical facilities there totaling 13,000 beds had only one attending doctor. More locally, at the Kinshasa Hospital there was an equally urgent need, and Kamanga immediately assigned doctors Tuttle and Wilson to take care of the 450-bed maternity ward. This was more than they could handle.

These conditions were indicative of the total collapse of health care in Zaire. At the end of 1960 of the seven hundred doctors that were in the country in June, only two hundred remained. Of these, fifty were missionary doctors who were in the bush, where most of the people lived. The rest had fled to urban areas where there was relative safety. The greatest need was in the countryside, and there the transportation network was completely disrupted.[2] Soon food shortages developed and the situation became desperate.

Seeing this tremendous need, the U.S.-based Christian Medical Society swung into action to recruit doctors for short-term service. They contacted Dr. Tuttle, and it was through him that Grady Parrott learned of the need for logistical support to reach the interior with food and medical supplies. Grady was not prepared to make any commitments for air support until he had seen the Zaire situation firsthand. A planned trip to Mali was quickly expanded to include Zaire.

"Operation Doctor"

In the meantime, the Congo Protestant Council brought some coherence to the various independent Protestant relief efforts that were springing up. From this came the Protestant Relief Agency, under which "Operation Doctor" came into being.[3] This was the agency MAF would serve.

When Grady Parrott got to Bamako, Mali, he reviewed the situation in that country since its recent independence. It had very restricted boundaries, compared to the vast territory formerly under French control. The prospects for a viable MAF program there were slim. When Grady shared this assessment with John and Erna Strash, who had been sent there to start a MAF program, Erna turned to Grady with the obvious question, "Why is it that the Lord would pull us out of Mexico where we had a very good operation, put us through a whole year of French language study and bring us to this?" Grady frankly answered, "I don't know." That was the simple truth at that point, but there would soon be a great need for French-speaking pilots in Zaire.

The first week of December Grady met Dr. William Rule, secretary of the Congo Protestant Council and Dr. Tuttle of the Christian Medical Society. They discussed the fluid Zaire situation at the Mennonite-sponsored Union Mission House, and Grady brought his experience to bear on how aviation might maximize the limited resources of the medical personnel who would be in "Operation Doctor." Dr. Rule suggested putting together a mobile medical team, using the plane, to begin in the Kwango district to the east of Kinshasa, where there was not a single doctor.

After the meeting two key people—Dr. Gorecki and Mr. Micuta—called on Dr. Rule. Dr. Gorecki was a private radiologist, and Mr. Micuta was a civil affairs officer in Kinshasa Province. The two related the urgency of restoring medical help to the people. Dr. Rule said he had just completed a lengthy discussion with Grady Parrott, president of MAF-US, about putting together a mobile team of doctors for that very purpose. The two were simply amazed, lifting their hands and exclaiming, "This is providential!" Dr. Rule agreed. "It was right remarkable that the same day that Grady arrived in Kinshasa I received this call just right out of the blue, from other people who wanted to talk about the same subject—medical aviation and medical services in the country."[4] The meeting was timely because Dr. Gorecki was an advisor to Dr. Tshibomba, acting head of the government's medical services.

Grady's concept of effective use of the doctors in this vast region was adapted from Jim Lomheim's use of the plane for the Institutes in Mexico. Grady proposed having teams of doctors move together. Using the airplane, these teams could be placed in separate clinics with little loss of time. With five teams and two planes, good medical emergency assistance could be given. Grady further explained that MAF-US had a pilot in Mali, a plane available in Fullerton that had been scheduled for Mali, and that Stuart King of MAF-UK might possibly make a Kenya-based plane temporarily available for "Operation Doctor."

Another meeting was called for the next day. As Grady came in, the hostess introduced him to Mr. Orie Miller, member of the Mennonite Central Committee and a shoe manufacturer. He was there to see the complex and was observing the people coming and going. Grady and the "Operation Doctor" planning group then started their session. Mr. Miller happened to sit within earshot of the team.

Joe Silvey at the Fullerton base preparing MAF's first Cessna 180 in support of "Operation Doctor" in Zaire.

The animated discussion of this group caught his attention and after a while he leaned over and asked, "Are your plans really going to get off the ground?" One of the doctors said the operation would cost one thousand dollars a month and they did not have the funds to get the program started.

Miller quietly replied, "Mr. Parrott, you send for your pilot and plane and I'll take care of the finances."

Grady was struck with the Lord's providential ordering of this plan. The medics were concerned about meeting the need of suffering people, then a plane and pilot were strategically located on short notice. Furthermore, Mr. Gorecki and Micuta, representing the government, were prepared to support the relief effort. Finally, the unexpected and unplanned presence of Orie Miller provided the finances. In this situation, despite the suffering created by violent men, the Lord was using people whom he had prepared to bring relief and medical care.

To get "Operation Doctor" off the ground the Strashes arrived in Kinshasa the first week of January 1961. Wes and June Eisemann, who had expected to serve with the Strashes in Mali, flew in from Paris a week later. They had been studying French and were ready to begin work immediately.

Johnny Strash went to Nairobi to fetch the MAF-UK 180 that Stuart King had offered to get the program started. The plane was marked with a large red cross on both sides of the tail to identify it with politically neutral medical assistance. Efforts were made to alert the villages to be visited as to the nature of the mission. Upon approaching one of them, Strash found four rows of gas drums lining the runway. This did not look good, but since the drums were not actually obstructing the runway, he touched down. As the doctor stepped off the plane, the local civilian administrator gave him a warm welcome. Shortly thereafter, a group of armed and angry rebel soldiers appeared. They demanded to know why the plane had landed. Fortunately, the local officials intervened and the soldiers backed away from the confrontation.[5] Strash flew out without further incident. In other places that Strash and Eisemann visited in the following months, they faced similar situations.

"Operation Doctor" was the beginning of a program that grew rapidly to meet the medical needs of the people of Zaire and pointed them to the Great Physician. Dr. C. Everett Koop, later U.S. Surgeon General during the Reagan administration, was one of the young American doctors who gave his time and talents in service. Wes Eisemann recounted a situation in which the medical team landed in a town and found one thousand Zairians gathered, many of them looking for medical help and all receiving portions of Scripture.

On another occasion fifty gathered around the plane to listen to the recorded music and a Christian message spoken in their native tongue. Eisemann said they did not know enough of the language to be able to preach, but by using a recorded message they were able to hold many "open air" services.[6]

This was the beginning of what became MAF-US's second largest operation after Dutch New Guinea. No permanent hangars or shops were constructed in Zaire until 1968 because of political instability that almost constantly threatened the program. By 1983 MAF's service to clinics provided five million Zairians with medical care.

Reentry into Eastern Congo

In 1964 central and eastern Zaire were again suffering from the anarchy that rebel soldiers had indiscriminately inflicted on their own people and missionaries. In the western part of the country, at Mukedi, an armed band had killed three Roman Catholic priests.[7] Wes Eisemann and Gordon Fairley flew out twenty-two persons from Mukedi, including six nuns.

In the east at Albertville, twelve British missionaries were captured by the rebels. It looked like their end had come when they were lined up for an apparent execution. Instead, their captors turned and walked away as though ashamed of what they had contemplated. Many prayers were raised for the safety of these missionaries, and the Lord answered.[8] The rebels captured the countryside, even though by spring 1965 the Kinshasa regime had secured the cities and towns. The outlying areas and the transport network were still unsafe. The use of the plane was still essential and strategic. It will be recalled that in 1948, when the first MAF-UK Zaire survey was made, road travel was deemed safe and in many places quite adequate. This was not so in 1965. The roads had gone unrepaired since the Zairian revolt and, given the climate of the region, they had deteriorated rapidly, making land travel precarious.

In the aftermath of those events, the African Inland Mission (AIM) called on Stuart King to see if MAF-UK could assist in getting missionaries back into stations in eastern Zaire that had been abandoned during the violence. Sid Langford, AIM's general director, wanted to assess the state of affairs of the stations bordering Uganda with headquarters at Bunia.[9] King recognized that since MAF-US was working in Zaire, Strash, the Zaire program director located at Kinshasa, had to be brought into the discussion. Grady Parrott readily agreed, and Strash was invited to the Nairobi Field Council to confer with a leadership that included Langford, Norman Weiss, and Dr. Becker, the seventy-two-year-old doctor from Oicha who had fled to Uganda before the rebel soldiers reached his clinic. The question was not only one of logistics but whether or not it was safe to go back to these stations.

The Nairobi Conference that Johnny Strash attended in July 1965 dealt with the question of AIM returning to these abandoned stations in eastern Zaire. The overall plan was to obtain permission from Kinshasa to reenter the Bunia region. The AIM stations still needed "air cover" and the British and American MAF organizations were going to coordinate this. In the meantime, Ken Schlehr went to Zaire to set up a radio network for the AIM stations.

As a first step, Hennie Steyn and Leslie Brown, MAF-UK pilots, flew in to give mobility to an AIM inspection team. Dr. Becker flew with them from Nairobi and met Sid Langford at Bunia. The latter went to Leopoldville to obtain the necessary permits. As planned, the mid-July inspection tour started at Bunia in Zaire, located just west of the Uganda boundary. This is a volcanic region with fourteen-thousand-foot cone-shaped mountains dotting the country.

Bunia, a modern-looking city, had seen over two thousand killed in armed clashes just a few weeks earlier.[10] Now life had taken on a semblance of normality, but the city still carried evidence of the recent struggle. Just outside the town stood an imposing hospital. The party was told that there was not one doctor on the premises and none could be found within a radius of one hundred miles. Given this great medical need, it is not surprising that Dr. Becker was prevailed upon to perform operations at a nearby mission station that was just opening again.

With Bunia as the center, Steyn flew the inspection party to outlying stations including Aba, Watsa, and Oicha, Dr. Becker's station. Oicha was a thirty-five-minute flight from Bunia, and there was a very good strip. It was evident that virtually everybody for miles around knew Dr. Becker. The hospital where he had worked was mostly deserted, except for a few rooms where his assistants carried on. The doctor's appearance was timely, as Leslie Brown recounts:

We had a look in one of the (operating) theaters and were met by the sight of a woman patient strapped down and two medical assistants already to perform an operation. They were greatly relieved when they saw the Doctor's face at the door. Not only were they overjoyed to see him back, but also because they were just about to tackle something which might have been a little too much for them. For years they had assisted Dr. Becker in his operations and had even been permitted to do minor operations by themselves, but this woman had been suffering from a strangled hernia for the past four days and was about to die if nothing could be done for her. So the Doctor was back to work immediately and spent the next two hours in the operating theater.[11]

In the meantime, news of the doctor's arrival spread like wildfire. In short order, several hundred people gathered outside the hospital, waiting for him to appear. Dr. Becker was overwhelmed by his warm reception.

This probe into eastern Zaire achieved all its aims. The mission stations were again safe for missionaries and doctors. However, one unanswered question remained: Could MAF-UK give support to these AIM stations through a radio network and periodic flights?

Parallel to these developments in the north, the mission organizations further south, adjacent to Lake Kivu, felt the same need. The American Consulate would only recommend reentry if there was air cover. Representatives from the Berean Mission, Glen Cruley, and the Conservative Baptist Foreign Mission Society, E. J. Kile, met with King in September. The outcome of their discussion was the decision that both the Bunia and Kivu areas needed similar air assistance. Having a plane come out from Nairobi, six hundred miles away, for rescue operations was too risky. The missions were prepared to reopen their stations, provided MAF-US would base planes in both the Bunia and Kivu regions. Fullerton agreed to supply these aircraft.

Until MAF-US was able to fill these flight needs, King saw to it that a Nairobi-based plane flew one week a month in the Kivu and Bunia areas.

Rapid Growth of Zaire's Program

In 1965 four new 185s were shipped from New Orleans and assembled in Kinshasa. Gordon and Kathy Fairley began serving the first interior base for the Mennonites at Tshikapa, a small diamond mining town in the savanna of Kasai Province. The existence of a government strip made it easy to service the base from Kinshasa. Sufficient disadvantages cropped up so that the program was moved to Nyanga to facilitate emergency medical flights to the nearby mission hospital at Kalonda.

Nyankunde to the east was the location of the Evangelical Medical Center. It became the base for another program that could be integrated with the transport needs of Kivu. This Nyankunde program, in addition to emergency medical flights, served AIM, Christian Missions in Many Lands, Conservative Baptist Foreign Mission Society, Assemblies of God, Worldwide Evangelization Crusade, and the Unevangelized Fields Mission.[12]

During this period of rapid reorganization and expansion, MAF-US was able to respond to the long-standing (1962) request of the Congo Inland Mission (now Africa Inter-Mennonite Mission). A Tshikapa-based plane serving in a cooperative flight program for the region filled this need.

From the Ubangi region in the northwest, where the Evangelical Covenant and the Evangelical Free Church worked, there came another call requesting a survey that John Strash later carried out. Each mission had a central hospital that served outlying clinics, and these were the mainstay for health care in the region. The Covenant Church's mission work, begun in the 1920s, had a hospital located at Karawa, where the plane was eventually based. The Free Church hospital was located at Tandala.

Wes Eisemann served the Methodists at Luluabourg in southern Kasai Province. The denomination had its own planes but was not satisfied with its flight standards. In 1966 they asked MAF-US to take over their Zaire flight program. As matters turned out, both the Presbyterians and Methodists at Luluabourg wanted to develop their own air arm. Their large flight needs justified such a program and by the 1970s they had a total of nine planes flying.

On balance, in 1965 Zaire was MAF-US's fastest-growing field of operations. By 1966, seven pilots were on assignment there. Besides the Strashes and Eisemanns, there were Gordon and Kathy Fairley, Ernie and Eva Doerksen, John and Margie Fairweather, Bob and Edy Gordon, and Paul and Carol Fogal. Ted and Beverly Ludlow were initially assigned to Zaire but directed to the work in Zimbabwe. Beverly Parrott Ludlow, daughter of Grady and Maurine, was the first second-generation MAF-US person to serve with MAF. Her brother Dick, who initially served in Irian Jaya, was right behind her.[13] The Ludlows joined Dave and Merilee Voetman at Karanda, Zimbabwe, where Norm Olson had initiated an air ambulance in connection with The Evangelical Alliance Mission's (TEAM) Gunderson-Horness Hospital at Mt. Darwin in 1964.[14] The entry of the second-generation MAF personnel into the work makes one realize that MAF was moving into its third decade of operation.

A Call from Laos

As part of a larger survey trip to the Middle East and Southeast Asia, in 1962 Grady Parrott spent ten days in Vientiane, Laos.[15] He discussed the aerial assistance needs of the region with the leadership of the Christian and Missionary Alliance, the Overseas Missionary Fellowship, and Swiss Brethren. His assessment was that there was an outstanding opportunity for a flight program to help C&MA with their work among the Meo people, more popularly referred to as the Hmong. They wanted to be able to move Bible teachers from village to village. Given the endless civil strife between the Communist insurgents (Pathet Lao) and the supporters of the government (Royalists), the future of expatriate missionary work was uncertain, at best.

The background of C&MA work with the Hmong is very interesting. These are the indigenous hill people who lived midway between the French on the eastern half of Indo-China and the British in Burma on the west. Laos and Thailand, in the middle of the peninsula, remained in splendid isolation. In the period following World War II, the Hmong came down into the towns to trade for goods. They also purchased transistor radios and began tuning in to the Far East Broadcasting Company's Christian programs. Without further outside contacts, the Hmong began to respond positively to the gospel. They followed up on the broadcast's invitation to contact the C&MA Bible school in Vientiane to receive more information about the gospel.

During this same period in the early 1960s, the Pathet Lao were expanding their Communist influence in Laos, particularly in the countryside. For the Hmong to reach Vientiane, they had to cross Pathet Lao controlled territory. Even so, they made their way to the C&MA school, where they met Ted Andrenoff, the mission's field leader. These people wanted more than tracts and asked

Andrenoff to come to their village to share the gospel in person. He and an interpreter courageously trekked back into the hill country accompanied by Hmong Christians. This trip marked the beginnings of a preaching circuit that yielded wide response to the gospel message.

Ed Gustafson, a C&MA missionary, observed these developments and followed-up the work using a single-engine plane. All went fine until it crashed and he and his wife were forced to trek over a wide area to maintain contact with the Hmong believers. This was time-consuming and dangerous, and they prayed that God would restore the air arm. The possibility of access to the Hmong became bleak when the Pathet Lao expanded further into the countryside and totally cut off Vientiane from the hill people. This is when Gustafson appealed to Grady Parrott for air support.

Grady responded by including Laos in the 1962 survey. What surprised Grady was the government's willingness to entertain such an aerial program. The head of Civil Aviation, who was the king's son-in-law, made it plain that MAF-US could come in anytime to do religious work.

In those years the Laotian government was seeking American military assistance to help them fight the insurgent Pathet Lao. There already existed a network of between fifty to seventy-five airstrips that the American Military Assistance Advisory Group (MAAG) had constructed for a fleet that consisted of Beavers, Twin Dorniers, and six Helio "Couriers," besides larger equipment. Helio "Couriers" flew from strips as short as six hundred feet.

At that time the rural population was being relocated into secure villages with Air America planes flying in supplies and equipment for the Laotian regime. A significant number of these displaced villagers were Christians. Grady recognized that an MAF plane could fly to the same villages as Air America, using the safe corridors around the Pathet Lao forces.

In reflecting on what MAF was doing in the Congo, Grady ventured that here was a place of service for MAF. Under the existing conditions it could play a "strategic part in keeping open the gospel lines in such crumbling situations." Certainly an element of risk was involved. Grady had a taste of that risk when he flew into contested territory in a Courier with a military pilot from

Riverside, California. On this mission the pilot received an emergency radio call to stop at certain strips to pick up and move military personnel. To do this, the plane skirted the Plain of Jarres, which was a staging area for the insurgents. The plain itself was surrounded by Royalist troops, although insurgents controlled its center. The flight took Grady two thousand feet up over a strip, to get out of range of rifle fire. He described the subsequent events this way:

> The strip was being abandoned because enemy troops now had it practically surrounded. Then over the High Frequency radio came a call from an American pilot in an Army Twin Bonanza reporting enemy troops moving from Nam Tha area toward the Thailand border. He was giving descriptive details of number, armaments, etc., including the fact that they had opened up on him but he had ducked behind a ridge![16]

The following morning, a slow Beaver went on a reconnaissance mission to take a look at the enemy advance. When it got back to Vientiane, it had rifle bullet holes in the fuselage. In spite of these troublesome realities, Grady noted that life went on in sleepy Vientiane as though nothing out of the ordinary was happening.

A year later, in July 1963, Grady returned to Laos. A coalition government was then running the country. The guerilla warfare had subsided in the countryside. Grady met with Ted Andrenoff, the C&MA field leader, who gave him a list of twenty strips in districts where C&MA wanted to minister. From government sources, Grady learned that two-thirds of these were only six hundred feet long.

Upon returning to New York, Grady recommended to Mr. Crisman, the C&MA treasurer, that a Wren be purchased for the Laos operation. The Wren was a short-takeoff-and-landing (STOL) craft that was especially good for the type of short landing strips of Laos. The craft cost thirty thousand dollars compared to ten thousand dollars for the PA-14. The price deterred neither organization, since the safety of the pilot was the first consideration.

Don Berry went to Vientiane to initiate the Laos program in September 1964, leaving his family in Manila. He assembled the Wren in Bangkok and flew it to Vientiane, Laos, in November to inaugurate flight service there. Phyllis and two of the children joined Don in January 1965 while their other two remained in the Philippines to continue their education.

Dave and Eleanor Swanson stepped into the Laos flight program in June and carried it forward. The Swansons came from the Midwest. Dave was a graduate of Moody's Technical Program; Eleanor was a Moody graduate who received her B.S. in nursing from North Park College.

During these years the Gustafsons were working in a number of areas, including the region of the China-Burma boundary known as the "Golden Triangle," reputedly a center of opium production. Swanson took Gustafson into that forbidden area and stayed with him several days. On one flight they came to "site 100" as identified on U.S. military maps of the country. No pilot had ever managed to land there five times in a row without some mishap. Swanson landed there over one hundred times, without one accident. The Air America men were so impressed with MAF's safety record that they referred to it as "Air-God." They suspected MAF had more than ordinary protection.

MAF experienced only one minor scrape and no major accidents in Laos during the stressful decade of its service there. On one occasion Dave was unable to stop the Wren fast enough on a downhill site. The plane went beyond the strip some fifty feet. It was pulled back by ropes without significant damage. Observing this superb flier, the CIA made Swanson a generous offer of three thousand dollars a month, a very attractive salary in those days. Swanson turned it down. He told them, "God called me to this ministry and I want to keep on doing what I am doing." Flying became more hazardous with each passing year. Even so, Swanson and George Boggs, the other MAF-US pilot who joined Dave, remained committed to this assignment until MAF made the decision to end the flight program in 1975. The new Communist-dominated coalition government precluded continued MAF work there.

Revolutionary settings by their very nature are filled with danger. Their essentially lawless character usually results in much unwarranted human suffering and misery. This was certainly the situation that unfolded in both Zaire and Laos in the 1960s. At the same time, these tragedies also created doors of opportunity for Christian service. Thousands of people in these countries who had suffered displacement and family decimation because of the civil strife became willing listeners to the good news proclaimed from the New Testament.

Such issues as whether or how one should minister in places of physical danger demand serious and prayerful attention. No organization should risk the lives of its workers. There has to be careful strategizing, and leaders have the responsibility to investigate firsthand all areas of possible service before assigning any to its dangers and challenges. Those assigned to these tasks must be shown that their service is crucial and can be performed with the least risk of harm. One has only to review the record of MAF-US involvement in Zaire and Laos to be convinced that all reasonable precautions for the well-being of the men and their families on these fields were taken. Admittedly, there was no guarantee that someone might not get injured or killed in the line of service. We know that the families that took the risk were fully apprised of its extent, yet they were willing out of love and commitment to Christ to serve in dangerous places. Indeed, all had counted the cost even before joining MAF.

Despite the ever-present possibility of catastrophe, no MAF personnel were injured in hostile action during this period. The protection of the Lord was with them.

Seasons of Service:
The Sudan and Ethiopia

Under Stuart King's able leadership, the work of MAF-UK in the Sudan was making steady strides. By fall 1959 the number of airstrips serving outposts had climbed to twenty. Flight service grew from four hundred hours a year in 1954, when there was only one Rapide, to one thousand hours with two Cessna 180s. This growth called for additional pilots to assist Gordon Marshall and Ernie Krenzin, an American pilot who had come to the Sudan before Betty Greene departed. Hennie and Adri Steyn from South Africa joined the work at Malakal in 1959. Later Tony Hollaway, a former British Navy pilot, joined the team.

As general superintendent, Stuart King had responsibility for the expansion and welfare of the entire work. Phyllis kept the accounts, an increasingly complex task that required extensive bookkeeping on such variables as the operational program in Africa, purchase of spares for the planes, insurance for the aircraft, finance for building new bases, and the personnel payroll.[1]

Getting Started in Ethiopia

Opening Ethiopia was very much on the mind of King in 1959. MAF-UK had served Ethiopian mission stations in the southern Sudan-Ethiopia border region for some years. King and Stevens had carried out a major survey there the year before for five missions: The American Mission, German Evangelical Mission, Swedish Evangelical Mission, Norwegian Lutheran Mission, and Sudan Interior Mission.[2]

Steve Stevens (visiting Africa from the London Office), Stuart King, and Betty Greene in Sudan discuss plans to survey western Ethiopia, 1958.

The survey showed that there was much potential for air service. The Sudan Interior Mission was eager to get started. Other missions felt they might make use of the service but were not initially its enthusiastic supporters. This was expected: Missionaries generally do not clamor for conveniences or service. They seem reconciled to using the same primitive means of transportation available to the nationals. Missionaries tend to view the airplane as a luxury that should not be used except in times of emergency. King's challenge was to change this attitude. Once a plane was in operation locally, however, missionaries took advantage of it and soon began to rely on it for routine travel.

To get started, King needed another pilot. Through correspondence with Fullerton, he received word that Bob and Betty Hutchins, MAF-US personnel who had served in New Guinea, were available. Hutchins had an unmarred safety record in New Guinea. Furthermore, the Hutchinses' home base, the Lake Avenue

Stuart King and Steve Stevens survey the Blue Nile region in southwest Ethiopia before starting air service there. King, in the foreground, is finding a way across the river for the missionary jeeps that follow.

Congregational Church in Pasadena, California, supported missionaries in Ethiopia. Having flown in Australia, Hutchins was a step closer to British air regulations than most other American fliers. Bob and Betty accepted this new challenge, which included learning a new language (Amharic) before joining the flight program in Ethiopia.[3]

Other factors indicated that this was a strategic time to set up this program. In the fall of 1959 Dr. Don McClure of the American Mission, who was stationed among the Anuak at Pokwo, gained an audience with Emperor Haile Selassie. The emperor not only supported missionary effort among his tribal people but opened up ten unreached tribal groups in western Ethiopia to Protestant missions.[4] McClure encouraged MAF-UK to assist in this pioneering venture.

These unreached peoples lived in a remote, mountainous, forested region centered at Gore. It was so inaccessible that very few of the people within a radius of fifty miles had ever left their villages. The area was densely populated. Gordon Marshall enabled missionaries Hoekstra, McClure, and Vandevant to gain a preliminary overview of the area by flying at five hundred feet throughout the region, where the mountains are around eight thousand feet. It was quite apparent that these people were culturally distinct from their neighbors, according to their dress, settlement patterns, and construction of their homes.[5]

Despite the potential of unreached peoples, several obstacles stood in the way of effective MAF mission service on their behalf. The Ethiopian government did not permit any private organizations to fly Ethiopian Air Line (EAL) routes. This was viewed as competition, even though MAF would only be flying missionaries. In the Sudan and elsewhere governments permitted MAF flights over the same routes as long as MAF limited itself to missionary personnel. Doing this required setting up a transceiver communication network similar to the one in the Sudan. Unless the government gave permission to set up this radio net, even emergency service would be difficult to provide.[6]

Getting Ethiopia to issue visas for the Hutchinses required gentle persuasion and much patience. Even though MAF-UK had received approval to fly in the country, the entry of even one pilot was not automatically approved. King was alerted to this stark reality when he heard the chairman of SIM mention that there were SIM missionaries who had been waiting to get into Ethiopia for over a year.

Howard Borlase, field secretary of SIM in Ethiopia, was assigned to check with the Ministry of Foreign Affairs in Addis Ababa on the status of the Hutchinses' visa application. He reported that progress in granting visas depended entirely on a certain Madam Martha, the director general of the ministry. Borlase contacted Madam Martha in the middle of June and found she was too busy to study the Hutchinses' file. He was persistent and phoned her again later in the week. She still was too busy. Then Borlase prevailed on another missionary to bring up the subject of the Hutchinses' visas when he visited her on another matter. This resulted in the same response. Nothing seemed to work.[7]

For the time being there appeared to be nothing anyone could do to speed up the process. Alistair Macdonald wrote to King and Parrott, "Really, it is something to rejoice about that we are *completely* dependent on Him over entry into Ethiopia."[8] Macdonald's assessment was that he was likely to get very little notice before the visas were approved. "They were likely to just suddenly pop up," he wrote.

But Macdonald was not one to give up easily. He made another visit to Madam Martha on September 2. At that time he was told that all the material related to the MAF files had been thoroughly studied and discussed. She revealed that MAF-UK operations were "approved on the broadest front." That meant that other departments had reviewed the proposed operation and given their approval. Madam Martha even promised that the Hutchinses' visas would be issued in one week. Macdonald remained somewhat skeptical. The only good news for MAF-UK those days was the arrival of the Ethiopia Cessna 180 at Mombasa, Kenya, in the middle of September.

In the meantime the Hutchinses arrived in London. On October 20, word came from Malakal that the visas were in hand. Without delay Bob, Betty, and son Bruce made their way to Aden on the southwestern tip of the Arabian peninsula. From there they collected their goods that had been shipped from New Guinea by sea and proceeded by air to Addis Ababa. They stayed there long enough to catch their breath and then moved to Nairobi, Kenya, where Bob worked with Ernie Krenzin to assemble the Ethiopia 180.

Through much red tape, prayer, and waiting, the Lord was swinging open the door to Ethiopia.

Expulsion from the Sudan

While MAF-UK was gaining entry into Ethiopia, the government began to restrict missionary work in the Sudan. In 1961 a dozen missionaries were expelled. The government simply declared these mission personnel superfluous and gave them several weeks to pack their belongings and move out. The growing number of expulsions issued at the outset of 1962 stunned King.

True, not all missionaries were forced to leave immediately, but by early January, six more families or individuals received "marching orders," as King termed the expulsions. Those expelled included the Maclaughlins, Thompsons, Adairs, Pollocks, Khoelers, Eleanor Vandervort of the American Mission, and Betty Cridland of SIM. The Harvey Hoekstras were ordered to depart in December 1962. This meant that Pibor, a very strategic mission station, had to be closed.

Despite these restrictions MAF-UK received recertification for continued work. That decision can only be understood in light of the valuable service MAF-UK was rendering to the country. The expulsion of missionaries under the Sudan "Missionary Societies Act" did not reduce the need for MAF-UK service to the missions. If anything, it increased it, inasmuch as fewer personnel were now obliged to cover wider territories.

In February 1964 the Khartoum regime expelled the remaining twenty-eight Protestant missionaries from the Sudan's three southern provinces and terminated MAF-UK operations.[9] This non-Islamic region had been seething with rebellion for some years, and the Muslim regime now seemed determined to use military force to quell the dissidents. They didn't want any Western eyes to witness the carnage, hence they closed the region to all outsiders. King asked Stevens to bring the situation to the attention of the British Foreign Ministry and members of Parliament for the purpose of exerting outside pressure on the regime and preventing a terrible slaughter of innocents.

MAF-UK's evacuation order came without warning. At that time both the Duckers and Becks, who had been serving with MAF-UK in the Sudan, and the one remaining Sudan plane, were in Nairobi. The entire MAF Sudan work was left hanging. The families had all their personal effects in Malakal. No provision had been made for their homes, the hangar, tools, and equipment. There were also the local nationals who worked for MAF. Marshall tried to make telephone contact with Khartoum from Nairobi but could not get through. Under these circumstances it was decided that Marshall, Ducker, and Beck would take a commercial carrier to Khartoum.

On March 6 they took Sudanair to the Sudan. Marshall decided he needed to talk to Norman Nunn in Addis Ababa, the Sudan Interior Mission senior man whom he had found to be a trusted counselor.[10] From Addis it was off to Khartoum, where the three asked the chief of police for permission to go to Malakal. That having been granted, the trio headed south, where the local police gave them permission to stay for only seven days.

There was much to be done in a short time. They asked the Shell Oil representative to recover fuel stocks stored on various mission stations and credit this to the MAF account. Then it was off to the American Mission, where they found Lowrie and Margaret Anderson closing down headquarters. The Andersons had only one day to make all the necessary preparations for their personal effects and the mission, including transferring mission responsibilities to Sudanese Christian leaders. Both had worked through the previous night and were exhausted.

Seeing Dr. Anderson again, after three years' absence from Malakal, brought back many memories for Marshall. It was Dr. Anderson who, in 1952, met Marshall at the airport when he came to take Stevens's place as pilot. Marshall met his wife Jean at the mission, and it was Dr. Anderson who had officiated at their wedding.

The MAF buildings were just a few hundred yards up the street. Here were the Kingstrand prefabricated homes that King had ordered from England and Marshall and Macdonald had toiled to erect. MAF-UK families had lived here, and their children had called it home. But now all had to be abandoned.

Poignant memories flooded Marshall's mind as he drove fourteen miles to see Hugh Beck's cook, and their own workers, to whom they brought a load of grain. Marshall recalled the night more than nine years earlier when a single light gave him hope as he flew north into Malakal while a late-afternoon storm broke over the city and darkened the sky. Only the glow of incessant lightning gave him some visibility and made it possible for him to make it safely back to the Malakal airport.

In recalling that incident Marshall recognized that it was the Lord who had protected him and the other pilots in their years of flying in the Sudan.

In the name of Christ they had come to serve the missionaries and the people of this land. Some of them were of the military and civilian elite; others were lowly peasants, some sick and dying, whom they carried to medical help. Marshall had come to love the land and its people; he was sad to see MAF-UK fold its tent, but there was no alternative.

On returning to Malakal the men set to work liquidating furniture, appliances, and much of their personal belongings. There was no time to sell their property. Given the circumstances, claims for compensation were filed with the government. Eventually MAF-UK received a payment of eight thousand pounds that was invested in making Jimma, Ethiopia, a first-class MAF-UK base. When the time came to leave, their African helpers stood around like lost sheep, weeping. Marshall wrote, "We were weeping too; it was a hard parting."[11]

The release of MAF-UK Sudan personnel gave some impetus to other understaffed MAF-UK programs. Even though the Sudan government had requested Ethiopia not to take in the expelled missionaries, that is exactly what happened. Among the MAF-UK staff, the Macdonalds and Becks transferred there. After six months of language study Alistair became the Ethiopia program manager. The Becks went to Jimma, where Hugh developed the Ethiopia shop facility. Tom Frank had already joined Hutchins and received orientation from him in preparation for taking over the Ethiopia flying.

The Ethiopia work was growing, and two planes were on active duty there in 1965. With all these changes in the wind and more to come, the Kings recognized the need to go to Nairobi, Kenya, and personally direct MAF-UK field operations.

Expansion in Ethiopia

Some of the missionaries dismissed from the Sudan who moved to Ethiopia began work among the ten tribes in the southwest that Emperor Haile Selassie had opened up to Christian missions. In 1965, Harvey and Lavina Hoekstra entered this pioneering ministry among the Mesengo people at Godare. Bob and Morrie Swart, also of the American Mission, settled among the Galeb tribe in southern Ethiopia.

The Hoekstras trekked seventy miles from Jeppi with native carriers and pack mules. This was a week's strenuous journey, provided the mules cooperated—which they generally did not. Once they reached the heartland of the Mesengo people, their lifeline to the outside world was the MAF plane.[12] Within an hour of their arrival at Godare, they set up their "Missavia" transceiver to guide the plane in for a supply drop. This startling innovation brought scores of Mesengo people to the Hoekstras' primitive camp. Just having these white people suddenly living in their midst was a marvel. To hear them communicate with the outside world was nothing less than a miracle. The Hoekstras' friendliness brought the Mesengo right into their living quarters. Hoekstra soon hired them as laborers to carve an airstrip out of the jungle. The Mesengos were most cooperative, and the natural landscape was transformed into a runway. Elizabeth Longley describes the scene:

> Day after day the ring of axes and the roar of the chain saw reverberated through the forest as the lush natural growth was forced aside, revealing the great beauty of the distant view. Giant trees up to twenty feet in circumference gave an awesome creak and crashed to the ground. Yard by yard the much-needed airstrip was cut out from the jungle. High above, in the tops of the trees, the black and white Colobus monkeys danced from branch to branch, their chattering mocking the men as they worked.[13]

During the early weeks of 1965, Tom Frank, the new MAF-UK pilot, was making familiarization flights as the Hutchinses prepared for their return to the United States. Frank made sixteen drops, bringing in well over three tons of supplies before the strip was completed.

Work on the strip had sufficiently progressed by the spring of 1965 for Hutchins to make the maiden landing at Godare, but first Tom Frank and Hugh Beck made a three-day trek into Godare to inspect the strip. They decided it was okay and Tom described its peculiarities to Hutchins over the radio. As agreed, Tom and Hugh marked the best touchdown area with white paper and placed flags on the places to be avoided until further work was done.

The stage was set for Hutchins to make the maiden landing on a bright sunny morning. All the natives waited with great anticipation for the plane to appear. Soon they saw a distant speck. As it approached in "gleaming red and white" against the blue sky, every eye was fixed on the plane. Tom Frank describes the final approach.

> Bob made a couple of circles overhead, and then several passes increasingly lower and slower in the direction of take-off, without quite touching his wheels. Then he came in the other way, and we knew that this was it: He was on final approach, and because of the slope, he was committed to make a landing. I think we all held our breath for the last few seconds as Bob came in over the trees: then he touched his wheels down lightly on the markers, slowed down, and taxied slowly to the top of the strip. The workers, cheering and clapping, broke into a run behind him, and soon we were all gathered round the plane excitedly talking in our various languages.[14]

The opening of the Hoekstras' American Missions station at Godare was one of many. Among others that opened were Waca, Gila River, and Adura. To the indigenous people who were caught up in this drama of penetration from the outside, the airplane represented exposure to an entirely new world civilization. They soon came into contact with medical care, the gospel message, education, and the fact that there was a great big world that lay beyond their experience.

In their first year among the Mesengo the Hoekstras also learned a great deal. They found out that the Mesengo tribal territory stretched over a seventy-five-square-mile region and they had one chief, whose word was law.

Harvey Hoekstra managed to bring a Land Rover into the outpost. He parked it near the airstrip and one day noted that someone had moved the vehicle. Harvey meandered down to the chief to find out what had happened. The chief, as was his custom, was drunk with honey water mixed into a bark brew. Given his frame of mind, the chief turned Hoekstra's inquiry into an altercation.

The upshot of this was that the chief verbally threatened Harvey and then sent for some of his men to apprehend the missionary. There was reason for caution, as this chief had shot his own son at point-blank range during a heated argument.

The Hoekstras and their missionary neighbors Betty and Larry Zudwig spent the night in a storage shed, praying and hoping that the chief would come to his senses and relent. The next day the Hoekstras took the initiative and sought peace. They brought gifts of salt and a bolt of cloth. This goodwill gesture paid off, and relations with the chief normalized.

During their time among the Mesengo the Hoekstras had the pleasure of welcoming their son Denny and his wife, Carol, as part of the MAF-UK team. Denny remained to complete ten years of flight service in Ethiopia (1967–76). Gordon Marshall, who had known Denny from his earliest years, having flown him and his parents during their work in the Sudan, now became Denny's mentor for flight orientation for Ethiopia.

Denny witnessed MAF-UK's explosive growth in Ethiopia. New airstrips were being opened at a fast rate, for various reasons. In a few cases, tribal people wanted the benefits of medicine and education. In other cases, Ethiopian evangelists saw fresh opportunities to reach new people. In still other areas, expansion was due to the encouragement of missionaries.

At the same time, the government wanted community development for the people: improved agriculture, better water systems, medicine, and education. The missions bent their efforts to supply these needs. Ethiopia's rugged terrain of high plateaus intersected by deep ravines and canyons made the plane the only practicable means of transportation. In this way the MAF-UK plane was a powerful factor in mission expansion as the chiefs sought the benefits of civilization, even though the national hierarchy of the Ethiopian Orthodox Church was not supportive of evangelical missions.

Some of the most geographically forbidding areas in Ethiopia lie to the north of Addis Ababa. The Munz people invited the Southern Baptists into their region in 1972 to help with community development. Sam Cannata, a senior missionary, began with a program of agricultural improvement, bringing in new breeds of cattle, sheep, and chickens. The Munz soon realized that the new sheep produced better wool and opened a mill to spin it. They produced more wool than they needed and used the surplus to weave rugs MAF-UK flew out to markets, helping the Munz gain the cash to buy items that had previously been out of their reach.

The Munz people belonged to the Ethiopian Orthodox Church; their language is Amharic. Their faith is highly ritualized; only the priests have access to the Scripture, and only altar boys learn to read the sacred text, which is hidden from the general population. They in turn become the next generation of priests. In this setting, Cannata bent every effort to teach the people the simple gospel. He closely identified with them by respecting their traditions, which included fasting and abstaining from eating certain animal fats. He found that the Orthodox priests were willing to study Scripture with him. Some believed and opened their local places of worship for gospel preaching.

The work in Ethiopia also expanded dramatically on the eastern frontier. Here the Red Sea Mission had forty-four missionaries helping people in the Danakil Desert as well as across the Red Sea in Yemen and Aden. Dr. Lionel Gurney wanted MAF-UK's help to reduce the time needed to go from station to station—generally a six- to eight-hour Jeep drive in the burning heat. This expanded work must be seen in the context of MAF-UK's wider responsibilities that, by 1970, included twelve mission agencies: Sudan Interior Mission, American Mission, German Evangelical Mission, General Conference of Baptists, Southern Baptists, Norwegian Lutheran Mission, Danish Evangelical Mission, Red Sea Mission, American Lutherans, Christian Missionary Fellowship, Swedish Evangelical Mission, and the Christoffel Blindenmission, a German agency.[15]

The plane opened unusual opportunities for Christian service across the Ethiopian highlands and beyond. In the decade that Denny Hoekstra flew in Ethiopia, evangelical mission work expanded from fifty to two hundred strips. Flight hours rose from thirteen hundred to thirty-one hundred hours a year. During this time, the number of planes increased from two to six.

Two technical developments that increased the safety margin in this rugged setting were the Robertson short-takeoff-and-landing (STOL) modification kit and the use of the Pilatus Porter. Adapting the patented Robertson STOL modification to the standard Cessna aircraft gave greater safety in landing and takeoff. Denny Hoekstra did not think this should allow the pilot to use strips that were unsafe without the kit. What the Robertson STOL did was give an extra margin of safety in this unforgiving terrain by offering better control at or near the stalling speed.

The Pilatus Porter was a Swiss-made plane used for taking skiers to the slopes. Its payload was five hundred pounds over the Cessna 206. By virtue of its larger cabin, the plane was ideal for hauling animals and building supplies. This plane became the workhorse; the performance trade-off was slow flight: Its maximum speed was ninety to one hundred miles an hour.

By 1972, five additional pilots had joined the Ethiopia program: John and Wendy Gray, Max and Sue Gove, Dave Staveley, and Bob Hedderley, all of whom were stationed at Addis Ababa. Verne Sikkema operated out of Jimma; Ronald Knight served as mechanic. Their reaction to this assignment can be appreciated best by reflecting on a brief note Ron penned after only three months in Ethiopia:

> There seems to be an impression in the world at large that the need for "traditional-type" missionaries is decreasing. My personal view is that the opposite is true. From my admittedly limited observations I would say that there is probably an even greater need here for "general" missionaries than there is for specialists.[16]

Unfortunately this good work was affected by the military coup against Haile Selassie in 1974. Two years later the new Marxist regime restricted MAF-UK operations. The pilots flew the planes to Nairobi to prevent confiscation, then returned to collect their families. The abrupt termination of this forward-looking program was tragic for those Ethiopian people living in dozens of villages who had come to trust MAF and to rely on regular contact with the outside world for medical and other purposes. Still, the good seed that was planted would bear fruit, and the spiritual harvest continues.

In reflecting on the developments in the Sudan and Ethiopia, one is impressed with the factor of timing. MAF-UK was given access to the roof of Africa as missionaries and flight programs had to abandon the Sudan lowlands. Other wonderful opportunities for service beckoned in Chad, Nigeria, and South Africa. One cannot help but note that MAF-UK's leaders and personnel were open to and capable of seizing new opportunities rather than bewailing the closing of regions where they had invested such a large part of their lives. Being expelled was a painful and trying experience, but in departing, MAF-UK only "folded its tent" and prepared to set it up in more hospitable territory.

Assisting in Chad, South Africa, and the Sudan

The mid-1960s saw transatlantic MAF organizations focus on the African heartland. MAF-US's work grew rapidly in Zaire and was planted in Zimbabwe. Calls from missions led the British to new work in the region of Lake Chad, leading to MAF-UK service in Chad and Nigeria. A new MAF work also came into being in South Africa under the impetus of Gordon Marshall. A turn of events in the Sudan led to MAF-UK's reentry there through its participation in a regional cooperative assistance program—the African Committee for the Rehabilitation of Southern Sudan (ACROSS).

Handling Crises

The growth in personnel in MAF-UK's Ethiopia program beginning in 1964 was a cause for rejoicing. Then came the accident of the Cessna 180 in October.[1] This came on the heels of an accident in Kenya and meant that of the five MAF-UK planes, only three were in operation. King might have blamed the pilots, concluded he had failed in supervision, or taken this as a sign that flight operations were not worth the risk. Rather, he wrote from London to the field personnel, saying how grieved he was by this turn of events. A situation of this seriousness coming on the heels of expulsion from the Sudan was a hard blow.

Under these trying circumstances, King counseled that the MAF-UK team "should have a day of prayer and humility before the Lord seeking His way and His wisdom and casting ourselves on Him."[2] Then he wanted an entire review of their operation. He wondered if perhaps they were operating on "margins that were too small," especially for new pilots. Despite the fact that there had been no bodily injury, he felt there were too many close calls.

One outcome of this spiritual exercise was Tony Hollaway's reassignment. This decision, an attempt to better serve the needs of MAF-UK, was for Tony to join Graham Macrae at Cranfield, England. Macrae was developing a flight training program for MAF-UK pilots. At the same time Tony was able to gain experience as flight instructor, studying for his airline transport pilot's license and making headway on developing the MAF-UK operational manual. The latter was something that Stuart had asked Betty Greene to work on during her two years in the Sudan. She made a good start, but more work was needed to update it and bring it to completion.

Marshall's upcoming furlough, King's felt need for closer day-to-day contact with the men, and the expansion into Ethiopia prompted King to move back to Nairobi.[3]

A most encouraging development that year was the coming of John and Ann Heywood. John came to help Jim Stack at the Nairobi maintenance base, while Ann devoted her talents to secretarial work. Leslie and Elaine Brown also came to Nairobi in 1965. Marshall worked with Brown on orientation and prepared him to take over while Marshall went to South Africa for furlough. Orientation also meant getting to know the Christians in rural Kenya. Elaine left a colorful record of one Sunday morning's outing to the village of Mukaa, located sixty miles southeast of Nairobi:

> Arriving at Mukaa, we were amazed to see an enormous gathering of Africans—all sitting on the grass around the missionary's house. One thousand people had come for the conference! The example of these radiant African Christians has been a challenge to us both. Their worship was completely spontaneous, quite evidently springing from pure love and devotion to God.
>
> Have you ever attended a service where three different offerings were taken up? But how lovingly the people gave and not always money, for we noticed eggs and fruit on the plate too! We were glad to be able to give a brief word of testimony at the meeting. After

three and one-half hours the service ended and then talking began! The friendliness of the people was overwhelming as they gathered around to greet us. Two dear old ladies pressed a shilling into my palm as they shook hands and others eagerly (and shyly) presented us with an assortment of gifts. I was a little amazed when an old lady handed me a live chicken! How humble we felt as we packed four oranges and lemons, thirty-three eggs and a large yellow pumpkin into the car. The people were simply poor peasants, and yet their hearts were overflowing with kindness and love. That Sunday we learned a lesson from these African Christians that will always remain a challenge to our hearts.[4]

A Call from Chad

In the spring of 1965 the personnel situation allowed MAF-UK's program expansion. At that point, it was a matter of waiting on the Lord to open doors. A letter came from Dr. D. Carling of the Sudan United Mission at the Bornu Leprosy Settlement at Maiduguri, Nigeria, located southeast of Lake Chad. Dr. Carling had begun a medical and evangelistic outreach in the Lake Chad region.[5] Some fifty thousand Buduma people lived on and around the thirteen-thousand-square-mile Switzerland-sized freshwater lake, which was dotted with many islands. During the rainy season, fierce storms inundate this otherwise parched land and make navigation on the lake extremely hazardous.[6] This landlocked body of fresh water is so strategically located that the boundaries of four nations touch its shores: Chad, Cameroon, Nigeria, and Niger. The indigenous people pay scant attention to the international boundaries, as they depend on cattle raising and fishing for sustenance.

Lake Chad is also strategically located from a religious and cultural perspective, since it straddles a cultural boundary running east-west across the Sahel from the Sudan to Senegal. North of this imaginary line live the Muslim people, while to the south live black Africans who have embraced the Christian faith in great numbers. Thus Dr. Carling and the United Sudan Mission viewed the medical work as an arm of the African Church with great potential for ministry to Muslims.

Initially, Dr. Carling's work consisted of dispensaries located on the south side of the lake. No good overland transport routes existed, and the doctor had to take a Land Rover for twelve and one-half hours of hard traveling from Maiduguri to Baga, located on the south shore. Since a sizable population inhabited the islands dotting the lake, the mission launched a thirty-one-foot cruiser to reach these people. Permanent islands are located mostly on the northern half of the lake. Dr. Carling made application to Chad for opening dispensaries on the north shore, centered at Bol. The government agreed. However, this compounded the overland transportation problem.[7]

When the Chadian government requested additional dispensaries to serve the north shore, Dr. Carling felt unable to accept this responsibility, since it took two to three days to reach the north shore by Land Rover. He made contact with Stuart King, who saw that existing commitments had already stretched Dr. Carling to the limit.

About the same time, King received a surprising request from AIM in the Central African Republic (just south of Chad), a halfway stop on the Chad survey. Early in 1965, it had become clear that MAF-US proposed service for the Lutherans at Enugu, Nigeria, even if immediately implemented, was too distant to include efforts to meet Dr. Carling's needs.[8]

Plans were therefore laid for Stuart King and John Ducker to fly through the Central African Republic (CAR) in July 1965 to survey the work centered around Lake Chad. It took two full months to obtain permission for this. With all paperwork in place, Ducker and King left on schedule and flew to Maiduguri. There they met Dr. Carling, who flew with them to Fort Lamy, Chad, to meet Sudan United Mission's Chad Field Secretary Wilfred Shore.

All four made an aerial survey of the lake area, including the north shore, to ascertain its population centers and the best locations for future dispensaries.[9] A survey of the lake revealed the need for access to the islands. One of the big questions from King's standpoint was whether a wheeled plane or floatplane should be used. Dr. Carling suggested the use of an amphibian, and existing conditions confirmed this would be the best option. The price was not attractive, but the ship's versatility was. With an amphibian, Dr. Carling could reach any place within an hour from Maiduguri. An amphibian could fly across the lake in perfect safety, land on the lake near population clusters, and eliminate the cost and trouble of making and maintaining airstrips. Such a ship could land next to the dispensary cruiser anywhere on the lake. Finally, from an emergency medical viewpoint, the amphibian could go wherever it was called to take someone into the hospital for treatment. Once the program started, the plane was used in other areas of Chad for river, bush, and desert service.

The MAF-UK commitment to move into Chad went forward in September 1966 with the coming of John and Mary Ducker and Tim and Elizabeth Longley. Tim was responsible for aircraft maintenance. He had wide engineering experience in the military and had gained civilian flying qualifications in Australia.

Both couples immediately realized that proficiency in French was needed for their work in Chad. Since they spoke only English they searched for someone with whom to converse. At Fort Lamy prices for housing and basic staples proved to be so high that the couples found eating to be almost a luxury.

For the simple dedication service of the Cessna 185 with amphibious floats, some five thousand to seven thousand people turned out. Radio Chad enthusiastically recorded the whole proceedings and the Sudan United Mission's fifteen-minute Sunday morning program was entirely given over to the dedication. "It seems," wrote Elizabeth, "that the plane has become a symbol of missionary advance."[10] The linking of the medical work, the plane, and a strong Christian witness certainly gave the gospel credibility, especially in a world that is easily impressed with and bent on gaining temporal benefits. In essence, the gospel gained a hearing because it addressed the needs of the people and had the ring of modernity.

Two years later in May 1968 Chris and June Emerson joined the Chad team. Emerson had studied at the Glasgow Bible Training Institute. Chris brought in a Cessna 206, and the two planes gave the program the means to effectively serve the needs of the region.

The Loss of Graham Macrae and Mike Melville

Before the Chad program got off the ground Graham Macrae suffered a fatal accident. For the past five years Macrae had trained MAF-UK pilots. He was an experienced pilot, holding an airline transport pilot's license—the highest rating possible. He held the rank of squadron leader when he left the RAF with the specific purpose of helping young Christian men prepare for service with MAF. The lack of such training programs in Britain had hindered the growth of MAF-UK. Macrae's generous help appeared to be on the brink of even greater effectiveness, since he had recently concluded an agreement with H. Fairweather and Co., Limited, the construction firm for which he flew. The company agreed to let Macrae devote all spare time to his prime task in life: working for his Lord in the sphere of MAF, training pilots. This arrangement gave promise of even more pilots being readied for MAF service.[11]

Macrae was instantly killed on the morning of Tuesday, June 14, 1966, in a midair collision between an RAF Varsity training aircraft and his plane. He was only forty-two. His wife, Helen, and children, Eleanor (seventeen), Stuart (fifteen), and Fiona (nine), felt a staggering loss. At this time of pain the larger MAF-UK family in London echoed the words of one of the widows who, in the aftermath of the Auca slaying, said, "The Lord has closed our hearts to grief and hysteria and filled us with His Perfect Peace."[12]

Funeral services were held at St. Andrew's Baptist Church, Bletchley, Bucks, where Macrae served as secretary. Mr. Adams, treasurer of MAF-UK, expressed MAF's deep appreciation for Graham.

> The name of Graham Macrae to us will always be synonymous with nobility of character, high purpose and above all sanctified and consecrated life. We are the richer for his friendship and his service with us and poorer for so great a loss. It is no exaggeration to assert that he could truly say in the words of St. Paul "this one thing I do," and like Moses "he had respect to the recompense of the reward," not a material reward, but the "Well done" of his Lord and Master whom he served so faithfully.
>
> Graham was a man sent from God at just the right time to play a vital part in the development of the work of MAF and this we can understand. Why he was taken from us in the prime of his manhood, at the peak of his powers and in the course of an unfinished task, we cannot understand. This is one of God's secrets. It is not

for us to know the times and the seasons which the Father has put in His power. We are but bondmen in the Master's service.[13]

Three years later, on the morning of June 21, 1969, Mike Melville was caught in bad weather and crashed into the Ngong Hills south of Nairobi. He and his four passengers were killed instantly. The purpose of the flight was to take architects and engineers to Musoma, Tanzania, one and one-half hours flying time from Nairobi, to conduct preliminary planning for a mission hospital there. Three of the passengers were with an architectural firm and the fourth, Alta Schenk, was the wife of a senior Mennonite missionary. Ruth Melville and her son Andrew chose to remain with the MAF-UK work in Nairobi after the accident. Evelyn Josling, MAF-UK secretary in Nairobi, wrote Grady Parrott, "I know that you will rejoice to hear that Ruth Melville is being wonderfully upheld by the Lord and is a challenge to all with whom she comes in contact."[14]

It must be noted that all accidents were investigated closely to see what lessons could be learned to prevent a repeat. Safety considerations had the highest priority, but there were accidents and fatalities. Nevertheless, God sustained his own to carry the work forward without paralyzing fear or provoking recrimination. These committed people had faith in God's providential rule, whereby all things work together for the good of those who love him.

MAF South Africa

From the early days of MAF-UK, South African pilots had come forward to serve. Steve Stevens, Gordon Marshall, and Hennie Steyn were all South Africans. In 1971, after nineteen years of service in the Sudan and East Africa, Marshall felt the Lord separating him from the work there. While the East African program encountered many problems and generated some tensions for Marshall, he and Jean did not view these as the reason for withdrawing from MAF-UK. Gordon explained to Tony and Ethel Hollaway that God used these tensions to cause them to raise questions as to what the Lord wanted them to do.[15] As they reflected on this, the direction God wanted them to take became increasingly clear. Marshall felt the family needed closer bonding with their children during this "vital time in their lives." Finally he felt the Lord pulling him back to South Africa to launch a South Africa MAF (SA-MAF) flight program.[16]

Gordon and Jean's family of four children were growing up rapidly. Their two oldest were in their teens. As they surveyed the future from their home in Nairobi, they wondered how things would be for them in South Africa, where racial unrest was mounting. "It is amazing to me," wrote Marshall, "how the Lord reveals to us only so much at one time, and then we need to exercise trust in Him. I go to South Africa not worried about the future because I know He will reveal it to us when we get there. Maybe this is just another opportunity for Him to teach us to rest in Him."[17]

Expecting to launch a SA-MAF operation, Marshall was aware of the solid support team MAF had built in South Africa over the years. Back in 1953 Brian H. Winter served as South African secretary and the Russell Mortons constituted the deputation team.

The possibility of starting SA-MAF came to fruitful discussion during Marshall's furlough in 1969, part of which was spent in America and Europe. At that time medical missions in the black homeland of Transkei approached Marshall on the possibility of establishing an air arm. Hennie Steyn did the actual feasibility study for flight work in Transkei, Ciskei, and Pondoland. His findings were positive for work in the Transkei, and the Steyns moved to East London, South Africa, to plan the details. A Transkei advisory committee met in February 1970 and decided to plan for the purchase of a Cessna 206, an additional used plane, and to build a house for the pilot's family. The need for forty-thousand rand to cover the costs led to a call for prayer.[18]

A year later the South African support team moved to create an independent South African MAF board chaired by David Luke. His wife, Beryl, kept the MAF accounts. South Africa wanted close links with MAF-UK, and both Gordon Marshall and Stuart King became board members. This is reminiscent of the close ties between New Zealand's and Australia's MAFs.

To get the program started Rev. Tallmage Wilson loaned MAF a plane. Soon arrangements were worked out with King to transfer

Gordon and Jean Marshall with two of their four children, Stephen and Mary, in South Africa (Joyce and Ruthann are not pictured).

one of the Ethiopian Cessna 180s to South Africa. Marshall ferried the plane down.

After withdrawal from MAF-UK the Marshalls made their home with Gordon's mother for six months. The new organization was further strengthened with the appointment of James Cole-Rouse as the full-time SA-MAF deputation secretary.

By the beginning of 1972 the Steyns had an adequate home and the plane a serviceable hangar. There were now six new strips in use. The work along the coast was given new impetus through pending applications for airstrips at Isilmela and Zithuleles.

And so the work grew. The Richardsons, David and Merle, and their two sons made application to SA-MAF in 1972 and actively joined two years later. David had qualified as a pilot in the South African Air Force (SAAF). He joined a crop-spraying firm and logged another 850 hours. This work was ideal preparation for service with MAF. By 1976 the Richardsons were getting further training in America for service in Africa. In 1980 he reestablished the Lesotho Flying Doctor Service,[19] giving doctors the mobility to visit scattered clinics.

Parallel to this was MAF-US's assistance to the Zimbabwe Baptist Mission hospital at Sanyati, 120 miles west of Harare. The American wing had served that hospital since 1965, when Baptist missionaries and MAF developed a medical service for people in an area of four thousand square miles within the Gokwe District. In a short time, nine clinics were opened as extensions of the hospital at Sanyati. This was the only access to medical help these people had. Dr. Rob Garrett and his wife, Eloise, cared for them until 1974, when they returned to the United States.

In the wider scheme of MAF services, MAF-US had effectively utilized dentists as well as medical doctors in missionary outreach to people in Honduras, Guyana, and northern Brazil. The plane really redeemed the time in these settings, by speeding critically ill patients to hospitals, giving a larger number of sick people access to hospital care, and reducing travel time of doctors so that they could give more hours to their actual ministry.

At each turn the Lord sent reminders that the work was his, but that it was contested by the enemy, sometimes through fatal accidents, at other times through his power to protect and preserve. The latter was true in the case of Gordon Marshall's 1974 accident in Zimbabwe. Gordon was ferrying two nurses in the Mt. Darwin area. Due to terrorist activities, the pattern was for pilots to fly either at high altitudes or at treetop level. On this occasion Gordon was flying low when the engine suddenly started making noises. He climbed to five hundred feet where the engine lost total power, and they glided to a grassy bank beside a nearby river. The speed allowed the plane to cross a wide ditch, but the undercarriage collapsed and the plane made a belly landing, sliding along the grass and coming to rest three feet from a large tree and steep bank. Gordon walked away from the plane without serious injury. Roy Parsons and Dave Steiger, who were in the region, came to assist in the plane's recovery. The latter commented, "Anyone who could walk away from a situation like this unscathed must have the hand of God upon him." Marshall had been wonderfully preserved for the work and for his family, who dearly needed both husband and father. We know that some MAF pilots in similar circumstances were not spared, but the mystery of God's ways in saving some pilots and taking others is beyond our finding out.

Gordon continued flying until 1981, when the family moved to Edenvale, South Africa. From then on he represented the work and spoke of the opportunities of SA-MAF to serve Christ in South Africa. His promotional endeavors gave visibility to the worldwide ministry of MAF.

African Committee for the Rehabilitation of Southern Sudan

The regional conflict that triggered the MAF expulsion from the Sudan in 1964 came to a political settlement in 1971 (the Addis Ababa Agreement). This was the setting: Ten million Arab Muslims in the north controlled the Khartoum government, to the great unhappiness of the three million black Africans who were animists or Christians living in the southern third of Africa's largest nation. With independence in 1955, civil war had broken out, with Islamic militants in the north intent on subduing the black population in the south. The result was the wholesale destruction of scores of southern villages, the fleeing of hundreds of thousands of people, and widespread suffering. Some 280,000 people took refuge across the eastern border in Ethiopia. Another 500,000 fled south into the bush country and became guerilla fighters that the Muslim north could not subdue.

The Addis Ababa Agreement gave the south a regional government at Juba, along with considerable autonomy within the republic. The widespread need for relief and rehabilitation led to the formation of a broad coalition of evangelical organizations to assist this government. This landmark cooperation between evangelical organizations forming the African Committee for Rehabilitation of Southern Sudan (ACROSS) received the Juba government's welcome, and MAF was once again flying there in 1975. Members of ACROSS were the Sudan Interior Mission, Sudan United Mission, African Inland Mission, and MAF-UK. These four had been in the Sudan prior to the expulsion of 1964. Joining hands with them were World Vision, Medical Assistance Program (MAP), TEAR Fund (Great Britain), German Missionary Fellowship, Australian Baptist World Relief, and the World Relief Commission. This unprecedented welcome and anticipated cooperation opened an era of wonderful help to the suffering people now returning to their ravaged land.

The immediate tasks for ACROSS were many: opening ten sites for medical dispensaries; reopening and staffing three hospitals at Doro, Bor, and Pibor; setting in motion a clothing program (Operation Dorcas) for the immediate dire needs of the people; starting an agricultural relief and rehabilitation program that included production of farming tools; developing a long-term public health program that included a medical strategy for controlling sleeping sickness, yaws, kalazar, and leprosy; finally, planning for long-term rehabilitation of the land that included town planning, reforestation projects, and primary education. Dr. Ken Tracey was the initial director of ACROSS. Its mission read: "The aim of ACROSS is to witness to the love of Christ by practical demonstration, trusting God to use this witness to encourage the church, to bring people to Christ, and as He sees fit, open the South once again to active missionary work."[20]

These immediate claims on the time and resources of ACROSS did not include the missionary task of preaching and teaching the gospel and the planting of churches. To meet the need for workers, the call went out for nurses, doctors, builders, agricultural and forestry experts, town planners, transport officers, secondary school teachers, and those who would dedicate at least two years of their lives to Jesus Christ in carrying out this good work. The door was wide open for a personal witness in word and deed.

What was unique about ACROSS, as Stuart King saw it, was the potential for promoting wide cooperation among independent evangelical parachurch groups to meet this crying temporal and spiritual need. It had been the mission of MAF since the Ecuador program to foster such efforts, and they had done so in virtually every program. ACROSS seemed to be a fitting transition medium to facilitate united service beyond that of individual mission objectives and forge a regional plan for attaining multiple societal objectives. MAF provided inter-mission communication and transportation services throughout the southern part of the Sudan.

The rapidly expanding work of ACROSS involved carrying larger payloads than any of the existing MAF-UK planes could transport. The purchase of the Cessna 402 (a twin-engine ten-seater) was a logical move to speed up shipping supplies from Kenya to the Sudan. An increasing number of locations were now operational. This cooperative ministry greatly strengthened the Christian witness of the Sudanese church and put feet to the gospel in a more concerted way and in a larger region than ever before. By 1982 MAF-UK was serving seven church, mission, and relief agency organizations with two planes and three pilots.[21]

Just when the work was progressing, the northern government suspended MAF's operating permit in August 1982. Hostilities between the north and south had erupted. The peace accord broke down, and the militant Muslim elements decided to subdue the restive tribal people of the south. This unfortunate situation required that MAF discontinue flights in all but the southern Equatorial Province, where service with ACROSS continued for another five years.

MAF's expenditure of money and effort in the Sudan may seem like a waste. Setting up flight operations that have to close after a mere seven years is hardly encouraging. Stuart King accepted that, as in regular warfare, spiritual battle incurs waste. At the same time there were also spiritual dividends in further encouraging the Christians among the Mabaan, Uduk, Dinka, and other tribes of the region during the years MAF was assisting them.

The decade of the 1960s saw the convergence of MAF-UK and MAF-US service on the African continent. The British expanded programs to Ethiopia and Chad and, through ACROSS, regained entry into the Sudan. The Americans started with "Operation Doctor" in Zaire, rapidly added air arms in that country, and supplied an air ambulance in Zimbabwe. In the meantime, SA-MAF, under the leadership of Gordon Marshall, began to serve the needs of that region.

During this period existing MAF programs in New Guinea and Latin America were moving forward and rendering wonderful service. MAF-US expanded the work further with five new air arms.

Entry into the Philippines, Suriname, Venezuela, Kalimantan in Indonesia, and Afghanistan

MAF-US operations expanded rapidly in the years from 1960 to 1972. New air services were launched in the Philippines, Suriname, Venezuela, Indonesia's Kalimantan, and Afghanistan. The latter two came about during Charlie Mellis's presidency. Even though vigilance for safety remained high, this growing work witnessed six in-flight pilot fatalities between 1968 and 1972.

The Philippines

Both Charlie Mellis and Grady Parrott made visits to the Philippines in the 1950s to assess missionary aviation needs there.[1] As part of a nine-month 1962 Middle East and Asia survey tour Grady and Maurine Parrott stopped in the Philippines before proceeding on to New Guinea.

From Grady's previous visit and correspondence, it appeared that the Lutherans, SIL, and New Tribes Mission (NTM) were open to cooperation with MAF. Once they conferred with the leaders in Manila, however, Grady found that NTM and SIL had their needs met for the time being. Only the Lutherans, Overseas Missionary Fellowship (OMF), and the Christian and Missionary Alliance (C&MA) were looking to MAF for help.[2]

In this connection, an attractive offer came from Glenn Peglau, a successful Chicago-based financier, who was keenly interested in furthering the Missouri Synod Lutheran overseas mission work. Peglau purchased a plane for service in the Philippines, and the

293

Lutherans contacted Grady as to the best way to use it.[3] Their work was centered in Baguio and radiated out northward in an arch of some fifty to seventy-five miles. Grady's meeting with Lutheran field director Nau and business manager Gudenshwager led to the conclusion that there was a need for about two hundred hours of flying time a year. There was a good possibility that NTM field chairman Lee German, the only pilot flying in the Philippines for that organization, would transfer to Palawan. In that case, Luzon would be open to MAF expansion.

There was no need to create a separate Philippine MAF corporation. American influence in the Philippines since the Spanish-American War and the American liberation of the Philippines during World War II made American corporations fully acceptable. Grady Parrott arranged to have MAF's California-based corporation registered in Manila, and all the legal paperwork was in place when Don and Phyllis Berry arrived in Manila in September 1962 to start the flight program. Don had been appointed area director of MAF-US programs in Asia and was slated to be involved in starting MAF-US work in Laos, so someone else was needed as director of the Philippine work. The big surprise was the return of Bob and Betty Hutchins to the Pacific area to take up this responsibility. The Hutchinses had served AMAF in New Guinea and then opened up MAF-UK's program in Ethiopia. They had yet to serve in a purely MAF-US program. Grady had discussed the possibility of serving in the Philippines with them while they were still on furlough. Faith Academy, in Manila, would be a good place for their children.

Other appointees to the Philippines were Cliff and Lenora Carlburg, who served in Mindanao, the Philippine's largest island. George and Beth Raney worked on Palawan.

While they were on furlough, Bob's parents celebrated their fiftieth wedding anniversary. Rather than have their friends and Lake Avenue Congregational Church members spend money on their pastor, the Hutchinses asked that all anniversary gifts be transferred to MAF. The result was a love offering of over $5,300.[4]

When it was known that Bob and Betty would be heading for the Philippines, the congregation looked for other ways to help them. At this time MAF had decided to open up work on Palawan, an island located in the extreme southwest of that island nation. A Cessna 180 was needed to launch this operation. On learning of this, the Lake Avenue congregation took on the task of raising the needed funds.

MAF purchased and modified the plane and had it ready even before the Hutchinses left. This gave rise to a novel idea: Why not take the plane to Pasadena and have a dedication service in the parking lot of the church? The disassembled craft was trucked up to Pasadena and set up for a Sunday dedication. The Lord performs miracles through his people, and Lake Avenue Congregational Church is a living example of the kind of people whom the Lord used to answer MAF's prayer.

Suriname

Roy and Katie Parsons opened up the MAF work in Suriname in 1964. From Paramaribo, the capital, the Parsons served the West Indies Mission (WIM), the Moravians, and the Pilgrim Holiness. WIM worked with the Trio Indians and had landing strips at Palamu, Papadue, and Lawa. The Moravians were a Dutch group who reached out to the over forty thousand Bush Negroes who still retained their African culture in the South American interior. SIL also worked among them, and Parsons supplied both agencies with transport.

There was a large cultural chasm between the Moravians and WIM. The former were Dutch in language and culture, specializing in medical work. Their less-restrictive Christian lifestyle condoned smoking and the use of alcohol. This cut cross-grain with WIM personnel, who viewed these practices unfavorably, and even caused some to question whether the Moravians were truly Christian. Parsons, who witnessed the spiritual integrity of both groups, sought to bring about better understanding between them by fostering regular interpersonal contact.

The initial major task for Parsons was developing new landing strips. This was a difficult undertaking entailing heavy physical labor. In the case of the Lawa strip adjacent to Walt Jackson's station, the Parsons themselves moved into the interior by canoe and worked side by side with the Wyana Indians. Digging out the tree stumps proved to be a most arduous task. The hard physical work totally sapped their energies. The Indians saw no reason for going to all the trouble of pulling up roots, but if a stump, hollowed out by termites, happened to lie under a runway, the safety of the runway was compromised.

As in Dutch New Guinea, the Dutch government greatly appreciated the MAF contribution to the spiritual and physical welfare of the indigenous people. However, the Cessna 172 that Parsons used was not well-suited for transporting patients. In 1965 the Dutch government provided partial funding for a 185 that had a large cargo door fitted for carrying stretchers.

Queen Juliana of the Netherlands, as part of a state visit to Suriname, came out to the landing strip in person to officially dedicate the plane as the *Flying Samaritan*. Grady Parrott had ferried the plane from Fullerton and was on hand for the occasion. The Queen was not content to stand on ceremony and asked to meet the pilots who were actually doing the day-to-day flying. By this time, another MAF couple, Bob and Francie Bowman, were in Suriname. The Queen canceled her other engagements in order to

Queen Juliana of the Netherlands and Roy Parsons at the dedication of the C185 in Suriname, 1965.

speak with Parsons and Bowman and learn firsthand how this air ambulance work was going to be carried out.[5]

Six months later the Dutch presented MAF with a second plane, a 206 Skywagon, a six-placer better suited for transporting people needing hospitalization. The Moravians were doing such an exceptional medical work that the Dutch government was happy to provide funds for still another air ambulance. Their support for the work continues today.

This "Dutch connection" over the years enabled MAF to receive assistance from SIMAVI, a private Dutch medical nonprofit foundation. Grady Parrott was introduced to the foundation through Dick Voss, the finance director of the Moravian mission. Chairman DeGroote of SIMAVI was most supportive of MAF's assistance to medical work in New Guinea and Suriname and paved the way for substantial foundation support for MAF in these fields. Parsons served in Suriname until he became program director in Zaire in 1967, replacing John Strash. Bob and Francie Bowman continued the work in the Dutch colony.

Venezuela

In 1950, Jim Truxton and Hobey Lowrance had carried out a full-fledged Indian population survey of Venezuela's interior. No MAF flight program had resulted from that effort. By 1964, the New Tribes Mission (NTM) began work in the upper Caura River to complement what UFM was doing on the upper Parima in Rio Branco Province in Brazil. On the Venezuelan side lived the Shiriana Indians.

Chuck Bennett, who was winding up the Tabasco program, was called to help launch this new work. He and his wife, Jane, were based at Ciudad Bolivar. From there they provided Don and Marilyn Roberson with solid orientation to the Venezuelan work. Don Roberson had joined MAF in 1959 after military service in Korea as a Navy jet pilot. He had graduated from Westmont and contributed much to the work and community life with the Berrys and Weirs in Honduras. The Robersons went to Venezuela in May 1965.

Once he had become familiar with the work, Roberson based the program at Puerto Ayacucho, where they could serve NTM in the interior. On October 6, 1967, Don's plane crashed. The day before, Don, Marilyn, and their three youngsters had celebrated Don's thirty-ninth birthday. The next morning while Don and Curtis Findley of NTM were flying from Puerto Ayacucho, the plane crashed. Pilot and passenger were killed. Hobey Lowrance, who led the search and investigated the accident, determined the engine had been running fine but that fire had broken out in the rear of the cabin. The cause of the fire was never determined. This was the first fatal accident in MAF-US's twenty-three-year history. Lowrance noted, "Possibly the Lord won't allow us to pinpoint the cause, so that we will tighten up our discipline in many areas."[6] Parrott followed through on this advice. Don Berry, who knew Roberson well, wrote this moving tribute:

> Don's motivation wasn't just flying, though he was good at that. It was somehow to be identified with the missionary in his problem, to help him to do a better job. Don was never just a pilot, a chauffeur. He was one of the group. He listened to the problems of others. He identified with the missionaries. He saw this as a rich area of service. He was that kind of guy.[7]

Later, the filmstrip *I Met a Guy* was based on the Roberson story. This was fitting because Don Roberson was a fine missionary pilot, but he was much more: He was a warm, loving husband and father, a professional in his work, and completely believable and human.

Kalimantan, Indonesia

It is fitting that we go back to Borneo, the land of the Dyaks, as we close the early history of MAF. This was the land where George Fisk's vision of using the airplane for missions first took hold. Fisk in turn had inspired Jim Truxton and a band of naval fliers to provide missions with an air arm. Following World War II Fisk was not able to resurrect the flight program in Borneo due to political and operational problems. However, at the request of C&MA, in 1960, Grady Parrott surveyed the eastern part of the island, renamed Kalimantan when it came under Indonesian control. The need for a flight program was there, but the Communist-leaning central authorities in Djakarta refused permission. Following the coup in 1965 the political climate changed. In 1969 Hank Worthington, Pacific area director, got the green light to start a program. The government not only agreed for MAF to come but added, "We welcome you!"[8] Dick Parrott, son of Grady and Maurine, was assigned to get the program started in the southwestern part of Kalimantan, centered at Pontianac. Other MAF pilots—Bob Johanson, Ken Simmelink, Jerry Reede, and Dave Hoisington—followed.

In 1973 the Indonesian national church and C&MA called a historic conference. Six thousand Christians gathered to pray for and plan a new extension education program that would send teams of lay preachers into remote villages. This program would give the church the tools to teach and train the 100,000 Dyak believers among whom George Fisk had labored. Ken Simmelink was now flying in Kalimantan (he later headed up Moody Aviation) and George Boggs soon joined him. MAF pledged to give such mobility to this church extension program that it would be able to link lay leaders and widely dispersed villages. At the conference, the villagers pledged to build airstrips. With twenty-eight strips then in place and another twenty soon under construction, the task of Christian education began to move forward in a way reminiscent of Jim Lomheim's circuit of flying pastors in Mexico.

Colombia

MAF also received a call to help the churches in Colombia. The invitation came from the Presbyterian Church, which was largely urban oriented. Even so, the conviction grew that it should begin to assist its neglected rural congregations. This "awakening" had been moving through the denomination in response to the vital spiritual ministry of Victor Landero, a profane man who had embraced Christ in 1958. In a period of three years the number of congregations grew from fifteen to thirty-six. The Presbyterians called on MAF to give them the mobility to help the lay pastors that the Lord had raised up through the ministry of Landero. Jack Walker was sent in with a Cessna 180.

Afghanistan

Assisting national churches was part of MAF's growing commitment in the late 1960s. This did not mean that MAF service to missions was abandoned, but there was an ongoing search for opportunities to serve churches in addition to sustaining the flight needs of overseas missions agencies.

The operation in Afghanistan was to assist the Medical Assistance Program (MAP), an agency that specialized in supplying Christian work with pharmaceutical and other medical supplies. From its Georgia base MAP was able to ship ten dollars' worth of supplies to medical missions abroad for every dollar donated. Its ministry in Afghanistan reached into isolated mountain villages where satellite clinics extended the outreach of the hospital in Kabul, the nation's capital. Given the severity of Afghan winters, especially in the Hindu Kush mountains, a Cessna 185 was specially modified with retractable skis. Other winterized features were an oil dilution system and an external engine heating system that prepared it for a quick start in subzero temperatures. This was the first time MAF was prepared to fly extended missions in winter weather. Don and Phyllis Beiter, who had served in tropical West Irian, were willing to accept the challenge of this high-altitude climate. By 1971 MAF service had reached a new geographic and service benchmark.

Flight Fatalities

The mobility of the MAF plane in advancing the Christian mission around the world was not without its hazards or cost. Fortunately the exceptional competence of the pilots and the care they exercised, reinforced by flight regulations, reduced the hazards. By the close of Grady Parrott's term as president, MAF-US planes had flown twenty-five million miles, equivalent to thirty-two round trips to the moon, and suffered only three fatalities. In the three years following Roberson's death, there were other fatalities.

George Raney served on the island of Palawan in the Philippines. Three days before Christmas 1969 he flew missionary Berle Buckingham of American Baptists for World Evangelization

Don Beiter with snow-covered C185, Afghanistan, 1972.

(ABWE) to his home base at Puerto Pincesa. Then it was off to the last assignment: a drop of food and mail to New Tribes missionaries at Tabon. Witnesses at the site saw the successful supply drop. Then, just when they expected to see the plane surge upward for the climb-out, the engine failed and the plane downed in a coconut grove, instantly killing Raney. Beth Raney continues to serve with MAF-US, and her son, Jonathan, flies in Kalimantan.

Within a week of Raney's fatal crash, on December 31, Menno Voth was flying six passengers to Mulia in West Irian from the south coast. On board was a MAF family, Gene and Lois Newman and their four children. Voth, returning on the same flight path he had taken that morning, noted a rapid cloud buildup over the highlands. He dropped under the cloud cover, believing he was on course for navigating through a gorge. The plane struck a ledge and crashed, killing him and five passengers. Only ten-year-old Paul Newman survived. He was well enough to walk away from the crash site and up a trail to the Yali people. A rescue helicopter flew there to safely retrieve Paul.

In February 1971 two other in-flight accidents took the lives of MAF veterans Paul Weir and Hatch Hatcher and their passengers. The first occurred in Honduras and the second in Southern California.

Paul Weir's terrain accident of February 9 occurred five minutes from his base at Siguatepeque, Honduras. He was returning with James Johnson and Dennis Mata from a service at Azaculpa when the plane struck a ridge at five thousand feet. Bad weather was a contributing cause. All three on board were killed instantly. Paul and Ruth Weir had served with MAF for eighteen years. Paul was a flight veteran of fifteen years in Honduras. Passenger Mata, a national, and Johnson had joined Weir in an evangelistic meeting, Mata giving his testimony in song and word. Johnson had just begun to serve MAF in the area of development and was in Honduras to gain a better feel for the work. His wife, Terry, and their six children were in Southern California at the time of the downing. The sudden taking of these three vibrant lives made an indelible impact on all who knew them. Ruth Weir's contribution to the Honduran church must not be overlooked: Her musical talent drew her into providing choral music that was used widely in worship.[9]

On February 17 Hatch Hatcher and John Wilson, a prospective MAF applicant, were flying in the mountainous area not far from MAF headquarters. John had been an Air Force pilot and flown heavy transports. He was working for United Airlines but found that "money isn't everything; being in God's will is." He looked toward service for the Lord with MAF. No one knows what caused the crash. The plane was discovered nose down; the men were killed instantly on impact. According to the accident report, there probably was "an inadvertent spin from either slow flight or stall exercises."[10]

Hatch was a veteran of twenty years flying in Mexico. His name became almost synonymous with MAF Mexico and "service with a smile." His winning ways set well with Mexicans and Anglos alike. Hatch was one of MAF's pioneers in Mexico and on the home base at Fullerton, where in the early years he began work on a flight manual. Many of his techniques were first tried and proven in Mexico and became standard for MAF fields. He had been called on to further develop MAF's technical flight orientation when Hobey Lowrance became Pacific area vice president. Hatch and Penny had six children, four of them still living at home when their father died. Penny continued with MAF, working in the home office. Hatch Hatcher's life, like that of Nate Saint, is still an inspiration for those who seek to serve the Lord with all their heart.

During Charlie Mellis's watch (1970–1973) there were three fatal accidents including Weir and Hatcher. Shortly after Mellis returned from a globe-circling tour of MAF fields, April 26–July 8, 1971, he faced the passing of Martin Kehle, a rookie on the West Irian team. Kehle was killed in a flight accident on July 17 in West Irian, on his way from Sentani to the highlands. The wreckage was found at eighty-six hundred feet in an area that was described as awesome. Kehle was somehow trapped in a treacherous cloud and terrain condition. The plane struck the side of a mountain, and he was killed instantly. A helicopter rescue team found the area so forbidding that they could not remove Kehle's body and had to bury him at the crash site. Dave Hoisington reported that "his name and the date of death were written on a piece of wing laid over his grave." A memorial service was held at Sentani.[11] Kehle was a native of Illinois and a graduate of Moody and the Spartan School of Aeronautics in Tulsa. He had served in the military two years. Hearing about Nate Saint and the missionaries who gave their lives to reach the Aucas had moved him to serve the Lord.

Even before Kehle's death, Mellis had reflected on God's ultimate intentions in the series of fatalities that had occurred. Many in the organization had raised questions: What is the Lord trying to tell us? Here are some excerpts from Mellis's response:

Is it testing . . . to test our dedication? Are we really willing to put our lives where our mouths are?

Is it instructional? Were we subconsciously drifting— despite all we said—to a place where we really felt a fatal accident wouldn't ever happen? Could this have induced a creeping decrease in vigilance? Did we need to be faced with stark reality to check a subtle drift?

Are we really as professional as we think we are? Are we living off our image?

Is it pride? With our words we insisted our long no-fatality record was of the Lord. But the true thoughts of our hearts often deceive us. They don't deceive the Lord.

Is it chastening ... to wake us up regarding some place or places where we're missing God's way for us? Particularly are we running ahead of Him or, in the wrong direction?

Could these incidents actually be evidence that we're on the verge of more effective service in the days ahead? Are we perhaps getting too close to real, current effectiveness for the Devil's comfort?

Historically we have some points of identification with that particular thought. We learned a lot of "lessons" through the Waco repair in 1946–47. But think of our feelings: one month flying; twelve-month repair. Even twenty-five years later it's hard to ignore the element of satanic attack on an emerging, since-proven, effective tool—at a point when we were potentially vulnerable. Yet God meant the attack for our good. We grew on it.

Is God, perhaps, giving us a fresh vision—and commission—as He did to Isaiah in the year of King Uzziah's death? "I saw THE LORD ... high and lifted up ... then I said, "Here am I! Send me." What do you think?[12]

Mellis left the answer for the reader to ponder. It is likely that he searched his own heart to see if any or all of the above possibilities might apply. We do know that the last possibility Mellis put forward is always true. As the hymnist wrote, "Prone to wander, Lord I feel it; prone to leave the God I love; here's my heart, O take and seal it; seal it for Thy courts above." As long as we live in our mortal bodies, there is always the need for drawing closer to God, whether in good or bad times. Given our many preoccupations, many times we just do not seriously think about our need until the Lord reminds us in gentle or jarring ways.

The Future Beckons

By 1970 the formative leadership of MAF-US had been carrying the responsibilities of the fast-growing organization for twenty-five years. During this period the executive committee had been welded into an effective five-member team: Charlie Mellis, Betty Greene, Jim Truxton, Hobey Lowrance, and Grady Parrott. This leadership team approached the ongoing work with prayer and open discussion and generally was able to make decisions by consensus. Naturally there were inevitable differences that had to be resolved.

More important, the executive committee members worked in close partnership with the field personnel. MAF was blessed with dedicated and giving leaders in Fullerton and equally committed and capable program managers, pilots, mechanics, and their wives. The latter provided additional essential support services. This was a team effort, and every person made important contributions.

Grady Parrott—who by 1970 had been president for twenty-one of the organization's twenty-five years—represents the quality of MAF personnel. He was a consensus builder and was admirably suited to serve in this position of trust by virtue of his spiritual commitment, love for people, exceptional competence, sterling integrity, gift for diplomacy, evenness of temperament, and caring spirit. His seemingly boundless energy, enthusiasm, and optimism were contagious. He loved nothing better than to meet with his men, roll up his sleeves. and pitch in to work where they worked and walk where they walked. His servant-leadership style reflected the spirit of cheerful giving that ran up and down the ranks of MAF. Grady tried to keep in contact with all

MAF-US personnel, and his almost continuous travel meant that his desk would have been piled high with correspondence had it not been for Dorothy Mount, the office manager, and her efficient secretarial staff.

As the accountant among the officers, Grady always had a dual purpose in visiting field operations. One was communicating with MAF staff and their families and the people whom they served. The second was checking the program accounts. A former public accountant, Grady devised an accounting system for MAF-US's far-flung programs, enlisting the pilots' wives, wherever possible, to keep the books. This gave the women a very significant role in the operation of each program. It must be remembered that the wives also usually handled the transceiver communication responsibilities that scheduled the pilots' flights and tracked them in the air.

The accounting structure that Grady had devised, combined with his visits to see the programs in operation, kept him fully informed. His visits to the field and close collaboration in the work of each program fostered the family spirit that characterized MAF. By the early 1960s, however, the work had grown to the point that Grady no longer could be in such close personal contact with each program.

An initial move at restructuring was made in the mid-1960s when four area directors were appointed (at first termed "supervisors"). Experience in Brazil, Dutch New Guinea, Mexico, and Zaire showed that these fast-growing programs needed local managers with authority to make decisions affecting their work.[1] As a result, Don Berry was appointed director of the Pacific region, which included Irian Jaya, the Philippines, and Laos. Jim Lomheim was assigned Brazil, and Hatch Hatcher headed Mexico, Honduras, Ecuador, and Venezuela. Roy Parsons had responsibility for the African area: Zimbabwe and the five programs in Zaire. The directors worked out of the Fullerton office, and each had a field operations committee that handled matters on the field. They still retained a highly centralized structure, but this reduced the need for Grady to communicate directly with the leaders of each program. In 1969 Hank Worthington succeeded Don Berry as Pacific area director and Berry became director of overseas operations in Fullerton.[2] In turn Charlie Mellis was appointed administrative vice president. These changes freed Grady from much of the operations task in which he had been totally immersed for twenty years.

Designation of area directors indicated that the founders recognized the presence of a new generation of young men, seasoned and available. The time had come to share leadership with these talented colleagues. At a special leadership retreat in 1968, Grady and the executive committee committed themselves to begin transferring the leadership load in the next two years. At that time it was also recognized that the decision-making process, particularly that of the executive committee, was no longer sufficient to handle the diverse decisions coming before the committee.

By 1969, these developments intersected with a wide range of related concerns. There were demands for the expansion of existing fields that required additional equipment and personnel. New global areas were requesting the help of MAF services. A pressing cash-flow problem remained, and questions were being raised about MAF's goals in a world that was focusing more on indigenous churches than on expatriate missionaries. The demand to clarify the goals of overseas Christian missions had come to the fore since the 1965 Interdenominational Foreign Missions Association (IFMA) Workshop on that subject for missions administrators. Possibly more than any other MAF leader engaged in operational problems, Charlie Mellis had been increasingly thinking about these larger missiological questions. Ever since Chuck Bennett had steeped himself in studies at Fuller Theological Seminary's School of World Mission, the leadership team had been exposed to a stream of mission-related insights and philosophies that touched the very heart of MAF's work.

The range of questions facing MAF led to the appointment of Norm Olson as chairman of a committee to consider and make recommendations on MAF's future goals.[3] Norm had served in Brazil and Zimbabwe and been involved in development responsibilities for MAF. He knew the heartbeat of the organization. Seeing the variety of issues on the table, Norm's committee gave high priority to MAF's need for organizational restructuring. At Grady Parrott's suggestion, they sought to contact Joe C. Profita, a management consultant. Grady had initially met and observed Profita in action at a Wycliffe leadership conference. Profita's advice to Wycliffe was that it move toward decentralizing its decision-making structure. This struck Grady as most relevant to MAF problems. His encounter with Profita was timely inasmuch as the MAF leadership team had committed itself to decentralizing its decision-making process as they brought younger men into leadership. What was needed was sound advice on how to reach this goal. Profita guided MAF to move to a new management format that reduced the executive committee's responsibilities. He also created department heads, each responsible directly to the president. The proposed reorganization format set the stage for the appointment of Mellis as president. He served as transitional chief executive officer for three years, 1970–73, and was able to put the new management structure into place.

International MAF Cooperation

Before moving on to Mellis's term as president it is good to note that the first quintennial international MAF conference was hosted at Fullerton, November 10–21, 1969. This marked a quarter-century of cooperation between the British, Australian, and American MAF wings.

The tangible benefits of the linkage among these MAF wings have been mentioned at various times in this story. It is good to spell them out in greater detail because of their importance. In this global partnership, MAF-US's ability to purchase Cessna planes at a substantial discount helped streamline MAF operations worldwide. From the outset, Fullerton had purchased its Cessnas through Air Oasis, a Long Beach-based Cessna dealership. All planes shipped to Australia and New Guinea came through this agency. As its business picked up, an Australian Cessna dealership sought to gain some of the New Guinea market. The Australians considered MAF-US's plane purchases and their shipment halfway around the globe an obvious infringement of their franchise.

For some months it appeared that the Australian dealership would prevail with their U.S. Cessna home office and that MAF-US would lose half the discount they enjoyed. The matter became a major prayer concern. To the great delight and jubilation of MAF, the company approved the continued MAF-US purchase of planes and their shipment to sister organizations, thereby overriding the objections of Cessna's franchisees. This breakthrough had significance for the future, inasmuch as Fullerton had also become the supplier of AMAF and MAF-UK planes. The standard MAF plane continued to be in the Cessna line. The benefits, however, were not one-sided. Through MAF, Cessna got its most advanced models out to distant parts of the globe far ahead of Piper, its competitor. In effect, MAF, as the largest private operator of Cessnas, showcased these planes worldwide, thereby greatly contributing to the expansion of the Cessna market.

Charter of Fellowship and Cooperation

The growing ties among the MAF wings and the benefits flowing from them was recognized in 1962. This led to the drafting of a Charter of Fellowship and Cooperation. Its objective was to show that the MAFs were parallel and cooperating organizations. Indeed, the British wanted a statement linking MAF-US and MAF-UK.[4] Originally, on the basis of informal agreements, the concept of MAF relationships, like Topsy, "just growed." Once formal discussions were launched, however, it was felt that the organizations should state their operational standards in such a way as to give some overarching control—ethical, if not legal—to prevent any interloper organization from springing up and using the MAF name.

Initially only MAF-UK was involved in this linkage, but by 1962 AMAF had entered the discussion. Once Australia joined the talks, New Zealand wanted to be involved as well. In this way, all the then-existing MAFs became linked in fellowship, shared operational standards, and performed simultaneous service to evangelical missions while retaining their independence as separate corporations.

All this had immediate relevance during the changing political climate and independence movements sweeping Africa and Asia. This made it necessary in the 1960s for MAF service to come from a wing whose nation was favorably viewed. A case in point would be New Guinea, where the presence of MAF-US in Irian Jaya was acceptable to Indonesia, while that of Australia was viewed less favorably. The preference had nothing to do with the MAF wings or their personnel per se; it had everything to do with international relations between the two countries. Another example may be cited in connection with the assignment of Australia's Ian and Joan Stacy to serve in Sarawak (North Borneo). Ian filled a pilot need for the Borneo Evangelical Mission in March 1963. An MAF-US presence would not have been welcomed there. In this way, the MAF coalition could serve without stirring up nationalistic feelings or inflaming international animosities that tended to get in the way of spreading the gospel.

At another level, the cooperation between Fullerton and Melbourne in the 1960s created a symbiotic relationship between the two transpacific wings. As already discussed, Fullerton purchased planes at a 20 percent factory discount and passed on these savings. They made all the necessary modifications to the aircraft heading for New Guinea. Melbourne, through MAF-Air, disposed of all used engines and purchased all used New Guinea aircraft. This division of labor benefited both organizations.

Unfortunately some of the AMAF field personnel did not see it that way and complained that Australia was getting American discards. Both Ambrose and Mellis took exception to this narrow nationalistic view of the work and pointed out the reciprocal benefits arising from the policy of assisting one another.[5] Given the enlarged technical possibilities for Melbourne, Ambrose anticipated doing more, not less, for the American wing. The fact that Mellis and Ambrose had worked so closely together in the field, no doubt, played a part in this continued close collaboration.

Cooperation between MAF-US and AMAF spilled over into a tendency to streamline everything from plane color (which changed from yellow to white with red trim in 1962) to flight regulations and service policy.

Operating Environments

Parallel MAF developments and collaboration should not cause us to lose sight of the distinctives characterizing each organization. Each worked in quite different operational environments.

The fact that AMAF operated largely in areas under Australian control made it much easier to engage in ancillary enterprises that raised revenue for the missionary flight program. The commercial ventures of AMAF were part of Melbourne's strategy to make AMAF increasingly self-supporting.

The American and British wings worked in foreign fields that barred them from setting up competing enterprises with nationals. Over the years, going back to Vic Ambrose, AMAF had cultivated commercial flight work to help pay for their missionary programs. Their intent was to make AMAF financially self-supporting, as far as possible. The commercial flight programs that were later developed on Bougainville and in North Australia had been profitable commercial lines that advanced a Christian witness in these areas. While in 1988 MAF-US needed to raise over 60 percent of its budget through donations from the Christian public, AMAF was obliged to raise less than 5 percent. This does not mean that MAF-US's flight programs were less efficient. Both Australian and American missionary flight programs require the same degree of subsidy. AMAF simply operates in an arena that embraces commercial work. This, plus the minimal mileage charge to missionaries using the service, pays for almost their entire missionary operation. As a result, in the 1960s AMAF became more and more economically self-sufficient.

Boundaries to Service

Service policy was another area of common concern to the MAF wings. The question of who should be served was not always easy to answer. For Melbourne in 1960 the question centered on flight service to the Anglican Church of New Guinea.[6] It was part of the High (Anglican) Church and received financial support from the Australian Board of Missions. The other branch, the Low Church (largely evangelical Anglican), received its mission support from the Church Missionary Society (CMS). Unfortunately, the Bishop of New Guinea would not allow CMS to work in New Guinea, and as Ambrose wrote, "expressly excluded any evangelical emphasis from his diocese." Their priests in New Guinea aligned themselves with Rome and considered the Reformation a big mistake.

Doug McCraw, the program manager at Wewak and an ordained evangelical Anglican priest, suggested AMAF not serve the Anglicans in New Guinea. In contrast, Max Flavel, field leader in New Guinea, believed that AMAF should extend its service to them, inasmuch as the church had both the High and Low wings. Ambrose also recognized that the New Guinea bishop was deliberately eliminating all evangelical emphasis, and this raised the question for MAF: "Should we use funds provided by evangelicals to help a work that opposes a fair bit of what we stand for?" If they truly represented both wings of the church in New Guinea, Ambrose saw no reason for refusing service.

As far as Charlie Mellis was concerned, the fact that the Anglicans had dissociated themselves from the evangelicals was seen as sufficient reason to exclude them from any cooperative AMAF flight service.[7] Charlie tossed all requests for Anglican flight service back to Ambrose for his decision. In his negotiations with the Anglicans, this matter was eventually resolved to the satisfaction of Doug McCraw, and MAF service was extended to the Anglicans.

In resolving such flight questions, it was the practice of MAF-US to extend service to core groups committed to the evangelical position. When new missions asked for service, Fullerton extended it, based on the concurrence of the local evangelical core group. In their earlier years, this meant not giving support to the New Tribes Mission because their unorthodox approach to frontier missions had alienated them from most evangelical mission agencies.

Once the MAF program was well established, MAF-US no longer entirely relied on a cue from other missions to decide who should be served, because it now could gain firsthand information directly. As a working policy, Mellis stated: "We try to get the cordial concurrence of all concerned before making such an extension and this has helped to get some groups working together that were at odds previously."[8] In medical emergencies, MAF was always willing to give flight support, regardless of faith or denomination.

The situation in Latin America, where the government and Catholic Church worked hand in hand, posed a more difficult problem. To retain the goodwill of the governments, SIL had freely carried priests on their planes. SIL justified it by saying that in supplying Catholics with assistance, they were fulfilling Christ's commandment to love all people. MAF-US leadership was not prepared to apply such a blanket rule, in view of their dedication to supporting those who were committed to the spread of the gospel message. MAF-US was willing to handle this on an ad hoc basis until some better policy could be found.

Theological differences were not the only reason for a MAF decision declining service to a mission. For instance, Venezuela and the Philippines were the first two fields in which MAF logistically supported the New Tribes Mission (NTM). There had been widespread criticism of the leadership of NTM for sending poorly trained people into frontier missions. By the mid-1960s NTM had changed its policy in this regard and earned membership in the IFMA.[9] Actually, a greater MAF-US reservation about NTM was over what appeared to be an undisciplined approach to aviation, leading to several plane crashes. Fortunately NTM responded constructively to these realities and beginning with the Philippine and Venezuela operations, MAF became increasingly willing to assist NTM in its frontier mission work.

This again raises the question about the groups MAF was willing to assist. The formal criterion was to cooperate with any evangelical organization engaged in any form of mission work based upon biblical principles. The working criterion was serving those organizations that were acceptable to the local evangelical core group. With respect to the Philippines in 1964, Parrott considered the core group to be the Far Eastern Gospel Crusade, Far East Broadcasting Company, the Christian and Missionary Alliance, Overseas Missionary Fellowship, and the American Baptists for World Evangelization.[10] When evaluating the acceptability of any other group to the larger constituency, MAF made its own decision for or against service. This was not a cut-and-dried process. In practice, MAF responded to all Christian groups requesting field service. Where a core group of missions had reservations about a new applicant, MAF would confidentially share the reported reservations with the applicant. At times these turned out to be myths rather than realities and MAF served as a bridge between mission organizations, leading them to better understanding and mutual cooperation.

If there were legitimate objections from the core group, and the mission in question demonstrated a need for aviation support, MAF counseled and even assisted the mission in developing its own flight program. MAF was eager to retain its cooperative flight service policies but remained unwilling to cast a negative reflection on missions that were not welcomed to participate.

This problem, of course, was not new. It was a fact of life in every field. In the Congo, rendering service to the Methodists was a concern to some.[11] From the standpoint of implementing programs, it was sometimes true that the more evangelically inclined were sometimes slow to take advantage of MAF's service. The more theologically liberal groups were often quick to see the value of air support. This was true in the Philippines. The situation made for difficulties, inasmuch as serving liberal groups would be the wedge that made evangelicals reluctant to seek MAF service. Thus there was a constant weighing of these factors whenever work in a new field was being negotiated. It must be remembered that there were Fundamentalists in 1960 who objected to MAF-UK's giving Billy Graham transportation in East Africa in his "Safari for Souls." Graham's cooperation with Christians of diverse views was looked upon as suspect, even heretical. MAF was sometimes viewed askance by some for its Christian inclusiveness. For MAF-US the executive committee promoted and succeeded in not letting MAF become a captive of narrow sympathies. Grady Parrott demonstrated a biblically informed Christian ecumenism in the face of pressures to abandon it.

MAF's unfolding history demanded that the organization be innovative while remaining essentially conservative. This combination allowed for flexibility within a context of strong commitment. This conservative bent was inevitable, because MAF's flight and radio service had been forged out of hard experience and careful reflection. One would not expect MAF to endorse either a careless aviation philosophy or the sort of theological speculation that encouraged faddism in missiological praxis.

This lengthy prologue to MAF's First International Conference gives some sense of the complexity of the inner workings of this fellowship. The MAF wings had settled on the Cessna as the plane of choice, but they operated in differing political and service envi-

First international MAF conference in Fullerton, California, November 1969. Participants included (left to right) Grady Parrott, Stuart King, Steve Stevens, Vic Ambrose, Max Flavel, Don Berry.

ronments that required unique adjustments to their varied settings. One can readily understand that periodic meetings would be beneficial to discuss areas that needed review or propose adjustments and changes. What is remarkable is that this first meeting in 1969 marked a quarter-century of service. As such, it was a celebration of the past, an assessment of the present, and a time to peer into the future and strategize how they might best serve the church worldwide.

Representing MAF-UK were Stuart King, Steve Stevens, Tony Hollaway, Alistair Macdonald, and Hennie Steyn. William Clack led the Australians, and he brought with him B. R. Redpath, chairman of MAF-Air Services, and Vic Ambrose, Alex Jardine, and Max Flavel. Major participants of the American wing were Grady Parrott, Betty Greene, Charlie Mellis, Jim Truxton, Don Berry, Jim

Lomheim, Hobey Lowrance, Hatch Hatcher, Roy Parsons, Norm Olson, Chuck Bennett, Bob Lehnhart, Wes Eisemann, and Hank Worthington.[12]

This first conference was especially productive in examining areas in which the respective organizations diverged in their practices. This exercise was undertaken with a view to understand the different approaches by these wings and benefit from one another. For instance, MAF-US had only charged for direct costs of service, which included fuel, insurance, maintenance, and depreciation. The cost of pilot support and equipment, as well as administrative overhead, was handled separately. Given the tight financial situation of MAF-US, they were ready to review this matter to see if pilot support should not be borne by the consumer. Shifting this cost, however, would create a greater burden on national churches who, it was agreed, MAF should increasingly serve.

Highlights of this meeting included the plenary address by Henry Hutchins, pastor of Lake Avenue Congregational Church of Pasadena, California. His son Bob held the distinction of having served on the field as pilot in all three wings. Chuck Bennett presented a research report, and professor Alan Tippett of Fuller Seminary spoke on missions and anthropology. Then there was a visit to the World Vision Research Center. For many, the highlights of the stay were the visits and fellowship with the MAF families who hosted the delegates in their homes. The conference strengthened MAF ties and generated a fresh sense of unity in serving the church in our day. Vic Ambrose wrote, "We have all come away with the feeling that the conference was a resounding success in every way."[13]

Charles J. Mellis Assumes the Presidency

Charlie Mellis became president of MAF-US in April 1970. At the same time Grady Parrott moved to the newly created position of chairman of the board. Charlie had been in the organization almost from the start, having served as secretary-treasurer since 1946. He was intimately familiar with all aspects of the work, having served on the executive committee for years. Grady regretted that Charlie had taken the helm at a time when MAF was experiencing severe cash-flow problems. However, as the newly appointed chairman of the board, Grady was quick to grapple with this problem and began working in such areas as deferred giving, foundation support, and related funding programs.

Charlie first took a well-deserved three-month sabbatical to catch his breath and reflect on a host of issues facing MAF. He also worked out the finishing touches of the previously approved management structure that was put in place with his tenure. To give himself time to think and plan, he instructed office manager Dorothy Mount not to forward any but the most significant personal correspondence. Dorothy knew just what to hold back and what to send on to Mellis. She had been with MAF since 1955 and was efficient and sensitive.

It was up to Charlie Mellis to set in motion the new management structure that had been conceptually hammered out during Grady's watch. There had been much talk of decentralization, and Charlie determined to make it happen. The area directors now became area vice presidents. They were to live on the field and have a fair degree of autonomy, being responsible for the planning and operation of MAF services in their respective geographic areas. Roy Parsons retained the vice president portfolio for the African area programs. Hobey Lowrance became the Asia area vice president. Hank Worthington was made the vice president for the Latin America area (both South and Central America). Jim Lomheim began to take over all responsibilities related to accounting and served as treasurer from 1966 to 1974.[14]

Charlie gave the vice presidents wider discretion in financial decisions affecting their operations. He intended to empower field operations, and he succeeded. By the time his successor, Chuck Bennett, took up leadership on April 1, 1973, the vice presidents who had control over field accounts were in enviable financial positions vis-à-vis Fullerton. To restore central control over MAF overseas funds, Chuck had to redraw the balance of authority in favor of Fullerton.

Despite his long experience with a centralized management style, Charlie was able to grow and change with the times. He had driven himself hard from the start. After over twenty-five years of working his heart out to accomplish whatever needed to be done at MAF, he saw a need for change in his own life and in the MAF management structure. He wrote Bob and Betty Hutchins, "It is my prayer these days that as we learn more of the reality of His acceptance, that our love will be expressed to those around us in terms of greater acceptance and patience. As you well know, that's not easy for an old choleric like me. It takes some working at. But working at it increases the blessing!"[15]

The impact on Mellis for change was driven home in close encounters with his five maturing children: John, Jim, Gordon, Gil, and Esther. The children were growing up in the sixties, a time when insensitive power structures were coming under the indictment of young people seeking caring relationships and human values. Mellis's children profoundly challenged him to reexamine old assumptions about all human institutions, including the management of MAF. Charlie Mellis recognized that in the closing decades of the twentieth century, when Western society was increasingly depersonalizing life, the Christian community had to provide a better model than the hippies and the flower children. Many young people became "drop-outs" in society, pursuing warm interpersonal relationships. Charlie understood their concerns.

Following his tenure as president, Charlie studied the nature of caring communities in the history of the Christian Church. He pursued an advanced degree in studies at Fuller Theological Seminary's School of World Mission and distilled his thinking in his book, Committed Communities: Fresh Streams for World Missions (1976).

As president, Mellis recognized that youth needed a new approach and encouraged Norm Olson to come out with filmstrips such as I Met a Guy, the story of Don Roberson, Changing Colors, and West Irian Story (now Irian Jaya).

The first generation of MAF leadership by virtue of its respect for one another placed people above the company. From the beginning they retained a collegial model for arriving at corporate decisions. This way of operating continued under Charlie's leadership. However, by 1970 the organization had grown to the point that the membership as a whole did not have a voice in decision making. With Charlie up front, MAF leaders became sensitized to the critique being leveled against centralized structures. Some saw the MAF executive committee as the ultimate locus of power that needed to be opened up to voices from the ranks of MAF. Charlie was very sensitive to this perception.

As a result, part of the reorganization—the centralized decision making of the executive committee—was modified. In its place emerged a board of directors partly chosen by the MAF membership. These directors established policies related to planning, budgeting, and candidates.[16] Carrying out these policies were separate departments located in Fullerton, each with a manager and an advisory committee. This new management structure diffused decision making through the creation of six departments, each headed by a senior officer: personnel, Don Berry; information services, Norm Olson; technical, Tom Albright; research, Chuck Bennett; new developments, Bob Lehnhart; and controller, Dave Ellichman. The departments supported field operations and assisted management at all levels.[17]

As personnel director, Don Berry received the files of accepted candidates from the candidate committee of the board. The personnel committee then gave particular attention to their placement on the field. This directly involved the area vice presidents. Mellis did not enter the process until Berry brought a recommendation before him based on all the work that had been done. At that point, Mellis would either approve or raise some questions about the recommendation. In this way, decision making became much more diffused throughout the departments. Final responsibility for field placement, however, still lay with the president.

Charlie Mellis's probing intellect impacted the entire organization during his tenure. He initially met with the directors every Tuesday morning, but these sessions were not confined to technical matters related to day-to-day operations. Charlie sent out reading material dealing with the larger issues of Christian concern, be it race relations in Zimbabwe or MAF's cooperation with the intelligence-gathering operations of secular authorities. However, he recommended and the board decided that MAF would not be involved in any way with such activities.

In pushing on to new conceptual horizons, Charlie moved ahead of many of the staff and field personnel who were geared to carrying out technical tasks with excellence and not eager to philosophize on a variety of issues unrelated to their tasks. A good many of the staff in remote places could not quite understand why they should be addressing larger questions related to the Christian mission in the world. While the staff members were keenly interested in practical operational issues, Charlie felt the need to think through and push others to a more "adequate theology of mission" which in turn was linked, as he said, to a "more adequate theology of the church." This was potent grist for even the ivory-tower mill of academia. In this connection, Charlie placed a high premium on the department of research headed by Chuck Bennett and the department of new developments headed by Bob Lehnhart. The latter implemented ideas approved by the board. It is, therefore, not surprising that Lehnhart has gone on to develop support for relief efforts through Air Serv International, an independent organization formed to give logistical support for relief in Marxist-dominated countries in Africa (e.g., the Sudan, Mozambique, Angola, Somalia, Ethiopia). Charlie was not one to let moss grow under his feet, and people like Bennett and Lehnhart were "steel sharpened by steel" in their encounter with him.

Charlie's lively intellect led to a reformulated MAF mission statement that may be summarized as "Serving the Church Worldwide" in contrast to the earliest statement, "A Servant of Missions." Accordingly, the masthead of the periodical shifted to "Mission Aviation Fellowship" in September 1971; the logo changed from the airplane with Bible and cross to the soaring dove.

These changes created tensions and considerable growing pains. In an organization in which the personal touch and a word of encouragement were on equal footing with a highly disciplined approach to mission aviation, Charlie's pursuit of ideas ruffled some feathers. For Charlie it was important to think Christianly about all issues, and he reflected on the true meaning of faith mission work, not just as it related to finance but in the objectives to be pursued. He bent his mind to thinking through, among other things, a retirement philosophy and wrote the draft of a book on money stewardship.

While Charlie gave attention to the theology of the church and of mission, he also gave close attention to detail. Charlie worked through the minutiae of reorganization problems with his man-

agement team. To give annual planning a firm base, MAF moved
to an annual budget. This set in motion a whole new way of
planning for MAF's annual financial program and personnel
commitments.

While Charlie was a penetrating thinker, he also had the gift of
administration. He carried through the entire reorganization package that literally overhauled MAF and poised it for additional
growth and future effective service. Incoming president Chuck
Bennett was the beneficiary of all that Charlie had accomplished.
Bennett himself built solidly on this legacy.

At the same time it must be recognized that Charlie's administration polarized the rank-and-file. Charlie opened the door to
member participation in the nomination and election of members
of the board. In many ways, he helped give the members a voice
and stake in the future direction of MAF. When it came time to
choose his successor, the issue became politicized, with a significant number wanting a president who epitomized the pilot-
mechanic rather than the philosopher. Hank Worthington (a doer)
and Chuck Bennett (a thinker) represented the two types of experienced and technically certified MAF fliers whose names came
before the board in the selection of Mellis's successor. Mellis gave
his blessing to Bennett, and the board closed ranks behind that
choice.

MAF-Canada

In moving toward the future, the founding generation of MAF
leaders did not sit on their laurels. They kept on building, even as
they turned the work over to the new generation. The transitional
years saw another MAF organization come to life. The coming of
MAF-Canada was natural because Canada had been sending a
good number of fliers into mission aviation through MAF-US.
Thus a growing support and prayer constituency was taking form
in Canada. In 1971 there were five Canadian MAF families: Hugh
and Norma Beck of Toronto; Herb and Eloise Morgan from Sun-
dre, Alberta; Neil and Meredith Bittle of Calgary; Judy and Walt
Mood from Saskatchewan; and Henry Warkentin from Clearbrook,
British Columbia.

Nurturing the Canadian constituency had been an ongoing task of Jim and Betty Truxton. The Truxtons had made four "Operation Handshake" tours of Canada by 1971.[18] Momentum for a Canadian MAF organization grew over the next year and, in August 1972, seven dedicated Christian men interested in MAF gathered in Regina, the capital of Saskatchewan, to discuss formation of MAF-Canada. Dr. Robert Thompson, member of Parliament from Langley, British Columbia, a Christian statesman who himself had flown missionaries in Ethiopia during the post–World War II era, moved that they proceed to organize. All agreed![19]

MAF-Canada has been an important addition. It has expanded interest in the work of mission aviation in Canada, enlarged financial support for Canadians serving with MAF, and created a home base for Canadian fliers.

Some Significant Observations

In reviewing the record of MAF's formative years, one gets a sense of the unique commitment of its first-generation MAF families. They had the usual daily concerns that preoccupy all of us, and they had their share of temptations and frustrations. They worked at having close-knit families, but they were not superhuman. One does note, however, that their hearts beat in tune with the apostle Paul who said, "This one thing I do," and that was to serve God and the human family to the best of their ability. One writer cogently expressed the purpose of the work this way:

> MAF exists to fly planes in the service of Christ. We have no other purpose. Running an airline for the worldwide Church is a complex business. So many pieces fit together in the jigsaw to make it possible for missionaries, pastors, relief and medical supplies to fulfill their saving and healing ministry.
>
> Aircraft and accountancy, radios and repairs, supplies and supporters, propellers and prayers—these and much more are essential for mission flights.
>
> MAF depends heavily on people. Men and women, personally committed to Christ, who work incessantly as pilots, engineers, buyers, accountants and communicators. They serve wherever

MAF is found—at the point of immediate need around the world and in the vital bases here at home.[20]

This very complex business called for people to work together as a team. The team spirit made for ownership of the work by those who ran the far-flung flight programs. To retain a sense of partnership and ownership in a growing organization is not easy. MAF-US encouraged this team approach by empowering field leaders and families doing the work in distant places.

Another distinctive has been MAF's lay leadership. Even though MAF served mission agencies, it did not bring into its ranks people with advanced theological education. With few exceptions pilots or mechanics do not seek ordination, although they have set themselves apart to serve Christ with heart, mind, and hand. They come together from varied theological traditions but with strong conviction that Christ is the Savior and the proclamation of his gospel is for all people. As a parachurch organization, MAF attracts Christians from a wide range of denominations. A review of their biographies quickly reveals that the evangelical impulse is the common denominator that unites them in service and propels them to build God's kingdom.

Their spiritual lineage may be traced from the apostles, Augustine, and the Reformers to Jonathan Edwards and William Carey, the eighteenth-century English cobbler and missionary who labored over his workbench with a map of the world in his shop. Carey crafted boots and prayed for the world and eventually made it to India to preach the gospel. This same evangelical spirit is what leads MAF families to invest their lives in flight work that promotes Christian mission.

The essential team dimension of this organization has been an important factor in structuring more recent regional, evangelical initiatives. MAF's local flight programs require cooperation. Over the years this approach has torn down barriers separating evangelical missions. Today we increasingly see Christians forming coalitions to meet the spiritual and temporal needs of whole regions. Such is the work of ACROSS in the Sudan and "The CoMission" formed to assist post-Communist Russia, the world's largest nation.

In the wake of the dissolution of the Soviet Union and the fall of the Communist Party in 1993, Russia called for assistance in building a new spiritual and moral foundation for its entire public education system. Russia's Ministry of Education asked for help in introducing Christian values and ethics in place of the materialistic ideology of Marxist-Leninism. Seventy Christian organizations, including MAF-US, responded to this unprecedented call to influence a whole generation of Russian youths. MAF's role in "The CoMission" is providing technical and communications support and mapping out the logistics for providing educational materials to "The CoMission" team members working with the Russian school system.[21] What future opportunities for service this initial step in Russia will bring is in God's hands. MAF's experience in the past has led to ever-wider opportunities for Christian witness.

MAF-US in Recent Years

Ghislaine F. Benney

For MAF-US the 1970s and 1980s were marked by growth brought about by church expansion, global crises, and strained social and political systems. It was a period of significant changes in the developing world. Colonies became independent countries; national churches were maturing and assuming indigenous leadership. MAF recognized that its most difficult challenge lay in responding to the needs of all the overseas churches in regions where it served. Evangelism was no longer the exclusive purview of North American and European missions. Missionaries were now being sent from many developing nations. The face of world missions was changing.

National Training and Local Autonomy

Soon after Chuck Bennett assumed the presidency in 1973, MAF set a course of rapid expansion and responsiveness to local needs. It was building a base for the future. The organization developed a policy of giving autonomy and authority to national boards wherever feasible. Two ways of developing local autonomy were established. One was to incorporate national pilots into the membership of MAF. The other was to establish separate national entities.

As MAF strove to work with a maturing national church as co-equals, nationals played a more prominent role. Training programs for pilots, administrators, mechanics, and avionics technicians were carried out locally, and some graduates joined MAF as career missionaries. This was a significant step. Although membership

325

in MAF confers voting privileges for board members and policies, it exacts the responsibility of raising personal support.

By the late 1970s and early 1980s the internationalization of personnel in MAF programs was well underway. Several nationals had attained positions of leadership. In Indonesia, the Irian Jaya program was co-managed by a national and an American; another Indonesian served as program manager in East Kalimantan. Two Redlands-trained national pilots were flying in Honduras and Ecuador. The Brazil program was nationalized under the direction of its own board of directors. Later on, the programs in Mexico, Suriname, and Guatemala also assumed autonomy, followed by other nations still in various stages of gaining independence. Although MAF continues to provide assistance in the form of staff, supplemental funding, or aircraft, program direction in most of these countries is established by independent boards.

New Functions to Support Growth

In carrying out its ministry MAF had utilized a number of aircraft models, always researching which would best serve each program. However, since Cessna planes were best suited, they became the standard, and by the 1970s, MAF operated the largest civilian Cessna fleet in the world. It was then that the organization began considering helicopters, and in 1974, the first MAF helicopter started flying in Mexico.

As requests for MAF services continued to increase, so did growth. In 1974, flight hours reached 23,574. Inquiries from potential missionary pilots poured in, many from the thousands of Americans who had read about MAF pilot Nate Saint and the four missionaries who had given their lives in reaching out to the Aucas of Ecuador. Between 1974 and 1980, the number of staff members had swelled from 125 families to 200, and flight hours had increased 53 percent. MAF had become an integral part of the worldwide Christian mission effort.

Such expansion made it necessary to intensify attention to staff training and equipment procurement. A technical department was established at headquarters in Fullerton. Theirs was the responsibility to assess candidates, conduct orientation training for newly

Test flight of MAF's first helicopter in Irian Jaya, 1976.

accepted pilots, repair and modify aircraft, and conduct flight evaluation for other mission organizations.

During the 1970s, MAF devoted significant efforts toward the
goals of increasing flight safety, aircraft durability, size of payloads, and improving crash worthiness. Later on, however, finding suitable aircraft became increasingly difficult. In 1985 and 1986
Cessna discontinued manufacturing the 185 and 206 models that
were so well-suited to bush flying. Larger planes could not accom-
modate short, dirt airstrips. As a means of finding needed aircraft,
securing attractive discounts, and generating additional income
for the ministry, MAF operated a Cessna dealership. This proved
to be a means of supplying aircraft to other mission groups and
sister MAF organizations.

A Time of Harvest

The course that MAF set for itself proved to be both challenging and most rewarding. Meeting the needs of local churches as
well as those of mission agencies helped the growth of national
churches and local missionary efforts. At times the cost was high
for these national Christians. In Irian Jaya, Indonesia, for instance,
during one year alone, thirty Indonesian missionaries lost their

lives in various circumstances while bringing the gospel to neighboring tribes.

The spiritual flame lit by the first wave of Western missionaries was now burning brightly. The zealous new believers had an intense desire to know the Scriptures and spread the good news. MAF planes helped make this a reality. In 1973 Theological Education by Extension (TEE) was enthusiastically set in motion by the national church in West Kalimantan, Indonesia. Thousands of local pastors throughout the world have since received their training from teachers flown in by MAF. It will be recalled that the idea of "Institutes"—using the plane to fly in pastors—was a technique that Jim Lomheim first introduced in Mexico. The wonderful mobility of the plane was extended to providing Theological Education by Extension to equip these shepherds spiritually, on location, in remote areas, even while they ministered to their flocks.

As evangelism bore fruit and touched the hearts of millions, social concern grew with it. Increasingly, local hospitals and clinics expanded their concept of medical care to include community health. Such programs focus on preventive aspects of health care, along with simple cures. In some areas, under the guidance of a health committee, health becomes the responsibility of the community and its chosen village health worker. These local workers are trained in their villages to use a few medicines that can usually treat up to 80 percent of local health problems, without the assistance of a medical professional or a hospital.

The airplane continues to be ideally suited for these programs. It flies health-care trainers and supervisors in and out of isolated villages, leaving village health workers to function on their own. The airplane becomes more than an ambulance—it becomes the lifeline that carries medical personnel and provisions to people without access to hospitals.

Responding to Unique Challenges

By 1980 the national church was coming of age in many regions. Pioneering ministries were giving way to development ministries. Increasingly, MAF flights for churches and missions were in support of relief and community development efforts. However, these

MAF providing transport with Cessna "Caravan" in Zaire, 1985. Nationals are loading bags of grain as part of a relief effort.

opportunities called for much wisdom. How could MAF respond to the cries of the needy, raise the necessary resources, and meet more stringent government requirements?

Planning and controlling the international flow of MAF resources had become a major dilemma. Which regions should receive the most help? What types of ministry deserve priority? How much of MAF resources should go toward indigenization? Which programs should become financially self-supporting? These questions and many more needed to be addressed.

MAF struggled valiantly in responding to needs, maximizing its resources, and balancing the budget. For years, expenses exceeded income. More staff, more fuel, more parts, more housing, more storage, and more ground transportation were always needed. Needs for MAF services in the Philippines, South Korea, Nepal, India, Burma (today Myanmar), Micronesia, China, Singapore, Pakistan, and Kampuchea could not be addressed. Reliance on God's providence has always been a hallmark of MAF. Nonetheless, it tugged at the hearts of MAF leaders and field personnel to be unable to give the needed help.

Famine and refugee relief became a larger part of total MAF activities. It was an MAF plane that flew the journalists who broke the news to the world about the famine in Ethiopia. When in Octo-

ber 1984 the American public suddenly became aware of that devastating famine, MAF experienced a dramatic response to its TV
and radio broadcasts. "Operation Flights For Life" raised more
than eight million dollars to help the relief efforts of the famine-
stricken in Africa. But donor fatigue to world calamities soon set
in, and the familiar budget struggles returned.

Adding to the pressures was the burden of new government
requirements or restrictions. In Latin America, for example, several governments were beginning to require that U.S.-based missions justify their entrance, presence, and activities in terms established by politicians and anthropologists. This remains particularly
true for those working with indigenous tribal groups.

Partners in Ministry

MAF has always looked to God first and then to churches and
individual partners to provide the means for ministry. Although
prayer letters from field staff to their supporters had long served
as the primary avenue for informing donors, the need was felt to
communicate on all areas of the ministry. In 1978, a fresh publication was inaugurated to report on MAF activities. *FlightWatch*,
which had previously been initiated as a newsletter to volunteers
across the U.S., grew to become one of the most important sources
of news to MAF partners and friends. MAF also used the pages of
FlightWatch as well as its *LifeLink* magazine to inform donors on
program activities and developments at home.

By the early 1980s a number of cost-cutting measures had been
implemented to reduce costs and increase effectiveness. Personal
computers were introduced in the field to help manage programs.
Accounting and flight operations were now "on-line"; headquarters, which had been divided between the Fullerton and
Ramona locations, were brought under one roof in Redlands, California, in 1980.

Renewed Vision

In 1985 Max Meyers was appointed president and chief executive officer, a post he still holds today. The former general direc-

tor of MAF-Australia, who had been serving on the MAF-US board, placed spiritual renewal and pastoral care of the staff among his top priorities. He explains: "The cry of the lost and the needy is loud—and heartrending. It is our privilege to be able to respond in so many ways. But the lasting, eternal value of the MAF response will be in direct proportion to our individual and corporate commitment to Jesus Christ. That is the priority!" Mr. Meyers also saw the need to redefine the purpose of MAF to include current and emerging technologies that could be harnessed for the organization's widening service.

MAF built its reputation by providing technical solutions for mission outreach. Consequently, mission organizations turn to MAF for such needs. It was this experience with communications technology that led to the establishment in 1985 of a shortwave radio network in Mali. This network supports nearly all missionaries serving there as well as health and development programs throughout the country. This same experience also spurred the 1992 invitation for MAF to manage logistics and electronic communications for numerous Christian groups operating in the newly opened countries of Albania and the former U.S.S.R. The CoMission discussed in the previous chapter is part of this initiative.

Today, as it continues to answer God's call, MAF-US extends its ministry around the globe. In more than twenty countries of Africa, Asia, Latin America, and Eastern Europe, the men and women of MAF use technology to serve the church worldwide. Aviation remains at the center of its ministry, but the communications technology that has served MAF aircraft for years is now becoming significant in its own right.

The ministry is carried on by more than 240 missionary families who serve in excess of three hundred Christian organizations. They operate sophisticated equipment that helps bring God's love and blessings to a world in pain. Their tools are ninety aircraft flying some four million miles each year, more than six hundred HF and VHF shortwave radios, two satellite terminals, and a global electronic mail network.

As the twenty-first century approaches, the "jungle mules" of MAF continue to fly missionaries, but the role of MAF has expanded to support local pastors and nationals. Some MAF staff trek for long distances in dense vegetation to show the *Jesus* film. Others help relief workers serve Rwandan refugees in hostile territory while maintaining contact with their headquarters via satellite. In one instance, a MAF pilot even settled a land boundary dispute by using his satellite-based Global Positioning System.

The work of Christ moves forward on many fronts, and our story of MAF glimpses the varied dimensions of this task. We have seen the worldwide Christian enterprise stretching from the jungles of Ecuador to the mountains of Irian Jaya, from the plateaus of Ethiopia back to the rain forests of Kalimantan. The mobility of the MAF plane and the communications link it provides has contributed greatly to the reality of the world as a global village. MAF, as the largest private air fleet in the world, is in some ways reducing the isolation of people in remote underdeveloped regions, comparable to what the transistor radio has done in spreading information generally.

MAF crosses barriers and helps to level them. In so doing it reaches a host of heretofore isolated groups of people and diverse "people groups." Its satellite link can virtually reach any location on earth, no matter how remote. Although many regions are still inaccessible because of topographical barriers or political decisions, with the help of MAF, the gospel can be preached anywhere. These possibilities are reason for great rejoicing as MAF celebrates its fiftieth anniversary in 1995. Indeed, much has been accomplished. To God be the glory! Yet much still remains to be done. As we stand on the threshold of the next millennium, MAF is committed to offer people the hope that comes from knowing the resurrected Christ. It is in his name that MAF moves out, as on wings of eagles, to meet the needs of suffering humanity.

Central to the heart and motivation of MAF is sharing the good news and making disciples. It is the driving force that gave birth to MAF and it continues to be its mission today.

The purpose of Mission Aviation Fellowship is to multiply the effectiveness of the Church, using aviation and other strategic technologies to reach the world for Christ.

Epilogue

Arthur F. Glasser

When I read this lucid account of the first decades of MAF, I was immediately struck by its similarity to Acts in the New Testament. Both record simple beginnings—the united prayer of a few dedicated people meeting in relative obscurity in urban settings. Both accounts cover approximately the same time period—about thirty years. Both are comprehensive and speak of vision and obedience, opposition and suffering, faith and victory. Both evolve into dynamic movements reaching out to the nations.

The chapters making up this record of MAF's early history were deliberately and wisely designed to focus on essentials. They begin with the vision that God simultaneously gave to several young Christians in various parts of the world in the early 1940s and trace the manner in which this vision slowly yet steadily was transformed into reality. How necessary steps of faith were taken, with God often responding with vigorous and often breathtaking answers to those who are just beginning the journey of faith. Then followed consolidation and growth as MAF entered the long haul in which faith was tested, obedience proved costly, and a growing sense of unity began to overtake the diverse few who had risked everything to become involved, welding them into a team that reflected genuine interrelatedness, supportive loyalty, and the growing maturation of each member. All this in spite of early setbacks and some grievous losses. And yet, always the joy of knowing that "their labor was not in vain in the Lord," for their overall strategic objective was to serve by all means those who were reaching out with the gospel into areas where air transport was a virtual necessity.

This narrative of the formative years of MAF embraces all the significant elements of its first generation, and it should serve as an indispensable resource for its future.

The MAF experience is a wonderful demonstration of what people like us can accomplish—under God—when we surrender to Christ's lordship and put heart and soul, strength and resources into the task of making him known. It is natural for us to ask ourselves what we have learned and personally appropriated from reading this book.

Here are the lessons that these chapters brought to me, and which I trust will make me more faithful in my "prayer association" with MAF in the days ahead. I am sure that after you go through my list you will feel that I have left out a few. So be it. "I see through a glass darkly," and my insights rarely achieve anything approximating comprehensiveness. Nonetheless, I am convinced of the following:

1. I should not "despise the day of small things" (Zech. 4:10) but rather be willing to listen to the concerns and dreams of young Christians. In the 1940s, only a few Christians were really impressed with the beginnings of MAF. Most were not on our Lord's missionary wave length! Just spectators! And think of what they missed!

2. I should concentrate my prayer support of MAFers on the vitality of their fellowship with God, their disciplined daily study of the Word of God, and their obedience to the command to be filled with the Holy Spirit (Eph. 5:17–18). We don't want any to be out of the will of God in these matters.

3. I should enter into the lives of MAF personnel and pray that they will not lose heart or despise the work in which they are engaged (Hag. 2:3). Much of the "service ministry" of MAF is repetitive, and vigilance is needed if one and all are to remain on top of each day's agenda, day after day. Let's pray that at the end of each day they will be able to lift their hearts to the Lord and thank him for enabling them to accomplish the work which he gave them to do (John 17:4).

4. I should not gloss over the temptations of flesh and spirit that beset all God's servants, especially MAF team members who are scattered widely over vast distances and are not sustained by par-

ticipation in the joys and challenges of congregational life, worship, and fellowship (Heb. 12:12).

5. I should not forget that although MAF personnel serve in just about the most complex and demanding mission organization in the world, God is continually bringing them in touch with people who need both the gospel and their personal witness to Jesus Christ (2 Tim. 4:5). May they always be quick to respond to the Spirit's leading that they take the initiative and speak on his behalf.

6. I should not forget the unusual demands Christian workers make of their leaders, expecting imaginative direction in ways that confirm God's guidance and blessing. Leaders of MAF must provide this in ways that convey wisdom and authority and reflect vital linkage with the living God (Eph. 4:11–14). All leaders need to be prayed for and encouraged.

7. I should not overlook the importance of MAF leaders being open in their interaction with one another, not forgetting that one of the most forward-looking MAF decisions was their need to heed Mellis's contention that the time had come for "missionary" to give way to "mission" in the MAF name. This change provided dynamic and necessary response to the changes then taking place in postwar missions (Acts 16:9–10).

8. I should pray that MAF leaders be kept from pursuing the novel to the diminishing of their involvement in the organization's primary commitments. The desire to be venturesome must be carefully controlled when new challenges call for exploration. All service that contributes to the priority task of evangelism—by word and deed—must be carefully protected. Strange as it may seem, Christian leaders tend to lose this sense of priority.

9. I should not forget that Satan and his hosts relentlessly attack by every means the holiness, unity, and effectiveness of an organization such as MAF. Fortunately, in our day evangelicals are realizing as never before their need to be more resolute in their resistance to "the powers" (Eph. 6:10–18). Discerning the spirits, resisting the devil, claiming the victory of the cross, wielding the sword of Holy Scripture, walking in the Spirit—all these are skills that MAFers must develop!

10. I must not overlook the demands "the ecumenical problem" poses for MAF personnel, scattered as they are throughout the

world. How should they respond to the diversity they encounter in the worldwide Christian movement when they find themselves working alongside those who also profess Jesus as Lord, but with whom they seriously disagree on matters of truth and practice? Will they be "swift to hear and slow to speak," avoiding judgmental polemics? Will they express the desire to engage with them in prayer and Bible study to work toward joint agreement on the issues that provoked disagreement? To refuse to enter this arena was hardly the position David assumed (Ps. 119:63).

11. I must not forget that MAFers on occasion are obliged to contact government officials in connection with their work. Although Caesar may not always be the friend of Jesus Christ, Christian duty demands that one renders to him the things that are his (Luke 20:25). This entails faithfulness to the demanding roles of "salt" and "light," to the end that glory will come to God (Matt. 5:13–14).

12. Finally, I find that I must pray that all MAF personnel are enabled to cope with the fact that on occasion *mystery* must be written large across all Christian experience and service. Political obstacles, costly accidents, unexpected fatalities, physical limitations, financial strains, spiritual dryness, disappointments in fellow-workers, on and on—the list is long. Only by faith can one accept with confidence the promise that God is working all things together unto his good that he may choose to disclose in his time and his way (Rom. 8:28).

So then, this is my prayer list for MAF and its leadership in the days ahead. And I am truly grateful for the ways in which this book has awakened me anew to my responsibilities related to the privilege of being part of the large family of "MAF Friends" who stand behind—by faith and sacrifice—just about the most wonderful and most effective missionary organization in the business today. Thank God that the mood of MAF is not to turn back, but to press on!

"Does the road go uphill all the way?"
—Yes, to the very end!
"And a day's journey, does it take the whole long day?"
—From morn till night, my friend.

                                                        Author unknown

Maps

Locations on these maps highlight places mentioned in the narrative.

1. Mexico
2. Peru and Ecuador
3. Africa
4. Sudan and Ethiopia
5. Colombia and Venezuela
6. Honduras
7. Australia, New Zealand and New Guinea
8. New Guinea
9. Northern Brazil, Guyana and Suriname
10. Zaire, Zambia, and Zimbabwe
11. Southeasrt Asia
12. Chad
13. South Africa
14. MAF-US Global Service, 1995

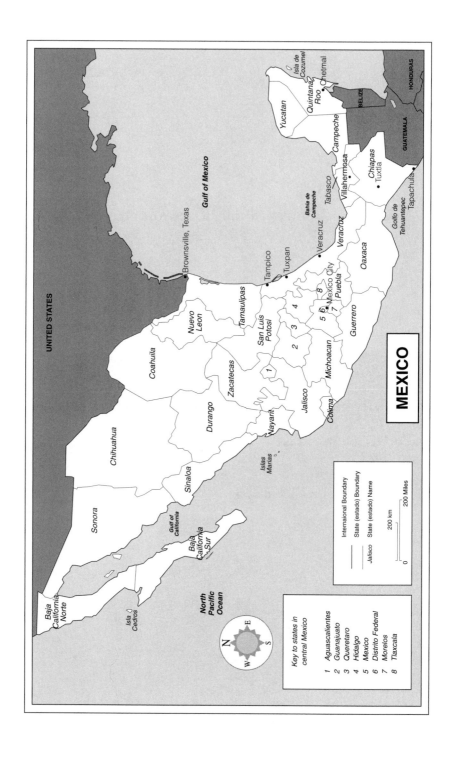

MEXICO

UNITED STATES

Baja California Norte

Isla Cedros

Baja California Sur

Gulf of California

Sonora

Chihuahua

Sinaloa

Durango

Coahuila

Nuevo Leon

Tamaulipas

Zacatecas

Islas Marias

Nayarit

Jalisco

Colima

Michoacan

San Luis Potosi

1

2

3

4

5 6

8

7

Guerrero

Oaxaca

Puebla

Mexico City

Veracruz

Tuxpan

Tampico

Brownsville, Texas

Gulf of Mexico

Bahia de Campeche

Veracruz

Tabasco

Villahermosa

Golfo de Tehuantepec

Chiapas

Tuxtla

Tapachula

Campeche

Yucatan

Isla de Cozumel

Quintana Roo

Chetmal

BELIZE

GUATEMALA

HONDURAS

North Pacific Ocean

International Boundary
State (estado) Boundary
Jalisco   State (estado) Name

0   100   200 km
0   100   200 Miles

Key to states in central Mexico
1 Aguascalientes
2 Guanajuato
3 Queretaro
4 Hidalgo
5 Mexico
6 Distrito Federal
7 Morelos
8 Tlaxcala

N E S W

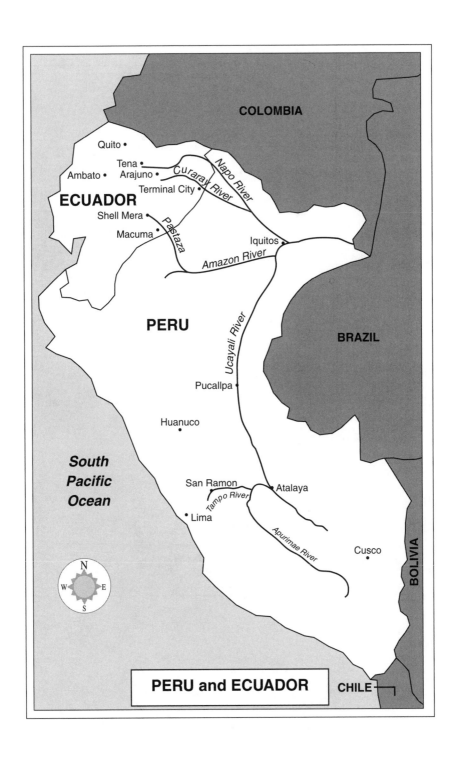

COLOMBIA

Quito •

Tena •
Ambato • Arajuno •
Terminal City •

ECUADOR

Shell Mera •

Macuma •

Curarak River

Napo River

Pastaza

Iquitos •

Amazon River

PERU

Ucayali River

BRAZIL

Pucallpa •

Huanuco •

South
Pacific
Ocean

San Ramon •
Tampo River
• Lima

Atalaya •

Apurimae River

Cusco •

BOLIVIA

N
W E
S

PERU and ECUADOR

CHILE

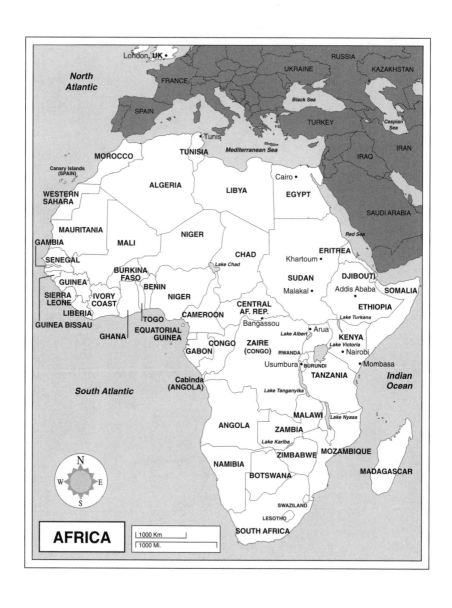

North
Atlantic

London, UK •

FRANCE

RUSSIA

UKRAINE

KAZAKHSTAN

SPAIN

Black Sea

TURKEY

Caspian
Sea

• Tunis

Mediterranean Sea

IRAN

MOROCCO

TUNISIA

IRAQ

Canary Islands
(SPAIN)

ALGERIA

LIBYA

Cairo •

EGYPT

WESTERN
SAHARA

SAUDI ARABIA

MAURITANIA

NIGER

Red Sea

GAMBIA

MALI

CHAD

ERITREA

SENEGAL

Lake Chad

Khartoum •

DJIBOUTI

GUINEA

BURKINA
FASO

SUDAN

SIERRA
LEONE

BENIN

Malakal •

Addis Ababa •

SOMALIA

IVORY
COAST

NIGER

ETHIOPIA

LIBERIA

CENTRAL
AF. REP.

Lake Turkana

GUINEA BISSAU

TOGO

CAMEROON

Bangassou

• Arua

GHANA

EQUATORIAL
GUINEA

Lake Albert

KENYA

CONGO

ZAIRE

Lake Victoria

GABON

(CONGO)

RWANDA

• Nairobi

BURUNDI

• Mombasa

Usumbura •

Indian
Ocean

Cabinda
(ANGOLA)

TANZANIA

South Atlantic

Lake Tanganyika

MALAWI

Lake Nyasa

ANGOLA

ZAMBIA

Lake Kariba

MOZAMBIQUE

ZIMBABWE

NAMIBIA

MADAGASCAR

BOTSWANA

N

W   E

S

SWAZILAND

LESOTHO

SOUTH AFRICA

AFRICA

1000 Km
1000 Mi.

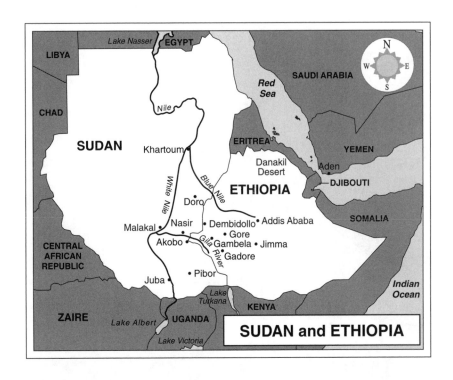

SUDAN and ETHIOPIA

COLOMBIA and VENEZUELA

BELIZE

Isal de la Bahia

Caribbean Sea

GUATEMALA

HONDURAS

Coco River

Siguatepeque

Bilhuascarma

Tegucigalpa

EL
SALVADOR

NICARAGUA

North
Pacific
Ocean

HONDURAS

100 Km

100 Mi.

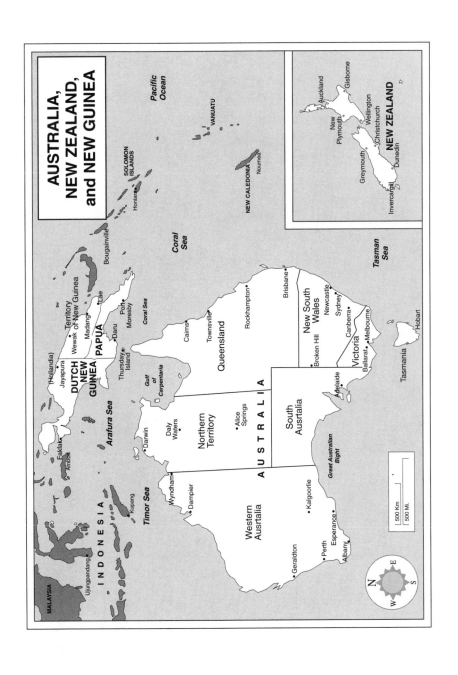

AUSTRALIA,
NEW ZEALAND,
and NEW GUINEA

Pacific
Ocean

VANUATU

SOLOMON
ISLANDS

Honiara

NEW CALEDONIA

Nouméa

NEW ZEALAND

Auckland

Gisborne

New
Plymouth

Wellington

Greymouth

Christchurch

Invercargill

Dunedin

Coral
Sea

Tasman
Sea

Bougainville

Territory
of New Guinea

Wewak

Madang

Lae

PAPUA

Port
Moresby

Daru

Coral Sea

DUTCH
NEW
GUINEA

(Hollandia)

Jayapura

Thursday
Island

Gulf
of
Carpentaria

Brisbane

Rockhampton

New South
Wales

Newcastle

Sydney

Cairns

Townsville

Queensland

Canberra

Broken Hill

Melbourne

Victoria

Ballarat

Hobart

Tasmania

Fakfak

Ambon

Arafura Sea

Darwin

Daly
Waters

Northern
Territory

Alice
Springs

South
Ausrtalia

Adelaide

A U S T R A L I A

INDONESIA

Kupang

Timor Sea

Wyndham

Dampier

Western
Ausrtalia

Great Australian
Bight

Kalgoorlie

Ujungpandang

Geraldton

Perth

Esperance

Albany

MALAYSIA

500 Km.
500 Mi.

N
E
S
W

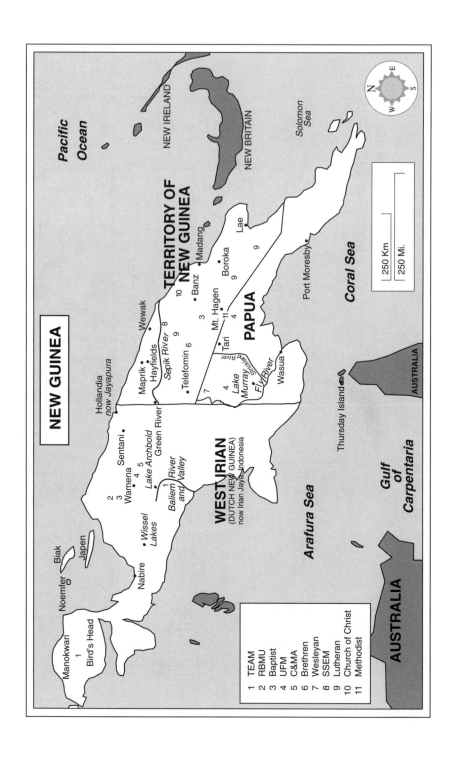

NEW GUINEA

Pacific Ocean

NEW IRELAND

NEW BRITAIN

Solomon Sea

TERRITORY OF NEW GUINEA

Manokwari
Bird's Head
Noemfer
Biak
Japen

Nabire

Wissel Lakes

Wamena
Sentani

Lake Archbold
Baliem River and Valley

Green River

WEST IRIAN
(DUTCH NEW GUINEA)
now Irian Jaya, Indonesia

Hollandia
now Jayapura

Maprik
Hayfields
Wewak

Sepik River

Telefomin

Lake Murray

Fly River

Wasua

Strickland River

Mt. Hagen
Banz
Boroka
Madang
Lae

Tari

PAPUA

Port Moresby

Coral Sea

Thursday Island

Arafura Sea

Gulf of Carpentaria

AUSTRALIA

AUSTRALIA

250 Km
250 Mi.

1	TEAM
2	RBMU
3	Baptist
4	UFM
5	C&MA
6	Brethren
7	Wesleyan
8	SSEM
9	Lutheran
10	Church of Christ
11	Methodist

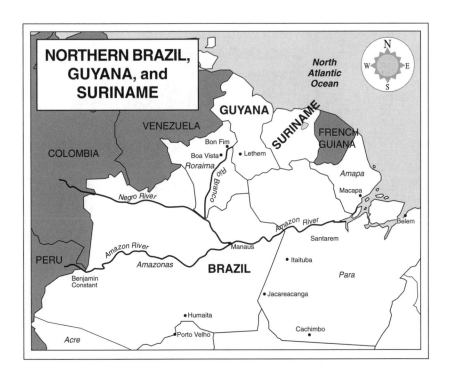

NORTHERN BRAZIL, GUYANA, and SURINAME

North Atlantic Ocean

N
W E
S

GUYANA

SURINAME

VENEZUELA

FRENCH GUIANA

COLOMBIA

Bon Fim

Boa Vista • • Lethem

Roraima

Amapa

Rio Branco

Macapa

Negro River

Amazon River

Belem

PERU

Amazon River

Manaus

Santarem

Amazonas

BRAZIL

• Itaituba

Benjamin Constant

Para

• Jacareacanga

• Humaita

Acre

• Porto Velho

Cachimbo •

CENTRAL AFRICAN REPUBLIC

SUDAN

ETHIOPIA
Lake Turkana

CAMEROON

UGANDA

• Karawa

Lake Albert

KENYA

Kisangani •

Bunia •

Lake Victoria

CONGO

GABON

ZAIRE (CONGO)

Lake Kivu

RWANDA

• Nairobi

BURUNDI

Cabinda (ANGOLA)

• Kinshasa (Leopoldville)

Kananga • (Luluabourg)

Kalemie • (Albertville)

TANZANIA

Tshikapa •

Lake Tanganyika

South Atlantic

N
W E
S

ANGOLA

ZAIRE, ZAMBIA, and ZIMBABWE

Lubumbashi •

• Kasama

Lake Nyasa

Kitwe •

ZAMBIA

MALAWI

Lusaka •

Lake Kariba

Mt. Darwin •

MOZAMBIQUE

Indian Ocean

NAMIBIA

BOTSWANA

ZIMBABWE

Harare •

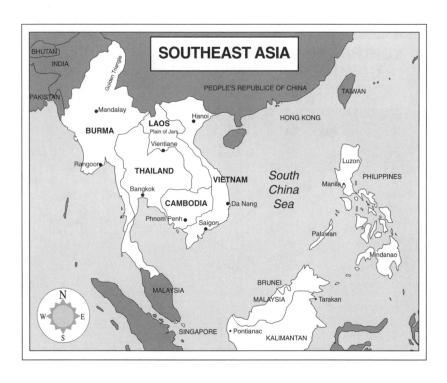

SOUTHEAST ASIA

BHUTAN
INDIA
Golden Triangle
PAKISTAN
PEOPLE'S REPUBLICE OF CHINA
TAIWAN
Mandalay
Hanoi
HONG KONG
BURMA
LAOS
Plain of Jars
Vientiane
Luzon
Rangoon
THAILAND
PHILIPPINES
VIETNAM
Manila
Bangkok
South
China
Sea
CAMBODIA
Da Nang
Phnom Penh
Saigon
Palawan
Mindanao
MALAYSIA
BRUNEI
MALAYSIA
Tarakan
SINGAPORE
Pontianac
KALIMANTAN
N
W E
S

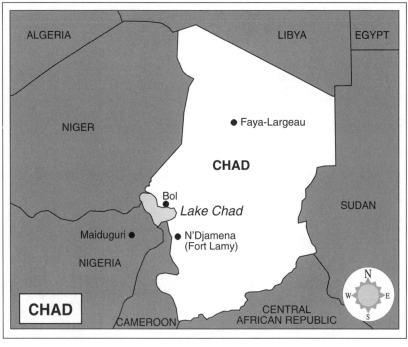

ALGERIA
LIBYA
EGYPT
NIGER
Faya-Largeau
CHAD
Bol
Lake Chad
SUDAN
Maiduguri
N'Djamena
(Fort Lamy)
NIGERIA
CHAD
CAMEROON
CENTRAL
AFRICAN REPUBLIC
N
W E
S

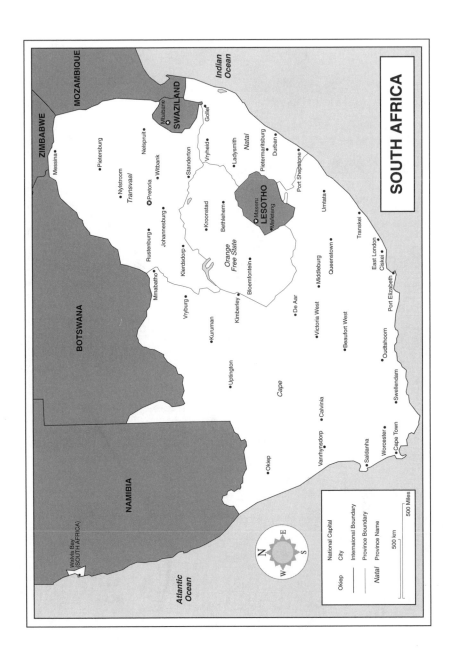

SOUTH AFRICA

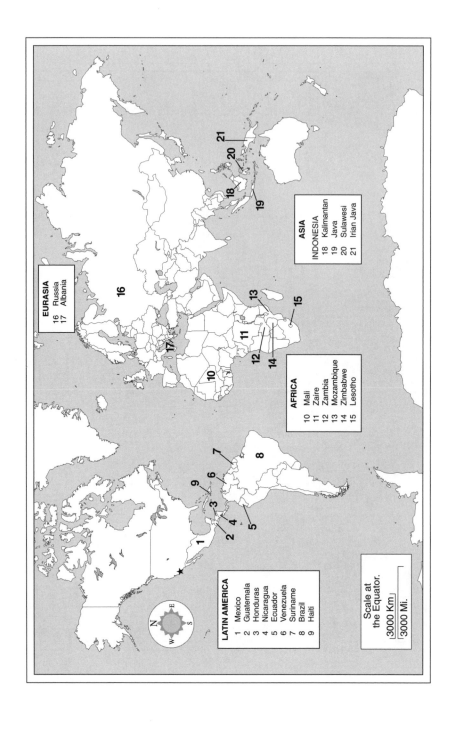

EURASIA
16 Russia
17 Albania

ASIA
INDONESIA
18 Kalimantan
19 Java
20 Sulawesi
21 Irian Java

AFRICA
10 Mali
11 Zaire
12 Zambia
13 Mozambique
14 Zimbabwe
15 Lesotho

LATIN AMERICA
1 Mexico
2 Guatemala
3 Honduras
4 Nicaragua
5 Ecuador
6 Venezuela
7 Suriname
8 Brazil
9 Haiti

N
E
W
S

Scale at
the Equator.
3000 Km
3000 Mi.

Notes

Chapter 1: Birth of a Vision

1. "C.A.M.F. Diary," *Missionary Aviation (MA)*, January–March 1946. The reference to the prayer meeting with Jack Wyrtzen should not be read to mean that the name Christian Airmen's Missionary Fellowship (CAMF) had been coined. The article allows us to say with certainty that the name CAMF was in use by spring 1944. Much of the information in this chapter came from interviews with Jim Truxton, Betty Greene, and Grady Parrott.

2. Truxton to "All Members of CAMF," September 1, 1945.

3. Truxton to Kendon, August 15, 1945.

4. Don Hoke, "Sketch of the Month," *His,* September 1944, 24–27; Betty Lee Skinner, *Daws: The Story of Dawson Trotman, Founder of the Navigators* (Grand Rapids: Zondervan, 1974).

5. Trotman to Truxton, June 29, 1944. Biola University is located twenty-three miles south of downtown Los Angeles in La Mirada, California.

6. Truxton to Trotman, July 4, 1944.

7. Ibid.

8. Ibid.

9. Ibid.

10. Trotman to Truxton, July 11, 1944.

11. Truxton to Trotman, July 17, 1944.

12. Ibid.

13. Trotman to Truxton, July 22, 1944.

14. Truxton to Trotman, July 28, 1944.

15. Ibid.

16. Christian Airmen's Missionary Fellowship, "Statement," 1944.

17. CAMF, "Speed the Light on Wings of the Wind," 1944; see Matthew 4:16; Psalms 18:10; 104:3 for references on this theme.

18. Truxton to Trotman, July 4, 1944.

19. Truxton to Rosenbaum, August 16, 1944.

20. Greene to Dietrich Buss, May 10, 1989.

21. Truxton to Rosenbaum, August 16, 1944.

22. Truxton to Trotman, September 5, 1944.

23. Fisk to Truxton, September 8, 1944.

24. Truxton to Trotman, October 21, 1944.

Chapter 2: In His Time and in His Way

1. Trotman to Greene, October 23, 1944. Much of the information in this chapter came from interviews with Jim Truxton, Betty Greene, and Grady Parrott.

2. Greene to Truxton, November 24, 1944.

3. Truxton to Greene, November 24, 1944.

4. Greene to Truxton, December 2, 1944.

5. Truxton to Greene, December 4, 1944.

6. Greene to Truxton, December 16, 1944.

7. Greene to Truxton, December 12, 1944.

8. Truxton to Greene, March 12, 1945.

9. Truxton to Greene, December 16, 1944.

10. Truxton to Greene, January 20, 1945.

11. Truxton to Parrott, April 29, 1945.

12. Greene to Truxton, March 12, 1945; Truxton to Greene, April 14, 1945.

13. Greene to Truxton, April 14, 1945.

14. Greene to Parrott, July 10, 1945.

15. Greene to Truxton, March 14, 1945.

16. Greene to Truxton, February 27, 1945.

17. Ibid.

18. Truxton to Parrott, March 8, 1945.

19. Greene to Truxton, May 2, 1945.

20. Greene to Parrott, August 3, 1945. The seal on the incorporation papers is dated June 4, 1945.

21. Truxton to co-workers, August 11, 1945.

22. Truxton to Fisk, Buyers, and Parrott, June 7, 1945.

23. *MA*, July–September 1945.

24. *MA*, January–March 1946.

25. Ibid.

26. "Report of the Missionary Aviation Fellowship of Mildmay Center, London, England," 1944.

Chapter 3: Launching Operations in Mexico

1. Truxton to co-workers, October 16, 1945. Much of the information in this chapter comes from interviews with Jim Truxton, Betty Greene, Grady Parrott, and Claire Mellis.

2. Mellis to Greene, August 22, 1945.

3. James and Marti Hefley, *Uncle Cam* (Waco, Tex.: Word Books, 1974), 82–85.

4. Greene to "Dear Co-laborers," October 1, 1945.

5. Minutes of the Board of Directors, January 7 and 10, 1946.

6. Truxton to Greene, March 11, 1946.

7. Truxton to "Dear Co-workers," February 18, 1946.

8. Greene to "Dear Co-workers," March 10, 1946.

9. "And Now . . . Mexico," *MA*, April–June 1946, 14.

10. Chicle huts are structures used for temporary storage of the latex extracted from tropical trees that produce chicle, a substance used primarily in the manufacture of chewing gum.

11. Greene to Parrott, March 27, 1946.

12. Russell Hitt, *Jungle Pilot* (Grand Rapids: Zondervan 1973), 48.

13. Ibid., 64.

14. Truxton to "Dear All," May 14, 1946.

15. Mellis to Greene, December 11, 1946.

Chapter 4: Clarifying the Mission

1. Truxton to "Dear Gang," May 28, 1948. Much of the information in this chapter comes from interviews with Jim Truxton, Betty Greene, Claire Mellis, and Grady Parrott.

2. Truxton to co-workers, April 2, 1946.

3. Truxton to Parrott, April 23, 1946.

4. Greene to "Fellow Workers in Christ," July 30, 1946.

5. Greene to Mellis, June 28, 1946.

6. Greene to "Dear Fellows," July 24, 1946.

7. Greene to Truxton, August 27, 1946.

8. Greene to Mellis, September 30, 1946.

9. Greene to "Charlie and Jim, et al.," October 5, 1946.

10. Ibid.

11. Truxton to co-workers, July 10, 1946, and August 17, 1946.

12. Mellis to co-workers, October 12, 1946. The elements of this package included the resignation of Jim Buyers as executive secretary, Elizabeth Greene as secretary-treasurer, and Charles Mellis as acting secretary. The responsibilities of executive secretary were simply absorbed by the secretary-treasurer.

Chapter 5: Agony and Ecstasy

1. Hefley, *Uncle Cam*, 145. Much of the information in this chapter comes from extensive interviews with Jim Truxton, Betty Greene, Grady Parrott, Darlene Lomheim, and Claire Mellis.

2. Truxton to Parrott and Mellis, July 17 and 21, 1947.

3. Charles Mellis, "Report, Missionary Aviation Conference," Summer 1947; "Wings of Praise and Prayer" (WPP), September 1947.

4. Truxton to Parrott and Mellis, July 28, 1947.

5. Greene to Truxton and Parrott, August 12, 1947.

6. Hefley, *Uncle Cam*, 157.

7. Greene to Parrott and Mellis, November 24, 1948; Parrott to Board, December 22, 1948.

8. Ibid.

9. Montgomery to Mellis, December 17 and 27, 1947.

10. Montgomery to Mellis, December 28, 1947; Montgomery to Truxton, December 29, 1947.

11. William G. Nyman to Truxton, June 19, 1948.

12. *MA*, March–April 1947.

13. Grady Parrott, "Development of MAF/Tabasco Flight Program," December 3, 1993.

14. Truxton to Parrott and Mellis, May 20, 1947; "What About Survey," *MA*, September–October 1947.

15. WPP, November–December 1947.

16. MAF *LifeLink*, 1993, 3, 19.

17. Truxton to Parrott and Mellis, December 2, 1947.

18. Truxton to Lomheim, October 30, 1947.

19. Truxton to Lomheim, November 6, 1947.

20. Truxton to Parrott and Mellis, November 11, 1947.

21. Ibid.

22. Truxton to Parrott, Mellis, and Greene, December 24, 1947.

Chapter 6: Founding of MAF in the United Kingdom

1. *Mildmay Outlook*, publication of MWE, March 1945. Much of the information in this chapter comes from an extended interview and correspondence with Stuart King. Publication of his *Hope Has Wings* (London: Harper Collins, 1993) adds much detail to the story beyond what is found here.

2. Kendon to Truxton, August 24, 1945.

3. "Report on the Missionary Aviation Fellowship of Mildmay Center, London, England," 1945.

4. H. Wakelin Coxill to Kendon, September 22, 1945.

5. Kendon to Truxton, November 6, 1945.

6. Ibid.

7. Kendon to "Friends of MAF," September 1946. In 1957, Stuart King and Charlie Mellis conducted a joint African survey.

8. Truxton to Kendon, October 8, 1946.

9. Parrott to Kendon, June 18, 1947.

10. Stuart King, "History of Missionary Aviation Fellowship From

Standpoint of British MAF."

11. Hemmings diary, January 23, 1948.

12. Banham, "Local Kenya Survey," March 4, 1948.

13. Hemmings, "Letter from Crew" #27; Banham, "Western Kenya Survey," undated (circa March 1948).

14. Hemmings, "Letter from Crew" #31; Banham, "East Kenya Survey," undated (circa March 1948).

15. Banham, "Letter From Crew" #35.

16. Banham, "Letter From Crew" #37, June 14, 1948.

17. Hemmings, "Accident of Gemini," August 8, 1948.

18. Malcolm Forsberg, *Last Days on the Nile* (Philadelphia: Lippincott, 1966), 73–80.

19. MAF-UK, "Sudan News Letter" #5, August 16, 1950.

20. Ibid.

21. Parrott to Hemmings, January 17, 1951. Back in London, Betty Greene stopped by the MAF-UK office in February 1951 on her way to fly for SIM in Nigeria. She met Bill Knights in the MAF-UK office. Betty was on her way to replace Clarence Soderberg as pilot in Nigeria. He was heading back to the U.S. for furlough. SIM now had three planes operating in the field.

22. King, "Provisional Basis for Operation of MAF Plane," January 1951.

Chapter 7: Ecuador: The First Year

1. Truxton to co-workers, February 11, 1948. Much of the information in this chapter comes from interviews with Jim Truxton, Hobey Lowrance, and Grady Parrott.

2. Lowrance to Mellis, August 25, 1948.

3. Truxton to "Dear Gang," July 30, 1948.

4. Truxton to Parrott, September 14, 1948.

5. Truxton to Mellis, November 6, 1948.

6. Truxton to Board of Directors, "Accident Report," December 31, 1948.

7. Lowrance to Mellis and Parrott, January 16, 1949.

8. Parrott to Saint, February 9, 1949.

9. Lowrance to Mellis and Parrott, January 16, 1949.

10. Parrott to Buss, "Ripple Effect of Plane Loss," December 12, 1993.

11. Lowrance to Parrott, January 13, 1949.

12. Saint to Truxton, March 28, 1949.

13. Parrott to Saint, July 27, 1949; August 4, 1949.

14. Parrott to Mellis, April 26, 1949.

15. Parrott to Mellis, May 14, 1949.

16. Lowrance to Mellis, July 23, 1949.

17. Lowrance to Parrott, Mellis, and Truxton, August 7, 1949.

18. Olivia and Hobey Lowrance to friends of bride and groom, August 1949.

Chapter 8: A Quickening Pace

1. Truxton to "Dear Gang," May 28, 1948. Much of the information in this chapter came from extended interviews with Grady Parrott, Jim Truxton, Hobey Lowrance, and Don Berry.

2. Ibid.

3. Parrott to D-2 (MAF personnel), November 22, 1949.

4. Parrott to Truxton, August 25, 1949.

5. Greene to Truxton, August 11, 1949.

6. "Plane Aids Evangelism," MA, June 1950.

7. Parrott to D-2, July 14, 1949. This fabric-covered, single-engine plane had remarkable acceleration for its day. With a payload of five hundred pounds, it took off on seven hundred feet of runway in just fourteen seconds.

8. Parrott to MAF personnel, October 29, 1953. The Piper PA-14 "Cruiser" was chosen for the Oaxaca work because of its better short-field handling at such altitudes. For this reason, Parrott said that the Pacer, with its clipped wings, landed like a "jet propelled brick." The Cruiser had near the load utility of the Pacer and, although it came with only a 108-horsepower engine, the CAA had allowed MAF to install one with 135 horsepower. This gave it much better "climb-out" performance.

9. Truxton to D-1 (MAF administrative staff), June 23, 1950.

10. Truxton to D-2, December 5, 1950.

11. Truxton to D-1, December 16, 1950.

12. Truxton to co-workers, September 24, 1950; Guillermo to Truxton, February 23, 1951.

13. Lowrance interview, October 7, 1985. The above described innovations to landing are an edited version of Hobey Lowrance's text dated May 30, 1994.

14. Ibid.

15. Lowrance interview, October 7, 1985.

16. Truxton to Lowrance, November 20, 1953.

17. WPP, July–August 1952.

18. Parrott to D-2, September 30, 1952. Among their number were Windsor Vick, Charlie White, Herman Matson, and Henry Walton.

19. WPP, September 1957.

20. Truxton to Greene, Lowrance, and Mellis, October 29, 1953.

Chapter 9: Australia Launches MAF

1. Vic Ambrose, *Balus Bilong Mipela: The Story of Missionary Aviation Fellowship, Australia and New Zealand* (Maryborough, Victoria: The Book

Printer, 1987), 13–15. Much of the information in this chapter came from interviews with Bob Hutchins and Grady Parrott.

2. Jim Truxton to Edwin Hartwig, April 1, 1946.

3. Hartwig to Mellis, undated letter received in Los Angeles August 29, 1947.

4. Hartwig to Mellis, undated letter of August 1947; Ambrose, *Balus Bilong Mipela*, 16.

5. Mellis to Hartwig, November 12, 1947.

6. Ibid.

7. Ambrose, *Balus Bilong Mipela*, 16–17.

8. Hartwig to Parrott, September 14, 1948.

9. Parrott to Hartwig, August 27, 1948; Hartwig to Mellis, December 22, 1948.

10. Parrott to Hartwig, January 5, 1949.

11. Hartwig to Parrott, February 10, 1949.

12. Hartwig to Mellis, May 27, 1949.

13. Una Dods to Mellis, September 26, 1949; Geoff Simondson to MAF-US, September 20, 1949.

14. Hartwig's report to AMAF, September 11, 1949; Final Report to AMAF; Hartwig to Parrott, April 3, 1950.

15. Herwig Wagner and Hermann Reiner, eds., *The Lutheran Church in Papua New Guinea: The First Hundred Years, 1886–1986* (Adelaide, Australia: Lutheran Publishing House, 1987), 574–77.

16. Hartwig to Parrott, May 16, 1950. Ecuador's aerial lifeline to stations of various missions became something of a prototype for the Lutheran work at Madang. The difference was that the Lutherans paid for the plane and contracted with AMAF to have Hartwig do the flying. This was not strictly a cooperative missions program. In some ways it was more like MAF-US's work with SIL in Peru, in that MAF agreed to fly for one organization. However the Lutherans, unlike SIL, did not enter into any agreement with the government limiting their freedom in the use of the plane; they were at liberty to make the plane available to fly for other missions as well. In that respect, it appeared to be more like MAF-US's Ecuadorian program.

17. Parrott to Hartwig, April 11, 1950. Besides the Stinson chosen for Ecuador, the Americans used the Piper "Clipper" and "Cruiser" in Mexico. Parrott felt that the more recent "Pacer" model was even better suited for MAF-US's bush operations because it had the advantage of adjustable wing flaps and a more powerful engine. Next to the Pacer, he suggested looking at the Cessna 170. This was an all-metal plane with good performance specifications, but it presented a great problem if damaged in an isolated area away from metal-repair facilities.

18. Hartwig to Parrott, April 21, 1950.

19. Hartwig to Parrott, July 6, 1950.

20. Hartwig to Parrott, May 16, 1950.

21. Parrott to Hartwig, July 8, 1950.

22. Hartwig to Parrott, August 4, 1950.

23. Australian *Missionary Aviation (MA)*, June 1951.

24. Hartwig to MAF-US, July 10, 1951; Grady Parrott to Hartwig, May 10, 1950. Compared to other MAF-initiated programs, this had a heavy workload. In Nigeria, Clarence Soderberg, flying for the Sudan Interior Mission, ferrying mostly personnel, logged around 50 hours per month. Hatch Hatcher in Mexico was averaging under 40 hours per month, and Nate Saint in Ecuador logged between 25–35 hours per month; some months considerably less. MAF-UK had just arrived in the Sudan with the Rapide, but had not yet begun to fly. In Australia, Harry Hartwig and Bob Hutchins logged 170 hours of flying time during the first two months, carried over twenty-two tons of cargo and seventy-three passengers.

25. Hartwig to MAF-US, July 10, 1951.

26. A report Edwin B. Hartwig was compiling at the time of his fatal accident, August 1951.

27. Ibid.

28. W. H. Knights, "MAF-UK Newsletter," November 1951.

29. Parrott to Margaret Hartwig, August 9, 1951.

30. King to Parrott, October 4, 1951.

31. Madang Airplane Advisory Committee, "Minutes of Special Meeting Held at Baitabag, August 8, 1951."

32. Parrott to C. W. Rout, October 30, 1951.

33. Ibid.

34. Ibid.

35. Rout to Parrott, November 21, 1951.

Chapter 10: Advance into Dutch New Guinea

1. Gavin Souter, *New Guinea: The Last Frontier* (Sydney, Australia: Angus and Robertson, 1963), 198. Much of the information in this chapter comes from interviews with Grady Parrott, Bob Hutchins, and Claire Mellis.

2. Souter, *New Guinea: The Last Frontier,* 195.

3. Parrott to Rout, January 4, 1952.

4. Shirley Horne, *An Hour to the Stone Age* (Chicago: Moody Press, 1973), 18–24.

5. Lumsden to Knights, February 7, 1952.

6. Lumsden to Parrott, February 7, 1952. The ever-closer cooperation between Melbourne and Los Angeles that was coming about as a result of Parrott's trip to Australia led Lumsden to suggest to Bill Knights, home secretary of MAF-UK, that the ties be strengthened between the three sister organizations through free exchange of information. In this way Lumsden suggested they could "forge links of common action between MAF Australia

and MAF England" in the same way as they had developed with MAF-US. Australia was willing to initiate some action in this direction and promised to send copies of the council minutes to London. Lumsden hoped that Murray Kendon, Grady Parrott, and he could hold extended discussions in Melbourne in conjunction with Grady's return from Dutch New Guinea. This did materialize in the end of March 1952. See Australian MAF Prayer Letter No. 18.

7. Grady Parrott, "Brief Confidential Report on Surveys of Mr. Grady Parrott in Territory of New Guinea and in DNG," May 1952.

8. Ibid.

9. Horne, *An Hour to the Stone Age*, 27.

10. Claire Mellis, *More Than a Pilot* (Redlands, Calif: Mission Aviation Fellowship, 1985), 30.

11. The Cessna 170 had a 145-horsepower engine, could carry twenty-two hundred pounds gross weight, and had a ceiling of 15,500 feet, well above the Auster. It had a cruising speed of 120 miles per hour and could make better time on cross-country flights.

12. Parrott to Rout, June 2, 1952.

13. Parrott to Rout, October 14, 1952.

14. Souter, *New Guinea: The Last Frontier*, 206–7.

15. Rout to Parrott, October 29, 1952.

16. Parrott to Rout, December 11, 1952; cf. L. E. Buck to Rout, December 19, 1952.

17. Bruce Lumsden to Parrott, December 22, 1952.

18. Rout to Parrott, December 16, 1952; Lumsden to Mellis, December 18, 1952.

19. Mellis to Rout and Lumsden, December 30, 1952.

20. Rout to Parrott, December 16, 1952.

21. Ambrose to Parrott, May 26, 1953.

22. Ibid.

Chapter 11: Charlie Mellis and Vic Ambrose

1. Ambrose, *Balus Bilong Mipela*, 39. Much of the information in this chapter came from interviews with Claire Mellis, Bob Hutchins, and Grady Parrott.

2. AMAF minutes of the thirty-seventh council meeting, February 13, 1953.

3. Mellis to Ambrose, February (undated) 1953.

4. Ambrose, *Balus Bilong Mipela*, 39.

5. Ambrose to Parrott, May 26, 1953.

6. Mellis, *More Than a Pilot*, 110.

7. Doug McCraw to Grady Parrott, June 15, 1954.

8. Mellis, *More Than a Pilot*, 116–18.

9. Australian *MA*, July 1955.

10. Ambrose, *Balus Bilong Mipela*, 43–44.

11. Australian *MA*, May 1955.

12. Doug McCraw to Parrott, March 16, 1955; cf. Parrott to McCraw, April 12, 1955. Douglas G. McCraw followed in the footsteps of Hartwig and Ambrose in the Melbourne home office. McCraw was an ex-RAAF pilot, an instructor who trained for and became a minister in the Anglican Church. He left his parish at Windsor, New South Wales, to become organizing secretary for AMAF when Ambrose left for New Guinea; see Australian *MA*, June 1954.

13. Mellis, *More Than a Pilot*, 153.

14. Ibid., 158. Clair notes that the Steigers arrived on March 9, 1955, and that coincided with putting the Pacer on floats. On March 13 Charlie wrote Clair, "While we were gone (with Al Lewis) Bob, Dave (who arrived with his family the afternoon before—at 6:20 P.M.!!!) and Bill (Widbin) hauled the plane down to the lake and launched it."

15. Mellis to Bruce Morton, May 30, 1955.

16. Ambrose to Mellis, July 25, 1955.

17. Australian *MA*, September 1955.

Chapter 12: Ecuador's "Operation Auca" and Its Legacy

1. Parrott to Saint, September 16, 1955. Much of the information in this chapter comes from interviews with Grady Parrott, Jim Truxton, and Hobey Lowrance. Dr. Everett Fuller provided much significant information in a taped statement.

2. M. Everett Fuller, "Address at the 25th anniversary of the Epp Memorial Hospital," May 8, 1983.

3. WPP, March–April, 1954.

4. Ibid.

5. Parrott to Saint, December 19, 1955.

6. MAF *LifeLink*, 1993, 3, 19.

7. Elisabeth Elliot, *Through Gates of Splendor* (New York: Harper and Brothers, 1957); Hitt, *Jungle Pilot* .

8. Parrott to Lowrance, September 19, 1956.

9. Elliot, *Through Gates of Splendor*, 244.

10. Parrott to Truxton and Mellis, January 16, 1956.

11. Ibid.

12. Parrott to Mellis and Truxton, January 17, 1956.

13. Parrott to Truxton and Mellis, February 14, 1956. The Crowell Foundation gave MAF ten thousand dollars to be used where most needed.

14. *MA*, May 1956; the citation went on to say: "This service is carried out without fear of the dangers and inconveniences which surround the task, in the true Christian spirit that motivates each one of the missionaries who have come from their distant countries to our jungle areas far from civilization and the Christian faith."

15. Parrott to D-1, January 17, 1956.

16. Parrott to Marj Saint, May 26, 1956.

17. Bob Moeller, "Lives Given, Not Taken," *Wellspring,* Summer 1989, 14.

18. Stephen Saint, "To the Ends of the Earth," *Guideposts,* January 1991, 24–28.

19. Parrott to Truxton, April 3, 1956.

20. Parrott to Hatcher, April 13, 1956.

21. Truxton to D-2, August 16, 1957.

22. WPP, October–November 1958; Elisabeth Elliot, *The Savage My Kinsmen* (New York: Harper and Brothers, 1961), 19.

23. Parrott to Derr, July 30, 1958.

24. Parrott to Derr, July 3, 1958.

25. Parrott to Truxton, August (undated) 1958.

26. Ibid.

27. WPP, October–November 1958; Elliot, *The Savage My Kinsmen,* 72–82.

28. Truxton to Lomheim, Berk, and Lewis, October 31, 1958. See p. 312.

29. Patrick Johnstone, *Operation World* (Pasadena, Calif.: William Carey Library, 1986), 162–63.

30. MAF *LifeLink,* 1990, 5.

31. MAF *LifeLink,* 1993, 3, 19.

32. Ibid.

Chapter 13: MAF-UK in the Sudan

1. MAF-UK Newsletter, March 1952. Much of the information in this chapter comes from interviews with Stuart King, Grady Parrott, Betty Greene, and Denny Hoekstra. Gordon Marshall provided much helpful information in the form of manuscript notations.

2. MAF-UK Newsletter, September 1952.

3. MAF-UK Newsletter, August 1953, January 1954.

4. Marshall to friend, September 18, 1970.

5. Ibid.

6. Marshall to Buss, June 16, 1989.

7. MAF-UK Newsletter, June 22, 1953.

8. MAF-UK Newsletter, August 1953.

9. Stuart King, "History of MAF: From Standpoint of British MAF," 6.

10. Stevens to Parrott, March 30, 1954.

11. MAF-UK Newsletter, August 1953.

12. Marshall to Buss, June 15, 1989.

13. King's prayer letter, August 11, 1955.

14. MAF-UK Newsletter, May 1955.

15. Stevens to Parrott, March 30, 1954; Marshall to friend, September 18, 1970.

16. Stevens to Parrott, June 21, 1952; Parrott to Stevens, July 11, 1952.

17. Kendon to Parrott, July 28, 1952.

18. King to MAF Sudan and London, "Report on the Discussions with Grady Parrott as to Possible British and U.S. M.A.F. Link-up," August 16, 1954.

19. Stevens to Parrott, March 30, 1954.

20. Russ Morton to "Dear Friends," July 2, 1954; Macdonald prayer letter, April 18, 1954.

21. Marshall to Buss, March 13, 1989; insert in correspondence: Lemuel Tew, "Encounter in Ethiopia," undated.

22. Parrott to King, April 25, 1955.

23. King to Parrott, September 20, l955.

24. Ibid.

25. Greene to King, October 24, 1955.

26. MAF-UK Newsletter, "A Day's Flying—Extract from Betty Greene's Diary," July 1956.

27. MAF-UK Newsletter, July 1956.

28. Stevens to Parrott, June 12, 1956; Truxton to Stevens, July 10, 1956.

29. King to Parrott, December 1956.

30. Mellis to King, December 21, 1956.

Chapter 14: The Challenge of Brazil

1. Truxton to D–2, November 23, 1949. Much of the material in this chapter comes from interviews with Jim Truxton, Hobey Lowrance, and Norm Olson. Separate taped statements from Mary Hawkins, Neill's wife, and his brother Bob Hawkins provided much helpful information.

2. Truxton to Parrott, July 22, 1954.

3. Truxton to Parrott, October 18, 1954.

4. Truxton to Parrott, August 9, 1955.

5. Truxton to D–1, January 26, 1957.

6. Ibid.

7. Truxton to Greene and MAF staff, February 8, 1957.

8. Ibid.

9. Truxton to Parrott and Mellis, February 20, 1957.

10. Truxton to Berk, January 29, 1959.

11. Truxton to Lomheim, April 28, 1959; Truxton to D–2, July 3, 1959.

12. Truxton to D–2, October 23, 1959.

13. Truxton to Eldon Larson, June 28, 1960.

14. Truxton to D–1, April 30, 1960.

15. Truxton to D–2, February 3, 1961.

16. Ibid.

17. Truxton to Parsons, July 28, 1960.

18. Ibid.

Chapter 15: Joining Hands to Reach New Guinea's Interior

1. Australian *MA*, October 1954. Some of the information for this chapter came from interviews with Bob Hutchins and Max Meyers. Harold Catto's taped statement about the work in Irian Jaya provided helpful information.

2. Australian *MA*, September 1955.

3. Ambrose to Mellis, February 1, 1956.

4. Ibid.

5. Mellis to Ambrose, April 20, 1956.

6. Ambrose to Rout, October 8, 1956.

7. Ibid.

8. Australian *MA*, June 1957.

9. Ambrose to Mellis, April 29, 1957.

10. Parrott to Ambrose, October 24, 1957.

11. Alex Jardine to Saint and Woolnough, February 1958.

12. Ibid; Parrott to Ambrose, September 13, 1957.

13. Hitt, *Jungle Pilot*, frontice piece.

14. MAF-NZ Newsletter, September 1958.

15. Australian *MA*, April 1957.

16. Ambrose, "Staff Report," September 4, 1958.

17. Ambrose to MAF-US, NZ, GB, December 19, 1960.

18. Ambrose to MAF-US, NZ, GB, December 12, 1960.

19. Ambrose, *Balus Bilong Mipela*, 89.

20. "M.A.F. Leases Former Air Force Station," *New Life*, October 26, 1961.

21. Ibid.

22. Ambrose, *Balus Bilong Mipela*, 90–92.

23. J. B. Bissett to Mellis, September 1962; Ambrose, *Balus Bilong Mipela*, 84–86.

24. "New Zealand News," Australian *MA*, August 1962.

25. Australian *MA*, May–June 1962.

26. Australian *MA*, August–September 1961.

27. Parrott to Mellis, December 25, 1959; Don Richter, "O Heathen Awake," a summary of his record for September 9, 10, 1959; Bill Mallon to Parrott, December 14, 1959.

28. Richter.

29. Parrott to D–1, November 21, 1959; Parrott to Mellis, October 9, 1959.

30. WPP, January–February 1960.

Chapter 16: A Christian Response to Changing Times

1. Parrott to Greene, June 23, 1958; the decision to have a Medical Committee came at the Annual Board Meeting on June 22, 1958. Much of the information in this chapter comes from extensive interviews with Don Berry, Chuck Bennett, Grady Parrott, Bob Hutchins, and Hobey Lowrance.

2. Truxton to Patton, March 6, 1963.

3. WPP, October 1963.

4. Charles Bennett, *Tinder in Tabasco* (Grand Rapids: Eerdmans Publishing Co., 1968), 126.

5. Truxton to Mellis, May 1, 1948; Parrott to Hatcher, September 13, 1961.

6. WPP, August–September 1960; Parrott to Truxton, July 12, 1960.

7. Parrott to D–2, January 13, 1961.

8. WPP, July–August 1961; WPP, September 1962; WPP, November 1962.

9. Parrott to Tom Gilmer, January 29, 1961.

10. Parrott to Mellis, April 12, 1962.

11. Parrott to D–2, March 1, 1963.

12. MAF-UK Progress Report, 1959.

13. Statement from Harvey Hoekstra, December 21, 1984.

14. MAF-UK Newsletter, March 1959.

15. Parrott to Truxton, October 12, 1955; Parrott to Harold Berk, December 29, 1955.

Chapter 17: Amid Danger: Zaire and Laos

1. Congo Christian Medical Relief Committee, "News Sheet," August 3, 1960. Much of the material in this chapter comes from interviews with Grady Parrott, John Fairweather, Roy and Katie Parsons, and taped statements from Dr. William Rule and Ed Gustafson.

2. William Rule to "Dear Friends," November 25, 1960.

3. Congo Christian Medical Relief Committee, "News Sheet," August 19, 1960.

4. Dr. William Rule, October 13, 1983, transcript of taped message, p. 2. Dr. Rule kept a record of events and in relating this story on tape he read this quote verbatim from his journal.

5. Parrott to D–2, February 17, 1961.

6. MAF-UK Newsletter, Winter 1961.

7. WPP, March 1964.

8. MAF-UK, "London Headquarters Prayer Meeting," November 19, 1964.

9. King to Johnny Strash, July 2, 19, 1965. Plans for this undertaking had been in the air for some time, but were actually set in motion at the AIM International Field Council held at Nairobi, Kenya, in mid-July 1965.

10. Leslie Brown, "Congo Flight," July 1965.

11. Ibid.

12. MAF-US, "Zaire Program Descriptions," 1989.

13. WPP, November 1965; Truxton to D–2, February 18, 1966; WPP, January 1966.

14. WPP, July–August 1964. The post office address of the TEAM hospital is Karanda but its physical location is Mt. Darwin, Zimbabwe.

15. Parrott to Truxton and Mellis, May 14, 1962.
16. Ibid.

Chapter 18: Seasons of Service: The Sudan and Ethiopia

1. Stuart and Phyllis King to friends, December 1, 1959. Much of the information in this chapter came from interviews with Stuart King and Denny Hoekstra.

2. Stuart King, "Siting Air Strips: Missionary Survey of Ancient Ethiopia," April 1958.

3. King to Mellis, July 22, 1959; Mellis to King, October 14, 1960. The decision for moving another family to serve MAF-UK paralleled a three-way MAF agreement dealing with equity on the question of personal support. It was felt that pilots should be neither penalized nor financially rewarded for service with a sister organization. A unified pay scale did much to bring about equity and was another indication of the degree of cooperation between the MAF groups.

4. MAF-UK Newsletter, Christmas 1959.

5. Marshall to Stevens and King, undated letter of 1959.

6. Gordon Marshall, "Report on Ethiopian Visit," June 3–7, 1959.

7. Macdonald to Fullerton, London, Nairobi, September 5, 1960.

8. Ibid.

9. MAF-UK London Headquarters Prayer Briefing, February 26, 1964.

10. Gordon Marshall, "Notes on 'Winding up of Sudan MAF'," April 1964.

11. MAF-South Africa Newsletter, April 9, 1964.

12. Elizabeth Longley, *Over the Mountains of Ethiopia* (London: Mission Aviation Fellowship, 1968), 7–8.

13. Ibid., 11–12.

14. Ibid., 13.

15. Stuart King, "History of MAF: From Standpoint of British MAF," 14.

16. Ronald Knight, "Personal Prayer and News Letter," August 1972.

Chapter 19: Assisting in Chad, South Africa, and the Sudan

1. King to Mellis, October 8, 1964. Much of the information in this chapter came from an interview with Stuart King and primary source information from Gordon Marshall.

2. King to Hutchins, October 9, 1964.

3. King to friends, December 1, 1964.

4. MAF-UK Newsletter, Christmas 1964.

5. Carling to King, undated letter circa March 1965.

6. King, "Operation Chad: A Sudan United Mission and MAF Joint Project," Summer 1969.

7. Carling to King, undated letter circa March 1965.

8. Parrott to King, April 21, 1965.

9. Stuart King, "Report on Chad Survey," August 1965.

10. MAF-UK Newsletter, Autumn 1966.

11. MAF-UK "Graham Macrae," Tuesday, June 21, 1966.

12. Ibid.

13. Ibid.

14. Josling to Parrott, August 12, 1969.

15. Marshall to Tony and Ethel Hollaway, November 7, 1971.

16. Ibid.

17. Ibid.

18. SA-MAF Newsletter, March 1970.

19. SA-MAF Newsletter, May 1975; February 26, 1980.

20. MAF-UK ACROSS, "Relief and Rehabilitation in Southern Sudan," September 1972; supplement of MAF-UK *News*.

21. King, *Hope Has Wings*, 280–81.

Chapter 20: Entry into the Philippines, Suriname, Venezuela, Kalimantan in Indonesia, and Afghanistan

1. Parrott to D–2, March 4, 1960. Much of the information in this chapter came from interviews with Roy and Katie Parsons, Hobey Lowrance, and Grady Parrott.

2. Parrott to Mellis, May 28, 1962.

3. Parrott to Mellis, July 4, 1965.

4. Parrott to D–2, June 24, 1966.

5. Parrott to Truxton, October 15, 1965; WPP, February 1966.

6. *MA*, February 1968.

7. Ibid.

8. *MA*, April–May 1969, *MA*, October–November 1969.

9. Mellis to Weir family and friends, June 1, 1971.

10. Mellis to D–2, March 4, 1971.

11. *MA*, September–October 1971.

12. *MA*, May–June 1971.

Chapter 21: The Future Beckons

1. Truxton to Greene, December 29, 1960; Truxton to Parrott, October 1960. Much of the information in this chapter has come from interviews with Chuck Bennett, Roy Parsons, Don Berry, and Grady Parrott.

2. *MA*, April–May 1969. In this period of transition, Berry next served as vice president with responsibility for personnel. Thereafter he was appointed department head for personnel in the new management structure.

3. Parrott, "Provisional Organizational Goals," May 1969; Parrott, D–2, May 23, 1969.

4. Mellis to Parrott, August 31, 1962.

5. Ambrose to Mellis, August 9, 1960; Mellis to Ambrose, September 1, 1960.

6. Ambrose to British and American MAF, October 20, 1960.

7. Mellis to Ambrose, December 7, 1960.

8. Ibid.

9. Parrott to Berry, June 30, 1964.

10. Parrott to Irv Allen, December 31, 1964.

11. Parrott to Eisemann, November 18, 1965.

12. WPP, January–February 1970; Ambrose to Parrott, June 17, 1969.

13. Ambrose to Parrott, December 2, 1969.

14. Darlene Lomheim interview, June 8, 1985. These were the years of growing up for Jim and Darlene's family of five children ranging in ages 14 to 2: Bruce, Terry, Joy Lynne, Carlos, and Tim. The parents wisely felt that the family unit should be together, as had the Marshalls in South Africa, half a world away. After 1974, Lomheim ably served on the board until his passing in October 1980 in the aftermath of a well-planned but mishandled heart surgery. This was a very heavy blow, but the Lord sustained the family through this incredible trial.

15. Mellis to Bob and Betty Hutchins, April 16, 1970.

16. Mellis to Parrott and Directors, April 15, 1970.

17. *MA*, July–August 1970; Hobey Lowrance to Buss, May 13, 1994.

18. Mellis, "To Our Canadian Friends," January 1971.

19. Mission Aviation Fellowship of Canada, "Minutes of the Organization Meeting," August, 10, 11, 1972; Richard Bittle to James Truxton, August 17, 1972. The initial officers selected were Leslie Harris, president; Leslie Hamm, vice president; Richard Bittle, secretary-treasurer. Dr. Robert Thomson agreed to serve on the board of directors together with Bob Gartshor of Alberta and Ralph Harman of Ontario. Jim Truxton served with the title of vice-president-at-large since the reorganization.

20. SA-MAF News #3, undated.

21. MAF-US Development Department, "MAF in the Former Soviet Union & with the CoMission," June 11, 1993.

Index

367

Dietrich Gotthilf Buss is professor of history and chairman of the department of history at Biola University, where he has taught history and geography since 1966. He was born in Tokyo, Japan, to German Liebenzell missionary parents. The family migrated first to the United States in 1952 and then to Canada. He received the M.A. from California State University (1965) and the Ph.D. in history from Claremont Graduate School (1976). He has served as director of missions at Cypress Evangelical Free Church (1984–91) and serves on the City of La Mirada Historical Heritage Commission. Publications include a business biography on Henry Villard and articles in *Fides et Historia, Dictionary of Christianity in America, Dictionary of Evangelical Biography,* and *Encyclopedia USA.*

Arthur Frederick Glasser is senior professor and dean emeritus of the School of World Mission at Fuller Theological Seminary. He is an ordained minister in the Presbyterian Church in America. He received his theological training at Faith Theological Seminary (M. Div.) and Union Theological Seminary (S.T.M.). Dr. Glasser wrote *And Some Believed* (Moody, 1946) on his experience as a U.S. Navy chaplain attached to the First Marine Division in the South Pacific War (1943–44). He served as a missionary to China (1946–51) and for years was a director of the Overseas Missionary Fellowship and the editor of *Missiology,* the journal of the American Society of Missiology (1976–82). Dr. Glasser's articles have appeared in such scholarly journals as the *International Bulletin of Missionary Research, Religion and Intellectual Life, Themilios,* and *Evangelical Missions Quarterly.* He wrote *Missions in Crisis* with Eric S. Fife (InterVarsity Press, 1961), and *Contemporary Theologies of Mission* with Donald A. McGavran (Baker, 1983).